What Writing Does and How It Does It

An Introduction to Analyzing Texts and Textual Practices

What Writing Does and How It Does It

An Introduction to Analyzing Texts and Textual Practices

Edited by

Charles Bazerman
University of California, Santa Barbara

Paul Prior
University of Illinois

2004

LAWRENCE ERLBAUM ASSOCIATES, PUBLISHERS
Mahwah, New Jersey   London

Lawrence Erlbaum Associates, Inc., Publishers
10 Industrial Avenue
Mahwah, New Jersey 07430

Cover design by Kathryn Houghtaling Lacey

Library of Congress Cataloging-in-Publication Data

What writing does and how it does it : an introduction to analyzing texts and textual
    practices / edited by Charles Bazerman, Paul A. Prior.
        p. cm.
    Includes bibliographical references and index.
    ISBN 0-8058-3805-8 (alk. paper) — ISBN 0-8058-3806-6 pbk. : alk. paper)
        1. English language composition and exercises: Study and teaching. 2. English
    Language Rhetoric Study and teaching. 3. Report writing Study and teaching.
    4. Discourse analysis. I. Bazerman, Charles. II. Prior, Paul A.

    PE1404.W456   2003
    808 .042 07—dc21

                                                                    2003052864

Books published by Lawrence Erlbaum Associates are printed on acid-free paper,
and their bindings are chosen for strength and durability.

Printed in the United States of America
10   9   8   7   6   5   4   3   2   1

Contents

Introduction   1
    Charles Bazerman and Paul Prior

PART I: ANALYZING TEXTS   11

  1.   Content Analysis: What Texts Talk About   13
      Thomas Huckin

  2.   Poetics and Narrativity: How Texts Tell Stories   33
      Philip Eubanks

  3.   Linguistic Discourse Analysis: How the Language   57
      in Texts Works
      Ellen Barton

  4.   Intertextuality: How Texts Rely on Other Texts   83
      Charles Bazerman

  5.   Code-Switching and Second Language Writing: How   97
      Multiple Codes Are Combined in a Text
      Marcia Z. Buell

  6.   The Multiple Media of Texts: How Onscreen and Paper   123
      Texts Incorporate Words, Images, and Other Media
      Anne Frances Wysocki

v

PART II: ANALYZING TEXTUAL PRACTICES   165

7. Tracing Process: How Texts Come Into Being   167
    Paul Prior

8. Speaking and Writing: How Talk and Text Interact   201
    in Situated Practices
    Kevin Leander and Paul Prior

9. Children's Writing: How Textual Forms, Contextual   239
    Forces, and Textual Politics Co-Emerge
    George Kamberelis and Lenora de la Luna

10. Rhetorical Analysis: Understanding How Texts   279
    Persuade Readers
    Jack Selzer

11. Speech Acts, Genres, and Activity Systems: How   309
    Texts Organize Activity and People
    Charles Bazerman

References   341
Author Index   357
Subject Index   363

Introduction

Charles Bazerman
University of California, Santa Barbara

Paul Prior
University of Illinois at Urbana-Champaign

THE STUDY OF WRITTEN TEXT AND WRITING

Discourse analysis has grown in popularity as a major analytical method in social science research fields such as communications studies, sociology, and anthropology. As well, it has been an increasingly popular method for research, practical applications, and pedagogical assessment in composition, education, and applied linguistics/ESL. Most discourse analysis has, however, been focused on spoken language. Yet a number of critical social domains involve significant written text. Think, for example, of schooling, scientific and disciplinary knowledge, cultural production in the arts, the everyday life of government and corporate institutions, the public spaces of news, the diverse worlds of electronic text on the World Wide Web, and other forms of widespread cultural self-representation. Looking at only the spoken interchanges in such educational, institutional, professional, and social settings gives a limited and potentially misleading picture of the ways that language enters into the dynamic unfolding of situations and events.

In extending the reach of discourse analysis to engage with written text, we would do well, however, to remember some of the lessons learned in analysis of spoken language: that language is emergent, multiform, negotiated in the process, meaningful in the uptake, accomplishing social acts. Analysis of writing must go beyond considering the written text as an inert object, complete in itself as a bearer of abstract meanings. Traditional forms of text analysis developed within school and in such academic disciplines as literary studies, rhetoric, and philosophy have told us much about what texts can mean. These modes of analysis, developed mainly for purposes of interpretation and criticism, by and large have not been brought into dialogue with discourse analysis as currently conceived and practiced within the social sciences. Yet they form the basic way most of us approach texts and represent what we are likely to think of as textual analysis. In order to understand how textual analysis can address issues beyond interpretation and criticism, we must be able to see the relationship between traditional forms of text analysis and the newer methods considered part of discourse analysis.

To understand writing, we need to explore the practices that people engage in to produce texts as well as the ways that writing practices gain their meanings and functions as dynamic elements of specific cultural settings. The absence of attention to writing as a social and productive practice has come about for reasons we discuss below. The effect, however, has been to severely limit the analysis of written text, closing off many lines of inquiry into how and why texts come to be as they are and what effects they have on the world.

WHY ANALYZE WRITTEN TEXTS AND WRITING?

Traditionally the motivation for analyzing texts has been to understand them more deeply and/or to examine the limitations of their meanings. **Text analysis** was earliest developed within scriptural religions, where people were highly motivated to find all the meaning they could out of holy books such as the Bible, Talmud, Koran, or Baghavad Gita. The emergence of philosophy and other intellectual endeavors involved criticizing claims of opponents, which motivated analysis of texts to find flaws in reasoning, confusions, or other limitations. Similarly as law became a matter of written law, written court precedents, and written legal briefs, it became important to determine what the law really said, what the loopholes were, how precedents could be used to argue one side or another, what the weaknesses and strengths were of opposing arguments. **Rhetoric** was first a productive discipline, concerned about how to make civic texts that would persuade others of an argument, establish the ethos (credibility and status) of the rhetor, or create a climate of feeling that would incline others toward certain views and actions. Rhetoric, however, also fostered a critical reading practice, reading civic texts for the means of rhetorical action, for the presence of tropes and topics, the signs of audience and authorial construction. Literary studies was premised on the importance of certain cultural texts, which may be difficult to understand because of their historical distance, cultural difference, profound meaning, or complex literary technique. Thus, it required ways of analyzing those texts in order to understand their meaning. Students, consequently, needed to be introduced to the techniques of analytical reading so as to have access to the culture of these texts. Cultural and historical criticism then served to characterize the particularity of the views and experiences in the texts. In all of these modes of analysis, the primary focus has been on uncovering or criticizing the meaning of the text. This concern for meaning is natural enough in reading and responding to other people's thought expressed in the writing. It is the natural stance, as it were, of the reader to be looking for meaning.

However, there are many other questions that can be asked about texts and we can learn many other things about texts beyond what they mean and whether we approve of the meanings. We can consider

- how texts direct people's attention to various objects and concerns;
- how different linguistic, rhetorical, and graphic resources make possible the creation of meaning;
- how texts depend on and use other texts; how texts influence people's beliefs and actions;
- how people learn to recognize, read, and produce genres (texts of certain types);
- how people actually go about producing texts; and
- how social systems of activity depend on and promote particular kinds of texts.

These questions focus on *what texts do* and *how texts mean* rather than *what they mean*. And these questions can be raised with respect to all types of texts, not just the texts traditionally privileged in particular disciplines. It is toward these questions that the modes of analysis introduced in this book are addressed.

Literary studies and rhetoric—when focused on the poetic, metaphoric, and narrative dimensions of language in particular—have explored how language produces effects on readers and listeners, questions that we normally ignore as we go directly for the meaning. With insights from recent linguistics, sociolinguistics, and semiotics, we can engage more deeply in this exploration, and we can extend it to types of texts that literary and rhetorical analysts have generally ignored. **For researchers**, discourse analysis provides **a means of examining communicative practice so as to uncover signs of social identities, institutions, and norms as well as the means by which these social formations are established, negotiated, enacted, and changed through communicative practice. For teachers of writing** in colleges and schools, discourse analysis provides **ways of going beyond the simple and perhaps confusing terminology of our everyday language for texts and writing**.

At one level, we all know that English (like other national languages) is actually composed of a variety of related codes, genres, and ways of communication linked to specific social situations and traditions. We all draw on this knowledge to navigate through everyday life, to understand or produce language that is formal or informal, that represents standard grammar or some colloquial dialect, that produces a letter, a poem, or a formal research paper. However, it remains a challenge to actually describe what we do. Likewise, as writers we learn a practical vocabulary for describing and evaluating texts, but that vocabulary may not give us the precise guidance we and our students need to improve our writing. For example, we might say a text flows or that it is convoluted, that it is awkward or direct, that it is formal or informal. Again, the challenge for discourse analysis is to figure out what makes a text flow. Finally, we know at some level that our writing influences people and accomplishes things in the world, but broad-stroke terms like "persuade" suggest that the only action writing accomplishes is to induce others to submit to our ideas. The challenge for discourse analysis is to identify the precise actions and means of action present in texts as they are used in the world.

Until the 1970s, there was no tradition for studying writing processes, the production and use of texts; however, there have been strong cultural models that shape how people typically imagine writing processes. For example, we learn to think of texts, at least certain texts, as having authors, a single person usually who thinks the thoughts and pens (or keys in) the words. However, in many cases, a careful **analysis of textual practice**, of where the words, ideas, and organization of a text come from, reveals a much more complex picture. It turns out that authors may be drawing on the organizational and thematic conventions of a genre, like that of the scientific article, that has been developed by thousands of writers over hundreds of years. The ideas in a text are also likely to rely on the general and specific influences of many other people and their texts. How can we begin to untangle the threads of so many voices in a single text? Here again the modes of discourse analysis in this book offer ways of both tracing processes and of exploring the variations, the textures of discourse, that exist within a specific piece of writing.

In short, discourse analysis offers ways of seeing texts and textual practices with greater clarity. Whether you are a writing teacher trying to find better ways of telling your students what they did well and what they didn't do well or a researcher interested in understanding how texts and textual practices in some social arena reflect and create certain social relations, **discourse analysis can offer a valuable toolkit, prompting careful examination of the details of language and its basic modes—of representation, production, reception, and distribution**.

WHAT MAKES THIS BOOK UNIQUE?

There are a number of books designed to introduce you to discourse analysis (many of which will be cited in this book). We believe that four factors at least make this book unique: its coverage of writing as well as text, its disciplinary grounding in North American Writing Studies, the breadth and diversity of traditions presented, and its focus on introducing *methods* of analysis.

Most introductions to discourse analysis have focused exclusively or heavily on ways to analyze talk and conversation. Introductions that deal with, or in a few cases concentrate on, written texts have looked exclusively at the textual product and not at the processes of production through which those texts were created. In this book, we treat both the writing and the text. Of course, no approach to discourse analysis can proceed without also considering contexts, and here again, we consider ways of analyzing the contexts of writing as well as the contexts of texts as received by readers.

Second, many fields have an interest in text analysis. However, the majority of introductions to text analysis reflect the disciplinary traditions of two fields: linguistics and sociology. It is important to recognize this fact because disciplinary tradition directs the goals of the analysis, the kinds of questions that an analysis addresses, and the kinds of disciplinary conversations that have shaped the approach. For example, Hoey (2001) is most influenced by a linguistically-informed interest in teaching English to non-native speakers of English. His book is oriented, explicitly and implicitly, to helping such learners to read English texts. Fairclough (1995), on the other hand, offers a sociolinguistic approach in his introduction to *Critical Discourse Analysis*, reading texts for the ways that they represent and produce larger social identities and relations. The chapters in this book, in contrast, have all been shaped by questions of how to teach and understand the work of writers, whether in school, the workplace, or the community. We believe that these chapters then will be of particular value to teachers of writing and to those in any field who are beginning to see the need to research the practices of writing (and how people learn them) as well as written products themselves.

Third, this book is not informed by a single theoretical orientation but represents diverse approaches to analyzing texts and textual practices. The chapters are written by various authors—each expert in their field and each providing a particular perspective. The book includes analytic approaches from linguistics, communication studies, rhetoric, literary analysis, document design, sociolinguistics, education, ethnography, and cultural psychology. Each chapter provides an introduction to large areas of research, theory, and practice. If you decide to delve further into the approach of any chapter, suggestions for further reading are provided near the chapter end. Because the authors of the chapters represent a range of perspectives, they will not always agree on every point, but we believe this diversity of perspective is a strength, revealing the comparative implications of the approaches. Nor is this book limited to examining one kind of writer or text or one scene of writing. The sample analyses include the writing of elementary and secondary school students, college students at the undergraduate and graduate level, professional writers, journalists, and academics.

Fourth, many introductions to discourse analysis spend considerable time explaining the theoretical frameworks and historical backgrounds of a method. We believe that theory and history are important; however, here we take a different approach. Each chapter of *What Writing Does and How It Does It: An Introduction to Analyzing Texts and Textual Practices* is organized around a basic question that can be used to interrogate a text, such as: What does the text talk about? How do texts influence audiences? And how do texts come into being? To answer each of the questions, you are introduced to an approach to text analysis (in the three examples earlier—content analysis, rhetorical analysis, and process analysis). Thus, in the course of the book you will become acquainted with 11 approaches to analyzing texts and will have developed motivated reasons for invoking each of the methods. Each chapter:

- previews the content and purpose of the chapter and the kinds of data and questions that the analysis is best used for; and introduces basic concepts, referring to key theoretical and research studies in the area;
- uses examples from educational materials, student writing, and other texts you are likely to encounter;
- presents one or more applied analyses, which include a clear statement of procedures for analysis and are illustrated by consideration of a particular sample of data; and
- concludes with a brief summary, suggestions for additional readings, and a set of additional activities.

Three Critical Issues for Analyzing Texts and Textual Practices

Before turning to the outline of the book, we need to discuss three critical issues, three areas where we anticipate possible obstacles because of the ways that text and writing are typically discussed in schools and in the popular culture.

The first issue involves our **definitions of texts**. In popular usage and in literature courses, text often means a formal publication: a book, an essay, an article in a magazine, a poem. However, **here we take text to include any written inscription**. Street signs, notes passed among students in a sixth-grade classroom, the words on a cereal box, a name carved into a stone monument or into a tree, an animated banner running across a Web page, a grocery list, the money and cards you carry in your wallet, a student paper written in a class, a teacher's responsive comments in the margin of that paper, a classified advertisement for renting an apartment, comments posted in an electronic chat space, an income tax form, all are texts—and all are written by people, with processes, genres, and contexts that may be quite different from what is normally thought of when people talk about texts and their authors. Seeing this incredible diversity of texts and textual practices is critical.

The second issue has to do with **how we conceive of writing as a process or activity**. In discussions of writing, we often think of writing as a solitary activity, with a writer sitting alone and in some way inscribing words into a document. We usually think first of writing on paper with pen or now on a computer screen with an electronic keyboard, but in fact the media can be diverse. People also inscribe text on t-shirts, in stone, on tree trunks, on metal, in the dirt. Tools of inscription include pens and pencils, computers and printing presses, lithographs and keyboards, knives and sticks. Furthermore, in most cases we equate inscribing a text with composing it, but of course a photocopy machine is also an inscription device yet involves no composing. Likewise, people sometimes compose a text in their heads or in conversation without inscribing it. The process of writing obviously includes the immediate acts of putting words on paper (or some other medium) and the material text or series of texts thus produced. However, the words have to come from somewhere and where they come from matters. Thus, the process of writing encompasses the inner thought processes of the writer(s) as well as exchanges (spoken or written) between people in which the content and purposes of a text are imagined and planned and even specific language may be "drafted" out. Thinking and interaction about texts may happen at any time or place and may be fleeting rather than sustained. Many writers describe ideas arising when they are jogging, riding on a bus, watching TV, taking a shower, in the midst of an apparently unrelated conversation, waking up from a dream, and so on. Finally, writers also routinely draw on other texts, most obviously through quoting but also as more indirect models, so it is important to consider the ways these other texts are read and used as a part of the writing process. In short, **when we look at writing as a process, we're really looking at a complex literate activity that includes reading and writing, feeling and thinking, speaking and listening, observing and acting**.

Third, **a central obstacle to analysis is the natural attitude toward texts and writing** that we develop as we become competent readers and writers. As language users, as participants in social interaction, we are always trying to understand what others try to communicate with us. If we have any difficulty, we stop to analyze what they say to help determine a meaning. Insofar as we feel uncomfortable with or disagree with what others say, we analyze their words to find out why we disagree, what is wrong, what are the weaknesses we might use to argue against them. This tendency to consider text analysis as interpretation and critique is reinforced throughout our schooling, from the earliest exercises in making sense of sentences and finding main ideas in stories to advanced instruction in literary technique and philosophical argument. This meaning-based approach to analysis of writing—what we are calling the natural attitude or stance—is so deeply engrained, so habitual, that we don't even notice it. It is hard for us to see things any other way. For text analysis, this means that it takes some effort and discipline to move beyond questions of what things mean to questions of what they do and how they mean. You might find that as you analyze a text you slide back into the natural stance of an everyday user, thereby losing your analytical orientation. As your attention focuses on what a text means, especially insofar as that meaning seems unproblematic or mundane, your attention goes past the text to think about the writer or the ideas. When you notice this happening, step back and remind yourself of the analytic question(s) that you want to answer, remind yourself to attend to the means that the text deploys, and ask how the words of the text and their organization are producing the effects you are perceiving. At first, it might be easiest to take an analytic stance to texts that you are not deeply engaged in or familiar with, texts that you can look at coolly and from some distance. However, if you can learn to see even the most familiar texts as strange objects worthy of close analytic attention, you will start to see the real benefits of text analysis, for you will understand texts in totally new ways. Breaking out of the natural attitude toward texts and textual practices is crucial to textual inquiry and analysis.

OUTLINE OF THE BOOK

What Writing Does and How It Does It is divided into two main sections. The chapters in Part I focus on ways of analyzing texts. In chapter 1, Thomas Huckin addresses content analysis, the question of what texts talk about. What texts talk about seems like the simplest thing to notice, the most like what readers do every day; however, analysis of the content of texts needs to get beyond simple summary. Huckin focuses on such issues as identification of themes and objects, ways of coding content, and qualitative and quantitative approaches to analyzing large collections of texts. He reviews a number of examples of content analyses and then illustrates one approach by considering depictions of homelessness in newspaper stories and editorials. In chapter 2, Philip Eubanks introduces poetics and narrativity, asking how texts create representations and tell stories. This chapter introduces types of close reading developed for analysis of literature, but now used in analyzing all kinds of texts. Eubanks introduces analysis of metaphor and other tropes and analysis of narratives. To illustrate these phenomena in non-literary texts (e.g., scientific and technical documents, student writing, media texts), he explores the narratives and tropes used in books, articles, and interviews to describe, praise, and criticize Microsoft chairman, Bill Gates. In chapter 3, Ellen Barton presents an introduction to linguistic analysis, asking how words and grammatical structures function in texts. Barton introduces linguistic approaches to discourse analysis, focusing especially on her approach to rich feature analysis. She illustrates this approach with sample analyses of awkward sentences and the use of evidentials in academic texts. In chapter 4, Charles Bazerman introduces the central notion of intertextuality, asking how texts rely on other texts. Bazerman introduces the concept of intertextuality in two streams: first, the way writers use the languages they find around them for their own purposes, and second, how writers explicitly quote or report the speech of others and position their own statement with respect to the words of others. He examines examples of intertextual practice from educational journalism and the writing of fifth-grade students. In chapter 5, Marcia Buell looks at code switching, asking how multiple codes are combined in a text. Work in sociolinguistics and the ethnography of communication has primarily investigated code switching in talk; here Buell considers the many ways that code switching appears in written texts. Buell applies this approach to the particular issues seen in writers for whom English is a second language. She illustrates this approach with a close analysis of the multiple codes present in the academic writing of a non-native speaker of English from Africa writing in a U.S. community college. Closing the first section, in chapter 6, Anne Wysocki explores multimedia, asking how texts incorporate words, images, and other media to produce their effects. Wysocki explores the nature of text as image (typography, script, page design, the material form of texts) and of images as text, particularly in electronic multimedia texts such as Web pages. To illustrate varied forms of multimedia analysis, Wysocki examines a features page from *Wired* magazine, the design of an interactive multimedia CD-ROM, print pages from traditional and experimental books, and pages from a website.

The chapters in Part II then turn more explicitly to considering the processes of writing, textual practices and their contexts, and what writing does. In chapter 7, Paul Prior considers ways of tracing the writing process, asking how texts come into being. Prior examines how to trace the production of texts, looking at processes of drafting and revision, oral and written response to writing and its uptake, the distributed nature of invention, scenes of writing, and the social organization of writing. To illustrate such process tracing, Prior presents a number of sample analyses of writing processes engaged in by graduate students and professors in several different fields. In chapter 8, Kevin Leander and Paul Prior explore speaking and writing, asking how talk and text interact. Leander and Prior examine the complex relationships between talk and text in context, considering ways that talk is transformed into, shapes, and occasions texts as well as the ways text is transformed into, shapes, and occasions talk. This chapter also introduces the analysis of talk, noting particularly the absence of representations of texts in existing transcription systems and suggesting strategies for addressing this absence. Sample analyses focus on response in a graduate seminar and particularly on talk and text in classroom and extracurricular activities in a high school. In chapter 9, George Kamberelis and Lenora de la Luna consider children's writing, asking how developing writers create symbolic meaning. Kamberelis and de la Luna present a framework for looking at the textual, contextual, and political dimensions of children's texts and textual practices. Methodologically, they describe the value of using ethnographically-informed experimental simulations as well as naturalistic observations of writing. They illustrate this approach through analysis first of a 5-year-old girl's response to an experimental request (in the classroom) to produce a "science report" and second of two fifth-grade boys collaborating to produce a quite hybrid report on their dissection of an owl pellet. In chapter 10, Jack Selzer introduces rhetorical analysis, asking how people act rhetorically, how they read and shape rhetorical situations and how they craft texts to influence people. Selzer introduces key notions from classical and modern rhetorics as he identifies two basic approaches to rhetorical analysis: the textual and the contextual. To illustrate these approaches, he analyzes the rhetoric of two texts, an essay by E. B. White on education and an open letter to Bill Bennett from Milton Friedman, in which he argues for the legalization of drugs. Finally, in chapter 11, Charles Bazerman concludes by asking how texts organize activity and people. Bazerman provides means to analyze how texts serve as actions within social contexts. Topics include speech acts, genre as typified social action, and texts within activity systems. He illustrates this systemic approach with an analysis of a complex 6-week curricular unit in a sixth-grade classroom on Mayan history and culture.

I

ANALYZING TEXTS

1

Content Analysis:
What Texts Talk About

Thomas Huckin
University of Utah

BACKGROUND

The logical starting point for analyzing texts is to consider the **meaning** of the text. All texts are about something (i.e., they have **content**); and the most direct way of taking account of this is through **content analysis**. Developed by communication scholars in the early 20th century, content analysis was first used to measure the objective features (article length, size of headline, etc.) of newspaper stories. During World War II its scope was broadened to include various forms of propaganda including non-print discourse. By the 1950s, content analysis had established itself in communication research as virtually synonymous with discourse analysis. Berelson's classic 1952 work defined it thusly: "Content analysis is a research technique that objectively, systematically, and quantitatively describes the manifest content of communication" (Berelson, 1952). In recent decades, however, as discourse analysis itself has evolved into a broad variety of approaches ranging from ethnomethodology to artificial intelligence, content analysis has lost its status as the prime means of analyzing texts. Although in specific cases it can still serve that purpose, today it is more often used in a supporting role for more sophisticated forms of discourse analysis.

Definition

Writing research is one such field where content analysis has proved to be a useful foundational methodology. Here it might be defined as follows: **Content analysis is the identifying, quantifying, and analyzing of specific words, phrases, concepts, or other observable semantic data in a text or body of texts with the aim of uncovering some underlying thematic or rhetorical pattern running through these texts**. The key distinguishing characteristic to this approach is its focus on surface features (or "manifest content"). However, content analysis's emphasis on semantic or **meaning**-based patterns distinguishes it from more purely formal stylistic approaches such as register analysis (Biber & Finegan, 1994) or textlinguistic stylistics (Sandig, 1986). Content analysis makes no claim to being a rich, definitive, or comprehensive method of analysis, as some critics have alleged. Given its limited scope, it cannot be so. Rather, content analysis typically serves only to provide empirical grounding for other more sophisticated methods, such as those detailed in other chapters of this book.

Conceptual Versus Relational

Content analysis has traditionally relied on two basic methods: conceptual analysis and relational analysis. In **conceptual analysis**, a concept is selected, coded, and counted for its presence in a text or corpus (set of texts). In **relational analysis**, the process goes one step further: it identifies a number of concepts and then examines the relationships among them. Also called "concept mapping," it is especially common in cognitive studies involving the construction of mental models (Carley & Palmquist, 1992). In conceptual analysis, meaning is assumed to reside in individual concepts, whereas in relational analysis, meaning is understood to derive from the relationship among concepts. The key step in both types of content analysis is the coding of concepts, for it is here that the analyst exercises considerable subjectivity. For example, if one wants to count all references to "children" in a set of texts, should that include *infants, offspring, youngsters, teenagers, kids, dependents*, and *youth*, or only some of these terms? The answer to such a question depends on the goals of the research. That is, the coding scheme used in content analysis should be determined based on its ability to shed light on the question that drives the research, on its ability to give the study *validity*; and it should be set forth explicitly, so as to facilitate interrater *reliability*.

Quantitative Versus Qualitative

Since the 1970s, content analysis has tended to combine quantitative ("objective") and qualitative ("impressionistic") approaches: "The hallmark of modern content analysis has become the maintenance of a balance between the objective and implied aspects of textual data" (Roberts, 1989, p. 148). A strictly quantitative approach takes into account only those words, phrases, or other linguistic tokens that belong to a predetermined list and thus can be tabulated reliably by a computer; it overlooks all implicit meanings that can be gleaned from the context. A qualitative approach focuses rather on both explicit and implicit concepts, and empowers the researcher to use his or her judgment in determining, on a case by case basis, whether a particular linguistic token references a particular concept in the given context. Roberts' paper on "Linguistic Content Analysis" illustrates an early effort to combine quantitative and qualitative approaches. Roberts hypothesized that a comparison of the Nazi party platform before and after the party gained power would reveal a rhetorical shift from utopianism to ideological pragmatism. For example, the preface to the 1927 platform begins as follows (English translation): "The 1926 party convention in Weimar has requested the publication of periodicals, which should deal in short, fundamental, and programmatic essays with all important areas of our entire political life." The positive, universal tone ("all important areas of our entire political life") bespeaks a utopian vision. In contrast, the preface to the 1933 platform refers to its periodicals as follows: "The Nazi Party does not have so-called 'time- or campaign programs.' The content of the 25 points [of the platform] is distinguished by a great determination, without someone having blocked tactical necessities in the process" (Roberts, pp. 156–159). Here the wording is more negative, more qualified, giving the statement a distinctly pragmatic tone. Examination of the 1927 and 1933 platforms using only quantitative, conceptual analysis failed to reveal a reliable difference. But re-examination of the same two texts using qualitative, relational analysis supported Roberts' hypothesis. By tabulating clause relationships rather than doing a simple word count, Roberts showed that in 1927 the concept *official Nazi literature* was used mainly (62.5%) as grammatical subject and semantic agent, reflecting the presentation of Nazi ideals as a force for utopian change, whereas in 1933 the concept was used overwhelmingly (87.5%) as grammatical object and semantic patient, reflecting its status as a now-established institution serving as a backdrop for people's actions. Based on this demonstration, Roberts claimed that "the coding of syntactic information improves on content analysis restricted to word count methodology" (p. 164). He also claimed that the qualitative work involved in syntactic coding is necessary to counterbalance the less insightful, if more reliable, quantitative work, cautioning however that "the coder must be familiar with both the context in which a statement is made and the cultural universe within which it was intended to have meaning" (p. 164).

This sensitivity to context, both local and broad, is something that writing scholars can appreciate. Indeed, many composition researchers have adopted some form of combined quantitative/qualitative content analysis in their work, typically using it to provide empirical evidence regarding certain kinds of rhetorical action, discursive practices, or sociocultural patterning. Rather than proceeding "bottom-up" (cf. Barton, chap. 3, this volume), they often start with some broad hypothesis and then use both quantitative and qualitative analysis to advance or abandon it. The remainder of this chapter discusses the basic methodological procedure, a number of exemplary applications, an assessment of the method, and some suggestions for reading and pedagogical activities.

METHODOLOGICAL PROCEDURE

Content analysis as practiced by composition researchers involves a synergistic blending of quantitative data gathering and qualitative analysis. The exact distribution and sequencing of these two activities will vary from one study to another: Some may start with a proposition and use data-gathering in a **deductive** manner to confirm or disconfirm the proposition, whereas others may be more exploratory, using qualitative analysis in an **inductive**, flexible manner. This section lays out the basic steps for either approach. One should bear in mind that researchers seldom proceed in simple linear fashion through this 6-step sequence; rather, most researchers find it necessary to cycle back through certain steps, perhaps several times, and revise them in light of what they have discovered in subsequent steps.

1. Pose a Research Question. Content analysis proceeds best if the researcher has a good research question to start with, one that: (a) addresses a topic or issue of likely interest to fellow members of the researcher's discourse community, and (b) constitutes a novel claim about this topic or issue. Finding a good research question can be a challenge, as it requires considerable knowledge of the domain in question. Usually the best way to begin is by reading extensively in one's area of interest, as this may reveal controversies, unanswered questions, or other "gaps" in the literature (see Swales, 1990, chap. 7, and Riffe, Lacy, & Fico, 1998, chap. 3, for good discussion). Also, it often helps to establish a small corpus of texts, preliminary to Step 3 below. Poring over a pilot corpus, even informally, may reveal patterns that suggest an interesting research question.

A research question becomes a **hypothesis** if it is sufficiently explicit to be tested and, if appropriate, refuted by empirical data. A deductive study requires a hypothesis, an inductive study does not.

2. Define the Appropriate Construct(s). A good research question will focus on one or more general concepts such as "writing quality" or "bias." Such a concept is the **construct of interest** for that study (MacNealy, 1999).

If the research question is worded in such a way that the construct of interest is not obvious, the researcher must make a special effort to clarify it. For example, a researcher who hypothesizes that more mature students tend to be more rhetorically sensitive than less mature students is implicitly working with two constructs, "student maturity" and "rhetorical sensitivity." These constructs will have to be defined, however, in a way that can be converted into measurable units. For example, "student maturity" might be defined in terms of age, years living on one's own, or some other variable; "rhetorical sensitivity" might be defined in terms of attention to purpose, attention to audience, and/or other parameters.

3. Select an Appropriate Text or Body of Texts as the Study Corpus. An appropriate study corpus is one that will provide a good test of the research question, which means (a) that all the texts included in the corpus correspond in some clear fashion to the research question, and (b) that these corpus texts are representative of some identifiable, larger body of texts. One way to start on requirement *a* is to use the constructs of interest generated in Step 2 as keywords in a computerized search. If possible, the corpus should consist of texts that represent the full range of those included in the research question or hypothesis. Furthermore, it should consist of a substantial number of texts. Although a single text can serve for a pilot study or a case study, multiple texts are the norm for a full content study. The size of the corpus should be manageable given the goals of the study and the constraints (time, expense, resources, etc.) impinging on the researcher. A project aimed at identifying only a small set of surface variables, for example, requires less time and effort per text than a project concerned with deeper, more complex variables; thus, a project of the former type should use a larger corpus than a project of the latter type.

4. Determine Appropriate Units of Analysis (Text Features), Using Multiple Raters if Possible. The units of analysis, or text features, to be quantified for content analysis must be those that emerge logically from the research question. They must have a direct bearing on the question, in the sense that the incidence of a feature will constitute either direct support or direct nonsupport for it. The categorization of these units of analysis should be readily identifiable and non-overlapping, so as to be codable with some degree of reliability. In cases where the unit of analysis is a specific type of lexical item, the coding is relatively straightforward; for example, a researcher investigating the incidence of sexist terminology in a corpus of texts could probably create a list of reference terms such as *manpower, stewardess, chairmen,* etc. prior to doing the actual count. On the other hand, a researcher investigating a more abstract concept, such as the use of certain themes or styles, would find coding to be a more challenging task. Working collaboratively with one or more other investigators can help resolve uncertainties and produce a sample list of reference terms. There should not be too many coding categories (which would make them unmanageable), nor too few (which would collapse some meaningful distinctions). Sometimes, especially in an exploratory study, identifying features is a multistage process involving several passes through the corpus. This allows important features to emerge that might otherwise remain unnoticed until too late in the study, or unnoticed altogether.

Once the units of analysis have been determined, two or more investigators should independently sort at least 10% of the data into categories, and then the respective sortings should be compared for interrater reliability. (See MacNealy, 1999, for useful discussion of these points; see Hayes & Hatch, 1999, for discussion of interrater correlation versus percentage of agreement.) If there is too great a discrepancy, the units of analysis should be re-defined and re-tested.

5. Gather Data. If the units of analysis have been narrowly defined in Step 4, data gathering should be a relatively straightforward matter of identifying and counting. For example, if sexist terms are the target features, the analyst can establish a master list of such terms and then simply go through the corpus (either by hand or by computer) looking for matches. On the other hand, if the units of analysis are more abstract—as discussed earlier in Step 4—the investigator may want to proceed in stages, checking with a fellow investigator from time to time. If the investigator is unsure about certain identifications, the units of analysis involved may need to be revisited and redefined, per Step 4.

In some situations it is worth noting not only those text features that are present but also those that are absent. For example, if a complete checklist of possible features can be identified for a corpus as a whole, the investigator can then examine individual texts for either the presence or the absence of those features. (See the discussion of Huckin, 2002, for an illustration of this technique at work.)

6. Interpret the Findings. The final step is to analyze the data against the research question, that is, to interpret the findings. With a deductive study, where the researcher has posited the existence of a certain pattern in the corpus, a statistical test can be used to determine if the data constitutes a statistically significant pattern (MacNealy, 1999); in cases where a predicted pattern is obvious, a statistical test may be unnecessary. With an inductive, exploratory study, analyzing the data is more open to interpretation. In particular, the analysis calls for speculation about the **context** in which the study texts were produced, disseminated, and consumed by their intended audience; such attention to context often yields insight into possible text patterns and reasons for them. In an inductive study, the research question is only tentative and may be in need of revision if it does not conform to the data. Indeed, the goal of such a study should be to construct and refine a research question that might stand up to a more deductive, follow-up study.

APPLIED ANALYSES

Modern content analysis can be largely quantitative, largely qualitative, or some combination of the two. This section illustrates the range of possibilities.

Mainly Quantitative Content Analysis

The studies described here are of the traditional type, consisting mainly of counts of predetermined text features with little qualitative analysis.

Ethnic Targeting in Food and Beverage Advertisements (Pratt & Pratt, 1995)

These researchers wanted to know if food, beverage, and nutrition advertisements in U.S. consumer magazines differed according to the ethnicity of the targeted audience. Accordingly, they examined 3,319 such advertisements published in 1980–1982 and 1990–1992 in *Ebony* and *Essence*, which are read mainly by African-American women, and *Ladies' Home Journal*, read mainly by Caucasian women. They coded advertisements according to product categories (fruits, vegetables, desserts, etc.), form in which the product was advertised (fresh, canned, cholesterol-free, etc.), and nutrition themes used in promoting the product (high in fiber, good for general health, good for weight control, etc.). A quantitative content analysis showed significant differences among these magazines in frequency and type of promotional messages being conveyed. For example, the African-American magazines had far more ads on alcoholic beverages (56%) than did the Caucasian magazine (1.6%) and had far fewer ads for vegetables (0.6% to 6.9%). In contrast, ads in the Caucasian magazine had far more nutritional information than those in the two African-American magazines. These empirical findings enabled Pratt and Pratt to comment on the ethics of advertising.

In this study, Pratt and Pratt's *research question* raised the issue of whether U.S. consumer magazines discriminated against African-Americans in food and beverage advertisements. Their **construct of interest** was "bias" and their **units of analysis** were product categories, advertised product form, and nutrition themes promoted. Their **study corpus** consisted of

3,319 such advertisements published over 6 years in three major consumer magazines with clearly identifiable ethnic readerships. Using multiple raters, they **gathered** their data and then **interpreted** their findings.

Learning of Shared Terminology in a Composition Class (Palmquist, Carley, & Dale, 1997)

This case study explored the evolution of a shared lexicon in a semester-long freshman writing class. The researchers constructed computerized maps of the 16 students' mental models of writing, both at the beginning of the course and at the end, and for comparison, a map of the course instructor's mental model. These maps were created as follows: First, a list of relevant concepts was gleaned from frequently occurring terms in student journals, interviews, class discussions, and the course textbook. Second, a text file of these terms was created for each student's text. Third, each such text file was converted into a map by a computer program called Map Extraction Comparison and Analysis. A primary rater coded all texts and a secondary rater coded 10% of the interview transcripts and journal entries; interrater agreement was found to be 95.5% for concepts and 70.7% for statements linking two concepts. The maps were then converted into data matrices that could be analyzed statistically for intersections of concepts and statements between students and between student and instructor. (For details, see Palmquist et al., 1997.) By tracking these maps over time, Palmquist et al. were able to show a steady increase in the mean number of concepts and statements shared between students and between students and the instructor.

Qualitative Content Analysis: Inductive, Exploratory, Emergent

In this section, we describe several studies that exemplify the qualitative paradigm (Altheide, 1987). In each of these cases, the researcher began with some notion of what might emerge, but not with a clear hypothesis. The study corpus was used therefore not for deductive (hypothesis-testing) purposes, but merely for exploratory purposes.

Assessment of Critique Writing in Disciplinary Writing Courses (Mathison, 1996)

To examine the question of what constitutes good student critique writing in upper level disciplinary courses, Mathison examined 2-page essays from 32 students in an upper division Sociology course. These essays were critiques of a 14-page academic article on "quasi-religions." This source text was parsed into a template of 216 topic-comment units. Student critiques were then compared to this template, according to the following measures: types of evaluative comments, types of support (disciplinary or personal) for comments, overall length, and text configuration (summary + commentary vs. integrated topics and comments). Four sociology professors provided holistic evaluations of each of the 32 student critiques. Mathison found that critiques were evaluated more highly if they found weaknesses in the source article, basing their judgments on disciplinary (rather than personal) knowledge and employing an integrated text configuration.

Progress Toward Gender Balance in Technical Communication (TC) Studies (Thompson, 1999)

Thompson wanted to explore thematic trends in articles about women and feminism in the leading technical communication journals over a recent 8-year period. Starting with all 1,073 articles published in the five leading TC journals from 1989 to 1997, she used keywords such as *feminist, gender*, and *women* to scan the titles and arrive at a provisional corpus. Multiple passes through the corpus using both computer and visual inspection yielded a study corpus of 40 articles. Thompson then analyzed these articles for commonly occurring themes. She found that five themes predominated, all calling for more inclusion of women in TC studies: eliminating sexist language, providing equal opportunity in the workplace, valuing gender differences, recovering women's historical contributions to TC, and critiquing previously uncontested terms and concepts. Thompson's conclusion from this study is typical of qualitative studies in its generality: "This qualitative content analysis shows that research about women and feminism has been accepted within the academic purview of technical communication as a discipline" (p. 175).

Formal Variations in the Use of Conceptual Metaphor (Eubanks, 1999)

Eubanks investigated the nature of conceptual metaphor by using an "emergent" form of data gathering and analysis. He started with a weak hypothesis, namely, that a broad sampling of instances of the conceptual metaphor TRADE IS WAR in contemporary public discourse would reveal formal variations in metaphoric mappings. He then developed a corpus of 180 naturally occurring texts from a variety of genres, all of which used in some way the TRADE IS WAR metaphor. Finally, he used focus groups and interviews to assist him in a qualitative analysis of these texts. (See Eubanks, chap. 2, this volume, for further discussion.)

Combining Qualitative and Quantitative Analyses

In this section, we describe several studies that exemplify a "grounded qualitative" paradigm—using quantitative content analysis to establish the basic data and qualitative analysis to interpret it.

Portrayals of Men and Women Managers in the Press (Lee & Hoon, 1993)

The rapid modernization of the Singapore economy in the past several decades has caused major societal changes for both men and women. Yet despite a rise in educational levels, Singaporean women continue to lag far behind men in gaining managerial positions. Lee and Hoon wanted to know if this problem with career advancement was due in part to portrayals of men and women managers in the press. Accordingly, they examined 65 articles about men and women managers published between 1980 and 1990 in Singapore's three leading newspapers. Coding was done according to three content categories: demographic profile (e.g., marital status, education), word typifications (e.g., "confident," "successful"), and problems and issues (e.g., "role conflicts," "management style"). To ensure reliability, three coders independently categorized and coded the data. After quantifying these data and noting gender-based asymmetries in them, Lee and Hoon constructed composite pictures, or what they call "rhetorical visions," for male and female managers in the Singaporean press. They noted, for example, that articles about women managers emphasized the role conflicts they faced and their dependence on support systems, while articles about men managers emphasized their managerial abilities and their independence.

Distinguishing Features of Strong and Weak Conference Submissions (Berkenkotter & Huckin, 1995)

In our study of "gatekeeping" at CCCC conventions, we wanted to know what text features differentiated high-rated abstracts (or "proposals") and low-rated ones. We developed a stratified random sample of 441 abstracts from three CCCC conventions, representing all subject areas for each year and all four levels of evaluation (two high and two low). Rather than identifying specific text features, we decided that holistic analysis would yield more insightful results. Accordingly, one of us examined all 441 abstracts, noting certain patterned text features that seemed to distinguish the high-rated abstracts from the low-rated ones. Another comp/rhet specialist, working independently, did likewise. The two analysts agreed on their findings, which were as follows: High-rated abstracts more often than low-rated proposals appeared to (a) address topics of current interest to the field, (b) clearly define a problem, (c) discuss this problem in a novel way, and (d) project more of an insider ethos through the style of writing. This study examined content across a large corpus, but did so in a distinctly qualitative, impressionistic way.

Insider Influence in the CCCC Selection Process (Faber, 1996)

Faber did a follow-up study using a large subset of the Berkenkotter and Huckin corpus. He was particularly interested to see if and how the CCCC selection process reflected the scholarly interests of organization insiders. He began with the following hypothesis: "Given the apparent ways in which institutions and organizations use language to structure and formalize relations of power and privilege, it would seem that we may learn much from an examination of jargon, acronyms, repetitions, and occasional and explicit citational practices within academic discourse" (p. 362). He then went through the entire study corpus looking for these kinds of features. As he did so, he noticed other, related features that seemed to more clearly reflect ways in which the language of these abstracts related to power and privilege at CCCC. Additional passes through the corpus reinforced this perception, and the result was a new tripartite taxonomy: (a) formal and generic features, (b) epistemic voice, and (c) expansionary rhetoric. Each abstract was then evaluated according to the specifics of these three categories. A co-rater highly experienced in the field went through 10% of this data and agreed with Faber's evaluation in 88%–92% of the cases. This is an excellent illustration of the inductiveness and flexibility of qualitative content analysis, in that Faber was willing to alter his initial hypothesis when he noticed that a more powerful, more explanatory hypothesis could be substituted for it.

Expert–Novice Differences in Written Argumentation Skills (Crammond, 1998)

Curious about the differences between expert writers and student writers in their ability to construct complex arguments, Crammond randomly gathered 36 argumentative essays from sixth-, eighth-, and tenth-grade students, as well as seven argumentative texts from professional writers. She then coded each text for the presence of Toulmin argument substructures, including Claims, Modal Qualifications, Constraint Qualifications, Subclaims, Data, Warrants, Backing, Reservations, Countered Rebuttals, and Alternative Solutions. This coding was done by mapping relationships between surface linguistic features and the Toulmin argument model. Because this involved some inferencing, a second rater was employed for reliability. Crammond found that the students used less argumentation than the expert writers, especially fewer warrants, countered rebuttals, and modals.

The Rhetorical Use of Citations in Scientific Discourse (Paul, 2000)

Scientific journal articles vie for attention in the scientific marketplace, and a key measure of their success is the degree to which they are cited by other researchers. In this longitudinal study, Paul traced the history of 13 journal articles about chaos theory over periods up to 20 years. Of the more than 3,200 citations identified, Paul isolated 609 for closer rhetorical analysis. Her principal construct of interest—scientific success—was operationalized mainly as "centrality to the scientific community," which was broken down into five features for each citation: location of the citation within the article, method of identifying the citation, level of acceptance of the concept cited, purpose or function of the citation, and discipline of the journal. Each of these features, in turn, was defined in a way that was measurable. For example, "method of identifying the citation" was defined as either including or excluding the author's name. For reliability, Paul had two other coders check a 12% sample of her corpus; correlations across the five features averaged 0.83. Paul then used rhetorical analysis to make sense of her findings. As this was an exploratory study, in cases where she encountered patterns contrary to her expectations, she was able to use qualitative analysis to revise her initial hypotheses.

Identifying Manipulative Textual Silences in Public Discourse (Huckin, 2002)

Rhetoricians and discourse analysts have long noted that one of the most powerful ways that writers can manipulate readers is to keep silent about certain relevant topics, that is, to restrict the universe of discourse. But the difficulty of identifying such manipulative silences has been a deterrent to full investigation. The goal of this study was to develop a systematic methodology for detecting such silences. Content analysis proved to be central to this effort. Because, by definition, manipulative silences occur when writers deliberately omit information that is relevant to a certain topic in a certain rhetorical situation, the key to detecting such omissions is to first determine the full set of sub-topics that are relevant to a certain topic. This can be done in the case of public discourse by first developing a corpus of public texts that deal with the topic in question. One then goes through this corpus looking for all terms and concepts that help characterize the general topic; let's call them **sub-topics**. This kind of focused content analysis enables one to get a comprehensive picture of the **general**

discourse on that topic (i.e., a full inventory of all the sub-topics that have been raised in connection with that topic). Finally, one can then do a focused content analysis of any **individual text** about that topic to see which of these sub-topics are unmentioned, thereby identifying the textual silences in that text.

In this case, I decided to use "homelessness in America" as my main topic, or **construct of interest**. My **research question** was, "How is homelessness depicted in American public discourse?" For my **study corpus**, I searched the Academic Universe online database to locate all newspaper reports, editorials, and feature stories on the topic of U.S. homelessness published in major U.S. newspapers during that month (January, 1999). Using the keyword *homeless** as my search term and hand-eliminating all texts that were not about human homelessness in the United States (e.g., homeless pets, homelessness in Honduras), I created a study corpus of 163 texts. I then prepared to go through each of these 163 texts, using content analysis to identify the relevant sub-topics, or **units of analysis**. As part of this effort, I read a number of books and articles about the topic, noting the sorts of sub-topics that experts kept citing when discussing homelessness. In addition, I noticed that four distinct categories seemed to dominate these discussions: causes of homelessness, effects of homelessness, public responses to homelessness, and the demographics of homelessness. I decided to use these same four categories in my own content analysis of the study corpus. I then examined each of these 163 study texts, looking for terms or concepts that fit into these four categories (including those that emerged from my earlier reading of books and articles). This **gathering of data** yielded a total of 51 sub-topics such as "vagrancy," "mental illness," "volunteers," and "shelter" (see Appendix), which I **interpreted** as reflecting the discourse of U.S. homelessness during that particular period of time.

After this quantitative part of my study, I then embarked on the qualitative part, the purpose of which was to **identify textual silences in individual texts**. The logic of this part was as follows: A knowledgeable author of a text on homelessness in the United States in January 1999 would have had 51 relevant sub-topics available for use; if he or she chose to discuss only, say, 30 of these, the other 21 would be omissions, or "textual silences." To illustrate this analytic process, I chose two individual texts from the study corpus. I then scrutinized each of these to see which sub-topics had been excluded. These missing sub-topics were interpreted as deliberately manipulative silences, since they were candidates for inclusion yet had not been included. Cognitive theory, rhetorical analysis, and social theory were then used to speculate on why the respective writers might have created these omissions.

Ethnographic Content Analysis (Altheide, 1987)

All of the studies described earlier have been strictly text-based studies. Writing researchers may be interested, however, in a variation of the qualitative/quantitative method known as ethnographic content analysis. In this method, ethnographic inquiry (e.g., interviewing, participant observation) is used as a discovery procedure to generate appropriate research questions and constructs; and then quantitative content analysis is used to code the appropriate units of analysis, gather the data, and perform reliability checks on the results. Although not a study of writing, Smith, Sells, and Clevenger (1994) serves as a good example of ethnographic content analysis. They used in-depth interviews of couples and therapists, and other ethnographic techniques, to study the use of reflecting team practice in therapeutic counseling. Viewed in conjunction with previous studies, these interviews revealed the emergence of themes in seven categories. Quantitative analysis validated the findings, demonstrating how multiple perspectives can produce greater stability and accuracy than one-dimensional studies.

ASSESSMENT

Content analysis has been criticized from various quarters for certain methodological shortcomings of both a practical and an epistemological nature. But these criticisms can be debated; furthermore, content analysis has some obvious virtues that defy criticism. This section discusses all of the pros and cons.

Criticism 1: Coding in Quantitative Analysis Is Too Surface-Based and Thereby Lacks Validity.   (Roberts, 1989). Such coding is said to valorize the textual artifact in unreflective fashion, ignoring the reader's or writer's engagement with the text (Anderson, 1973). As Van Dijk (1997b) put it, content analysis is "a method which in fact has less to do with meaning than with the more observable aspects—mostly words—of discourse" (p. 9; see also Kepplinger, 1989). On this view, quantitative content analysis reductively fragments human phenomena into artificial categories, making the analysis invalid as a reflection of human meaning making. In short, by restricting its attention to formal text features, quantitative content analysis ignores rhetorical, social, interpersonal, and other contextual aspects of written communication. Thus, quantitative analysis cannot account for much of what matters to most writing researchers.

The force of this criticism depends, of course, on the nature and extent of the claim being made by the analyst. In some cases, as in the Pratt and

Pratt and Palmquist studies described earlier, the claims put forth are limited in such a way that a purely quantitative approach works. Most current topics of interest in writing research, however, involve subtleties that exceed the reach of quantitative content analysis, and in such cases a researcher would be unwise to rely on such analysis as the main investigative instrument. Quantitative analysis *can* be useful as an adjunct to more qualitative analyses, as shown in most of the earlier studies.

Criticism 2: Coding in Qualitative Analysis Is Subjective and Thus Lacks Reliability. (Roberts, 1989). Given its exploratory, inductive nature, qualitative content analysis typically includes implicit concepts among its units of analysis. Identifying and coding such concepts can be quite impressionistic, requiring subjective interpretation on the part of the analyst. For example, in Eubanks' study of the TRADE IS WAR conceptual metaphor, he reports having identified hundreds of instances of this metaphor in his corpus of 180 texts. But this metaphor, like other metaphors in general, does not present itself *tout nu*; rather it is something that is perceived by the analyst. In some cases, such as those where the term *trade war* is used, the metaphor may be straightforwardly identifiable. But what of the following example cited by Eubanks? "Our real problem is not access to Japan's markets but Japan's destruction of ours. We're erecting tombstones over U.S. industries—semiconductors, machine tools, robotics, computers—targeted for extinction by Japanese government–business collaboration. Our high-tech economy is looking more like an industrial graveyard" (p. 190). Is this an instance of the TRADE IS WAR metaphor—or isn't it? It uses terms such as *destruction*, *tombstones*, *targeted*, and *graveyard* (all highlighted by Eubanks in citing this example) but is that sufficient for it to trigger the idea of international trade as "warfare"? Different analysts could reasonably come to different conclusions about this.

To guard against this problem, discourse analysts should gather independent judgments from one or more additional raters and then apply correlation measures to determine the interrater reliability. (See Step 4 under Methodological Procedure; see also Hayes & Hatch, 1999, and the references cited therein.) If the correlation coefficient is too low, the units of analysis may have to be revised.

Criticism 3: Content Analysis Is Labor Intensive. MacNealy (1999) cautioned that there is often a great deal of time and energy involved in doing detailed text analysis: "Defining categories, dividing texts up into recording units, and sorting the recording units into the categories consume large amounts of time. Also the individual tasks are not so easy. For example, defining categories can be a very frustrating task because, even though you think you have set up enough categories and defined them so carefully that another researcher can use them and achieve the same results you did, you will soon learn that you overlooked something. That is why user-testing your categories with a piece of similar text is essential" (pp. 143–144).

There is no disputing the fact that content analysis is labor intensive. But this also has certain positive aspects, inasmuch as the very labor involved imposes a degree of thoroughness that is often missing in other types of research.

On the other hand, content analysis has many *virtues*, including the following:

Virtue 1: Content Analysis Requires the Researcher to Examine Actual Writings in Systematic Fashion. MacNealy (1999) makes this point in regard to text analysis in general. Writing research is as much about the products of writing as it is about the processes that produce and interpret them, and focusing on the text itself should be something that writing researchers welcome. Indeed, it can be argued that in recent years many writing researchers, in their zeal to study the sociocultural context in which writing takes place, have neglected the linguistic text itself. If so, content analysis, especially of the hybrid type favored here, can be seen as a healthy corrective.

Virtue 2: Content Analysis Can Be Done at a Time and Place Convenient to the Researcher. Unlike most other methodologies, such as ethnography, experimental research, or focus groups, content analysis does not require coordinating with other people or using special equipment other than, in most cases, a personal computer and modem. The one exception concerns testing for reliability, which involves using one or more colleagues to serve as raters (see Step 4 under Methodological Procedure).

Virtue 3: Content Analysis Yields Information No Less Valuable Than That Provided by Other Methods, and Does So With Greater Objectivity. Thomas (1994) argued persuasively that content analysis has been misrepresented and unfairly maligned by its critics. She notes that although content analysis does not provide direct access to an individual's meaning-making processes, it is no different from any other technique in this regard. Rather, *all* research techniques involve the gathering of data that are then interpreted by the analyst. Making an important distinction between individual meaning making and cultural meaning making, Thomas argues that written artifacts "are important means by which [societal] customs and beliefs are collectively expressed" (p. 686). The interpretation of texts encompasses "the regularity and pattern of human experience," and as such, "to deny or discard that patterned experience is to deny culture, not to celebrate it" (p. 688).

Having made the case for the value of artifactual analysis in explicating cultural meaning, Thomas then makes the case for content analysis in particular. Her argument revolves around the following central claim: "There is no kind of information that can be encoded into the forms of other conventionally written scholarship about artifacts that cannot also be presented in a research report relying on content analysis" (p. 690). Responding to the complaint about content analysts typing and thereby "fragmenting" human phenomena, Thomas states that people in their everyday social interactions do likewise and that every other form of artifactual analysis does so as well. "The big difference between what is done in content analysis and these other circumstances is that with content analysis the typing is done consciously and publicly (read: manifestly) and is systematized for quantitative synopsis" (p. 691). Content analysis provides data in the form of frequency and distribution measurements that is unavailable using other text-analytic methods. Furthermore, in basing its investigations on observable data, it offers a greater level of objectivity than other methods. She concludes: "All scholars studying the content and form of artifacts in the context of culture—regardless of technique—are, at some level, performing the same functions. *All* studies involve sampling, analysis, and interpretation of analytic data. What makes content analysis 'objective' is that, as much as possible, the researcher is obliged to make public the bases for the sampling and analytic choices" (p. 694).

ACTIVITIES

1. To help students see the *prima facie* value of content analysis, have them discuss the findings of the Pratt and Pratt (1995) study. How harmful is it for a particular group to be deluged with ads for alcoholic beverages? How can such a situation be averted in a market-driven society?

2. Have students do a "mini-replication" of the Pratt and Pratt (1995) study, using small samples from a current *Ebony* or *Essence* and *Ladies Home Journal*. Or, have them do a similar study substituting different readerships (e.g., ads in teenage girls' magazines versus those in magazines for mature women).

3. Eubanks's study of the TRADE IS WAR conceptual metaphor is based on a corpus of texts gathered from the early 1990s. More recently, international trade has often been discussed in terms of "economic globalization," a discussion that sometimes invokes conceptual metaphors different from those analyzed by Eubanks. Have students search the Internet using the term "economic globalization" and create a small corpus of study texts. Then have them do a content analysis of these texts, looking specifically for conceptual metaphors.

4. Have students identify some other conceptual metaphor in public discourse (e.g., POLITICAL CAMPAIGNS ARE HORSE RACES), and do a qualita-

tive content analysis of it. Books by George Lakoff (*Metaphors We Live By*, *Women, Fire, and Dangerous Things*; *Moral Politics*) could be consulted for ideas.

5. Have students read Barton's (1995) article, "Contrastive and non-contrastive connectives: Metadiscourse functions in argumentation," in *Written Communication, 12*(2), 219–239, and apply the same methodology to a sample academic text (e.g., one of the chapters in this book).

6. Using the list of subtopics from the homelessness corpus (see Appendix), have students find a public document (e.g., editorial, feature story, news report) on homelessness and identify its textual silences. Then have students use rhetorical analysis (see chap. 10) to speculate on why the author created such silences.

7. Have students think of a public issue that concerns them (e.g., the voting system, clean energy, globalization), log on to the Academic Universe database (part of Lexis-Nexus) and, using one or more keywords, create a small corpus of about 30 texts addressing that issue. Then have them do a quantitative content analysis of this corpus.

8. Using the same search as in #7, have students each summarize one of these sites and then discuss their summaries in class.

9. Have students search the Internet using "content analysis" as their search term. Have them examine the first 10 sites listed and see how these readings conform to (or depart from) the instruction given in this chapter.

FOR FURTHER READING

Riffe, D., Lacy, S., & Fico, F. G. (1998). *Analyzing media messages: Using quantitative content analysis in research*. Mahwah, NJ: Lawrence Erlbaum Associates.

This is an excellent resource that provides thorough instruction in how to do quantitative content analysis. After some historical background and then a precise definition of **quantitative content analysis**, the book has chapters on research design, measurement, sampling, reliability, validity, data analysis, and the use of computers. The writing is clear and comprehensible throughout, with good use being made of well-chosen examples. Of particular value is the chapter on research design, which raises the following key questions: What is the phenomenon or event to be studied? How much is known about the phenomenon already? What are the specific research questions or hypotheses? What will be needed to answer the specific research question or test the hypothesis? What is the formal design of the study? How will coders know the data when they see it? How much data will be needed to test the hypothesis or answer the research question? How can the quality of the data be maximized? What kind of data analysis will be used? And, has the research question been answered or the research hypothesis tested successfully? These questions serve as a scaffold for the rest of the book, constituting a general research model; and although the book itself is devoted to quantitative content analysis, a researcher interested in **qualitative content analysis** can learn much from the rigor of the approach taken here.

Titscher, S., Meyer, M., Wodak, R., & Vetter, E. (2000). *Methods of text and discourse analysis*. Newbury Park, CA: Sage.

This book analyzes 10 different empirical approaches to the study of text and discourse: content analysis, grounded theory, ethnographic methods, narrative semiotics, critical discourse analysis, conversation analysis, membership categorization device analysis, functional pragmatics, distinction theory text analysis, and objective hermeneutics. Although content analysis is only one of these, the volume as a whole is of relevance to the content analyst by virtue of the fact that each method is compared to the nine others. Thus, this book, more than any other, allows one to get a sense of how content analysis fits into the larger world of text and discourse study.

APPENDIX
Subtopics Mentioned in 163 Articles on Homelessness Published in Major U.S. Newspapers, January 1–31, 1999 [100,264 words]

Causes	Weighted Totals
substance abuse	83
mental illness	43
poverty	42
shortage of jobs/loss of job	28
lack of affordable housing, available shelter	22
desire for independence	18
domestic abuse	14
bad luck, medical emergency, etc.	12
low wages/low min. wage	11
racism, discrimination	10
welfare cuts	9
self-destructive behavior, bad choices	9
criminality	8
failure of the healthcare system	6
transportation problems	5
lack of life skills	3

Effects	
exposure to severe weather	66
hunger, sickness, or death	62
crime/violence	52
vagrancy/loitering	47
begging/panhandling	23
psychological/emotional effects	20
bad grooming	17

(Continued)

APPENDIX
(Continued)

Public Responses	Weighted Totals
shelter/beds	158
funding (govt)	67
donated food	62
religious support	50
transitional/affordable housing	45
police sweeps, 'cleanups,' harassment	42
criminalization/jail or fines	40
funding (private)	39
jobs or job-training	38
politics	35
volunteers	30
medical care	29
donated clothing	25
treatment for substance abuse	26
donated blankets/sleeping bags	25
redevelopment, property values, NIMBY	25
treatment for mental illness	23
outreach workers	17
unspecified services, counseling, rehab	15
education	15
entertainment, toys, art	14
moral or legal issues	10
transportation, communication needs	9
life skills, parenting training, etc.	8
demand for personal responsibility	6
childcare	5
media/publicity	5

Demographics	
Types of homeless: families/children	78
Numbers of homeless	47

2

Poetics and Narrativity: How Texts Tell Stories

Philip Eubanks
Northern Illinois University

Language scholars have traditionally associated narrative, metaphor, and other figures of speech with literary texts. But in recent decades there has been a shift away from that traditional view. Most scholars now see narrative, metaphor, metonymy, and a host of rhetorical figures not as "devices" for structuring or decorating extraordinary texts but instead as fundamental social and cognitive tools. In other words, a growing number of writing researchers, rhetoricians, literary critics, linguists, and cognitive scientists are studying poetics in order to make sense of wide-ranging social processes and the workings of the mind.

This shift in perspective has opened productive avenues for the study of everyday texts. As scholars have begun to show, texts such as experimental articles, business reports, daily conversations, and even student compositions, to name a few, are often shaped by over-arching or embedded narratives and figures. Analyses of these narratives and figures proceeds somewhat differently from analyses associated with more traditional poetics.

Because—in general—novels and dramas are obviously stories, and poems manifestly figurative, traditional poetics describes unrecognized characteristics of recognized forms. Everyday texts, however, sometimes hide their narrative and figurative dimensions, making it necessary for scholars to read the situations and silences that attend these texts in order to analyze, or even to recognize, their "literary" elements. To make matters yet more complex, theories of narrative and figuration are evolving quickly. Thus scholars may often do more than apply known theories; they may contribute new theories of narrative and figuration that are suggested by new data.

In this chapter, we take a brief look at some ways of studying narrative and figuration in everyday texts: narrative first, metaphor second, and other figures after that. Bear in mind that the order of discussion does not imply an order of importance or logical priority. In fact, narrative, meta-phor, and other figures are profoundly intertwined.

NARRATIVE: BASIC CONCEPTS

Many theorists distinguish between a story and a narrative this way: A story is what happened, and a narrative is the way what happened is re-counted in words. That distinction can be important at times, but in this chapter I use the terms more or less interchangeably—an ambiguity, I note, that is in keeping with much current commentary.

What, then, is a story? Simply put, a story consists of two or more re-lated, sequential events. "My sister is a teacher" is not a story; it is merely a statement of classification. On the other hand, "after four years of college, my sister became a teacher" is a story. It's not much of a story, but it has the minimum a story requires: two related, sequential events (my sister's going to college and her becoming a teacher). Most stories—at least, those that capture people's interest—also have a complication. For instance, it may be somewhat more interesting to hear, "While my sister was in college, *she ran out of money*, but in the end she became a teacher." The story still consists of sequential, related events, but because of a complicating event the situation at the end of the story resolves the situation that precedes it.

Stories, of course, can be vastly more complex. Numerous theorists have explained the varied structures of stories—along with the convolutions of recounting them (e.g., Bal, 1997; Prince, 1987; Propp, 1968). But no matter how abundant a story's characters and events, and no matter how round-about the telling, all stories—from novels to newspaper items—are com-posed of structures similar to the my-sister-became-a-teacher story. That observation has at least two important implications for researchers of ev-eryday texts. First, if we define narrowly what counts as a story, we can broaden significantly the number of places where stories may be discov-ered. Second, because stories exhibit a distinct structure, many scholars see story-based discourse and thought as distinct from other forms of dis-course and thought.

That is, scholars have for a long time assumed that narrative (story-based) and non-narrative (usually argumentative) texts are different *in kind*. Writing in the mid-1980s, for example, the cognitive psychologist Jerome Bruner (1986), even as he makes a case for the importance of narrative in thought, claims, "A good story and a well-formed argument are different natural kinds. Both can be used as means for convincing another. Yet what they convince *of* is fundamentally different: Arguments convince one of their truth, stories of their lifelikeness" (p. 11). Although this premise is not always asserted so explicitly, it has tacitly informed much study. Especially with respect to school composition, arguments have been considered not just different from stories but more important as something to teach—and, in turn, more interesting as something to investigate.

Many current researchers, however, are finding that narrative and non-narrative texts and thought are profoundly woven together. And because of continuing work on the social, cultural, and cognitive import of narrative, the anti-narrative bias no longer holds sway. More typical of the current view is that of Jane Perkins and Nancy Blyler (1999), who "foresee a burgeoning of interest in narrative, as the factors contributing to its devaluing increasingly lose their influence and researchers, teachers and trainers, and workplace professionals are freed to recognize narrative's considerable strengths" (p. 28). If narrative is as important as current researchers claim, the question that follows is, Important in exactly what way? There are two main, not unrelated, answers to that question.

The first answer is provided by postmodernism. Postmodernism is attuned to **grand narratives** or **metanarratives**—stories that pervade, shape, and, it is often asserted, delude cultures. Postmodernists argue that the very prevalence of some narratives makes them largely invisible and, at the same time, inescapably intermingled with institutions, practices, and texts. Even so-called non-narrative scientific texts—and thus science itself—cannot escape the molding power of grand narratives. As Jean-Francois Lyotard (1979) points out early on,

> What do scientists do when they appear on television or are interviewed in the newspapers after making a "discovery"? They recount an epic of knowledge that is in fact wholly unepic. They play by the rules of the narrative game; its influence remains considerable not only on the users of the media, but also on the scientist's sentiments. (pp. 27–28)

In other words, whereas science claims to construct texts that represent an objective, impersonal reality outside itself, scientific texts are made legitimate by culturally pervasive stories, such as science's discovery story.

Science's discovery story is, of course, familiar to us all—we know its typified sequence of events. Scientists face an incomprehensible world, but through observation, experimentation, and rejection of ignorance and superstition, they make the world ever more explainable. So old and familiar is this story that we don't need to recount it in detail, or perhaps not at all, for it to be understood. It is summed up in the phrase "scientific progress." As Lyotard (1979) puts it, "Consider the form of popular sayings, proverbs, and maxims: they are like splinters of potential narratives, or molds of old ones, which have continued to circulate on certain levels of the social contemporary edifice" (p. 22).

The scientific discovery story is only one of many grand narratives that tacitly pervade non-narrative texts. One of the main tasks of studying narrative in everyday texts is to document and analyze tacit narratives—narratives that legitimate, direct, and constrain discourse and practices in institutional and professional settings. In that respect, the study of narrative is the study of culture. Moreover, as we enter a *post*-postmodern phase, more and more scholars do not attach a stigma to grand narratives. Instead, these pervasive narratives are seen as important cultural tools that may operate for good or ill, but need to be recognized in either case.

Narrative is also important in a second and complementary way. Cognitive scientists are interested in the structure and function of language as an indicator of the workings of the mind—or, some would prefer to say, the brain. Along with metaphor, narrative is one of the most observable ways we conceptualize experience and organize memory. Over the past couple of decades, cognitive scientists have studied story grammars, the specific structures of stories, and they have concerned themselves increasingly with the social aspect of cognition.

Roger Schank and Robert Abelson, for example, argue that memory is not just partially structured by narratives but is fundamentally narrative in nature. They suggest that memory functions through the telling of stories—that memories are formed in the social act of rehearsing stories of our experiences. In a similar vein, literary critic and cognitive scientist Mark Turner (1996) argues, "Narrative imagining—story—is the fundamental instrument of thought. Rational capacities depend upon it. It is our chief means of looking into the future, of predicting, of planning, and of explaining. It is a literary capacity indispensable to human cognition generally" (pp. 4–5). Thus, cognitive science is beginning to help us explain why, in a biological sense, the grand narratives critiqued by postmodernists can reasonably be credited with broad social power.

It is against this background, a background of multiple, complementary approaches to narrative study, that researchers interested in everyday texts are working. Not surprisingly, the work is diverse. But these diverse approaches hold in common a growing sense that the study of narrative suits more texts and settings, and should be more central to the study of everyday texts, than ever before.

NARRATIVE: APPLIED ANALYSIS AND METHODS

In this section, I analyze stories told by and about Microsoft chairman Bill Gates. Given the many possible perspectives, any narrative analysis needs to be prefaced by an explanation of the practical and theoretical approach—an explanation of what data are being examined, what procedure was used for analyzing the data, and what "lenses" are being employed for viewing the data.

Extending a larger case study of the discourse surrounding Bill Gates (Eubanks, 2000), I gathered three interviews given by Gates in the 1990s. I selected these interviews for analysis here because each offers insight into Gates's, and hence Microsoft's, rhetorical response to the federal antitrust suit that long plagued the software giant. The first is an extended interview that appeared in *Playboy* in 1994, just as the antitrust suit began to take shape. The second two are brief interviews that appeared in *Time* in 1998 and 1999, after the suit was well underway.

My procedure for analyzing these texts was as follows:

After selecting the texts for relevance and interest, I read them repeatedly, identifying all of the stories I could and making notes in the margins. To make the notes useful in a practical way, I jotted summary notations in the margins: "story about developing software," "story about the Internet," and so on. These summary notations simply drew attention to relevant passages so that they could be found again. In addition to summary notations, I recorded questions and tentative observations. Marginal notes don't have to represent in fact, should not represent—the final word on a text. But they're an excellent tool for discovering patterns and developing interpretations. Observations can be refined, reconsidered, or cast aside in second, third, and fourteenth passes. And they're almost always refined even further during the composition and revision of the culminating research paper.

After taking as many notes as I reasonably could, I sorted the identified stories into analytic categories, attempting to see not just how each story could be understood on its own but how the stories related to each other rhetorically. These analytic categories were similar to, but not the same as, the categories I used in my summary notations. That is, at the outset I used concrete classifications such as *story about developing software* and *story about the Internet*, but when it came time to analyze the stories in relation to one another, I categorized both the developing-software story and the Internet story as *business-development stories*. The difference may seem subtle, but the process of categorization is both crucial and potentially messy. As you will see, I've emphasized the business-development story embedded in many of Gates's statements. But other categorizations are possible, and other stories undoubtedly inhabit the same passages. In texts, as in the world, stories melt into one another, pile one on top of another, provide context for each other.

The procedure I've described—note-taking and categorizing—may seem so natural that it is not a method at all. But, of course, it *is* a method—one that differs substantially from other possible ways of treating the same texts. Consider the things I did not do—such as quantify the number or type of stories, search for key words or concepts, analyze the specific ways the stories were put into words, and surely more. To put it another way, my approach was similar to rhetorical analysis as described in chapter 10 by Jack Selzer, who explains how texts can be usefully understood in light of rhetorical principles, classical and contemporary. I read the Gates interviews in light of rhetorical theory and, of course, in light of the narrative theory outlined earlier: I was guided by my understanding of what counts as a story, what possible importance can be attached to stories, and how stories can function as part of a text or corpus of texts.

The stories embedded in the Gates interviews, I suggest, function as part of a larger strategy of narrative-making that has been used by Microsoft to shape its public defense against both the federal government and competitors who have worked with the Justice Department. My analysis of this strategy is twofold.

First, as Graham Smart (1999) points out in his examination of stories at the Bank of Canada, one function of stories told in organizations is to develop coherent representations of problems. In that sense, storytelling is both a matter of consensus building and of what is lately called **distributed cognition**, cognitive frameworks that allow people to think and work together. At the bank of Canada, economists collaborate to create past, present, and future stories of monetary policy. Similarly, in his role as chairman of Microsoft, Bill Gates uses stories to give cognitive shape to and build consensus about the company's mission. To it put more plainly, Gates tells stories in order to define what problems his company aims to solve. Not surprisingly, perhaps, many of the stories that Gates tells in *Playboy* and *Time* are echoed in Gates's books, in speeches to his stockholders, and in Microsoft's other public relations efforts.

Second, Gates's stories have an argumentative function. They are told not spontaneously but rather in response to other stories told about him and his company, antagonistic stories that not only disparage Gates himself but also provide an opposing cognitive model of what Microsoft does and hopes to do. Thus, Gates's stories are as much matters of refutation as they are matters of problem setting.

Gates is well aware of his role as a public storyteller, a role that permits him to influence the way the public imagines the inner workings of Microsoft. Of course, without the benefit of extensive ethnographic data, we should not speculate as to whether Gates's representation is fair—some say it is not. But by looking at his public utterances, we can gauge what Gates would like the public to believe, and we can observe how persistent he is in attempting to shape those beliefs. Asked by *Playboy* why he granted an interview, Gates responds with a jumble of what seems to be public-relations boilerplate and disarming, some might say clumsy, frankness. His reason for speaking:

> For the message that personal computers can do neat things, that software is great stuff, that there's an exciting opportunity here and Microsoft is involved in it, that's a worthwhile message for Microsoft to get out. And if you want to just put Microsoft spokesman next to all those comments, that would be fine, except I know that people are more interested in human stories than they are in what technology can do for them. (*Playboy* Interview, 1994, p. 68)

Gates may, in fact, want us all to know about the exciting future of computer technology, but more surprising is his candor about telling personal stories to promote Microsoft's objectives. To reveal stories about himself is to fashion the public image of his company.

He also understands the importance of crafting personal stories carefully, as he demonstrates when responding to commonly repeated tales of the young Bill Gates—such as the doubtful tale, told by Gates himself, that he made a large profit on McGovern–Eagleton campaign buttons after Thomas Eagleton was dropped from the 1972 Democratic ticket, the story that Gates once spent $242 on a pizza delivery in the hardcore days of his upstart company, or the story that Gates once received three speeding tickets from the same officer on his way from Albuquerque to Seattle. With evident irritation, Gates corrects the details and reinterprets the meaning of each episode. Gates is irked most by a version of his personal success story that begins with his having a million-dollar trust fund while he attended Harvard. He not only denies the story's substance, but also wonders aloud why such a story would be spread:

> You think it's a better myth to have started with a bunch of money and made money than to have started without? In what sense? My parents are very successful, and I went to the nicest private school in the Seattle area. I was lucky. But I never had any trust funds of any kind, though my dad did pay my tuition at Harvard, which was quite expensive. (*Playboy* Interview, 1994, p. 67)

An appropriate myth is, indeed, what Gates is after. But the myth he wants to create is not just about himself but rather about Gates and his company, merged into a single (id)entity.

If Gates does not want people to believe he began life with too many advantages, he even more vehemently resists stories that emphasize Microsoft's advantages. According to Gates, such stories obscure Microsoft's fundamental task, which is twofold: first, to provide consumers with products they want; second, to stay a step ahead—and perhaps no more than a step ahead—of fast-gaining competitors. Describing Microsoft's role with emerging technologies, Gates frames his Microsoft myth in both corporate and personal terms.

Because we've had leadership products, we've had an opportunity to have a role [with the Internet]. But this would have happened without us. Somebody would have done a standard operating system and promoted a graphics interface. We may have made it happen a little sooner. Likewise, the information highway is going to happen. If we play a major role it'll be because we were a little bit better a little bit sooner than others were. . . . If we weren't still hiring great people and pushing ahead at full speed, it would be easy to fall behind and become a mediocre company. Fear should guide you, but it should be latent. I have some latent fear. I consider failure on a regular basis. (*Playboy* Interview, 1994, p. 153)

Gates's story is a good one, it seems. In it, the hero (Gates-Microsoft) is both victorious and benevolent, and "he" is not invincible, just hard-working. It is a problem-setting story that emphasizes not Microsoft's gains but its contributions.

That is, no doubt, why Gates tells the same problem-setting story again and again. In the late 1990s, in an interview about the federal antitrust suit, he tells *Time*: "The only right we've asked for is to be able to listen to customers and add new capabilities based on that input. Was putting a graphical interface in Windows a good thing? Font management? File-system management? I think so" (Exclusive, 1998, p. 58). Here the story is abbreviated, almost tacit, but a fuller story is strongly implied. Microsoft is being hindered from its basic mission, the mission encapsulated in its problem-setting story. Customers need software that has more features and is easier to use. Microsoft learns of that need and fills it by adding such things as a graphical interface, font management, and file-system management to Windows. The customer receives the benefit of Microsoft's work. All of this amounts to a story because we can identify a sequence of related events and a complication that is resolved in the end. Of course, the role of the competitor in the story is unexpressed, but we can easily guess what that role is.

One year later, Gates's story is the same, but the role of the competitor is suggested more directly:

At the heart of this case is a principle that's pretty important: our right to add features to Windows. We have been taking things that people demand, whether it be adding a graphical interface or support for networking, and building it into the operating system. Doing that has been why the PC revolution has done so much for consumers. . . . Without innovation, *given the intense competition out there*, Windows would become irrelevant. Not only would that be a tragedy for the shareholders, it would be a tragedy for consumers. (They're Trying, 1999, p. 65, emphasis added)

Perhaps more revealing than what this problem-setting myth says is what it does not say. Microsoft's problem-setting story does not rely upon the standard plot of business success stories, which usually focus on an individual's or a company's struggle to acquire money and position. To *Playboy*, Gates points out that he does not want to be seen as a business person but as a scientist or "technologist." He remarks, "When I read about great scientists like, say, Crick and Watson and how they discovered DNA, I get a lot of pleasure. Stories of business success don't interest me" (*Playboy* Interview, 1994, p. 60). But stories of Gates as a business person—indeed, as a ruthless business person—abound. As much as Gates may want to narrate Microsoft's chief problem as outpacing the competition in its effort to please the consumer, many of his competitors tell a different story—the story of a powerful company that uses its power in unethical ways.

The federal antitrust suit was based, largely, on the disparaging stories of competitors. What Gates frames as innovations that benefit the consumer, Microsoft's competitors frame as unfair business practices. In particular, Gates calls adding features to Windows a beneficial innovation; his competitors, backed by the federal government, call it "bundling," a way of pre-empting the competition. In short, competitors construct Microsoft's success story not as one of a hardworking company pleasing customers faster than its competitors but as a monopolistic corporation eliminating competition in order to gain industry power.

Because these tales are difficult—impossible—to ignore, Gates's stories are necessarily rebuttals: They have an argumentative function. Here it is important to point out that the legal arguments in the antitrust suit often take a standard argumentative form that includes careful statements of principle, definitions, reasoning, and evidence. But as Gates makes his case to the public, it is paramount for Gates to replace ruthless-business-person stories with benevolent-technologist stories.

In print, Gates's preferred narrative almost always appears side-by-side with stories of Gates's ruthless business practices. The introduction to the *Playboy* interview presents unhappy competitors' counter narrative:

> His competitors accuse Microsoft of unfair business practices, and his allies consider themselves fortunate to be on his good side. Given the fluidity of partnerships and strategic alliances in the computer industries, today's friends could easily become tomorrow's foes and vice versa, if Gates thinks it advantageous. (*Playboy* Interview, 1994, p. 55)

Time runs Gates's interviews without comment. But no *Time* reader could easily miss the magazine's unflattering feature stories.

The week following Gates's 1998 interview, *Time* reports on Justice's "fairly persuasive argument" that, among other things, "Microsoft executives visited Netscape's lovely office park in Mountain View, Calif., and, like conquistadores carving up the New World, offered to split this emerging market down what they tried to define as the middle.... At which point Microsoft proceeded to do everything it could think of to sweep its rival into the dustbin of Internet history" (Krantz, 1998, p. 32). In a subsequent edition, *Time* juxtaposes Gates's words with a sidebar that narrates Microsoft's effort to combat the government's antitrust suit by hiring Republican lobbyists and contributing to the campaigns of Republican attorney generals (Novak, 1999).

By themselves, none of these stories—not Gates's, not his antagonists'—can be understood well. Rather, each story is part of a narrative strategy that is pursued in relation to the other narrative strategy. It may be true that Gates is not particularly interested in business-success stories, but even so, were it not for his antagonists' unrelenting narrative of Gates as a business bully, he would be free to claim them as at least a part of what explains his and his company's achievement. Certainly, business leaders who are not under such narrative attack have laid claim to stories of tough marketing and management. The automotive industry's Lee Iacocca. General Electric's Jack Welch. But Gates's narrative options are limited by an ongoing narrative onslaught. Persistent accusatory stories tint Gates's stories of innovation and goodwill with a defensive, if not disingenuous, color.

Moreover, the stories told by Gates and his antagonists have cultural resonances that make them particularly potent as argumentative weapons. These resonances are, in part, metaphoric in character—a point I take up later in this chapter.

METAPHOR: BASIC CONCEPTS

Like narrative, metaphor is increasingly considered fundamental to culture and thought. As George Lakoff and Mark Johnson (1980) put it in their influential book, *Metaphors We Live By*, metaphor is not "a device of the poetic imagination and the rhetorical flourish—a matter of extraordinary rather than ordinary language," but is instead "pervasive in everyday life, not just in language but in thought and action" (p. 3). Indeed, over the past couple of decades, we have witnessed a sea change, to speak metaphorically, in the way metaphor is studied.

Standard definitions of metaphor no longer hold, not even those offered by rhetoric's patron saint, Aristotle. Aristotle defined metaphor in two main ways. In the *Poetics*, he calls it an *alien name*, a word that is transported from one location to another. For example, in the metaphoric utterance *corporate battle*, the word *battle* is an alien name because it ordinarily refers to a fight between soldiers but is used to name competition between businesses and business people. *Battle*, thus, migrates from its familiar setting to an unfamiliar one.

In the *Rhetoric*, Aristotle equates metaphors with similes, observing that all good metaphors can be made into good similes, and vice versa. In other words, if we can say interchangeably either *corporate battle* or *corporate competition is like a battle*, then a metaphor is merely an elliptical simile, and a simile is a metaphor that uses an explicit term of comparison. Many current theorists would agree with Aristotle regarding the metaphoric quality of similes. But few would defend without qualification Aristotle's underlying assumptions about the way metaphors work. Both in calling metaphors alien names and in equating them with similes, Aristotle assumes that metaphor is merely a matter of wording—a way of making meaning elegant, not a way of making meaning.

One of Aristotle's most influential critics is Max Black, who extends the work of the early 20th-century rhetorician I. A. Richards. In the early 1960s and again in the late 1970s, Black argues that Aristotle's view is predicated on erroneous "substitution" and "comparison" theories. That is, Aristotle assumes (1) that metaphors can be precisely restated in literal terms and (2) that when we speak metaphorically, we do no more than recognize preexistent similarities. If that were the case, the phrase *corporate battle* would merely be a stylish way of saying *corporate competition is similar to battlefield competition because both kinds of competition are very aggressive, which is to say that they share the characteristic of brutality*. But there is little reason to think that metaphors really work that way.

Black points out that metaphors are, at least in a loose sense, creative. They are creative because the two parts of a metaphor—the literal referent and the metaphoric term—interact. Metaphors, far from merely making use of obvious, preexistent similarities, emphasize some similarities and ignore others; they also suggest similarities that would not be apparent without the metaphor. To continue with the example of *corporate battle*, business competition (the literal referent) and *battle* (the metaphoric term) have many resemblances that are not made salient by the application of *battle* to business competition: both battles and business competition are carried out by human beings, both can be measured in units of time, both can be interrupted by unexpected developments, and both are, by turns, celebrated and vilified. These similarities may exist prior to the metaphor, but they are not especially relevant to it. On the other hand, although we may have a preexisting idea that corporate competition is aggressive, when we liken it to a battle, corporate competition takes on a new quality. It comes to seem "violently" unrestrained.

Black would take the analysis a crucial step further. Not only does the metaphor alter our idea of corporate competition, but it also alters our idea of battle. Just as battle and business have similarities that are not useful in the metaphor, battles have important elements that do not correspond well with corporate competition—elements such as the longing for home and

family, physical discomfort, an atmosphere of explosion and chaos, and, often, moral justification. When we ignore these elements for the sake of the
metaphor, how we think of battle shifts. The literal referent and the metaphoric term work on each other to heighten awareness of some elements
and to draw our attention away from others. They interact.

Once we recognize that metaphor creates meaning, it is impossible to
maintain that metaphor is just a tool that speakers call upon for effect. To
speak metaphorically is not merely to dress up literal meanings by using
alien names. Furthermore, when we examine the process of highlighting
and suppressing elements, we begin to see that metaphors do more than
apply isolated features from—to use current terminology—the source onto
the target. Instead, metaphors set in motion a complex, meaning-making interaction between domains of activity. When we utter the phrase *corporate
battle*, we are not making a comparison between static notions of two kinds
of competition; rather we are evoking dynamic systems of activity that have
many elements, some relevant, others not. Therefore, to make sense of so
conventional a metaphor as *corporate battle*, we need to examine a range of
business-as-war metaphors—to consider an abundance of expressions that
reveal how a single metaphoric concept is made and remade, again and
again.

This systematic, interactive view of metaphor is key for proponents of
conceptual metaphor such as George Lakoff, Mark Johnson, Mark Turner,
and others. But if the interaction theory is an important corrective to the
Aristotelian view, conceptual metaphor theory makes a thorough break
from almost all time-honored assumptions about metaphor. Many students
of metaphor would be sorely tempted to agree with Gerard Steen's (2000)
tongue-in-cheek hyperbole: "In the beginning was Aristotle. Then there
were the Dark Ages, which lasted until 1980. And then there was Lakoff. And
there was a Johnson too" (p. 261). Steen points out that the history of metaphor theory is more complicated than that. But it is, nonetheless, accurate
to say that, in 1980, Lakoff and Johnson's *Metaphors We Live By* proposed a
radically new understanding of metaphor that has attained considerable influence in every discipline concerned with metaphor and mind.

The conceptual metaphor view argues that specific expressions do not
constitute a metaphor at all; rather metaphoric expressions recruit larger
metaphoric concepts, such as Love Is A Physical Force, The Mind Is A Container, A Nation Is A Family, and so on. These concepts, on one hand, provide a fairly stable projection of abstract similarity from one domain onto
another and, on the other, permit a good deal of flexibility in the way any
specific utterance is formulated. In other words, a conceptual metaphor
such as Business Is War projects the **image schema** of war—an abstract or
skeletal shape of war—onto business. That image schema consists mainly of
contending sides aiming to conquer or defeat the other. It does not tell us

much about the specific actions a side may take, nor does it provide us ways of valuing the activity of business or war. However, when we recruit the war image schema and project it onto business, we can hardly do so without also attaching specific actions and values. We recruit the metaphor in the abstract and make use of it in highly specific ways.

Perhaps more than any other explanation of metaphor, conceptual metaphor theory suggests a full integration of language and thought. Conceptual metaphors are stable cognitive structures, rooted in bodily and social experience, without which we do not, and perhaps cannot, think. Consider Business Is War again. We cannot imagine contending sides without calling upon the embodied perception of containment, something perceptually presupposed by pushing, destroying, and capturing. We must imagine important elements of the metaphor—nations, companies, markets—as entities that have insides and outsides, that are unitary, that are tangible. Otherwise, it would make no sense to *penetrate* a market, to *take over* a company, or to *demolish*, *crush*, or *kill* a business competitor. Business Is War has other bodily, perceptual requisites, too. To make sense of it, we need to think of forward motion, exertion, resistance, and so on.

But to reduce the metaphor to just bodily, perceptual requisites would be to sell it short. Conceptual metaphors have cultural origins and implications. Business Is War is a conceptual staple of much English-speaking culture. In fact, it is part of a conceptual ensemble that, taken together, defines business. To be sure, war is not the only way we conceptualize business. And many of us may not like the concept very much. But an English speaker who cannot readily comprehend business as a warlike activity does not know what everyone else knows. In English, in our historical time and place, Business Is War helps to tell us what business *is*. Likewise, we have many conceptual metaphors that bear integrally upon seemingly literal concepts. Try to understand life without thinking about journeying. Try thinking about success without thinking about moving upward. Try thinking about happiness without thinking about warmth. For English speakers, it's tough to do.

METAPHOR: APPLIED APPLICATION

Let us return to the example of Bill Gates. In this analysis, I will consider not just the three interviews that I took up earlier, but rather attempt to make sense of the give and take of metaphors that intermingle with Gates's and his antagonists' stories. I will be most interested in conceptual metaphors that populate texts closely related to the Gates interviews. Specifically, my concerns will be (1) to consider the relationship between prominent conceptual metaphors and (2) to take into account their problem setting and argumentative functions. Just as the applied analysis of Gates's stories was related to a more extensive case study, this analysis is an extension of a larger study of business metaphors (Eubanks, 2000).

Let me pause here to note that my procedure for analyzing these texts was much the same as for the narratives in the Gates interviews. I selected promising texts, read them repeatedly, noting as many relevant metaphors as I could, and placed the metaphors into analytic categories. Of course, identifying metaphors is not always a straightforward matter because it presents the challenges discussed by Thomas Huckin in chapter 1. Concepts may be expressed in various and sometimes indirect ways. And metaphors, in particular, are found in more than just the canonical "A is B" form. If I say to you, "Your point is coming into better focus for me now," I may not have stated, in so many words, "Knowledge is a visible object." But I have, nonetheless, recruited the conceptual metaphor Knowing Is Seeing.

Searching out **conceptual metaphors**, then, is not just a matter of cataloging clever non-literal expressions. It is a process by which we gain insight into the ways people think—the way they approach their professions, the way they construct their culture, the way they understand themselves. Like the stories people tell, conceptual metaphors reveal a rich and various landscape of shared and sometimes contested assumptions that operate so pervasively that the users of these metaphors can hardly imagine their worlds any other way.

In and around the stories told by Gates and his detractors, there are numerous metaphoric expressions to be found, expressions that recruit entrenched conceptual metaphors. Like the stories they are associated with, these conceptual metaphors help to define the problems that Gates and Microsoft must solve, and they refute other metaphors. Although these conceptual metaphors are stable cognitive structures, they necessarily operate concretely, as part of an actual discourse and debate filled with individuated metaphoric expressions. Most prominent in the give and take are the conceptual metaphors Business Is War, Business Is A Game, and Business Is A Journey.

Gates's critics persistently denounce him by calling upon the conceptual metaphor Business Is War, a metaphor that is today a rhetorical pariah. That is, when expressions such as defeating competitors, conquering markets, and killing off the competition are taken seriously, reputable business people do not ordinarily claim that these metaphors fittingly describe their actions or beliefs. Business is not really about destroying competitors, they say; it's really about benefiting consumers within a competitive system. On the other hand, if Business Is War is used to characterize someone else's actions or beliefs, the metaphor serves a problem-setting function in the sense that it ascribes a problem-setting scenario to someone else.

Business Is War suggests a hyper-competitive, disreputable way of doing business. First, its image schema entails that business competitors direct hostile action at one another. If that is so, the main problem for businesses is not to serve the customer but to harm or eliminate the competitor—the enemy. Second, its image schema entails a view of markets as contained. If markets are contained, like nations or theaters of war, they are likely also to be viewed as finite. Contained, finite markets mean that business competition is zero sum: When one company gains, another must lose. And third, its image schema encourages us to view some elements as more important than others. While it is possible to imagine a role for customers in a war between businesses, that role is likely to be peripheral. The customer is a third party who may or may not benefit from the actions of the main actors.

Because war metaphors are rhetorically intense, they bolster accusations that Gates engages in unethical and possibly illegal behavior—a set of business practices that are not explicitly named by the metaphor, such as excessive price-cutting, one-sided or coerced agreements, double-dealing, and the like. Of course, Business Is War is sometimes ascribed to Gates in whimsical ways. Above an article on competition for control of Internet technology, *Time*'s illustration shows Gates astride a tank that represents the Windows operating system, a helmet on his head and a cigar protruding from a clenched-toothed sneer (Ramo, 1996, p. 58). Its cartoonish appearance signals hyperbole meant to amuse. But more sober ascriptions of the Business Is War abound. A few months after Gates's *Time* interview, the magazine muses, "Is he the brilliant innovator who has brought the wonders of the information age to millions of satisfied customers? Or is he the *rapacious* capitalist leveraging his software monopoly to *crush* competitors?" (Cohen, 1998, p. 58, emphasis added).

Although Business Is War is the dominantly ascribed metaphor in anti-Gates discourse, we should note that it does not operate discretely. Numerous metaphors have a rhetorical affinity with Business Is War. Thus metaphors of fighting, crime, and evil-doing, all noteworthy in the discourse of literal war, are woven into accusations of business misconduct by Gates. In court, federal prosecutor David Boies accuses Microsoft of wanting to "gain a *chokehold* on the Internet" (Cohen, 1998, p. 61, emphasis added). Former Netscape CEO James Barksdale, a key witness against Microsoft, claims that Microsoft "set out to . . . *cut off Netscape's air supply*" (Cohen, 1998, p. 61, emphasis added). He also describes a meeting in which Microsoft "implied that we should either stop competing with it or [they] would *kill* us" (Cohen, 1998, p. 61, emphasis added). Another Netscape executive likens a meeting with Microsoft to a visit from the Godfather character, Don Corleone: "I expected to find a *bloody* computer monitor in my bed the next day" (Cohen, 1998, p. 61, emphasis added).

Metaphoric hyperbole of this earnest variety is part and parcel of antagonism toward Gates. As *Time* notes, in the 1990s anti-Gates Internet sites routinely portrayed Gates as evil, not-so-playfully calling his company "the

Evil Empire" (Cohen, 1998, p. 59). The knowledge that these metaphors are common anti-Gates parlance no doubt motivates Microsoft attorneys' in-court objection that federal prosecutors are depicting Gates as "the Great Satan" (Cohen, 1998, p. 59). (To understand better how these references to *The Godfather* and the words of Iranian ayatollahs found their way into court, see chapter 4 by Charles Bazerman.)

These unrelenting anti-Gates metaphors provide the context in which we ought to view Gates's self-ascribed metaphors. When Gates metaphorizes himself, he is not speaking *de novo*; he is replying to the metaphors so frequently used to characterize him. Most notably, Gates responds with the culturally potent metaphors Business Is A Journey and Business Is A Game. By putting forward competing metaphors, Gates accomplishes at least two things. First, his metaphors contradict the problem-setting assumptions ascribed to him as entailments of Business Is War. Second, Gates's metaphors are rhetorically cooler than Business Is War, allowing him to appear more reasonable than his detractors.

Let us look at Business Is A Journey first. Business Is A Journey is a standard trope in business discourse. Its entailments are roughly these: A businessperson or a company begins at a defined starting point, travels forward via a pathway, and ends at (or at least aims toward) a destination. This is usually called the **source–path–goal image schema**. It is the same abstraction that underlies Life Is A Journey and various journeying metaphors that help us conceptualize portions of life. The journeying image schema fits Gates's purposes well because it emphasizes forward motion, comports with visionary claims, and does not make eliminating competition an ultimate goal.

Describing Microsoft's and the digital world's future in his book *The Road Ahead*, Gates (1995, p. xiii, emphasis added) offers this version of Business Is A Journey: "We are all beginning another great *journey*. We can't be sure exactly where this one will *lead* either, but I'm certain it will touch many lives and *take us all even farther*." But the metaphor does not have to be explicitly spelled out in order for us to recognize its logic. For example, asked in the *Playboy* interview what he plans to do for "an encore" (*Playboy* Interview, 1994, p. 154), Gates figures his business career this way:

> Encore implies that life is not a continuous process, that there's some sort of finite number of achievements that defines your life. For me, there are a lot of exciting things in front of me at Microsoft, things that we want to see if we can make happen with technology. There are great people here who are fun to work with. And in the next decade the most interesting industry by far will be information technology, broadly defined. . . . That will be my focus for the foreseeable future.

Although Gates does not use obvious Aristotelian alien names such as *journey* or *voyage* or *the road ahead*, expressions such as "things in front of me" and "the foreseeable future" call upon a conceptualization of events in a linear sequence, with past events tracing a path backward toward the source (not his birth, but the beginning of his business career), and with upcoming events leading toward the goal (the end of his business career).

Gates also ascribes to himself the metaphor Business Is A Game, a metaphor that is almost always rhetorically cooler than Business Is War. Business Is A Game can in some evocations align with the hostile-action image schema of Business Is War. Football metaphors often have this quality. However, Gates typically recruits Business Is A Game in a way that aligns with Business Is A Journey: business as a race. Consider the metaphoric dimension of one of the stories he told to *Playboy*. Insisting that Microsoft's behavior ultimately benefited the consumer, Gates says in 1998, "If we play a major role it'll be because we were a little bit better a little bit sooner than others were. . . . If we weren't still hiring great people and *pushing ahead at full speed*, it would be easy *to fall behind* and become a mediocre company" (Exclusive, 1998, p. 58, emphasis added). Racing is not evoked explicitly in his 1999 *Time* interview, but Gates nonetheless describes actions and motivations that suggest a racing view of business:

> We have been taking things that people demand, whether it be adding a graphical interface or support for networking, and building it into the operating system. Doing that has been why the PC revolution has done so much for consumers. . . . Without innovation, given the intense competition out there, Windows would become irrelevant. (They're Trying, 1999, p. 65)

In both the racing version of Business Is A Game and in Business Is A Journey, Gates–Microsoft is directed toward a goal that is not the destruction of its competition: the consumer's benefit. Thus Business Is A Journey and Business Is A Game seem to offer a plausible alternative to the war metaphor so often ascribed to Gates. If Business Is A Journey and Business Is A Game are strong enough to withstand Business Is War's cultural and ideological force, then Gates might reasonably expect his retorts to be successful. However, the success of his metaphorical parries, as with so many arguments, may come down to credibility.

Gates's credibility suffered at least once because of his choice of metaphors. I noted at the outset of this analysis that Business Is War is a pariah among metaphors, that no respectable businessperson claims its ideological baggage in earnest. That is why the revelation of one of Gates's intracompany emails became, according to news reports, crucial in the federal antitrust case that accused Gates–Microsoft of anticompetitive practices. Regarding the use of a competitor's product, he writes: "Using Sun is just declaring war on us. If either of these things are the case, then these guys are really at [war] with us and we should do the most extreme things we can" (U.S. Judge, A4). If private utterances are taken to be more genuine than public ones, then Gates erred badly.

OTHER FIGURES: BASIC CONCEPTS

The brevity of this section reflects, perhaps, the amount of research into figures other than metaphor. But figures such as irony, metonymy, and others are receiving increased interest. Although metaphor has often been seen as the master trope, future research is likely to carve out a place for figures that have not received as much notice. Let me consider here just metonymy.

Metonymy is often confused with metaphor when important figures are discussed, but it is not the same thing. Metaphor involves a projection of image schemas and attributes from one thing to another. It is about the recognition or creation of similarity. Here, on the other hand, is a frequently used example of metonymy: A waitress refers to her customer as the ham sandwich. She is associating the customer with item he ordered. That's a metonymy. But it's not a metaphor because there is no suggestion that the customer has any of the characteristics of a ham sandwich.

Metonymy is always about contiguity. But contiguity may take various forms such as substituting the place for the population or activity (e.g., Wall Street), the part for the whole (e.g., all hands on deck), the thing for the maker (e.g., the report argues), and so on. Moreover, metonymy is not always expressed in noun form. In the phrase *deadly poison*, the adjective and noun are related by metonymy (cause and effect). I should note, too, that I have, as many do, conflated metonymy and synecdoche, the figure that substitutes the part for the whole.

Metonymy may seem to be mainly a matter of language. But like metaphor, metonymy is also a matter of thought. Furthermore, metonymy does not operate discretely. It often works in tandem with—woven within or around—metaphor, narrative, irony, and perhaps other linguistic and conceptual forms.

APPLIED ANALYSIS: METONYMY

I continue here with the example of Bill Gates and the Microsoft antitrust suit.

It is a familiar trope to personify companies. I use the general term "trope" advisedly because the concept that companies are people is simultaneously metaphor and metonymy. The conceptual metaphor Companies Are People tells us that companies have the qualities of a person. It projects onto companies the image schema of a human being. Like humans, according to the metaphor, companies are unitary beings who make rational, moral, and emotional decisions. Of course, as with all metaphors, some characteristics of the source domain are not projected—that human beings are mammals, are bipeds, have eyebrows, and so on. When we metaphorize a company as a person, we usually do so by making the company the agent of human-like action: companies decide, reconsider, hesitate, move ahead, and so on.

The personification of companies is buttressed, if not set into motion, by the metonymy Companies For People. After all, companies are made up of people (along with financial and physical assets). Thus the proximity of the legal fiction of a company to its human composition makes it possible to think of everything a company does as the collective action of people. It is then a short step, via the conceptual metaphor Groups of Things Are Singular Things, to the notion that the collective actions can be understood as individual actions. Moreover, because companies are typically organized hierarchically—with one person at the top who speaks for the collective and for whom the collective speaks—Companies For People often tells us that the company is a particular person, usually a founder or CEO such as Bill Gates.

This metonymy-metaphor has important rhetorical consequences in the debate surrounding the Microsoft antitrust suit because the metonymic dimension of Companies Are/For People permits Gates and his critics to refer to Microsoft as Bill Gates or, alternatively, to refer to Bill Gates as Microsoft. Let me suggest briefly what a few of the rhetorical consequences of that might be:

- When antagonists refer to Microsoft as Bill Gates or otherwise emphasize Microsoft's juxtaposition with Bill Gates, alleged illegalities become the act of a single, morally sentient being. Antagonists thus can fix moral blame unambiguously. Gates is assigned responsibility for the collective acts of his company. And Microsoft's collective acts become extrapolations of Gates's acts.
- When Gates's defenders (particularly his lawyers) refer to Gates as the recipient of attacks, accusations of illegality seem unduly harsh. The effect is just the opposite of naming Gates as the metonymic actor, as in the bullet point above. When Gates seems to be the recipient of aggression that should be directed at Microsoft, he seems less powerful, more fully human.
- When Gates refers to his own rights as his company's or employees' rights, he enhances the worthiness of his claim. Generally speaking, people are suspicious of excessive personal power or ambition. Thus government limitations on Gates's personal prerogatives might seem

warranted. But it seems less warranted to limit the activities of the many individuals who make up Microsoft, especially if they are being hindered from serving the customer. The government's limitation of rights is multiplied.

- When Gates refers to Microsoft, rather than himself, as an actor, he disperses the responsibility for what may be seen as overly aggressive or unethical acts. The company shoulders widely dispersed responsibility. Although collective action is often conceptualized as singular or unified, collective action nonetheless must meet the moral standards of many autonomous individuals.

The rhetorical consequences of the Gates–Microsoft metonymy may not be exactly—or at all—as I have stated them. Only more research could enlighten us about that. But there is one point of which I feel certain. When we look at the conceptual and rhetorical consequences of metonymy and metaphor, we cannot dismiss metonymy as a mere alternate name for a fixed reference. The Gates–Microsoft metonym has important consequences precisely because, in the context of the Microsoft antitrust suit, it is often unclear what the reference is. "Gates" may refer to Gates himself or to Microsoft. "Microsoft" may refer to the company as a legal entity, to all of its employees, to some of its employees, or to Gates. That ambiguity, made possible by a combination of metonymy and metaphor, is a powerful conceptual and rhetorical tool.

CONCLUSION: THE RELATIONSHIP BETWEEN NARRATIVES AND FIGURES

It has always been known, I suppose, that narratives and figures are related somehow. Allegories are metaphorical stories, and stories have usually been expressed in figurative language. But that recognition has not informed much formal study into the nature of narrative, metaphor, or other figures. Rather, in keeping with the linguist Roman Jakobsen, most theorists and researchers have treated narrative, metaphor, metonymy, and other figures (to the degree they are discussed at all) as intersecting but distinct. In other words, narratives, metaphors, metonymies, ironies, chiasmus, and any number of other figures may exist within the same text, but they are treated as independent elements that can be studied one at a time.

That view has some sense to it, in part because of the way we so casually conflate various figures. In everyday language—and in some scholarly studies—stories and metonymies are carelessly called metaphors, and metaphors are carelessly called symbols. In rigorous studies, it is important to identify accurately what textual elements we are focusing on. At the same time, theorists and researchers today, not the least those who study the poetics of everyday texts, are well situated to discover the relationships between narratives and other figures—relationships that are cognitive, social, linguistic, and rhetorical. I suspect that a better understanding of the relation between narrative and figuration is on the horizon.

But short of that, researchers are increasingly recognizing that studies of narrative, metaphor, and other figures are not just concurrent or collocated but inherently connected. Moreover—and I say this recognizing how difficult it is to sort things out—the study of narrative, metaphor, and figures is probably relevant to all of the other issues raised in the far-flung chapters of this book. How the study of narrative and figures might enhance other kinds of textual analysis is almost certainly a worthwhile direction for research.

ACTIVITIES

1. Newspaper editorials make points by telling stories. Select an opinion piece from the "op-ed" page of a well-regarded newspaper and identify as many stories as you can. Which of these stories seem to be retellings of master narratives (such as David and Goliath or the scientific discovery story)? What kinds of stories would the same editorial writer be unlikely to recount and why?

2. Newspaper editorials are often written in highly metaphoric language, too. Select an opinion piece from the "op-ed" page of a well-regarded newspaper and identify as many metaphors as you can. Which of these metaphors seem to be novel, not just in the way they are expressed but in their underlying thought? Which seem to be instances of conceptual metaphors?

3. Stories and metaphors almost never operate without reference to other stories and metaphors. Locate a few opinion pieces on the same topics as the ones you examined in exercises one and two. Are their stories similar or different? Are their metaphors, especially the conceptual metaphors, the same or different? Do the stories and metaphors seem to be related or "conversing"?

4. Select a text unlikely to present obvious narratives, metaphors, or other figurative constructions. What narratives, metaphors, and figures are implied? To what extent (if at all) do these elements pertain to the overall logic or argument of the text?

5. In a well-known text in your area of study, identify one of the most important recurrent metaphors. Analyze the structure of the metaphor (1) by sketching a diagram of its image-schema, (2) by writing a paragraph about its

logical assumptions, and (3) by listing salient attributes that are mapped from source to target.

6. Consider the metaphor you analyzed in Exercise 5. What from the source is not mapped onto the target? Could these attributes be mapped? If so, what rhetorical difference would it make? If not, why not?

7. Stories and metaphors are not always conveyed in words. For example, in chapter 6, Anne Frances Wysocki analyzes a video game called "Eve" that evokes the Biblical story of the creation, the world's move away from the Garden of Eden, and its eventual restoration. Select a video game or board game and analyze the stories and figures that make it meaningful. Pay special attention to images and all of their suggestive detail.

FOR FURTHER READING

Narrative Theory

Bal, Mieke. (1997). *Narratology: Introduction to the theory of narrative* (2nd ed., C. van Boheemen, Trans.). Toronto: Buffalo, University of Toronto Press.

Bal offers a comprehensive introduction to narrative and its elements. The book considers not only written literary narratives, but also nonliterary narratives and narratives in visual media.

Lyotard, Jean-Francois. (1979). *The postmodern condition: A report on knowledge*. Minneapolis: University of Minnesota Press.

Lyotard's analysis of scientific and technological knowledge remains influential long after its publication. Lyotoard argues that science and narrative are fundamentally in conflict and, among other things, examines that way grand narratives belie the usual understandings of what scientific knowledge is. Like many postmodern critiques, this book seeks to reveal and disassemble social and cultural constructions. Unlike too many postmodern works, it is quite readable.

Propp, Vladimir. (1968). *Morphology of the folktale* (2nd ed.). (Laurence Scott, Trans.). Austin: University of Texas Press.

This widely read book was first published in 1928. Propp, a structuralist's structuralist, takes apart the Russian folktale piece by piece, giving us a detailed blueprint of every possible twist and turn a simple tale might take—in *sequence*. He also explains more comprehensive elements of the folktale.

Turner, Mark. (1996). *The literary mind*. Oxford, England: Oxford University Press.

Also an important contributor to cognitive metaphor theory, Turner regards narrative as a basic constituent of thought. Drawing upon recent work in cognitive science, he demonstrates how narrative combinations—what he calls "creative blends"—help us to make sense of time, place, self, and others. Because Turner uses fairytales and fables to illustrate his argument, *The Literary Mind* makes a good companion to Propp's *Morphology of the Folktale*.

Metaphor Theory

Ortony, Andrew. (Ed.). (1993). *Metaphor and thought* (2nd ed.). Cambridge, England: Cambridge University Press.

First published in 1979, *Metaphor and Thought* includes twenty-six essays, including such notables as Max Black's "More on Metaphor," Michael Reddy's "The Conduit Metaphor: A Case of Frame Conflict in our Language About Language," and Sam Glucksberg and Boaz Keysar's "How Metaphors Work." The collection represents a wide range of approaches to metaphor and covers topics such meaning, representation, understanding, science, and education.

Lakoff, George, & Johnson, Mark. (1980). *Metaphors we live by*. Chicago: University of Chicago Press.

This disarmingly readable book lays out one of the most influential theories of metaphor to date. Many important conceptual metaphors are discussed, including More Is Up, Happy Is Up, Argument Is War, Love Is A Physical Object, and others. For people interested in metaphor, this is a must read.

Lakoff, George, & Johnson, Mark. (1999) *Philosophy in the flesh*. New York: Basic Books.

In this carefully argued book, Lakoff and Johnson present "multiple, converging evidence" that supports the conceptual metaphor view. They also contend that a group of related metaphors form the conceptual basis of most Western philosophy.

Poetics Today. (Winter 1992) 13:4; (Spring 1993) 14.1; (Fall 1999) 20.3.

Poetics Today's special issues on metaphor provide a wide variety of commentary on metaphor from literary critics, cognitive psychologists, linguists, rhetoricians, and others.

Selected Research

Fahnestock, Jeanne. (1999). *Rhetorical figures in science*. New York: Oxford University Press.

Examining instances of figurative language and thought from various scientific disciplines, across centuries, Fahnestock demonstrates the rhetorical and conceptual import of figures *other than* metaphor. Because Fahnestock is critical of the attention metaphor has received at the expense of other figures, and because she draws heavily upon classical sources, her work make an excellent counterbalance to much other work on figuration.

Nerlich, Birgitte, Clarke, David D., & Dingwall, Robert. Clones and crops: The use of stock characters and word play in two debates about bioengineering. *Metaphor and Symbol, 15*, 223–239.

Nerlich, Clarke, and Dingwall argue that "a Lakovian approach to metaphor can certainly help us to become better hunters, gatherers, and interpreters of metaphors" (p. 237), but that approach should be combined with linguistic, literary, anthropological, and sociological perspectives.

Perkins, Jane, & Blyler, Nancy. (Eds.). *Narrative and professional communication*. Stamford, CT: Ablex.

This collection of research essays explores the role of narrative in research methods, science, management, health care professions, websites, and society at large.

Sheridan-Rabideau, Mary. (2001). The stuff that myths are made of: Myth building as social action. *Written Communication, 18*, 440–469.

Sheridan-Rabideau examines myths and counter-myths as they operate at a community-based organization for school-aged girls. She argues that productiveness of myths is understood best when we pay attention competing myths' hidden dialogicality.

3

Linguistic Discourse Analysis:
How the Language in Texts Works

Ellen Barton
Wayne State University

As Thomas Huckin pointed out in chapter 1, one starting point for the analysis of texts is meaning. This chapter begins from a different starting point for the investigation of texts, which is the analysis of language through a method known as discourse analysis. In this chapter, I introduce **discourse analysis as a method for analyzing the ways that specific features of language contribute to the interpretation of texts in their various contexts**. Discourse analysis, broadly defined, is the study of the ways that language is organized in texts and contexts; discourse analysis can investigate features of language as small and specific as aspects of sentence structure, or it can investigate features of texts and contexts as large and diffuse as genres and sociocultural world views. Discourse analysis can be practiced either quantitatively or qualitatively, or with an emphasis on linguistic structure or contextual function, although most discourse studies utilize a combined design of qualitative–quantitative and structural–functional methods and analyses. There are currently a great many approaches to discourse analysis because it is practiced by many researchers in different fields, but we focus here on discourse analysis as it has been developed in the field of linguistics and practiced in the field of composition studies. This chapter first covers basic concepts and approaches in discourse analysis, reviews the literature on one seminal issue within the field, and then describes a method for discourse analysis of written texts called rich feature analysis.

BASIC CONCEPTS AND APPROACHES
IN DISCOURSE ANALYSIS

Discourse analysis developed originally within the field of linguistics, so it may be helpful to introduce linguistics briefly as the scientific study of language.[1] One of the ways that I as a generative linguist introduce linguistics to students new to the field is to note that many linguists investigate language as both a cognitive and social object, viewing language as a set of structures and a variety of functions. Under this view, speakers have internalized the rules and constraints that underlie the grammatical structures of their language, and they have learned various conventions that underlie situational and contextual functions of language in use. Two key terms in linguistics, then, are **structure** and **function**: a structure is a unit of language (sound, syllable, word, phrase, clause, sentence); a function is a use of language for a particular purpose, whether that purpose is informational, expressive, or social (Schiffrin, 1994). A crucial issue in linguistic theory in-

---

[1] I use a few terms from linguistics in this chapter:

- syntax—rules of sentence formation in a language: rules for combining phrases and clauses into sentences
- semantics—system of meaning In a language (e.g., ideas in sentences)
- clause—subject-predicate structure
- dependent clause—subject-predicate structure that is embedded into a larger sentence
  - types of dependent clauses:
    -subordinate clause—begins with a subordinating conjunction
       (e.g., I ate lunch *after I went to class*)
    -relative clause—begins with a relative pronoun, modifies within a noun phrase
       (e.g., I attended [the class *that I hate*])
    -participle clause—headed by a verbal participle
       (e.g., *Running to class*, I lost my notebook)
    -infinitive clause—headed by an infinitive (to + V)
       (e.g., I hate *to miss class*)

I also use some terms from discourse analysis in this chapter:

- register—a variety of a language that occurs in a specific context (e.g., scientific discourse); a register typically has a set of co-occurring features associated with it (e.g., the passive in scientific discourse)
- genre—a conventionalized variety of text structure in a language, either oral (e.g., a sermon) or written (e.g., the IMRD [Introduction, Methods, Results, Discussion] structure of a scientific research article)
- relationship between register and genre—some discourse analysts make a distinction between the investigation of registers as focused on the sets of co-occurring linguistic features in a variety, and the study of genres as focused on the rhetorical form of texts, but other discourse analysts see the terms as describing virtually the same phenomenon of oral and written varieties within a language (cf. Atkinson, 1999, pp. 9–11)

volves the complexities of the interaction of structure and function, and different linguistic theories take different approaches to seeing structure or function as primary, or to seeing them as relatively separate or inherently fused (Newmeyer, 1986b, 1998).

Traditionally, structural linguistics has focused primarily upon **language as a cognitive object**, investigating **the rules and constraints that make up a language** (and language in general) by trying to account for the creativity of language that allows speakers to produce and understand utterances they have never heard before (in generative linguistic theories, notably those derived from the work of Noam Chomsky, this is called speakers' **linguistic competence**; cf. Newmeyer, 1986b, 1998). The rules of language, in this sense, are not conscious directions that are taught to speakers but deeply internalized and highly abstract principles that make up speakers' knowledge of their language(s). An example of a structural rule of language is word order. Some languages, for example, English, structure their sentences with a subject-verb-object order, but other languages use different word orders: Japanese, for example, structures sentences with a subject-object-verb order, while Irish structures sentences with a verb-subject-object order. No speaker, even a child learning language, is ever consciously directed to form sentences in a particular order (no one tells a toddler learning English, "Now the rule is to put the object after the verb; obey it"), but every speaker internalizes the word order rules for the language(s) that he or she speaks, and uses the rule again and again to produce and understand new sentences.

At the same time that modern structural linguistics developed, anthropological linguistics and sociolinguistics came to focus primarily upon **language as a social object**. Some sociolinguists investigate the variation in language that arises when groups of speakers learn the same language in different dialects, with a recent focus on how variation in language leads to language change (cf. Trudgill, 2001). Other sociolinguists and some anthropological linguists investigate language in a social perspective more broadly, focusing on how speakers know how to make choices and follow practices of using language appropriately in various sociocultural contexts (in some theories, notably those derived from the work of Dell Hymes, this is called speakers' **communicative competence**; cf. Saville-Troike, 1989; Schiffrin, 1994). Variation in language is sometimes described in terms of rules (e.g., regional dialect pronunciations), but much variation in language arises from speakers making and following choices about the uses and functions of language in different contexts, choices that can be described in terms of conventions of language use. An example of contextual variation in this sense is the level of formality speakers choose to use in a given situation: The features of language in the setting of informal conversation (e.g., clipped pronunciations like *bringin'* instead of *bringing*, elliptical syntax like sentence fragments) would not conventionally be chosen for the more formal situation of written academic discourse. **Conventions of language** in context, in this view, are not matters of simple surface correctness (or what linguists would call prescriptive rules in the sense of stylistic dictates taught in school) but complex connections between the use of a linguistic feature and its function and interpretation in a text or context. Sometimes these choices and conventions are the result of active attention by the speaker to his or her use of language (e.g., telling a story differently to different audiences), and other times these choices and conventions are the habituated results of community practices of language use (e.g., answering greetings appropriately). In other words, conventions describe a relationship between the repeated or typical use of a feature (e.g., the recitation of a Bible verse) and its function in a context (e.g., to signal the beginning of a sermon).

Structural linguistics typically focuses on units of language at or within the level of sentence, since **structural rules describe the possible combinations of basic linguistic units into grammatical sentences** (e.g., word order). In anthropological linguistics, sociolinguistics, and discourse analysis, as we see shortly, the focus is on uses of language in context (e.g., formal/informal variations), and **conventions refer not to matters of grammaticality, strictly speaking, but to the connections between features of language and their functions in context** (e.g., the Bible verse and the sermon).

Discourse analysis developed from a number of traditions in linguistics, some of which were concerned primarily with linguistic structure but most of which were concerned primarily with linguistic use. For example, early work in anthropological linguistics by Dell Hymes (1972) on what he called the ethnography of communication suggested that discourse analysts look at the ways in which language in different communicative events functions to create and reflect aspects of culture, including world view; his work also suggested that discourse analysts look at communication cross-culturally (Scollon & Scollon, 2001). In another example, early work in sociolinguistics by William Labov (1972a) on oral narratives by young African-American speakers suggested that discourse analysts look at the ways in which oral language is structured within units that are larger than a sentence, such as stories and other genres; Labov's work also suggested that discourse analysts look at the organization of language and dialects in minority social and ethnic groups (Wolfram, Adger, & Christian, 1999). More than 30 years of research has taken the field in many different directions, but most work in discourse analysis somehow considers the structure of language and its functions in social and cultural contexts. The field called discourse analysis, then, poses a number of questions: How do speakers and writers organize language to function at or beyond the level of the sentence? How do speakers and writers organize language to function in texts and contexts? In what specific ways? For what purposes? With what effects?

A number of theories and methods of discourse analysis have developed over the years, approaches that often reflect the interdisciplinary configurations of their practitioners. For example, the **ethnography of communication**, which aims at describing how communication works within different cultures, draws from linguistic anthropology, and looks at issues such as language socialization (Saville-Troike, 1989; Schieffelin, 1990; Schieffelin & Ochs, 1990). **Interactive sociolinguistics**, which describes language within smaller social groups, including gender groups, looks at conversations, arguments, and other interactions conventional to those groups (Schiffrin, 1984b; Tannen, 1984, 1993). **Genre analysis**, which describes the structure of texts in the contexts of discourse communities, especially academic disciplinary communities, focuses on the ways that texts reflect the social nature of disciplines in the natural sciences, social sciences, and humanities and draws from applied linguistics to pay special attention to the texts of second language speakers and writers (Johns, 1997; Swales, 1990; cf. Bazerman, chap. 11, this volume). **Systemic linguistics**, developed by M.A.K. Halliday as one of the earliest and most elaborate discourse theories, draws upon theories of social semiotics to describe the structure of clauses, sentences, and texts with a focus on textual structure (Halliday, 1978, 1998). More recently **critical discourse analysis** draws from various social theories to analyze the complex interactions of language and ideology in various contexts (van Dijk, 1998).

These different approaches to discourse analysis have also focused on different kinds of data for investigation. Work in the ethnography of communication, for example, often collects data from cultural performances of oral traditions, such as narratives told by a culture's storytellers (Scollon & Scollon, 1981). Work in interactive sociolinguistics also looks at narratives, but primarily narratives that arise in ordinary conversation (Schiffrin, 1984a). Genre analysis, as noted, often uses academic discourse as data when it investigates the natural and social sciences, although other work has looked at texts in the contexts of business and legal systems (Bhatia, 1993). Systemic linguistics draws its data from many sources, but recently has emphasized language and genres in educational settings (Halliday & Martin, 1993). Critical discourse analysis also draws data from many sources, but has developed a focus on language in the public and political domains by examining language in the news and in bureaucratic settings such as parliamentary debates and official reports (van Dijk, 1991, 1993; Wodak & van Dijk, 2000).

THE ANALYSIS OF ORAL–WRITTEN LANGUAGE
IN DISCOURSE ANALYSIS

To give a sense of the research conducted within discourse analysis, consider the investigation of one particularly interesting issue—the systematic differences between the features and functions of oral and written language. Some of the earliest work in discourse analysis, work that defined the emerging field, looked at the intriguing differences between the ways people talk and the ways they write, and work on this topic has continued in discourse analysis within a variety of approaches and methods.

Using an **inductive methodology** based on the close examination of samples of oral and written language, Wallace Chafe has been prominent in arguing that oral and written language exist upon a structural and functional continuum, with different features typical of either end (Chafe, 1982, 1994; Chafe & Danielewicz, 1987). Consider the following utterance from oral language (the dots are to be read as pauses—two dots for a short pause, three dots for a longer pause):

> . . . And . . . she was still young enough so I . . I just . . was able to put her in an
> . . uh—sort of . . . sling . . I mean one of those tummy packs . . you know. (Chafe
> & Danielewicz, 1987, p. 89)

The features of this utterance in oral language include its many false starts and hesitations (repetitions, fillers like *uh*), its many informal mitigations (*sort of*, *I mean*, *you know*), its basic-level vocabulary (*sling*, *tummy pack*), its short and simple syntax in 5- to 7-word units expressing one idea (phrases and simple clauses bounded by pauses), and its basic connectives between units (*so*, *and*). Compare this utterance to a sentence from written language:

> Language change has occurred when the utterances of some members of that
> community have characteristics demonstrably different from those in utter-
> ances of previous generations. (Chafe & Danielewicz, 1987, p. 98)

The features of this sentence in written language include its length (24 words), its lack of disfluencies and mitigations, its elevated vocabulary, and its complex syntax with syntactic embedding of multiple ideas in a single sentential unit, complete with punctuation (e.g., modification and dependent clauses).

Although Chafe's close investigations of many language samples have confirmed the basic features of the ends of the continuum, it is important to note that he argues not for an absolute characterization of oral and written language. In other words, not all oral language is characterized by the presence of all of the features listed above, and not all written language is characterized by the presence of contrasting features: Academic lectures, for example, are a type of oral language that draws upon features of written language (e.g., complex vocabulary), and informal letters (and more recently, email) are a kind of written language that draws upon features of oral language (e.g., simple syntactic units that are not necessarily complete sentences). Speakers and, especially, writers can draw upon the repertoire of features in oral and written language to function for different purposes and effects in different texts and contexts.

Chafe's methodology for discourse analysis is primarily **qualitative and inductive, with basic quantitative verification**: he collected and examined many language samples that he thought would be illustrative of different kinds of oral and written language, identified features of interest through close qualitative analysis, verified the occurrence of these features across the corpus of samples through basic quantitative analysis, and presented the results of his analysis primarily using examples to relate structural features to functional and contextual dimensions. In discussing why oral and written language typically have different structural features, for example, he suggests a functional explanation based on the different contexts of oral and written language: Oral language takes place in a context of involvement—face-to-face interaction between speakers, interaction that is constrained by the limits of short-term memory, hence its conventionally short and syntactically simple utterances with basic vocabulary; written language, on the other hand, takes place in a context of detachment—no immediate interaction between an author and a non-present audience, a situation that allows careful composition and editing to achieve the complex lexical and syntactic features of written discourse.

Recent work in linguistics on the analysis of oral and written language by Douglas Biber has developed a more **systematic quantitative methodology**, based on large corpora of language samples selected for their representativeness and analyzed using a statistical technique called **Multidimensional Analysis** (a form of factor analysis, for those familiar with statistical methods; Biber, 1988). The overall method is too complex to summarize in full detail here, but the basic idea is that different registers and genres of oral and written language are characterized not by single features but by sets of **co-occurring features** (cf. fn 1). To analyze features in sets, Biber worked with a large **corpus of texts** (his baseline analysis utilized 481 texts in 23 different genre/register categories). Atkinson (1999) gave a simplified, but illustrative, example from this method. One of the linguistic features included in this analysis is simple past tense. Simple past tense, it turns out, co-occurs at a high rate of frequency with several other features, including third person personal pronouns, perfect-aspect verbs (i.e., verbs that describe actions or events completed in the past), and verbs that report communicative acts (e.g., *report, claim*). This set of linguistic features, Biber argued, is constitutive of the functional category narrative; in other words, this set of features is characteristic of registers and texts, including written texts, that are narrative, such as romantic fiction and biography. Other registers and genres, such as academic discourse, for example, are not typically characterized by the features of narrative (although that is not to say that these features never occur in academic discourse). The crucial point here is that it is not a single feature that characterizes different registers and genres, but multiple, co-occurring sets of features. Biber (1988) identified five key dimensions of variation: involved vs. informational production, narrative vs. non-narrative concerns, situation-dependent vs. explicit reference, overt expression of persuasion, and non-abstract vs. abstract information. In the results of his numerous studies, face-to-face oral conversation is characterized by involved production and non-abstract information, while written academic discourse is characterized by informational production and abstract information.

THE ANALYSIS OF ORAL–WRITTEN LANGUAGE IN COMPOSITION STUDIES

The qualitative work of Chafe and the quantitative work of Biber, then, converge in support of a view of oral and written language on a structural–functional continuum, with different structures conventionally associated with different functions in context. Their work further suggests that written academic discourse has a number of structural features that have complex functions in the construction of knowledge in the context of the academy, which is one special interest in the field of composition studies. Work on oral–written language specifically and work in discourse analysis generally, then, has long been influential in composition studies, with early work leading to detailed investigations of academic discourse written by student writers and by scholars and researchers in different disciplines. Mina Shaughnessy's (1977) classic work *Errors and Expectations*, for example, drew extensively upon the discourse analysis of oral–written language to argue that basic writers may not be familiar with the conventions of written language in the academy. One of the earliest anthologies in composition studies, Kroll and Vann's (1981) *Exploring Speaking-Writing Relationships: Connections and Contrasts*, included many innovative studies of student writing from the perspective of the oral–written language continuum, including Anne Ruggles Gere's (1981) thoughtful discussion of the connections between oral and written language and sociocultural ideas about literacy. These early studies contributed significantly to the field's view of student writers as linguistic and rhetorical practitioners working in what may be an unfamiliar and even potentially alienating context of academic discourse.

More generally, discourse analysis of written language in a wide variety of academic and non-academic contexts became prominent in the early development of composition studies as a field, and still occupies an important place in research today. Charles Bazerman's (1981) seminal study "What Written Knowledge Does: Three Examples of Academic Discourse," for example, described the different features and functions of texts in the contexts of the natural sciences, the social sciences, and the humanities; Susan Peck MacDonald (1994) took up this kind of description in her study of three fields in the social sciences and the humanities (psychology, history, literary theory). Dwight Atkinson's (1999) historical study of the evolution of scientific discourse in the publications of The Royal Society of London (1675–1975) drew upon Biber's statistical analysis in combination with rhetorical discourse analysis to show how the conventions of the scientific article changed over time. Paul Prior's (1998) studies of orality in written discourse explored the complex ways in which oral language contributes to the writing process (cf. Leander & Prior, chap. 8, this volume). Researchers in technical and professional communication have been particularly active in describing the structure of texts and their functions in institutional contexts: Jennie Dautermann's (1997) study of nurses writing procedural manuals in a hospital, for example, showed how the texts were shaped to reflect the organizational and political realities of the field of nursing in contemporary medical care. All of these studies, and many more, draw implicitly or explicitly upon work in discourse analysis to develop structural–functional analyses of written language in context. Most of these analyses are qualitative, although the field has grown increasingly interested in combined qualitative–quantitative methodologies. In the following section, I describe such a combined qualitative–quantitative method of discourse analysis that I use to work within composition studies.

RICH FEATURE ANALYSIS

In an earlier work entitled "Context Sensitive Discourse Analysis," Thomas Huckin (1992) described the basic methodological procedures for undertaking a discourse analysis within composition studies:

1. **selecting an initial corpus** that is of intrinsic interest to the audience (in composition studies, many researchers begin with a corpus of student writing, a collection of disciplinary articles in the sciences or humanities, or a set of texts from an institutional workplace);
2. **identifying salient patterns**, usually by scanning texts holistically;

3. **determining "interestingness"** (how are the identified patterns interesting in composition studies?);
4. **selecting a study corpus** (sampling);
5. **verifying the pattern** (coding, counting, and other forms of empirical analysis);
6. **developing a functional–rhetorical analysis** (explaining the significance of a pattern in its context).

Working within this framework, my own work elaborates Step 2, describing what makes up a salient pattern in more detail. In this approach, I define a pattern as the conventional relationship between a structural feature and its function, meaning, or significance in context. This relationship is centered upon what was earlier described as a convention: A convention is an interpretive association between the typical use of a feature and its meaning in context (recall the example of a Bible verse conventionally signaling the beginning of a sermon). In the approach I call rich feature analysis, then, I look for particular features in a text or a set of texts that are associated with conventions of meaning and significance in context. I call these **rich features**. Rich features are defined as those features that point to the relation between a text and its context. Rich features have both **linguistic integrity** (i.e., they are structural features of language, so they can be defined in linguistic terms and then categorized, coded, counted, and otherwise analyzed empirically) and **contextual value** (i.e., they can be conventionally connected to matters of function, meaning, interpretation, and significance). The connection between a feature and its contextual value is a convention of language use. In this method, then, the connection between structure and function is the primary focus of analysis.

A rich feature can be any linguistic feature in a text or a set of texts that points to the way that meaning is embedded into that text in connection to its context. Rich features, in other words, are the basis for conventions of meaning and interpretation in context. Features can be as small as individual sounds, as in an analysis of alliteration in rap music lyrics, or features can be large as the types of narratives male and female academics use in lectures. A feature is rich, though, because it conventionally connects to meaning in context. Meaning arises in part out of the repetitive and patterned use of rich features: If a feature is repeated within and across texts, it is likely to be typified and conventionalized as to appearance and significance, and these conventional relations between features, patterns, and meanings are the ways that rich features both reflect and shape the context of its text.

Methodologically, rich feature analysis utilizes a recursive and circular process of bottom-up (or data-based) and top-down (or theory-based) analysis as discourse analysis is often practiced in composition studies. **Bot-**

tom-up discourse analysis seeking rich features involves looking at texts, inductively identifying their rich features and associated conventions, and then using these features and conventions as examples in a descriptive argument in support of some generalization(s) or claims(s) about the interpretive relations between features, conventions, texts, and their contexts. **Top-down discourse analysis** interpreting rich features and their conventions of significance associates these descriptions with larger social, political, and cultural frameworks, such as gender theory, organizational communication, social construction, or other theoretical frameworks that are described in this volume (cf. chapters in this volume by Bazerman and by Prior). Rich feature analysis is not already embedded within a particular theoretical framework, so it is compatible with many theories and approaches now available. Rich feature analysis is also a method that can be used in original research by students newly trying out discourse analysis, as is shown in the following examples of rich feature analysis that lead to the practice activities at the end of this chapter.

EXAMPLES OF RICH FEATURE ANALYSIS

Rich feature analysis is particularly useful in the analysis of academic discourse, particularly in the analysis of student writing and in the comparison of texts written by inexperienced writers (students, or new members of a disciplinary community) and experienced writers (established members of a disciplinary community). It should be noted that it is not uncontroversial in composition studies to use categories like inexperienced and experienced writers. Susan Miller (1992), for instance, argued that these categories are reductive and regressive, but I would argue that they are categories of significant intuitive value, especially within considerations of composition theory and pedagogy. Further, it should be acknowledged that it has been a popular practice, particularly in composition studies, to debate the existence of such a thing called academic discourse (Cooper, 1989; Harris, 1989; but cf. Swales, 1998), given that the kinds of writing done in the university vary from basic writers in remedial classes to research writing by teams of scientists to performance art created by a poet-in-residence in a fine arts program. But the applied linguist Ann Johns (1997) provided a contextually based characterization of academic discourse that also has considerable intuitive value:

> There may be some general academic discourses, language, values, and concepts that most academics share. Thus faculty often identify themselves with [the academy] and its language and values, as well as with the more specialized areas of interest for which they have been prepared.... [Within] this

broad academic identification, . . . many faculty believe that there is a general academic English as well as a general set of critical thinking skills and strategies for approaching texts. (p. 56)

Specific professional and pedagogical genres—the personal essay, the summary, the research paper, the critical essay, the argument, the research article, and so on—fit under this broad characterization of writing and texts within the context of the academy, a context that includes both experienced and inexperienced members who write different kinds of texts. Like the concept of continuum for oral–written language, however, with its acknowledgment that features and types of language are not absolutely defined, the concept of academic discourse may be best characterized by a continuum, perhaps thought of in the philosopher Ludwig Wittgenstein's well-known concept of family resemblance, where it is not specific shared features that deterministically define the category but general resemblances across different texts that underlie what we intuitively call academic discourse.

Given these caveats, studies of student writing and of texts by inexperienced or experienced writers are nevertheless of special interest in composition studies (Huckin's first and third criteria above), and discourse analysis is an excellent method for investigating bodies of texts produced in the context of the academy. Let me introduce two studies from my own work that serve as examples of rich feature analysis. Both of these studies arose out of my own experience in working with student writing. In my early years as a composition teacher, I had two bothersome questions about the ways students typically wrote: I wondered why they wrote such awkward sentences, and I wondered why they wrote in such general form.

Awkward sentences, as any composition teacher will agree, are one of the most common and most vexing problems in student writing. Awkward sentences are not sentences with simple grammatical mistakes that can be corrected with a quick reference to a handbook (e.g., sentence fragments, comma splices, subject-verb agreement). Awkward sentences seem to have grammatical problems, but they defy easy description: As a composition teacher, when I encountered one of these sentences I would usually either rewrite the sentence or simply mark it with the correction symbol *Awk*, neither of which was instrumental either in my understanding the nature of awkward sentences or in my helping the student writer learn to recognize and revise them. The analysis of awkward sentences, then, seemed like a good focus for an interdisciplinary project in linguistic discourse analysis and composition studies, in part because their description involved grammatical analysis and in part because their explanation would be interesting and important for composition pedagogy.

Developing a discourse analysis of awkward sentences led me to form a small research team of composition teachers to identify and analyze exactly what kind of sentences were labeled awkward in student writing and why (Barton, Halter, McGee, & McNeilley, 1998). We began with a collection of 100 student essays written for a university proficiency examination, and we identified awkward sentences by each reading the corpus separately and marking sentences with the correction symbol *Awk*. The rich feature of the analysis, then, was this feature *Awk*, with its conventional categorization of a sentence with serious syntactic problems in the context of academic discourse. Through our reading, we created a **corpus** of almost 300 sentences that reflected the intuitive categorization of awkward sentences among composition teachers. Sentences marked awkward included the following examples:

(a) Many years go by and sons and daughters do not even live in the same state any more only to come back for the holidays.
(b) I say this because the candidates that have no extracurricular activities, he/she may only want the title to glamorize themselves.
(c) Normally these discussions involve insights on who is the prettiest girl on campus, who is the most popular guy with the girls and if they are outgoing or not.
(d) Father[s] started out poorly in the 1970's make up only 1.1% of the "head of household."

We then moved **from data collection to analysis** by using a descriptive grammar of English (Quirk, Greenbaum, Leech, & Svartvik, 1985) to **categorize and code** each individual awkward sentence, and we combined similar sentences into what turned out to be four major categories:

(a) **Problems in Embedding Dependent Clauses**
College student[s] have a lot of pressure on them *being high achievers.*
(b) **Problems in Predication**
The data represents /*eighty-five percent of the automobiles*/ are moving or obeying the laws of driving an auto.
(c) **Problems in Parallel Structure**
Family life is eroding because of gender liberation, divorse [sic], teenage sex, and lastly, *because of people[']s morals just aren't what they used to be.*
(d) **Problems in Incorporating Source Material**
Single-parent headed households, *24.0% which includes mother only*

with 21.6% and father only 3.1%, so sadly to say that with the divorce
rate on the rise [and] high unemployment[,] some fathers are choosing to leave their families so that they can find employment in other
places.

In general, we determined, awkward sentences could be defined overall as
sentences in which clausal syntax and semantics were mismanaged: in
other words, students wrote awkward sentences when they mismanaged
sentences with multiple grammatical embeddings or multiple ideas. The
four categories identified the specific ways in which sentences were mismanaged. For example, a sentence like (a) above has problems in embedding its dependent clause: the sentence is awkward because the second
idea in the sentence is in the dependent clause *being high achievers,* but it is
not grammatically established either as an initial (participial) modifier
which should be moved close to its subject (*Being high achievers, college students have a lot of pressure on them*) or as a modifier (infinitival) for *pressure*
(*College students have a lot of pressure on them to be high achievers*). A sentence like (b) has a problem in predication called a syntax shift: the sentence begins with one subject, *the data represents,* but instead of moving
into a predicate for that subject, the sentence shifts into another entirely
different subject–predicate structure, with a different subject, *eighty-five
percent of the automobiles,* followed by its own predicate, *are moving or obeying the laws of driving an auto.* A sentence like (c) violates the convention of
parallel structure, in which items in a list are in similar syntactic form: the
list here begins with three noun phrases, *gender liberation, divorce,* and *teenage sex,* but the final element is an awkward subordinate clause *because of
people's morals just aren't what they used to be.* Finally, a sentence like (d)
has an awkward integration of source material: the material from the question here is incorporated in incomplete syntactic forms, *24.0% [of] which include [a] mother only, with 21.6%,* and *father only 3%.* In sum, the analysis
showed that awkward sentences resulted from the mismanagement of
clausal syntax and semantics, two key features of written language (recall
Chafe's earlier description of the sentences of written language as syntactically and semantically complex). The analysis of the study developed detailed grammatical descriptions of the kinds of awkward sentences students
wrote when they mismanaged syntax while trying to embed multiple ideas
into one sentence.

This discourse analysis was based on a relatively straightforward relationship between structure and function: The grammatical structure of
these sentences led to their functional categorization as awkward (by composition teachers, at least). The value of identifying the grammatical structures of awkward sentences was in the connection between the awkward
sentences and their significance in the context of academic writing: Student

writers write infelicitous sentences under the specific circumstances of managing multiple, closely connected ideas, and these infelicities and their circumstances, once identified and explained, can be addressed in pedagogy. A pedagogy to identify and edit awkward sentences, we then argued, would need to teach students what dependent clauses are and how to embed them within sentences grammatically.

To recap this study, then, in terms of the steps of discourse analysis in general and the method of rich feature analysis in particular, the methodology of the study was basically qualitative, though with quantitative verification (the report of the full study included tables with numbers for each category, showing how the analysis covered all of the data). We began with **a corpus of interesting texts** (student writing) with **an interesting problem** (awkward sentences), **holistically identified a salient pattern** by looking at sentences to identify those with the **rich feature** *Awk*, **analyzed a corpus** (using grammatical description) to **develop categories that account for the data** (types of awkward sentences), **verified the coding** through multiple codings by different researchers, and **described the structural–functional relationship** of the study (the functional category awkward sentences can be defined as sentences in which student writers mismanage multiple clauses or multiple ideas).

The other question I had about student writing, however, the question of why student writers so often write in such general form, required a rich feature analysis with a much more complicated relationship between structures and functions (Barton, 1993). For this project, I wanted to focus comparatively on essays written by inexperienced student writers and experienced academic writers, because of my intuitive sense that student writers write in much more general terms than experienced writers in an academic context. Selecting a corpus for the comparison of inexperienced and experienced writers, however, is a difficult matter, as these writers typically write very different kinds of texts in very different contexts. I eventually chose texts based on the criteria of genre and audience: I selected persuasive essays that were written for that well-worn clichéd group, "a general academic audience." That is, I selected texts by both experienced and inexperienced writers that were not addressed to specific disciplinary communities, such as chemists, or ESL teachers, or marketing professors, because I wanted to investigate how these different writers presented their ideas and evidence when they were writing in an academic context defined broadly. I thus chose as my corpus a set of writing proficiency examinations that asked for persuasive argumentative essays and a set of opinion essays written by academics for *The Chronicle of Higher Education*, a weekly publication aimed at university and college faculty and administrators. So that my work would be based on a good sampling, I collected 100 *Chronicle* essays and 100 proficiency essays. As I read my sets of texts over and over, looking inductively for salient patterns of rich features and conventions of presenting ideas in more or less general form, I found contrasting ways of using what linguists call evidentials.

In linguistics, **evidentials are defined as words that express a writer's attitude toward knowledge**. Evidentials are a particularly interesting unit across languages: Many non-Indo-European languages have specific words, suffixes, prefixes, or particles that express speakers' attitudes toward what is said and their evaluation of its reliability. In Central Pomo, for instance, a Native American language spoken by only a small remaining number of speakers in Northern California, there are a variety of suffixes that express evidentiality by attaching to a verb: The suffix -*ka*, for instance, indicates knowledge arising from an inference (in English, translated something like *must have*), the suffix -*ma* indicates factual, general knowledge, and the suffix -*?do* indicates knowledge via hearsay rather than direct observation (Mithun, 2001, pp. 45–48). English, however, does not have specific lexical units or grammatical structures that exclusively express evidentiality, as noted by Wallace Chafe (1986), who proposed a functional definition: "everything dealt with under this broad interpretation of evidentiality involves attitudes toward knowledge" (p. 262). Chafe (1986) identified three general categories of evidentials. First, **degree-of-reliability evidentials** evaluate the reliability of knowledge, with expressions such as *probably*, *certainly*, *generally*, and *virtually*. Second, **evidentials specifying the mode of knowledge**—belief, induction, deduction, sensory evidence, and hearsay—cover a range of expressions. Evidentials indicating knowledge based on belief, for instance, include *I think*, *I believe*, and *in my opinion*. Evidentials indicating type of reasoning include <u>seem</u> (induction) and <u>thus</u> (deduction). In written language, evidentials of hearsay include the conventions of citation. Third, **contrast evidentials** mark contrasts between knowledge and expectation, and include hedges and other contrastive expressions such as *of course*, *in fact*, *oddly enough*, *but*, *however*, *nevertheless*, and *actually*. In this discourse analysis, then, identifying evidentials was a matter of moving from function to structure, reading sentences to find words or phrases being used to express attitudes toward knowledge. The identification of an evidential was thus not an exact or absolute matter: A word like *clearly* can be used to express an attitude toward knowledge, as in a sentence like *Clearly the evidence pointed to the butler*, in which case it is functioning as an evidential, but not all uses of the word *clearly* are evidentials, as, for example, in the sentence *The butler could see clearly that the door was open*.

As in the previous project, the move from intuitive observation (that evidentials are used differently by experienced and inexperienced writers in academic discourse) to analysis involved identifying all of the evidentials in the corpus of essays and inductively formulating categories that account for this particular data. Contrasting examples below illustrate the use (or non-use) of evidentials in three categories (the first sentence in each set was taken from a *Chronicle* essay, the second from a student essay):

(a) Editorials and commentaries from the political left, right, and center seem to agree on at least one point—that a crisis exists in the way we determine the collective priorities and policies that make up our public culture. . . . There is little agreement, *however*, on how to revitalize public debate in the United States. (Kaye, 1991, p. A40)

(b) Nicholas Xenos states the character of political figures is an important factor in their ability to responsibly judge political issues. Therefore, journalists attempt to reveal personal information about political figures and reference "the Character Factor" to justify their inquiries. "The Character Factor" is overused and the relevance of personal actions by political figures is overestimated.

(c) As a developmental psychologist, *I believe that* . . . (Damon, 1990, p. A48)

(d) *I think* we as mature adults who enjoy sports should all take part in non-aggressive sports.

(e) Some critics of corporate relationships *assert* that. . . . The view *seems to assume* that . . . (Gray, 1990, p. A48)

(f) In Johan Huizinga's excerpt from *Homo Ludens, he states*. . . . *Huizinga also states* . . .

In (a), the evidential of contrast *however* is used by the experienced writer to emphasize the contrast between background sentences and his perspective on those sentences, but in (b) there is no evidential of contrast despite the same pattern of background and contrasting sentences written by the student writer. In (c) and (d) there are evidentials of certainty which describe how certain a writer is about his or her statement (*I believe, I think*). In (e) and (f), there are evidentials of citation (*assert, seem to assume, state*). In academic discourse these different evidentials served different functions in academic discourse (yet another layer of structural–functional complexity in the analysis): Evidentials of contrast emphasized the author's problematization, as in (a); evidentials of certainty function within the author's persona, as in (c) and (d); evidentials of citation, as in (e) and (f), establish the critical (*assert, seem to assume*) vs. descriptive (*state*) perspective of the author in talking about the work of others. The study moved further into the analysis by coding the data to see how many evidentials of each type were used by experienced writers and inexperienced writers within the functional categories of problematization, persona, and citation.

In this analysis, evidentials became a rich feature because their use systematically established a difference in the ways that epistemological stance is conventionally expressed by experienced vs. inexperienced writers in academic writing. Epistemological stance is a perspective on knowledge or knowledge-making. Experienced writers use evidentials to point to their epistemological stance that knowledge is oppositional, the product of contrast and competition. For example, in (a), the experienced writer uses *however* as an evidential of contrast to problematize previous knowledge and emphasize the need for a new perspective (his own); in contrast, the inexperienced student writer in (b) uses no evidential of contrast to highlight his third sentence either as the identification of a problem or as a comparison of a general view to his own view. Experienced writers use other kinds of evidentials to establish a focus on knowledge as specialized: In using evidentials of certainty like *I believe*, the experienced academic writer in (c) embeds the evidential within his credentials (*as a developmental psychologist*) so that the *I believe* carries the full authority of his academic persona within his discipline; in contrast, the inexperienced student writer in (d) embeds his use of *I think* within the set of general members of society (*we as mature adults*). Grammatically, there is not too much difference between *I believe* and *I think*, but the effect of the statements in (c) and (d) is quite distinct, based on their embedding within a specialized or general persona. Experienced writers keep their focus on oppositional knowledge throughout their essays: in (e), for example, the author uses evidentials of citation to emphasize his critical perspective on the opposing literature, which *asserts* or *seems to assume*, two rather noncomplimentary terms within the domain of academic argumentation where authors are supposed to prove and explain; in (f), however, the inexperienced writer simply describes the literature in a summary with neutral citation forms like *state*, not establishing his own perspective on the literature as critical in any way.

In sum, although experienced writers use evidentials to point to their **epistemological stance** that knowledge is oppositional and specialized, inexperienced writers use evidentials to point to their epistemological stance that knowledge is general, the product of shared agreement by all members of society. Hence, ideas, claims, arguments, and evidence are presented generally by inexperienced writers rather than critically or argumentatively as they are by experienced academic writers. So evidentials became a rich feature in this analysis not simply because they are a type of repeated linguistic form but also because the conventionalized patterns of their use point to an important aspect of meaning in an academic context— epistemological stance, how writers express their attitudes toward knowledge. Experienced academic writers use their epistemological stance to establish and maintain their authority as individual knowledge-makers. Inexperienced academic writers, in contrast, use their epistemological stance to establish and maintain general society as the authority over knowledge. This conclusion was an interesting one for the field of composition because it proposed an understanding of how student writers express attitudes that are in contrast to the assumptions of the academy, a contrast which can lead to their writing being misunderstood and devalued. This contrast between inexperienced writers' identification with general society and experienced writers' identification with the academic community is one of the classic conflicts between professors and students, experts and lay people, town and gown.

In conclusion, then, a **rich feature analysis** of academic discourse looks at texts with the idea of identifying rich features that are significant in the context of academic writing. The method identifies a rich feature or a set of related rich features; defines the feature(s) linguistically by focusing on structure, function, or both; describes the conventional meaning or significance of the feature(s); establishes and verifies the patterns of the feature(s) within a set of texts; and explains how the resulting discourse analysis is interesting for the field of composition theory and pedagogy. It is a method of discourse analysis that focuses closely on the investigation of language in texts and contexts, and it holds the promise of uncovering new knowledge about what written language does and how it does it.

PRACTICE ANALYSIS

Now it is time for you to practice rich feature analysis. Following is a reprinted essay written by an experienced academic writer and published in the *Chronicle of Higher Education* (see Fig. 3.1). Figure 3.2 is a reprint of an essay written by a student writer for a common writing genre in the college years, an argumentative essay written for a writing proficiency examination (this essay is reprinted from the coursepack of advice for students preparing to take the proficiency examination). Read these essays slowly and carefully, trying to identify rich features and their conventionalized meaning and significance in the context of academic discourse.

You may look for rich features that were discussed in the chapter, such as features of oral–written language, awkward syntax, or evidentials. Or you may look for other rich features you may be familiar with from the research literature (e.g., features mentioned in other chapters in this volume). You may also look to identify rich features inductively by yourself, perhaps features that have not been previously identified or discussed in detail. You may work bottom-up, by focusing on structural features in order to develop functional explanations, or you may work top-down, by looking in the texts for rich features that reflect your functional expectations of texts in this

POINT OF VIEW
For Students on Welfare, Degrees Pay Dividends

By W. Ann Reynolds

Two years ago, Linda Howard was homeless, riding the New York City subways at night to keep her children out of dangerous city shelters. Through her determined efforts over eight months, the two children were kept clean, never missed a day of school, and never went hungry. Ms. Howard went on public assistance after she was laid off from her job and her unemployment benefits ran out; she became homeless when her welfare payments did not cover her rent. But her grit and determination led her to apply to a special certificate program in practical nursing, designed for parents on welfare, at Medgar Evers College of the City University of New York. She recently completed the 18-month program and began a full-time job as a licensed practical nurse at Jamaica Hospital. Her annual salary: $30,000.

Ms. Howard was luckier than others in her situation today. The federal welfare law enacted in August makes little mention of education and training, in contrast to the 1988 Family Support Act, which encouraged welfare recipients to attend college. The new law makes getting an education much more difficult. It requires welfare recipients to perform "work activities" for at least 20 hours a week to maintain their benefits. Although one permissible activity is enrollment in "vocational educational training" for up to 12 months, this would not permit a student to earn even an associate's degree. Because the law does not mention "higher education" specifically, it is unclear whether enrollment in a college program will be permitted under this 12-month clause.

The provision effectively forces student recipients to make a Hobson's choice between remaining on welfare so that they and their families can survive financially, and gaining the credentials that can get them off the welfare rolls forever. This feature of the law is jeopardizing the careers and futures of hundreds of thousands of students striving for degrees at colleges and universities across the country.

To call national attention to this critical issue, 65 presidents and chancellors of colleges and universities have joined with me to form the National Coalition for the Education of Welfare Recipients. We have come together out of concern for the students and would-be students whose careers are being truncated or jeopardized by welfare reform, not only by the federal provisions but also by state and local interpretations that can further restrict opportunities. For example, in the absence of federal regulations stating otherwise, in some localities welfare recipients who want to pursue higher education have been told that they can enroll only in short-term vocational training, not in programs that lead to an associate's or bachelor's degree.

FIG. 3.1. *(Continued)*

Many members of the coalition head institutions in urban areas and other poor communities. We all share a sense of urgency and concern about the draconian aspects of the federal law, and we intend to speak out wherever possible about the shortsightedness of these policies. Coalition members are urging elected officials at all levels of government to work to modify the federal law, and we are recommending that the Department of Health and Human Services issue regulations that will allow welfare recipients to pursue college degrees. We also will press for local rules that make it easier for student recipients to fit the work assignments they must perform into their college schedules.

For those able to earn them, college credentials offer the best hope for permanent freedom from a lifetime cycle of poverty. Allowing welfare recipients to earn degrees will pay dividends, as is demonstrated by the former welfare recipients who are working in virtually all fields, from health care and business management to academe and the law. Denying degrees to public-assistance recipients imperils our national economic health by condemning countless individuals to low-paying, dead-end jobs.

At CUNY, this national predicament plays out daily for about one in 10 of our students -- for nearly 20,000 students who, like Linda Howard, receive welfare. The new welfare law, formally known as the Personal Responsibility and Work Opportunities Act of 1996, also haunts teen-agers hoping to go on to college from New York City public schools, where 450,000 students -- approaching half of the public-school population -- come from families that currently receive welfare benefits. Yet many studies confirm that higher education is the best way to break the cycle of welfare dependency and help recipients achieve self sufficiency. Our research shows that people with bachelor's degrees from CUNY earn $690,000 more over their lifetimes than high-school graduates -- and, obviously, pay much more in taxes.

As written, the welfare law is replete with hidden obstacles to success. It erects barriers to education for women, since the majority of A.F.D.C. recipients are female. Unfortunately, it is still the case that women frequently need bachelor's degrees to get jobs that men can obtain with less education. The law also will inhibit the success of members of minority groups by assuring that they remain in low-paying, unskilled positions -- the only ones available to individuals lacking postsecondary education and training. In terms of class, the law promises to widen the growing income gap between rich and poor that threatens our society's stability.

Several changes are needed in the federal welfare-reform law, as well as in state and local policies, to assist disadvantaged students who are seeking broadened career opportunities through higher education:

* Even if the provision in the statute referring to 12 months of *vocational* education is interpreted to allow a year of community-college study, this is not enough time to earn an associate's degree. Thus, students making satisfactory academic progress should be given enough time to complete that degree while still receiving benefits.

FIG. 3.1. *(Continued)*

77

* Welfare recipients who gain associate's degrees and who qualify academically should be encouraged to work for bachelor's degrees, which are essential for the best jobs. Under the law, recipients must perform mandatory work assignments for at least 20 hours a week, and although the law may not consider such advanced study a "work activity," as it does "vocational educational training," student recipients could be allowed to perform work assignments on their campuses, similar to the jobs that students receiving payments from the federal College Work-Study program perform.

Such work assignments now are often located at sites far from a welfare recipient's campus or home, causing problems in attending scheduled classes and taking up hours in transportation time, thus preventing progress toward a degree. All campuses should be designated as work sites at which students may fulfill their work requirements and retain their benefits. College job sites also can offer work that relates to students' career goals, unlike the low-skilled jobs to which welfare recipients are usually assigned.

* Just as child care is made available to welfare recipients during their mandatory work assignments, it should be available when recipients attend college classes not designated as a "work activity."

* Legal immigrants must not be penalized by welfare rules that are different from those applied to native-born citizens. Now, under the federal law, native-born recipients of welfare can receive food stamps and temporary-disability insurance, but legal immigrants cannot. Clearly, this can undermine the immigrants' ability to continue college studies. At CUNY, some 30 per cent of students on welfare are legal immigrants. Many other institutions enroll similarly large numbers of immigrants.

President Clinton is insisting in his fiscal-1998 budget proposals that two years of postsecondary education should become the norm in this country, so that all citizens can secure a stable niche in the labor market.

In fact, the 1,400 community colleges throughout the United States are well equipped to offer education and training in many fields to welfare recipients who want to gain marketable skills. Many two-year colleges already have experience and solid track records of success in doing this. The nearly 2,200 baccalaureate-granting institutions offer even greater options for academically qualified students. A few simple revisions in the new welfare law could open doors to individuals eager to escape public assistance — and strengthen our nation's work force in the years ahead.

W. Ann Reynolds is Chancellor of the City University of New York.

FIG. 3.1. *The Chronicle of Higher Education,* March 21, 1997, p. A68.

We unemployed share a social stigma similar to that of the rape victim. Whether consciously or unconsciously, much of the work-ethic-driven public feels that you've somehow "asked for it," secretly wanted to lose your job and "flirted" with unemployment through your attitude—possibly dressed in a way to invite it . . .

But the worst of it isn't society's work-ethic morality; it's your own. . . . You find out how much self-satisfaction was gained from even the most basic work-related task: a well-worded letter, a well-handled phone call—even a clean file. Being useful to yourself isn't enough.

Student Response

The Out of Work Stigma

As Jan Halvorsen says in the article "How it feels to be out of work," the unemployed share a social stigma not unlike that of a rape victim. Society views those out of work as having asked for it. Whether it is conscious or unconscious this attitude of the work-ethic driven public persists. It is as if they believe those without a job secretly sabotage their own employment. Whether this is in the form of on-the-job attitudes, or dress style or attendance. Though whats worse than societies moralizing judgment is that of the out of work themselves. One finds out when unemployed just how much self-satisfaction was obtained from the simplest work related tasks. A minor thing such as: a well written letter, a nicely handled phone call or even orderly clean files can come to mind when unemployed. One thinks if there were something they might have done better.

Society doesn't help this second guessing. One can't get rid of the feeling emitted that somehow "you" were at fault. Not unlike a crime victim today, no compassion or understanding for the situation is extended. It is a social problem which isn't seen as such. Just as the rape victim doesn't seek being raped, so also the jobless don't seek unemployment.

A factor not mentioned in the article abstract is that of regaining a job once one has been lost. A job for the sake of a job is nothing. Though society appears to feel any job is okay, as long as there is employment. This isn't true. If one comes from a position which paid more than what is now offered, an employer who will hire is hard to find. Again a case of no-fault unemployment, but society still treats you like a pariah.

FIG. 3.2. *(Continued)*

This work-ethic driven attitude is part of us all, even the job-less. This can be the hardest part of being without work, even meaningful work. The thought comes into the mind "Did I do all that I could to keep my job?" It is a very difficult question to answer. In most cases you are too close to the situation to be objective. Social conditions or economic situations may have taken presedent, and unemployment results.

Without a job one has time to reflect on what their own work ethic is, how much did the job mean. Was there a sence of satisfaction in doing even mundane tasks. Was there a feeling that only what was asked would be done, or was there a willingness to do a bit more even if not recognized. This the part that cuts the deepest. Then self-recrimination whether justified or not.

Society is constantly judging the jobless. This pressure to succeed is always at the heels of the unemployed. Perhaps this pressure is good to some extent, but it can be devastating if not coupled with compassion and understanding. Society has to stop generalizing and view each case of joblessness individually. This will take unnecessary blame from the shoulders of the out of work. Enough blame and recrimination is generated by those people themselves.

I disagree with the tone of the last sentence in Jan Halvorsens article. The idea "of being useful to yourself isn't enough" seems to imply the author in some way does blame the work ethic of the jobless. It seems to say society demand one to extend in order to keep one's job. Thus shifting the burden back onto those out of work. Again fueling self doubt.

Being out of work is a social problem as much as an individual one. Society must become aware that it is a shared blame. As in crime the victim isn't a victim because he wants to be, he doesn't do it by himself.

FIG. 3.2.   From "How It Feels to Be Out of Work" by Jan Halvorsen. Sample essay from proficiency examination preparation materials.

genre and context. You may wish to use some of the following questions to guide your analysis:

- How can you describe the rich feature(s) linguistically, that is, as units or structures of language (sounds, words, phrases, sentences, discourse features)?
- What is the pattern of the rich feature(s) and conventions of meaning and significance in these texts?
- How can you describe the conventions of interpretation for these features?
- How are these features distributed across the texts written by the experienced and inexperienced writer?
- From this initial analysis, can you formulate a claim or generalization?

- Given this claim, can you point to some representative examples of rich features and their conventions of meaning in the texts?
- Are there any counterexamples to the pattern you've identified?
- What are the implications of your study for writing effective persuasive essays? For teaching writing? for the description of academic discourse? For thinking about writing in the context of the academy?

FOR FURTHER READING

For an overview of linguistics written for the general public, see Stephen Pinker's (1994) *The Language Instinct* (a linguistics book that resided on the *New York Times* best-seller list for some time). For more on language as a cognitive object, see any introductory text in linguistics. George Yule (1996), in *The Study of Language*, provides a basic-level introduction to the field. Victoria Fromkin (2000) provides an upper-level introduction to current linguistic theory in *Linguistics*. For an account of the way that linguistics has developed as a field, including detailed discussion of the concepts of structure and function, see *Linguistic Theory in America, Politics of Linguistics*, and *Language Form and Linguistic Function*, all by Frederick Newmeyer (1998, 1986a, 1986b).

For more on language as a social object, see any introductory text on sociolinguistics or anthropological linguistics. Peter Trudgill's (2001) *Sociolinguistics: An Introduction to Language and Society* is a standard text, as is Allessandro Duranti's (1997) *Linguistic Anthropology*. For further reading on standard and non-standard dialects, see *Dialects in Communities and Schools* (Wolfram, Adger, & Christian, 1999). For a sociolinguistic approach to discourse analysis, see John Gumperz's (1982) *Discourse Strategies*. For a classic description of language in context by an anthropological linguist, see Shirley Brice Heath's (1983) *Ways with Words: Language, Life, and Work in Communities and Classrooms*.

For more on systemic linguistics, begin with Halliday's (1998) *An Introduction to Functional Grammar*. Additional texts include Eggins's (1994) *An Introduction to Systemic Functional Linguistics*. To read about Halliday's use of social semiotics in systemic grammar, see his *Language as Social Semiotic* (Halliday, 1978).

For more on discourse analysis in linguistics, see *Discourse Analysis: An Introduction* by Barbara Johnstone (2002) and *Approaches to Discourse* by Deborah Schiffrin (1994), which provide comprehensive overviews of the field of discourse analysis within linguistics. A shorter introduction is Deborah Cameron's (2001) *Working with Spoken Discourse*. For an excellent collection of essays on the various theoretical approaches to the analysis of discourse, see Teun van Dijk's (1997d) *Discourse Studies: A Multidisciplinary Introduction*, Vols. 1–2.

For more detail on Chafe's work on oral–written language, see his articles cited in the References and the volume *Discourse, Consciousness, and Time* (Chafe, 1994).

There has been much work on the analysis of academic discourse in composition studies. Especially important is the work of Charles Bazerman, particularly his volume *Shaping Written Knowledge: The Genre and Activity of the Experimental Article in Science* (Bazerman, 1988). For additional discourse studies of writing within the disciplines of the academy, see Dwight Atkinson's (1999) *Scientific Discourse in Sociohistorical Context: The Philosophical Transactions of the Royal Society of London, 1675–1975*; Carol Berkenkotter and Thomas Huckin's (1995) *Genre Knowledge in Disciplinary Communication: Cognition/Culture/Power*; Susan Peck MacDonald's (1994) *Professional Academic Writing in the Humanities and Social Sciences*; Greg Myers' (1990) *Writing Biology: Texts in the Social Construction of Scientific Knowledge;* Jack Selzer's (1993b) *Understanding Scientific Prose*; and John Swales' (1990) *Genre Analysis: English in Academic and Research Settings*. Swales has a well-known and influential discourse analysis of the introductions to research articles.

For an excellent methodological description of discourse analysis within composition studies, see Thomas Huckin's "Context Sensitive Text Analysis" in Kirsch and Sullivan's (1992) *Methods and Methodology in Composition Research*. Keith Grant-Davie (1992) has a thoughtful article on the process of coding discourse data in the same collection. For examples of a variety of approaches to discourse analysis in composition studies, see my collection co-edited with Gail Stygall, *Discourse Studies in Composition* (Barton & Stygall, 2002). For further description of rich feature analysis, see my chapter there entitled "Inductive Discourse Analysis: Discovering Rich Features."

4

Intertextuality: How Texts Rely on Other Texts[1]

Charles Bazerman
University of California, Santa Barbara

Almost every word and phrase we use we have heard or seen before. Our originality and craft as writers come from how we put those words together in new ways to fit our specific situation, needs, and purposes, but we always need to rely on the common stock of language we share with others. If we did not share the language, how would others understand us? Often we do not call attention to where specifically we got our words from. Often the words we use are so common they seem to come from everywhere. At other times we want to give the impression that that we are speaking as individuals from our individuality, concerned only with the immediate moment. Sometimes we just don't remember where we heard something. On the other hand, at times we do want to call attention to where we got the words from. The source of the words may have great authority, or we may want to criticize those words. We may want to tell a dramatic story associated with particular people with distinctive perspectives in a particular time and place. And when we read or listen to others, we often don't wonder where their words come from, but sometimes we start to sense the significance of them echoing words and thoughts from one place or another. Analyzing those connections helps us understand the meaning of the text more deeply.

    We create our texts out of the sea of former texts that surround us, the sea of language we live in. And we understand the texts of others within that

---

[1]Thanks to Beth Yeager for classroom data.

same sea. Sometimes as writers we want to point to where we got those words from and sometime we don't. Sometimes as readers we consciously recognize where the words and ways of using words come from and at other times the origin just provides an unconsciously sensed undercurrent. And sometimes the words are so mixed and dispersed within the sea, that they can no longer be associated with a particular time, place, group, or writer. Nonetheless, the sea of words always surrounds every text.

The relation each text has to the texts surrounding it, we call **intertextuality**. Intertextual analysis examines the relation of a statement to that sea of words, how it uses those words, how it positions itself in respect to those other words. There may be many reasons for analyzing the intertextuality of a text. We may want to understand how a school district's policy statement is drawing on or speaking to educational research and political controversies. We may want to see how students in their writing are expressing knowledge of what they are learning from biology. We may want to understand what techniques are necessary for students to comment intelligently and critically on what they read in history. We may want to understand how students learn to write arguments informed by the best knowledge available, or we may want to see how some popular texts are deeply parts of contemporary culture.

Learning to analyze intertextuality will help you pick through the ways writers draw other characters into their story and how they position themselves within these worlds of multiple texts. It will help you see what sources researchers and theorists build on and which they oppose. It will help you identify the ideas, research, and political positions behind policy documents. It will help you identify what students know about negotiating the complex world of texts, what they have yet to learn, and how their need for particular intertextual skills will vary depending on the tasks they are addressing. Finally it will help you see how students and schools are themselves represented, made sense of, and given identity through intertextual resources that characterize students and schools.

AN EXAMPLE

To give you a concrete sense of how intertextuality works, consider the following opening of a section from *Education Week* of October 5, 2000, on the current state of the middle school.

> The Weak Link
> By Ann Bradley and Kathleen Kennedy Manzo
>
> The middle grades are feeling the squeeze. For the past 30 years—and with particular intensity since the late 1980s—educators have labored to create distinc-

tive middle schools, whose mission is to attend to young adolescents' social, emotional, and physical needs as well as their intellectual development.

Yet both proponents of the middle school model and critics of the approach recognize that too many such schools have failed to find their academic way. Instead, the original concept has been undermined by ill-prepared teachers guided by ill-defined curricula.

Middle-level education is now squarely on the defensive. The standards and accountability movement is placing unprecedented demands on the middle grades, typically 6–8. So far, middle schools don't have much to boast about when it comes to student achievement.

The spotlight has been particularly harsh since 1996, when the Third International Mathematics and Science Study [TIMSS] was released. While U.S. elementary students scored above average, middle and high school students' scores lagged. The study faulted the American curriculum for being "a mile wide and an inch deep."

The National Assessment of Educational Progress [NAEP] and most state tests reveal similar patterns, with minority students tending to fare even worse.

"The middle school is the crux of the whole problem and really the point where we begin to lose it," says William H. Schmidt, a professor of education at Michigan State University and the U.S. coordinator for TIMSS. "In math and science, the middle grades are an intellectual wasteland."

The article doesn't have a fragmentary quotation until the end of the fourth paragraph and a full quoted sentence until the sixth, yet from the beginning it creates an intertextual web of statements that place middle schools in the center of a controversy and define particular problems that middle schools need to address. The first paragraph in setting out the movement that created the current concept and practice of middle schools evokes the many discussions, philosophical statements, developmental studies, policy papers, school bond initiatives, mission statements, curricular guidelines, training documents, parental information sheets and myriad other documents which guided and made real, and carried on the work of the middle school around the whole child concept.

The second paragraph, again without identifying a particular climate, evokes an extensive atmosphere of controversy between "proponents" and "critics." Further it passes judgment on certain curricula and training (which rest on plans and materials) as inadequate. There is also the implied hint of studies or reports that definitively establish the inadequacy of training and curricula, so that it is implied that both proponents and critics would agree to the inadequacy as the root cause of schools having "failed to find their academic way." Thus, in general language the paragraph not only establishes a controversy but specifies a problem and root causes that all statements on both sides have already agreed to.

The third paragraph adds another intertextual context for the pressure on middle schools: the standards and accountability movement. This evokes the political battles over education in many states and the nation, as well as particular legislative initiatives undertaken in the name of standards and accountability. The fourth through sixth paragraphs then alight on particular tests, their results, and statements interpreting them to establish with social scientific certitude that there is a specific problem with the middle schools. It is only after all this preparation that we get a direct and forceful quoted statement to drive home the point in the sixth paragraph.

The journalists have created a drama of a movement and its critics, supported by scientific studies to define a problem and take a side in the controversy. The journalists seem to be adopting a neutral, objective voice of simply reporting on a controversy, but they have assembled the characters and recounted the tale so as to focus the issue and then put the words of one powerful critic at the climax. The reporters use the voices of the people and groups they report on to tell their story as much as a novelist uses characters or a ventriloquist uses dummies. Of course if there weren't a TIMSS or a NAEP with their results or prominent academics making statements the reporters would not have had powerful resources to tell their story, nor would they have likely to have come to the same conclusions. Yet of the many ways these and other potential materials could have been used to create an overall statement and position of this article, the authors/reporters chose this particular way of putting the voices together in a story.

BASIC CONCEPTS

Intertextuality. The explicit and implicit relations that a text or utterance has to prior, contemporary and potential future texts. Through such relations a text evokes a representation of the discourse situation, the textual resources that bear on the situation, and how the current text positions itself and draws on other texts. Although this is now a widely recognized phenomenon, there is not a standard shared analytic vocabulary for considering the elements and kinds of intertextuality. The terms I introduce next are an attempt to capture key dimensions and aspects of intertextuality.

Levels of Intertextuality. For purposes of analysis we may distinguish the different levels at which a text explicitly invokes another text and relies on the other text as a conscious resource.

1. The text may draw on prior texts as a **source of meanings to be used at face value**. This occurs whenever one text takes statements from another source as authoritative and then repeats that authoritative information or statement for the purposes of the new text. In a U.S. Supreme Court decision, passages from the U.S. Constitution can be cited and taken as authoritative

givens, even though the application to the case at hand may be argued. In the example discussed earlier, the title of the news article "The Weak Link" invokes and takes at face value the old adage that "a chain is only as strong as its weakest link."

2. The text may draw **explicit social dramas** of prior texts engaged in discussion. When a newspaper story, for example, quotes opposing views of Senators, teachers' unions, community activist groups, and reports from think tanks concerning a current controversy over school funding, they portray an intertextual social drama. The newspaper report is shaping a story of opponents locked in political struggle. That struggle may in fact preexist the newspaper story and the opponents may be using the newspapers to get their view across as part of that struggle; nonetheless, the newspaper brings the statements side by side in a direct confrontation.

3. Text may also explicitly use other statements as **background, support, and contrast**. Whenever a student cites figures from an encyclopedia, uses newspaper reports to confirm events, or uses quotations from a work of literature to support an analysis, they are using sources in this way. In the foregoing example, the reporters use the TIMSS and NAEP data to back up their assertion about troubles of middle schools.

4. Less explicitly the text may rely on **beliefs, issues, ideas, statements generally circulated** and likely familiar to the readers, whether they would attribute the material to a specific source or would just understand as common knowledge. The constitutional guarantees of freedom of speech, may, for example, lie behind a newspaper editorial on a controversial opinion expressed by a community leader, without any specific mention of the Constitution. The news article discussed earlier relies on the middle school mission "to attend to young adolescents' social, emotional, and physical needs." This phrase relies most directly on familiar discussions about how schools can serve the whole child, calls for schools and other institutions to deal with the problems of youth, and journalistic, academic, and policy presentations of school programs that succeed and fail. The statement more indirectly relies on common and oft-restated beliefs about the difficult transitions of adolescents as well as fictional, journalistically embellished, and honestly factual accounts of troubled youth and youth violence.

5. By using certain implicitly **recognizable kinds of language, phrasing, and genres**, every text evokes particular social worlds where such language and language forms are used, usually to identify that text as part of those worlds. This book, for example, uses language recognizably associated with the university, research, and textbooks. In the earlier example, paragraph by paragraph the news article moves us through the worlds of school and administrative policy, political contention, statistical analysis, and contentious policy debate.

6. Just by using language and language forms, a text relies on the available **resources of language** without calling particular attention to the intertext. Every text, all the time, relies on the available language of the period, and is part of the cultural world of the times. In the example news report, the opening sentence relies on familiarity with the "middle grades" concept, which came out of the mid-20th-century movement to create middle schools. It also relies on familiarity with the idiomatic phrase "feeling the squeeze," which had its origins in underworld language and then worked its way into sports and business.

Techniques of Intertextual Representation. These levels of intertextuality can be recognized through certain techniques that represent the words and utterances of others, starting with the most explicit:

1. **direct quotation.** Direct quotation is usually identified by quotation marks, block indentation, italics, or other typographic setting apart from the other words of the text. Although the words may be entirely those of the original author, it is important to remember that the second author, in quoting the writing, has control over exactly which words will be quoted, the points at which the quote will be snipped, and the context in which it will be used.

2. **indirect quotation.** This usually specifies a source and then attempts to reproduce the meaning of the original but in words that reflect the author's understanding, interpretation, or spin on the original. Indirect quotation filters the meaning through the second author's words and attitude and allows the meanings to be more thoroughly infused with the second writer's purpose.

3. **mentioning of a person, document, or statements.** Mentioning a document or author relies on the reader's familiarity with the original source and what it says. No details of meaning are specified, so the second writer has even greater opportunity to imply what he or she wants about the original or to rely on general beliefs about the original without having to substantiate them, as the news reporters do with respect to proponents and critics.

4. **comment or evaluation on a statement, text, or otherwise invoked voice.** The reporters in the earlier example accept as truthful and definitive the TIMSS and NAEP studies, although they have been in fact criticized. They also see "the original concept undermined" and they pass judgment on curricula as "ill-defined."

5. **using recognizable phrasing, terminology associated with specific people or groups of people or particular documents.** In the example article, William Schmidt criticizes middle-grade math and science education by the phrase "an intellectual wasteland" that recalls Newton Minnow's famous statement of the 1960s calling television "a vast intellectual wasteland." This

echo not only evokes major public controversy over educational issues, but also implicitly suggests that middle-school education has no more value than television as an educational tool.

6. **using language and forms that seem to echo certain ways of communicating, discussions among other people, types of documents.** Genre, kinds of vocabulary (or register), stock phrases, patterns of expression may be of this sort. The reporters of the example article clearly are writing within the forms of journalism over public policy controversies. As mentioned previously the language of that article brings us through worlds of educational planning, political movements, statistical evaluation, and policy controversy.

Usually the most explicit purposes and formal expressions of intertextuality (those at the top of the previous two lists) are most easily recognizable and therefore most easily analyzable. It is with these more explicit forms we introduce intertextual analysis here, and only suggest the possibilities for examination of the more implicit forms of intertextuality.

Intertextual Distance or Reach. Intertextual relations are also usually most easily recognizable when the textual borrowings involve some distance in time, space, culture, or institution. Phrases that are common and unremarkable in sports such as "stepping up to the plate"—just part of the ordinary way of talking that everyone shares—become a bit remarkable when they start appearing in political contexts, such as when a congressperson talks about the courage to take a stand on an issue by talking about "stepping up to the plate." This phrase, used metaphorically, can signal us that the political situation is being viewed like a sporting event and that the standing up for a position is being viewed as an individual competitive performance. It would be even more likely to be noticed and remarked on if the term turned up in a piece of legislation. How far a text travels for its intertextual relations we can call the **intertextual reach**.

Often a document draws on bits of text that appear earlier in the text, echoing and building on it, in what we might call **intratextual reference**. A text can reach a bit farther, but stay in a limited domain when a company memo refers to and relies on a previous memo from the company on the same case. We might call this **intra-file intertextuality**. Interesting questions rely on the way texts within a file or other collection pull together to make a representation of a case or subject—we might call such a phenomenon the **intertextual collection**. A classroom might equally create a fairly closed world of **classroom intertextuality**, between the lectures, the textbook, assignment sheets, class discussion, and student exams and papers. Classroom intertextuality broadens as students and teachers bring outside reading to bear, refer to other courses, start discussing applications to issues found in the newspapers or television documentaries. Some research disciplines are fairly contained, relying only on an explicit **disciplinary intertextuality** (although there may be unnoticed reliance on other fields), whereas others have a much larger interdisciplinary reach, and those have a broader **interdisciplinary intertextuality**.

Outside of the academic disciplinary world, we might speak of **intracorporate** or **intraindustry intertextuality**, but again the reach may broaden into **intrasystem intertextuality**, if, for example, corporate documents attend to larger corporate policies, government law and regulations, documents of other companies, economic predictions, consumer culture, and so on.

Finally we should notice **intermediality**, when the resource or reference moves from one medium to another, as when talk, or movies, or music is alluded to in a written text.

Translation Across Contexts/Recontextualization. Each time someone else's words, or words from one document or another part of the same document, are used in a new context, the earlier words are recontextualized, and thereby given new meaning in the new context. Sometimes the **recontextualization** goes unnoticed as the earlier meanings are not far from the meaning in the new context. Sometimes, however, the shift is significant as when the name of a medical procedure, developed among surgeons and used within hospitals gets brought up in financial discussions with insurance companies, when the procedure then becomes a matter of costs and who will pay. When the term travels to discussion of medical ethics it takes on new meanings and concerns. Then the same term when put into a public debate over medical policy comes to carry a host of other meanings, particularly when the procedure may involve reproductive rights or some other similarly controversial issue.

Sometimes the recontextualization may also put the words into a less friendly or more critical context, or some context that comments on, evaluates, or puts the other words at a distance. An opponent of an abortion rights act may call it the "so-called reproductive choice act." The phrase *so-called* signals a criticism of the way his opponents use the word choice. In talking with his friends a teenager may mock his teachers just by repeating their favorite phrases using an odd tone of voice. The philosopher in a scholarly book, by identifying a set of ideas as Locke's theory of the senses, holds those ideas up for examination and possible criticism. In such recontextualizations the current author takes a stance, adopts an attitude, comments on, or evaluates the original words. We might call such recontextualizations **intertextual comment**.

Finally within specific genres (see chap. 11) there may be typical and expected patterns of intertextuality. For example, as John Swales (1990) has shown, in research article introductions, authors cite the previous litera-ture to establish that a problem exists and what is known, and then identify a needed new kind of study not covered by the previous work. This defini-tion of the limits of previous research creates the research space of the new work.

Another example of generically expected intertextuality occurs in the news story about a controversial issue, where you can expect quotations from people on opposite sides of the issue, or the newspaper story about a disaster where you can expect quotations from witnesses or victims.

METHODOLOGICAL ISSUES

As with any form of research and analysis the first and most important task is knowing **why you are engaged** in the enterprise and **what questions you hope to answer** by it. Intertextual analysis might, for example, help you identify which realm of utterances an author relies on and how, or how an author tries to ensure the readers see the subject through a certain set of texts, or how an author tries to position himself or herself in relation to oth-ers who have made statements, or to understand how a researcher is at-tempting to characterize, rely on, and advance prior work in her and re-lated fields, or to understand how students are assimilating and developing a synthetic or critical understanding of subject materials. Although one may begin with broad exploratory questions the sooner one can determine what one is looking for, the more one can refine one's analysis so as to probe more deeply into the material.

Once you know what you are looking for and why, the next task is to **identify the specific texts you want to examine**, making them extensive enough to provide substantial evidence in making claims, but not too broad to become unmanageable. Often intertextual analysis is quite intensive, so you may limit your study to a single short text, at least at first, to focus your inquiry. However, if you decide to use very visible and obvious markers of intertextuality, such as considering only the works cited list to see which authors some individual or groups rely on, than you might be able to do a broad quantitative study on a large corpus. After doing an intensive pilot study on a small text you may have identified a small set of easily identifi-able features that are relevant to your question and you want to focus on, so you may then move to a more extensive study. But remember if you move to more extensive analysis, do not try to answer questions that re-quire detailed intensive analysis.

Having identified your corpus the next step is to **identify the traces of other texts** that you wish to consider. This is most easily done when you wish to examine explicit overt references to other authors, as revealed in direct quotation or formal scholarly references or works cited lists.

If you are working with explicit references you might underline or high-light each such reference in the text and then create a list of all instances, leaving open adjoining columns to add in further observations and interpretations. You might in the next column list how it is expressed whether through a direct quotation, indirect quotation, or just paraphrase or description—but still attributed. Then in the next column you may begin interpreting the intertextuality, making comments on how or for what purpose the intertextual element is being used in the new text.

Then, from these basic facts, you may start **making observations and interpretations** by considering the reference in relation to the context of what the author is saying. Depending on the purposes of your analysis, you might ask why the writer is bringing in the reference, how the person referred to relates to the issue or story at hand, whether the writer is expressing any evaluation or attitude toward the intertextual resource, how the original may have been excerpted or transformed to fit the author's current concerns, and whether the reference is linked to other statements in the text or other intertextual references.

If your analytical purpose leads you to look at unattributed or background intertextuality, you will need to look for **more subtle clues**. Some distinctive words, well known now or at the time of the original writing and circulation of the document can suggest that the author was evoking a whole realm of language and attitudes, so you might look for similar or related words. Thus if we see an author appealing to "the inalienable rights of citizens" we would look in a more orderly way for other words and concepts echoing the Declaration of Independence. We may even pull out our copy to remind us of all the terms and concepts we might search for.

In the same way if a word or phrase seems out of keeping with the general tone, level, or sets of words, we might wonder where these words came from, what other kind of document they might reflect, and if there any other similar borrowings in the text.

Again you would then do well to **make a list** of such words that evoke some world or group or actors outside the text. Then in the second column you might list who those words evoke and then how they are used here to give a particular impression; then in a further column you may interpret the evocative words in relation to the context they are used in.

Whatever the focus of your analysis, from your examples you should start **looking for a pattern** from which you start developing conclusions, which again would depend on the purpose of your examination. If your aim is to examine how the author coordinates intertextual elements into a single coherent statement, your focus will be on the techniques the author uses to draw the voices of others into the central argument and relate them to each other through the overall perspective being developed. If your aim is to examine the degree of manipulation in the intertextual borrowing, you may wish to consult the original sources and compare the original presentation to the way the new author represents his or her sources.

APPLIED ANALYSES

The most visible intertextuality occurs when people comment on some other's words, as they frequently have to do in school assignments. In a fifth-grade class, for example, which was assigned to write responses to Ray Bradbury's story "All Summer in a Day," a student referred to the following passage from the story:

> And they had written small stories or essays about it.
>
> > *I think the sun is a Flower*
> > *That blooms for just one hour.*
>
> That was Margot's poem, read in a quiet voice in the still classroom while the rain was falling outside.
> "Aw, you didn't write that!" protested one of the boys.

One student, C, quotes the lines directly, and then rephrases the meaning in a personal way to explain how he connects to the feelings of the character.

> I think she felt really, really bad, as much as I did, because she could just remember the sun. She wrote in her poem, "I think that the sun is a flower that blooms for just one hour." That line made me think of a beautiful flower that blooms for just one hour.

The quotation and the personal rephrasing of what is evoked in his imagination brings C into relation with the meanings of the text and articulates a bond of feeling for the character. In his commentary, C aligns himself very closely to the character Margot.

Another student in another year, writing about the same story, references the same passage, but to make a different point and adopt a different position with respect to the character and story. The student R, to support her claim that "the way Margot was treated in the story was not nice," draws inferences about behaviors described in the story.

> I say that because of the way the kids were treating her, like when Margot wrote her poem: "I think the sun is a flower that blooms for just one hour." A kid did not like her just because she remembered the sun and he was jealous. He told her that she did not write the poem.

R, in addition to quoting the couplet from the story also paraphrases an additional line about the response of one boy; she also makes an interpretive statement tying the two statements and characters together in an emotional drama, which she has then framed in an evaluation of the boy's behavior. In doing so she does done more than extract and sympathize with one character's thought; she has made judgments about the meaning and morality of both words and events portrayed in the story. She also has attributed meaning to more than the words of one or two characters—she has attributed meaning to the author of the story who has created the dramatic incident. (Data collected by Beth Yaeger.)

CONCLUSION

This classroom example along with the earlier journalistic example strikingly display that **intertextuality is not just a matter of which other texts you refer to, but how you use them, what you use them for, and ultimately how you position yourself as a writer to them to make your own statement**. People can develop adeptly complex and subtly skilled ways of building on the words of others. Such complex intertextual performances are so familiar we hardly notice them.

ACTIVITIES

1. An Academic Article: Locate a research or scholarly article for your own field. Analyze how the article uses, builds on, takes a position with respect to, and adds to prior publications.

2. News: Analyze a short newspaper story to examine how it creates a social drama and forms a journalistic standpoint by the way it organizes its representation of words of others. Find a short editorial piece on the same topic. Examine the intertextuality in that piece and compare it to that which you found in the news story.

3. A School Essay: Analyze an undergraduate paper you wrote in relation to the material presented in the lectures and discussions, textbook, assigned readings, special readings, or things you may have learned before. Consider how you assembled all these resources to come up with your own statement. What position did you take to all these materials? In what way did you create something novel? What was your value added, your critical, evaluative, synthetic contribution? In what way might those critical analytical or synthetic actions also have had their intertextual sources? To what extent was the teacher or reader of the paper concerned with the accurate portrayal of material in the course and to what extent on the additional work you did?

FOR FURTHER READING

The best overview of intertextuality from the perspective of literary theory is Graham Allen (2000), *Intertextuality*. Allen provides a roadmap to theorists Vladimir Volosinov, Mikhail Bakhtin, Julia Kristeva, Roland Barthes, and Gerard Genette, largely framed around the question of originality of texts and their dependence on an existing discursive field. Volosinov's (1986) *Marxism and the Philosophy of Language* is the most foundational of the theoretical works. Not limited to literary concerns, it examines how all utterances are located within and take attitudes toward a social field. Genette's works are worth consulting for his distinctions of the various relations one text may adopt with respect to other texts (what he calls the text's transtextuality): intertextuality (explicit quotation or allusion), paratextuality (the relation to directly surrounding texts, such as prefaces, interviews, publicity, reviews), metatextuality (a commentary relation), hypertextuality (the play of one text off of another familiar text), and architextuality (generic expectations in relation to other similar texts). Genette offers detailed analyses of literary texts in relation to these categories in *The Architext* (1992), *Palimpsests* (1997a), and *Paratexts* (1997b). Jack Selzer (1993a) provided a briefer introduction to literary theoretical approaches to intertextuality and begins to put the literary issues in relation to rhetorical investigation, as did Jim Porter (1986).

Exemplar rhetorical analyses of how intertextuality is concretely used in nonliterary texts are by Amy Devitt; Carol Berkenkotter, Tom Huckin, and James Ackerman; and Charles Bazerman (1991, 1993). Devitt's (1991) study of the writing of tax accountants revealed that all genres they use have strong intertextual connections with the legal tax code, but those intertextual connections are displayed and used differently in different genres. For example, in letters of tax protest to the Internal Revenue Service a technical discussion of the interpretation of specific parts of the tax publications is typical. Letters of response to clients only have occasional mention of reference numbers in the tax code to indicate that the accountant's view is based on law, but the body of the opinion is presented as the accountant's advice, although we can assume that awareness of the law is implicit throughout. In all documents exact terms and phrases from the tax code are used without quotation, because those terms take on authoritative, technical, and consistent meaning; however, quotation marks are used at times for specific rhetorical effect. Berkenkotter, Huckin, and Ackerman (1991) have studied how a graduate student learns to use the literature of his discipline in ways approved by the professors and then develops a position from which to discuss and contribute to that literature. The student, in learning how to appropriately represent the intertextual field and in developing a strategy for representing his own work in relation to the field also develops his own professional identity and direction for his work. Bazerman (1991) examines the origin of modern review of the literature and citation practices in science by looking at the writing practices and social beliefs of Joseph Priestley, who saw that attending to the aggregate experience of humankind was necessary for advancing knowledge. Bazerman (1993) compares the rhetorical presentation of cited materials in an unusual modern scientific article to the texts of the original articles to uncover the way in which the two coauthors construct the intertextual field to position their own argument as a powerful antidote to mistaken directions taken by their discipline.

The linguist Per Linell (1998) and the essays that follow in the special issue of *Text* provide the most extensive examination of the issue of transformation through recontextualization in a new text. John Swales (1984) presents his well-known model of how the introductions of scientific papers locate themselves within intertexts. Bazerman's (1995) textbook *The Informed Writer* in the chapter "Analyzing the Many Voices in Writing" provides further detailed advice for writing an essay analyzing the intertextuality of a piece of writing.

5

Code-Switching and Second Language Writing: How Multiple Codes Are Combined in a Text

Marcia Z. Buell
University of Illinois at Urbana-Champaign

PREVIEW

Sociolinguistics and the ethnography of communication have represented major areas of language scholarship over the past 40 years. These areas have focused on language use in specific settings and specific communities. Researchers ask questions about the relationships of language to society, such as how a particular variety of language signals a social identity, an attempt to affiliate with a group or institution, or an attempt to exclude participation by others. Sociolinguists and ethnographers of communication have been particularly interested in code-switching[1] because they have repeatedly found that **shifts in coding point to or index social identities, relationships, and contexts**. When a speaker uses or changes a code, she is signaling who she is, how she relates to listeners or readers, how she understands the context and what communicative tools are available to her. **In fact, code-switching does not simply reflect context, but operates to establish the relevant contexts of a situation.** Because codes are developed through histories of interaction, they also map onto sociocultural groupings and domains of activity. The picture that emerges from such research is of language as a complex patchwork of codes linked to diverse

---

[1]A keyword search for code-switching of the *Linguistics and Language Behavior Abstracts* database turns up over 1,300 articles, chapters, and books that address code-switching between 1973 and October 2001.

arenas of social life and of language users as nimble code-switchers. While code-switching represents a general framework from which any kind of writing might be analyzed, in this chapter we explore code-switching and code hybridity in relation to the special case of second language writing. Code-switching offers particularly rich insights for examination of second- (multi-) language or dialect speakers and writers who must not only negotiate across recognizably distinct languages or language variants, but also must work through the complexity attached to learning and using an unfamiliar set of codes.

BASIC CONCEPTS

Codes and Code-Switching. The basic notion of a code seems relatively straightforward when we are looking at shifts between languages or distinct dialectal varieties. **Code-switching** has generally been explored as a phenomenon in which speakers switch back and forth between two separate languages or dialects to include or exclude other participants, to portray a particular nuance or to establish solidarity (Schecter & Bayley, 1997). Alternatively, some code switches are less intentionally rhetorical or audience focused and may occur because a speaker has no other means of communication available (Hancock, 1997). Code-switching can be as brief and fleeting as a single word from another language included in an utterance, or it can appear in larger units of discourse and be a sustained, even stabilized, practice (e.g., routine use of Latin in a Catholic church service). In short, code-switching across languages occurs for many reasons.

Although studies of code-switching have generally focused on oral language, cross-lingual and cross-dialectal shifts can also be seen in written language.[2] Figure 5.1 shows several examples, which suggest the complex and diverse social meanings of such shifts. Using Latin classifications for biological terminology is a convention signaling technical precision and may not appear as a strongly marked code switch. Richard Rorty's (1979) use of classical Greek in a philosophical text, often without translation or even transliteration, indexes an expectation his readers would be of the elite class where such knowledge is assumed. This contrasts with Gloria Anzaldúa's (1987) politically charged use of marginalized languages to illustrate how language and culture can be richly hybrid or fused. These examples illustrate that code-switching across languages is a feature of written texts and that the motivations for such shifts are complex and need investigation.

---

[2]The emphasis on speech rather than writing has not been motivated by any particular theoretical principle. Instead, it reflects the overwhelming historical tendency of sociolinguists and ethnographers of communication to focus on talk.

From Biology: (Myers, 1990, p. 154)	From Philosophy (Rorty, 1979, p. 44)	From Literature (Anazaldúa, 1987, p. 45)
We have demonstrated that (i) *Heliconious* females respond to the presence of eggs; (ii) this response has a strong visual basis (8) although chemical cues are not altogether excluded and (iii) the response to egglike structures of *Passiflora* and to real eggs both reduces the possibility that real eggs will be laid after host discovery and increases the time required to oviposit.	But the sense that the nature of reason is a "permanent problem" and that anyone who doubts our uniqueness should study mathematics persists. The θυμός which quickened the Homeric heroes, St. Paul's πνεῦμα, and Aquina's active intellect, are all quite different notions.	*Soy nopal de castilla* like the spineless and therefore defenseless cactus that Mamagrande Ramona grew in back of her shed. I have no protection. So I cultivate needles, nettles, razor-sharp spikes to protect myself from others.

FIG. 5.1. Examples of code-switching across languages in written texts.

Code-switching, however, is not limited to changes in language or dialect. Dell Hymes (1974) defined code-switching as "alternate use of two or more language varieties of a language, or even speech styles" (p. 103). Under this definition, even when speakers use what is recognized as a single language, ways of using language vary. **Such shifts in style, register and voice, whether in spoken or written language, can then be included in a broad definition of code-switching.**[3] It is important to note that sociolinguists and ethnographers of communication have proposed a variety of

_____

[3]Hymes (1974) noted: "Whole-language choice is important and salient, but not in practice or in principle fundamental. The true structure of choice of linguistic means, of a theory of the creative aspect of their use, lies deeper. Thus, shift in the provenance of linguistic means (e.g., from German to Italian), while striking, goes together with shift in any component of speaking, as prospective evidence of underlying organization: shift between normal voice and whispering, between direct and indirect address, between deliberate and hurried tempo, between one topic and another, etc." (p. 105).

finer terminological distinctions, sometimes distinguishing between such notions as code shifting, style shifting, and code borrowing. In this chapter, I use code-switching in its broadest sense—what Saville-Troike (1989) called variety-shifting.

Although it is easy to recognize separate languages juxtaposed against each other, there are also more subtle types of code-switching which occur within the same language, in both speaking and writing. (For examples of speaking shifts, see Labov, 1972b.) For shifts in writing, Greg Myers (1990) explored how biologists changed codes when they went from articles in technical journals to articles in popular science magazines. With different audiences and genres, Myers found that in addition to lexical or syntactic choices, these scientists shifted content and organization so much that they produced very different representations of what science is and of the kind of authority the scientists might claim. Such shifts are not the domain of professional writers alone. David Bartholomae (1985) showed how basic writers flounder when they must write with authority in an academic context but do not have the appropriate resources or models to enact authoritative voices. The result is often a hybrid code that moves uncomfortably between informal and didactic phrasings.

When speakers or writers switch codes, whether they do so adeptly or with difficulty, they index identity and affiliation on multiple levels. This may take the form of competing identities that simultaneously come to the fore (Goffman, 1981; see also Leander & Prior, chap. 8, this volume). Although speakers or writers may shift the identities they foreground by altering code, such shifts may also occur in reception, that is, in the ways a recipient understands and takes up the language (e.g., Irvine, 1996). In a broader sense, recipients of text can perceive or not perceive the use of certain codes, depending on their backgrounds and relationships within the context.

For sociolinguists, **code-switching is a key marker of social identities, relations, and contexts**. Writers, for example, may vary tone or style to match their perceptions of audience expectations, but this variation is mediated by the writer's own understanding of language use, of the context, of social relations, and of aspects of identity she wishes to highlight. Code-switching then functions within what Carol Myers-Scotton (1998) defines as negotiations of rights and obligations in an exchange. In this construct, participants employ **unmarked**, or ordinary, forms when they believe they are sharing the same set of rights and obligations. If one speaker perceives a need for a new set of rights and obligations, he or she will change to a more **marked** form. However, because perceptions of rights and obligations may not match, speakers must constantly negotiate with each other to establish parameters for interaction. Of course, many of these perceptions and negotiations are tacit aspects of discourse practices, not conscious acts.

Negotiation may be focused on issues as simple as word choice or as complex as determining which larger textual or cultural codes dominate. Language groups, academic disciplines, and other discourse communities hold varied preferences of the way discourse should be laid out, so that salient points in one style of discourse may not be seen as legitimate in another. Activating a code that is different from the one listeners or readers expect can result in a negative reception of the text or in communicative breakdowns (Gumperz, Aulakh, & Kaltman, 1982). From a sociolinguistic perspective, misunderstandings of this type still serve social functions, marking and building relations of affinity and distance, and inclusion and exclusion, across social groups.

Frameworks for Studying Second Language Writing

Though conversational code-switching between two or more languages receives widespread attention in language acquisition studies, code-switching has not been a major research framework in studies of second language writing (with notable exceptions, such as Baynham, 1993). For second language writing, the dominant research and pedagogical paradigms have focused on errors in vocabulary and syntax or on cultural influences in organizing text. Theories of code-switching operate in conjunction with these existing paradigms, so it is worthwhile to briefly examine major tenets of these frameworks for second language writing.

Two basic accounts have been offered for language errors in second language writing and talk. Starting in the 1950s, U.S. researchers looked at syntactic and lexical errors through the lens of **contrastive analysis**, which held that errors occurred because of differences between a learner's native language and the language she was trying to learn. For example, contrastive analysts would argue that native Japanese speakers and writers often have trouble including the "s" to mark third person (e.g., "I work" vs. "he works") because the Japanese language does not alter verbs to show person. However, it soon became clear that such differences between languages cannot account for all the variance that arises with language learning. An alternative to this concept of language interference is the notion of **interlanguage** (Selinker, 1974). Interlanguage theory postulates developmental psycholinguistic processes in language learning whereby individuals create structures that neither mirror the learner's first language nor follow the usual patterns of the target language.

Moving beyond sentence-level lexical and syntactic issues, work in **contrastive rhetoric**, begun in the 1960s, has examined cultural influences on written texts, to account for why some texts could be (or could be made) grammatically or semantically correct, but still have a "non-native" feel.

The paradigm of contrastive rhetoric has attempted to uncover broad rhetorical differences rooted in cultural differences between national or supranational groups (e.g., Japanese vs. American, Asian vs. European). It has focused especially on differences in modes of organization and development within specific genres, in ways that audiences are addressed, in ways that authors achieve credibility, and so on, with the claim that different ethnic cultures have preferences for how these things are done (Connor, 1996; Kaplan, 1966). As contrastive language analysis led to contrastive rhetoric, interlanguage analysis suggests a notion of **inter-rhetoric**, where learners of new rhetorical codes may creatively produce novel, border zone forms, new combinations and transformations that mimic neither the code they are learning nor the code they already know.

Moreover, reasons for rhetorical and other discourse practices may be multilayered and contradictory. Tying rhetorical difference only to ethnic or national culture ignores the diversity of codes operating within diverse genres. Likewise, salient rhetorical differences are not limited to modes of organization, style, questions of audience, and forms of argument, but also involve specific topical resources with deep intertextual roots, use of metaphors and other tropes, complex voicing, ideologies, and so on. For instance, research by Casanave (1995) and Prior (1998) points to the challenges first and second language writers alike face as they work to learn the multiple and fluid codes found in graduate seminars and disciplinary fields.

Analyzing second language learning and writing through the lens of code-switching complements and extends these existing traditions. It offers a framework that anticipates the possibility of **heterogeneity**, of multiple codes being present in a text. It highlights, as other theories do not, the **social significations of linguistic and rhetorical codes** in terms of how they both reflect and produce social identities, relations, and contexts. It emphasizes **the negotiability of discourse**, the ways, for example, that the actual work, as well as meaning, of a text is reshaped in the uptake of a reader. It may as well point to **motives for second language learners' code switches** that are not reducible to knowledge or lack of knowledge of a public code. Because of the complex interaction of language and social factors, theories in code-switching offer fertile ground for analyzing how multiple discourses co-exist and potentially signal a kaleidoscope of identities emerging as second language writers define their worlds. Again, code-switching is a framework that applies to first language writing and talk as well. Thus, it posits that second language writers and first language writers share the same basic types of challenges and draw on the same basic types of resources and strategies in their textual and rhetorical work, although the magnitude of the challenges and the nature of the specific resources may differ greatly.

METHODS OF ANALYSIS

The first step in this type of analysis is to **identify** the codes and where code-switching is occurring. The second, more important, step is **contextualization**, exploring the functions, and significations of codes and code-switching. Analysts may pursue three basic strategies in studies of code-switching in writing:

- **interpretive analysis** of a text, which relies on the analyst's existing knowledge of codes and their functions;
- **intertextual analysis**, which involves explicit comparison of multiple texts to identify or confirm patterns of codes and code-switching, a strategy that might lead the analyst to expand her knowledge; and
- **ethnographic methodologies** (observation, interviewing), which go beyond the analysts' knowledge by observation of *in situ* practices and by eliciting participants' perceptions of, and reflections on, language use.

These three strategies work in concert to produce a rich reading of the codes of a text and the contexts of their use. They are not three steps in a linear process (though in some cases, analysts may move from a single text to multiple texts and then outward toward ethnographic contextualizations); instead, it is best to think of these strategies as three phases of a recursive process of inquiry.

Interpretive analysis may be as straightforward as noting the occurrence of a shift from one language to another, or it may require closer reading to identify subtle variations in style, register, voice, or world view. One key to reading for code-switching with second language writers is to **expect variation**, and to look for those points where the text takes on an unfamiliar sound or feel. Code-switching may range from the fleeting invocation of a code in a single word or phrase to large blocks of text where a specific code is realized, or even to switching codes across different texts. As Myers (1990) found with different kinds of narratives biologists employ, many **dimensions of a text** may be involved (singly or in conjunction) in code switches: differences in the **topics** discussed, in the kinds of **textual representations** produced, in adherence to certain **world views**, in **images and other modes**, as well as in patterns of **textual organization** and **specific lexis and syntax**. In the analysis that follows, several potential code switches stood out as variant from usual forms in English academic writing. They included cross-lingual grammatical and semantic shifts, cultural shaping of essay structures, decisions about academic conventions and examples of competing world views. These factors were rich starting points for this set of data, but I must emphasize that other data sets would highlight other aspects of language and culture.

While identifying points which appear as changes in code, or as codes in competition with each other, it is also important to consider the motives for, and contexts of, such shifts. As an analyst, you need to ask if the shift appears to be deliberate or unintentional and if there are factors in the text, or in the production of the text, which facilitate a code switch. Looking for these facets moves an analysis away from simply labeling where a code switch occurs to viewing code-switching as a social function of language embedded within other linguistic social functions.

One approach to uncovering motivations behind code switches would be to draw on some theoretical framework. Analysts who wish to start within such a framework may find Myers-Scotton's (1998) description of rights and obligations useful, in that it lays out conversational goals that a speaker may try to realize through code-switching. If you take this theoretical construct as a model, you can then draw on it to help explain conversational or textual moves that are manifest as code switches. Alternatively, analysts may wish to examine texts in a more speculative way and develop broader hypotheses, which are not tied to any one theory, and seek to explain why the shifts occur where they do. The following analysis leans more toward the second approach although it has some grounding in theoretical constructs.

Though interpretive analysis of a text may lead an analyst to identify codes and suggest possible interpretations of the functions and significations of their use, **intertextual analysis** allows the analyst to expand the range of data to triangulate and test the consistency of code identifications, motivations, and interpretations across texts. Of course, in a fundamental way, by default, intertextuality already comes into play in any interpretive reading of the text. If you are looking at the function of certain codes in academic writing, you must first be able to recognize academic writing, both in canonical and noncanonical forms. This recognition emerges from experience with texts and guides to the construction of such texts. Repeated experience with text, in effect, creates expectations for what a class of texts should look like. In addition, to examine shifts across languages, you may draw on understandings of cross-cultural communication and second language writing. Analysts lacking experience in these areas may have to rely on intuitions at first and then test observations with learners of English or with more experienced colleagues. This would still require noting where text varies from your expectations and then categorizing where that variance appears to lie.

Intertextual triangulation may involve reading one text against other texts by the same writer(s), perhaps through texts appearing in different forums (as Myers did in looking at popular and technical articles from the biologists), against texts by other writers in similar contexts, such as other students in the same class, and against texts produced in response to a writer's work, such as, in the case of the sample analysis, texts that an instructor produces in evaluating a student's work. (For more on intertextual analysis, see Bazerman, chap. 4, this volume.) In this case, I did not have available texts that other students wrote. However, the texts the participant submitted included the written responses of the instructor. This response text—what was responded to *and* what was not—is important because it displays another reading of the text and it suggests what the instructor had expected of the task.

Another form of intertextuality, relevant to this analysis, is a writer's handling of **source texts**. In other words, particularly in academic settings, writers often produce texts that somehow respond to another piece of writing, whether it is responding to ideas presented in another source, or incorporating quotations or paraphrases from the source to discuss a concept in further depth. Some texts index sources more overtly than others, and the range of influence or incorporation is vast. As a methodological starting point, it may help to question if another source might possibly be influencing the production of a text, although potential answers may never move beyond the realm of speculation. The following analysis postulates an oblique, rather than direct, influence of a source text, illustrating how code choices are located within a mosaic of experience and knowledge of the world.

Interpretive and intertextual reading offer many ways to identify code-switching, but to gain a fuller perspective, it makes sense to also seek out the perceptions of the writer(s) and of other readers to both identify and contextualize the codes. **Ethnographic methods** may include questionnaires about language use and social networks, observation with field notes or mechanical recordings, and varied types of interviews (see chapters by Prior, Leander & Prior, and Kamberelis & de la Luna, this volume). These methods offer potential windows into context, purpose, and functions of texts or parts of texts. Interviews in particular allow for confirmations or refutations of the analyst's interpretations and for participants to introduce alternative readings of the texts, codes, and contexts. If you interview the writer of a text, she or he may be able to persuasively argue why a particular form is being used, offering reasons that are simply unavailable to an analyst who is limited to the immediate text. If you survey other writers engaged in similar practices in similar situations, you may be able to uncover factors that were unique to the local community of writers but do not necessarily translate into other situations. In a similar fashion, other readers of a text may complicate, in productive ways, the analyst's reading by identifying other possible code switches or not seeing a code switch, or naming code switches and their consequences differently.

In the following analysis, I used two ethnographic methods. The first was an interview with the creator of a piece of text, and the second called for response from a group of readers who had nothing to do with the production of the text. Questions for the interviews emerged after laying out initial interpretations through close reading of the text and by comparing the work with other pieces of writing the same student had produced over time. The interview questions highlighted possible codes that butt up against each other and set conditions for shifts. To pinpoint shifts and their underlying motivations, I used principles of qualitative/inductive data analysis, allowing major classifications to emerge from the data (Patton, 1990). Such classifications arose from this particular data set, so the potential categories will apply only to this piece of writing. Analysts engaging in similar studies would first have to identify interesting features of the texts they select and then set interviews based on the features they have observed. Categories for discussion are not necessarily predetermined, although existing research can suggest categories as starting points.

The applied analysis in the next section elaborates on the kinds of methodological reasoning involved in analysis of code-switching. It also illustrates some of the ways that interpretative and intertextual analysis can work with text-based interviews to produce a rich description of codes and code-switching in a text.

TRACING MULTIPLE CODES IN KWASSY'S TEXT: A SAMPLE ANALYSIS

The data for this analysis come from Kwassy, a student from the Ivory Coast, who studied ESL and math at a community college in the United States for $2\frac{1}{2}$ years, before entering a 4-year university in electrical engineering. Before coming to the United States, Kwassy had acquired working knowledge of English grammar and speaking while studying in high school in the Ivory Coast. Knowledge of English makes him trilingual, adding to French and Baule (his home language). Linguistically and culturally, he clearly has multiple influences that affect his language choices and that have shaped his world view.

Kwassy provided me with essays he had written in 1998 and 1999, including five final drafts from the first semester of a two-semester ESL composition course; three essays from a Humanities course in African studies; summaries, a research proposal and a research paper from the second sequence of freshman composition; and a computer science paper written primarily in computer codes. After reading through all the texts, I chose one of the essays, "Analysis of Museum Artifacts," from the Humanities course for intensive analysis because it most clearly illustrated code use as-

Analysis of Museum Artifacts

[1]As I drove on Peabody Drive by the Krannert Art Museum on Friday afternoon, which I entered for the first time, I was expecting to see some of the many artifacts that I used to go by the side of in Cote d'Ivoirvre. [2]The day looked clear with a blue almost whitened by flocks of clouds dispersed all over a sky already heated by an angry sun. [3]I was very exciting. [4] Even the spirits of the objects I was going to meet, did not allow my enthusiasm to weaken, when I first figured out that the Krannert Center on Matthews avenue does not shelter any museum. [5] I guess they were determined to make that day "[an enjoyable] learning experience" for me. [6] The spirits? [7]Why I am disserting about spirits of items that are supposed to be only "objets d'art" displayed in a museum? [8] How does it come that inanimate things like a Wee mask from Liberia and Cote d"Ivoire, or an Akua'ba figurine from Ghana can bear dynamic and living soul? [9]Perhaps one can truly state that the idea of the "objet d'art" in the Western view; "that is, and object created more for the sake of its beauty than its utility, does not exist in Africa." [10]But I have come to believe that, the art of the of the object along with the love of aesthetic contours are more "present in daily life [ ] in Africa" than anywhere else.

(Note superscript numbers were added to the beginning of each sentence for reference in the analysis.)

FIG. 5.2. Kwassy's introduction.

sociated with second language writing on the multiple levels listed above. Specifically, I focus here on the first paragraph of Kwassy's essay (see Fig. 5.2). To explore these aspects, I begin by considering some of the shifting codes that became visible through interpretive analysis, then move to considering how intertextual analysis offered additional perspectives, and finally turn to some additional insights and corrections that arose from text-based interviewing and discussion.

Exploring Kwassy's Codes: Close Reading as Interpretive Analysis of the Text. Close reading involves paying careful attention to the details of language in the text. It is a slow, focused noticing and marking of a text. What is noticed and what interpretations are initially made are necessarily grounded in, and dependent on, the analyst's knowledge. Thus, I begin here with an account of features I noticed and initial interpretations I made. However, such interpretations do not go far enough to explore the reasons driving the code switches and may not identify unfamiliar codes, so a second function of the interpretive phase of analysis is to identify features of interest or questions that could then be pursued through intertextual analysis or with ethnographic methods (in this case, text-based interviews).

Although there is much more to analyzing second language writing than looking at syntax and lexicon, these forms do offer one starting point for this analysis. In Kwassy's first paragraph there are several points where we can see shifts to another language code. He refers to the Ivory Coast as the "Cote d'Ivoire" (Sentence 6) and the "Cote d'Ivoirvre," (Sentence 1), the first close to a standard French spelling (lacking only a diacritical mark above the "o" in Cote) and the second including an apparent typographical error. The use of the proper name in French seems somewhat unconventional because "Ivory Coast" is the typical Anglicization of the term. However, as it follows the proper name, it is not a particularly marked code shift. Kwassy also twice switches to the French phrase "objet(s) d'art," (Sentences 7 and 9) in both cases marking this phrase with quotations. This phrase could reflect Kwassy's Francophone heritage;[4] however, it is more likely marking a typical use of this phrase in English discussions of art. "Objet d'art" is used regularly enough in such contexts that it is found in English dictionaries.

I also noticed a few places where syntactic or lexical forms might be read as not native sounding:

> . . . artifacts that I used to <u>go by the side of</u> in Cote (Sentence 1)
> I was very <u>exciting</u>. (Sentence 3)
> Why I am <u>disserting</u> about spirits . . . ? (Sentence 7)
> How does it <u>come</u> that . . . ? (Sentence 8)

Most of these sentences follow syntactic rules but display an unusual choice of words. The phrases "go by the side of" and "how does it come" follow English syntactic rules of word order and are comprehensible, but not typical forms of expression. The sentence "I was very exciting" displays an English word (exciting), but not in the regular syntactic form (excited) that this context appears to call for.[5] Problems with participle use are a fairly common occurrence in second language writing, and may simply be based on interlanguage processes rather than indexing some sociolinguistic or rhetorical intention.

Finally, the language of Sentence 7 (the third example shown) does not display conventional word order for questions and incorporates a word "disserting" which follows the expected syntactic form but is not a regular English word (neither as standard nor usual nonstandard varieties). However, because of the context, I can guess that Kwassy either meant "digressing" as he was moving away from the narrative he had started, or "disser-

---

[4]Of course, making this interpretation depends on the analysts' having, in this case, sufficient knowledge of French to recognize "Cote d'Ivoire" and "objet d'art" as French. In this case or similar ones, an analyst encountering such phrases may only be able to infer that these phrases are foreign, not English, or not conventional.

[5]Alternatively a suitable sentence could read "It was very exciting."

tating," because he introduces a topic which he then elaborates on as he states a thesis.

All these language variants could be traced to influences of the other languages that Kwassy speaks (as in contrastive linguistic analysis), or to the emergent and developmental character of his English (as in the interlanguage analysis). However, the question here is whether these kinds of features signal a code shift. Certainly, I have already discounted certain "errors," such as the spelling of "d'Ivoirvre" as a typographical error. To explore other possibilities, I could compare these examples to the regular syntactic or lexical forms in French or Baule, or I could analyze a broader sample of Kwassy's writing and speech to see if they represent some interlanguage patterns (assuming these to be stable). I might also speculate that Kwassy is foregrounding his Francophone African heritage, building his ethos as a knowledgeable cultural critic. Finally, from the perspective of native readers, these forms could collectively signal a code switch not so much *to* another stable code, but *away from* English, marking the text as second language writing, and in some cases, drawing attention to the surface errors (e.g., see Prior's 1998 discussion of the case of Betty).

In addition to indexing a cross-lingual influence, Kwassy's use of "disserting" coincides with a broader shift in codes. "Disserting" appears at the point where Kwassy shifts from telling about his trip to the museum into a series of three questions (Sentences 6, 7, and 8) about art and culture that lead toward a more generalized claim (perhaps the thesis of the essay) in Sentence 10. Embedded in a question, "disserting" introduces a key technical concept "objet d'art" and the specific objects he will analyze. This point also appears to mark a change of register with the surrounding words. For example, the register in this paragraph is marked by the repeated use of first person pronouns (with 12 instances of "I" or "me" in the first 239 words, appearing in 6 of the 10 sentences) that might point to a personal narrative. However, in Sentences 8 and 9, there are no first person pronouns but a use of the relatively formal pronoun "one" as well as a long quote, perhaps indicating a shift toward a more academic register. The shift from personal to expository also appear to signal double-voicing in the textual identity of the writer. As Goffman's (1981) discussions of footings would suggest, the "I" Kwassy writes in these two sections of the first paragraph seems to shift significantly. In the first sentences, the "I" seems to point to the person who was driving to a museum and thinking about his task, while the two instances of "I" in the last five sentences both point to Kwassy as the writer of the paper in the current context of the class. Thus, a careful reading of multiple features of the first paragraph finds a kind of global shift in code between the first six sentences, which offer a descriptive and narrative account of Kwassy trying to find the museum, and Sentences 7 to 10 where we see a more expository and less personal discussion of art, with the word "disserting" appearing to mark the boundary of the shift.

Because this shift in the first paragraph seemed more significant than spelling or syntactic structures, it became one feature that I marked to discuss during the text-based interview. Specifically, I wanted to ask Kwassy about the word "disserting," to test out my sense that it was a significant marker of the code switch (and also to test my interpretations of the form). These switches, especially the rhetorical shift at Sentence 7 from a personal narrative to academic exposition, also led me to wonder to what extent Kwassy's introduction displays the generic discourse features of U.S. academic writing and academic register and to what it extent it reflects a personal or cultural variation, questions that I then pursued in both the intertextual analysis and the text-based interviews.

There are also interesting shifts in Kwassy's handling of the existence of spirits in objects. Some of his sentences appear to take their existence as a given (Sentence 4) while others (Sentences 6–8) question it. This tension could be related to conflicts in world views that Kwassy discusses and the representation of identity he wants to present. While contrastive rhetoric can account for patterns of development, styles of argument, source use, ways that audiences are addressed, and ways that authors are represented (or not) in texts, rhetoric in its broadest sense may ask how a text locates itself in relation to existing conversations and ideologies (see Gee, 1999; Eubanks, 2000). Kwassy's treatment of the spirits of the masks is an example of how code-switching might operate in this sense. In the first three sentences, Kwassy seems to be operating within a common Western ideological framework. He is driving to a museum, noticing what kind of day it is, and talking in unremarkable ways about his feelings. However, in the fourth sentence Kwassy introduces another sociocultural discourse, one which espouses the existence of "the spirits of the objects," which apparently might be dangerous in some sense (since he notes that even these spirits did not weaken his enthusiasm). The codes at play here, like other codes in general use, are constituted out of ideological worldviews as well as linguistic forms. Certainly, the notion of spirit is familiar in the West, although less typical is the notion that a place or object might have a spirit. However, the notion that material objects house spirits and that such spirits are likely to cause some anxiety is not part of what I take to be the usual worldview of natives of the United States. This worldview also crosses the code shift from personal narrative to expository academic writing as Kwassy again presupposes that the objects "can bear dynamic living soul" in Sentence 8 of the introduction. In my reading, to operate within the dominant academic ideology of the United States at present, the question in Sentence 8 would have to ask how Africans *believe* that such objects house living spirits. Sentences 9 and 10, however, seem to step back into familiar Western worldviews, shifting codes again, as Kwassy talks about a common Western classification that would divide art from utilitarian objects and that would associate art with heightened aesthetic concern. In short, world views seem to be colliding in the presupposition that the spirits exist, versus a presupposition that it is a belief under discussion. Uncovering worldviews and ideologies can be a fruitful venture in understanding why second language writing moves in some unexpected directions. Here again, such interpretations can be strengthened or challenged by input from the writer or others. The deep cultural codes of worldviews and ideologies often operate at such a tacit level that they may be easy to miss, easy to misconstrue, and difficult to articulate. Consequently, Kwassy's invocation of spirits became one of the questions that I wanted to explore in my interviews with him.

Even from this partial interpretive analysis, it is clear that Kwassy's paper presents a mix of codes. It includes French and English—and conventional and unconventional forms of both. It displays a mix of personal narrative and abstract exposition and appears to involve differing cultural–ideological codes (as in the treatment of spirits). Where a contrastive language and rhetoric approach would lead us to search for explanations for any differences in Kwassy's native language(s) and culture(s) and an interlanguage–interrhetoric approach might suggest ways that Kwassy's text displays unconventional developmental patterns, attention to multiple codes and code switching—without rejecting either of the other types of explanation—allows for and expects a more complex, hybrid text and keeps open the question of which codes are best suited to the purposes of the writer and most appropriate for the context. In this fashion, I could continue to read Kwassy's text to identify its codes and code-switching from the level of individual words to that of worldviews. However, as I have already begun to suggest, this close reading could be complemented by an intertextual analysis that sheds further light on the play of codes.

Some Intertextual Analyses. As this was a graded essay, it was presumably evaluated on how it met certain expectations. In this case, the instructor gave the paper a "C," but included few comments about the writing. In the introductory paragraph, the instructor only changed a few grammatical points, such as changing "exciting" to "excited." Repeatedly, she asked how Kwassy's descriptions of museum artifacts tied back to TFA (what I learned through interviewing was Achebe's [1959] *Things Fall Apart*, a novel that was a source text for the class). The instructor's response text converged with some of the second language or unconventional features I had identified, although not with others. It also led to a new question I had not initially been aware of, the absence of direct and explicit reference to Achebe's novel. The absence might simply signal a breakdown in understanding the task expectations; however, variations on how a task is com-

pleted often seem to index the identities a student is projecting and the social relations of the classroom.

The instructor's references to *Things Fall Apart* point to another potential
direction for intertextual analysis—examining if and how Kwassy's text links
up with Achebe's novel. Treating the spirits' existence as a given indirectly
reflects Achebe's incorporation of spiritual power. Characters within the
novel respond to the spirits as if they are real and their existence is not
questioned. When a ceremony to settle a dispute takes place, the characters in *Things Fall Apart*, especially the women and children, respond in fear
to the spirits among them (see p. 94). Since Achebe incorporates myth and
deities into the story, the invocation of spirits in Kwassy's introduction
could be read as an implicit link to the reading. However, the instructor
seems to have been looking for another kind of intertextuality that Kwassy,
for whatever reason, did not produce. Yet, Kwassy's thesis is not the existence or even the roles of the spirits, as much as the crossing of aesthetics
and utility. It appears that although his body paragraphs show how the
spirits interact, his real interest is in showing the beauty of the objects, and
so the intertextuality with the source text remains hidden.

In examining Kwassy's texts, I also found that the introduction to the
"Analysis of Museum Artifacts" displayed a general and, in my opinion,
somewhat sophisticated pattern that appeared in Kwassy's introductions
for other assignments in other classes. In his introductions, he often seems
to employ analogy to approach a broad topic, philosophically linking a detailed concept to the analogy and then connecting the overall concept to a
particular thesis which had not been mentioned previously. Because
Kwassy follows this pattern for most of the essays in the sample, and because this approach represents a variation from the way that the general to
specific funnel is often taught in U.S. composition classes, I speculated that
such a technique could be a culturally preferred style of development.
Without access to texts produced by other writers from Ivory Coast (another possible direction for intertextual analysis), I could not confirm or
rule out this possibility. Alternatively though, it could also be an "interlanguage" pattern in that it is embedded within an essay format taught in
some English writing classes, but with cultural or rhetorical influences
shaping the move from general to specific.

The intertextual analysis then helped to clarify certain issues while leaving others open and raising new ones. A single feature of a text may result
from a complex interplay of linguistic, rhetorical, and cultural codes and it
may be motivated by many interacting social and personal contexts. An analyst with sufficient familiarity with the contexts and genres can identify a
number of possible interpretations for a feature of the text. However, because of the complexity behind codes and code-switching, it is important to

seek out the writer's and others' perceptions and accounts to enrich the interpretation of texts and their contexts.

Ethnographic Methods: Text-Based Interviewing and Participant Accounts. Ideally, I would have liked to interview the instructor and the students in the class as well as Kwassy to gain a fuller picture of the context for these assignments. Insight into her grading processes could have helped show where Kwassy was accommodating course goals and consequently taking on that persona in his writing, and where he was not accommodating these goals. Unfortunately, because 3 years had passed since Kwassy had written the essay, and for other logistical reasons, I could not set up such an interview. I was, however, able to interview Kwassy to elicit his interpretation of class goals and comments that the paper received.

To prepare for the interviews, I wrote up initial analyses based on the features which interpretatively or intertextually appeared as non-native or as elements of code-switching across an array of frames. These initial analyses became the bases for my interview questions, which included:

1. To what extent did Kwassy view the essay, or specific sections of the essay, as academic or personal?
2. What was his previous experience with writing introductions?
3. What did the word "disserting" mean to him and how did he come to use it in the first paragraph?
4. What did he think about the notion of spirits and what were his intentions in introducing them as he did in the essay?

In Kwassy's introduction to "Analysis of Museum Artifacts" I perceived code switches reflecting syntactic and lexical items, as well as rhetorical and cultural structures for essay introductions. (See Swales, 1990, for how introductions are shaped in other genres.) Rhetorical structures included ways that introductions and essays are organized, questions of a personal or academic voice, and use of sources. Cultural structures would include world views, ways of approaching topics, and even acceptable topics for discussion. Just as these matrices overlap in domain, code shifts across domains do not necessarily occur as single events. For example, it is possible to have cross-lingual shifts that also index or coincide with personal or academic changes, or to have a rhetorical/organizational shift that coincides with one reflecting a cultural world view.

In addition to answering specific questions about codes and shifts, I also asked Kwassy to supply contextual information about the course and his writing. In this case, although he had not expected the course to be overly demanding, Kwassy reported that he found the complexities of examining his own culture while studying in a foreign culture had pushed his intellectual and emotional capacities, although not always in ways expected by his instructor. Thus, while he did not make the explicit connections with the novel that his instructor evidently expected, Kwassy reported that the reading and writing led him to make strong connections with the novel and others texts, along with many of his own observations and experiences.

Kwassy expressed an almost epiphanic enthusiasm for his realization of the beauty in everyday African objects, as illustrated by this sentence in his final reflection for the course: "The experience at the Krannert Art Museum marked a primary percussion of a flagrant revelation that never crossed my mind before." This enthusiasm came through in his interview, even though he was talking about the essay 3 years after he had initially written it. Yet, he was aware of tensions between the relatively easy flow of ideas when he looks at Africa as an African, in contrast to the more difficult task of writing up a systematic analysis for a class. Because of these tensions, he defined the essay as a blend of personal and academic writing. Thus, it is not unreasonable to see elements of both coming through in the introduction of "Analysis of Museum Artifacts." Interestingly, Kwassy also claimed that the introduction was the section most representative of himself as a writer and learner.

In the interview, Kwassy reported that he sees introductions in general as important parts of an overall essay. Nevertheless, when he began writing essays in English, he did not feel he had learned a precise method, so he drew on techniques he had learned when studying French in the Ivory Coast. In the Ivory Coast, French is an official language and the language of higher education, so students must attain a high level of proficiency in both speaking and writing. Through rather rigorous training, Kwassy came to believe that the way to write an introduction was to open with a general subject and narrow it down to a specific thesis. However, he sees that these are not direct, simple approaches from a general focus to a specific one, so he lays out a detailed, sometimes philosophical, background as a way to make the generality feel more connected to the specific point. Supplying a fair amount of detail reflects Kwassy's view of "what people used to do back there," in reference to the Ivory Coast, but he also sees it as a personal way to enter into the topic. In other words, without detailed explanation of a theoretical background, he feels he cannot make the connections he needs to move toward a thesis. Consequently, he reported that his process of forming the introduction reflects some contrast of cultural conventions for shaping writing, but also it illustrates code-switching principles as he attempts to merge the French interpretation of the funnel introduction with his interpretation of an English one and to establish a framework where he feels comfortable as a writer and thinker.

Additionally, the potential of French training and knowledge to influence English writing appears with Kwassy's use of unique words. Just as Kwassy drew on French organization styles when he was unsure about how to proceed with an English essay, he also pulled out the French language to help express a meaning in English. As a general lexical strategy, Kwassy says that when he cannot find an English word, he picks the meaning for what he wants in French and then checks a dictionary for the appropriate English word. Because French and English share a good number of cognates or near-cognates, this technique works fairly well for Kwassy. That is, it works well except when the dictionary cannot supply the word he wants to fit the meaning. Then, he will anglicize a French word in hopes that it will convey the intended meaning. In this case, he knew *dissertation* as an English word and was familiar with how verbs sometimes form nouns (as in *discuss* and *discussion*), so he employed a back-formation strategy to arrive at "disserting" rather than "dissertating." More than the word itself, this process shows how even cross-lingual code-switching is a mediated process, where words may take shapes that hover in between one recognizable language and another, but can still imply meaning when embedded into context.

I had speculated earlier that the use of "disserting" signaled a change in discourse structure. Because I was examining the text as academic writing mixed with a personal style, I saw it as signaling a move from a narrative to a more formal style. In the interview, I told Kwassy this interpretation, since, unlike experimental designs where researcher's goals are often hidden, this was an open interview where we were constructing meaning together. By explaining what I was seeing, he had the chance to say where my observations coincided or conflicted with his sense as a writer.[6]

To some extent Kwassy agreed that "disserting" shifted the focus of the introduction, but he felt the personal/academic continuum was outside of his writing goals. Although he had expressed a liking for the introduction and noted that it reflected who he was, he saw his processes on the more general level of adhering to the general/specific framework he felt essential to introductions. He felt the meaning of *disserting*, to talk more deeply about, signaled that he was moving into the heart of his discussion, which had previously been set up by a narrative. Use of *disserting* served as a writing strategy to help move the essay along.

In discussing his own strategies and the presentation of spirits in this essay, Kwassy noted that local culture in the Ivory Coast embeds the possibility of a world view that accepts spiritual activity. In traditional Ivory Coast

---

[6]One drawback of such open interviewing is that stating my observations at this point could color how my interviewee sees the work. Nevertheless, though it may influence perceptions, it does not force perceptions and potentially takes some of the mystery out of research goals, especially if the statement of intentions opens the pathways for further discussion. There were points where he rejected my interpretations of switches and their significance.

society, the roles of ghosts and spirits are taken seriously among some members of the population. In his interview comments, as in the essay, Kwassy's shift from treating spiritual existence as a given to talking about it as a belief system may reflect his own ambiguity about accepting or rejecting such a point of view. In Bakhtin's (1984) sense of double voicing, he may be simultaneously occupying the subjectivity of one who acts within that local world view, while at the same time, he occupies the position of one who questions it. Identity positions, as Goffman (1981) stated, do not have to be clearly one thing or another and indeed, can be several at once.

Classroom context also sheds light on how the spirits are invoked in this case. Without considering classroom context, it might appear that Kwassy's invocation of the spirits is idiosyncratic to his writing style or to this particular assignment. In fact, Kwassy's interview indicates he refers to the spirits because of their centrality to classroom discussions. Referring to the spirits in the text signaled a reference to his classmates so he could play with the concept of spirits embodied in objects, and use the shared knowledge and lexicon of his classmates to build a story. Upon rereading the essay 3 years after he had written it, Kwassy noted that his story about getting lost allowed him to bring up spirits in a playful way, so that he could set up a joke as a way of entering into the topic and also better represent who he was as a person. He noted that although he is a hard worker, he wants his writing to show him as creative and having a sense of humor even about serious or difficult topics.

Analyses of text, as shown in many chapters in this book, can go in a number of directions. Yet relying solely on the readings of one analyst and on the text itself can be severely limiting. Kwassy's interview exposed a richer, more nuanced interpretation to the text and its creation than I could have found through interpretive analyses alone. In particular, we begin here to see how codes remain ambiguous and complex in this text (infused with multiple voices), how Kwassy was working through his language to produce and project multiple identities (as a student, an African, someone who is creative and funny), and how this text, connected to the instructor's response, points to a complex pedagogical space, filled with multiple ideologies, goals, and discursive expectations.

To triangulate Kwassy's and my own readings of the text, I also elicited interpretations from other people who were not involved in its production and were reading the paragraph for the first time. In a colloquium for graduate students and professors in composition studies, I presented a basic definition of code-switching as being a change from one language variety to another in conversation or text which can occur across languages, dialects, or monolingual contexts and can be deliberate or subconscious. Then I showed Kwassy's introductory paragraph and asked for quick first reactions. One person pointed out the error with "exciting" and another questioned the meaning of "go by the side of." Someone wondered about "disserting," believing it to be a word she did not know as opposed to an error, while another participant immediately identified it as a back translation, a technique of modifying a word in the speaker's first language to look like a word in the target language, in hopes that it will resemble an actual word. This participant recognized the strategy because, as he later explained, it was one he used when writing in French as a second language. There were also comments about how Kwassy's shifts from personal narrative to academic thesis were very similar to Bartholomae's (1985) observations about basic writers, in that students, in both instances, try on the language of academe before they are able to use it convincingly. These observations all aligned more or less with my initial analysis. However, along quite different lines, one audience member saw a sophisticated and melodic essay which resisted—in form as well as content—the utilitarian orientation of Western writing and art theory and defended African art as simultaneously utilitarian and aesthetic. Finally, in a later discussion, one participant also identified another sort of resistance, noting that he appreciated Kwassy's incorporation of spirits, because he saw it as a sophisticated way of challenging discourse expectations.

These responses illustrate diverse codes and identities that the readers perceived, even with a quick first time reading. The reader who noticed the misuse of "exciting" may have been struck by how second language writing differs from the writing of native English speakers. The reader who recognized the translation strategy may have been struck by how a writing strategy in a different context mirrored his own. The reader who made the intertextual link to Bartholomae may have been observing that such unfamiliarity with an academic genre does indeed cross boundaries between second language and first language students, while the readers who spoke about resistance may have been seeing the clash between poetic or cultural preferences juxtaposed to a more rigid style of academic writing. Any one of these points of view could be added for further analysis of how code-switching operates within and across texts and audiences. While several of the responses pointed to elements that I had identified in earlier analysis, there were also interesting absences and divergences. These differences in focus point back to the Bahktinian notion that recognition and responses to codes and code-switches rests in the readers themselves as well as in the text and the writer.

CONCLUSION

As the sample analysis indicates, **interpretive, intertextual, and ethnographic approaches can work together to enrich an understanding of codes and code-switching in written texts**. Code-switching has proved to be a rich framework for research in speaking, and it holds equal potential as a means of analyzing writing, especially when we not only consider the codes themselves, but examine the contexts of, and potential motivations for, such switches. Such analysis is necessarily somewhat speculative because analysts, writers, and readers cannot fully articulate the codes present in a text. As Bakhtin (1986) suggests, the meanings of a text cannot be finalized because they are always part of historical dialogues, always open to further interpretation. The goal of analysis then is not to definitively state the boundaries of monolithic codes and what type of switch occurs, but to explore the discursive possibilities of a text. By examining where disjunctures to expectations or convention occur, we can begin to see multiple levels where meaning can be located both for writers and for readers. I hope it is clear that **this approach to analyzing codes and code-switching in texts is one that can be used in any analysis of writing as well as one that offers rich resources for considering second language writing**. Especially with second language writers, we can begin through this framework to see shifting textual codes as marking a range of practices and world views, instead of seeing them reductively as temporary deficiencies in knowledge or ability.

ACTIVITIES

1. Following are two excerpts from a journal that a female Japanese student kept while working on a group project for an MBA program. The first excerpt comes from her first entry, where she expresses some concern about how her group members made rapid decisions and how she felt unable to participate. The second excerpt was written 2 months later as part of a wrap-up assignment. In this assignment, she had to read back through her journal to assess how decision-making processes and group interaction evolved during the course of the semester. This excerpt responds to the question, "If this group were to continue, what could I do to improve my own effectiveness?"

Working in small groups, use the two excerpts to identify code switches intertextually. Use these questions as a guide.

- What language shifts do you notice within or across the texts?
- What are places where identity appears to shift between the two texts or within either text?
- Did you observe any shifts in world view within or across the texts?
- For each of the shifts you identified, what are possible motivations behind these shifts and what might they imply to the writer and other readers?

Share your interpretations with other groups.

September 1999

I found out in order to have a good discussion, you need to have an imagination and wide over view. I thought my group members lacked imagination. I am also nervous about the group project and discussions since I am the only international student. Sometimes I can not understand clearly what the other members said. I also wonder if my ideas are wrong because my background is so different from the other members. So I can not make comments immediately. I have to worry that what I feel is because of the fact I am Japanese. In that case, I should not tell them my idea or comments. As a result, my goal as an MBA student in this program's course is to develop the skills that will allow me to discuss business issues with Americans and I feel comfortable about doing it. This goal seems really different from the others in the group.

November 1999

One of my goal as an MBA student in this program's course is to develop the skills that will allow me to discuss business issues with Americans and I feel comfortable about doing it. This goal is also I would contentiously focus on improving. Furthermore, I would like to not only become equal to American but also enable to contribute to the group dynamics because from my different view of point. I would like to make best use of my all past experience such as living in many countries, speaking many languages, and getting well with decertified environment. Unfortunately, we just had one semester group activity, so that I could not contribute my uniqueness positively to group work. I was handicapped because of cultural barrier and English language skill. But if this group were to continue, I could show much variety of ideas and contribute to the group work to help all the member to better understand different ideas. Since American organization no longer exist without diversification now and future, people must learn the different people and different ideas and managers has to educate the workers to understand those difference.

2. Gloria Anzaldúa (1987) code-switches throughout her book *Borderlands: La Frontera*. In one chapter, she writes of prejudices against the different languages and dialects she speaks. In this excerpt, where she switches from English to Spanish is marked traditionally with italics for the Spanish words.

- What are possible implications for the switches across languages?
- Aside from switching actual languages, what other shifts do you notice in register, style or other ways of marking identity?
- Why do you think these shifts might be occurring where they do?
- What additional types of data might you need in order to make a fuller analysis?

"*Pocho*, cultural traitor, you're speaking the oppressor's language by speaking English, you're ruining the Spanish language." I have been accused by various Latinos and Latinas. Chicano Spanish is considered by the purist and by most Latinos deficient, a mutilation of Spanish.

But Chicano Spanish is a border tongue which developed naturally. Change, *evolución, enriquecimiento de palabaras nuevas por invención o adopción* have created variants of Chicano Spanish, *un nuevo lenguaje*. *Un lenguaje que corresponde a un mode de vivir*. Chicano Spanish is not incorrect, it is a living language.

For a people who are neither Spanish nor live in a country in which Spanish is the first language; for a people who live in a country in which English is the reigning tongue but who are not Anglo; for a people who cannot entirely identify with either standard (formal, Castilian) Spanish nor standard English, what recourse is left to them but to create their own language? (p. 55)

Spanish glosses (These are my own. Anzaldúa does not supply translations.) *Pocho (derogatory):* overly-Americanized; *evolución, enriquecimiento de palabaras nuevas por invención o adopción:* evolution, enrichment of new words through invention or adoption; *un nuevo lenguaje:* a new language; *Un lenguaje que corresponde a un mode de vivir:* a language that corresponds to a way of life.

FOR FURTHER READING

There are numerous articles and books on code-switching. Two good anthologies that address motivations and affective functions of code-switching are John Gumperz's *Language and Social Identity* (1982b) and Carol Myers-Scotton's *Codes and Consequences: Choosing Linguistic Varieties* (1998). Both are collections of research written by analysts in diverse fields. The authors in Gumperz's collection focus on cross-cultural misunderstandings that impede the use or uptake of tacitly understood codes for community outsiders (such as Gumperz, Aulakh, and Kaltman's discussion of competing notions of appropriate discourse strategies among British and Indian businessmen), and that involve selection of codes to signal acceptance or rejection of power relations (such as Monica Heller's discussion of Francophone and Anglo Canadians).

The authors in Myers-Scotton (1998) look at code switches more through the lens of the markedness model to explore how individuals select codes to change perspectives and accrue benefits within a given situation. The markedness model holds that speakers and writers will use unmarked or neutral language until they feel there is a need to use special forms to define social relations, establish solidarity, take on authority, or signal nuances. However, what is considered marked varies across situations and speakers as illustrated in discussions of literary moves and cross-lingual translations (Kreml, "Implicatures of styleswitching in the narrative voice of Cormac McCarthy's *All The Pretty Horses*"; Wilt, "Markedness and references to characters in Biblical Hebrew narratives"), interactions within families or workplaces (Mishoe, "Styleswitching in southern English"; Bernstein, "Marked versus unmarked choices on the auto factory floor"), and perhaps of most interest to second language researchers, transactions between non-native speakers of English and their native speaker counterparts (Sroda, " 'Not quite right': Second-language acquisition and markedness"). Sroda explores how native speakers and non-native speakers of English evaluate politeness forms in requests, finding that native speakers have more variance in their preferences than non-native speakers have come to expect.

Also of interest is *Code-Switching in Conversation: Language, Interaction and Identity*, edited by Peter Auer (1998). Auer and the other contributors to this volume argue against both traditional sociolinguistic perspectives on code-switching and against Myers-Scotton's markedness model. Instead, they argue for an ethnomethodological approach to seeing how code-switching works in situated conversations and for emic, more open, and less definite approaches to identifying what codes are.

Second language writing is a growing field. For a discussion of current developments and perspectives, see the collection edited by Tony Silva and Paul Kei Matsuda called *On Second Language Writing* (2001). Also of use for multiple perspectives on second language academic writing is Diane Belcher and George Braine's *Academic Writing in a Second Language* (1995). Of most relevance to this chapter in Belcher and Braine's collection is Christine Pearson Casanave's "Local interactions: Constructing contexts for composing in a graduate sociology program," which discusses how writing expectations are shaped within courses and other local contexts and how writers have to negotiate among these expectations as they progress in their studies. Casanave's (2002) book, *Writing Games: Multicultural Case Studies of Academic Literacy Practices in Higher Education*, offers richly detailed case studies of first and second language writers at varying academic levels (undergraduate to professor).

A great deal has been written about the grammar of speakers of English as a second language. For an overview of research paradigms in grammar acquisition, including contrastive analysis and interlanguage, see Rod Ellis' linguistics textbook *Understanding Second Language Acquisition* (1986). For a theoretical discussion of interlanguage, see Selinker's simply titled chapter "Interlanguage" (1974).

Readers who want to know more about developments in contrastive rhetoric should start with Ulla Connor's *Contrastive Rhetoric: Cross-Cultural Aspects of Second-language Writing* (1996). She discusses major developments and considerations in the field since its inception with Kaplan in 1966. In *Bootstraps: From an American Academic of Color*, Victor Villanueva (1993) gives a personal account of his discovery and application of principles of contrastive rhetoric, especially the notions that Hispanic writers have a cultural predilection for non-direct writing. In contrast, for critiques of contrastive rhetoric, see Vivian Zamel's (1997) article "Toward a Model of Transculturation" and Ron Scollon's (1997) article "Contrastive Rhetoric, Contrastive Poetics, or Perhaps Something Else?" Zamel argues that writers do not necessarily depend on one clearly delineated set of cultural influences, but are much more apt to merge voice and preferences across cultures. Scollon argues that contrastive rhetoric severely limits the kinds of texts open for study and therefore fails to uncover the richness and diversity of a variety of texts across cultures.

6

The Multiple Media of Texts: How Onscreen and Paper Texts Incorporate Words, Images, and Other Media

Anne Frances Wysocki

Michigan Technological University

PREVIEW

Every day we encounter texts that hold together words, drawings, colors, charts, photographs, animations, sound, video, and so on; sometimes these texts are a single page or screen, and sometimes we have to navigate through many pages or screens to gain sense of what the texts' creators hope to achieve. This chapter offers a rhetorical approach (using both textual and contextual analysis, as Jack Selzer describes in his chapter on rhetorical analysis) for analyzing texts made up of multiple media, tied primarily to the visual presentations of pages and screens. The chapter raises questions about relations among the visual/material presentations of our texts and particular values of our time and place, such as efficiency, clarity, consumption, and standardization—and the "seriousness" of words and the non-seriousness of images—as a way of contextualizing the analysis and composing of texts that use different visual strategies.

BASIC CONCEPTS

Assumptions Underlying the Arguments of This Chapter

The visual presentation of a page or screen gives you an immediate sense of its genre.

When you see 8½″ by 11″ white pages with double-spaced type, you probably see the pages, without having to think about it, as a "school paper" or "unpublished manuscript"; printed academic books are usually printed on smaller sized sheets, and with lines of type that are closer than double-spaced. When you see a large page with brightly-colored drawings, you probably think "children's book." Think of how—without having to study it—you know whether a webpage has been designed to sell you something or present you with news.

When you first look at a page or screen, you initially understand its functions and purposes because it follows the visual conventions of a genre.

All page- and screen-based texts are (therefore) visual and their visual elements and arrangements can be analyzed.

Some texts, such as academic texts, try to 'hide' their visuality in order to meet a reader's expectations: A reader of these pages is not supposed to be aware of the layout of a page or the typefaces used. Think about how strange an academic page would look were its lines of type not straight, were it to contain many colors and typefaces, or were it not to have page-numbering. Precisely because you come to an academic page bringing expectations about how that page should look means that the page has had to be visually designed to fit your expectations. This doesn't necessarily mean that the design has been much attended by the designer: When you write a paper for a class, for example, you probably do not consider the size of paper you will use or how to indent your paragraphs; instead, you use whatever paper is in the printer and you follow the page-layout conventions for margins and headers and paragraph indentation and page-numbering you were taught in high-school English or a first-year writing class or handbook.

Meanwhile, we expect other texts—comic books, children's books, web pages—to highlight or even celebrate their visuality, using multiple typefaces and many colors and different kinds of images and visual arrangements.

That we associate particular visual arrangements with different genres of writing means that the visual arrangements do some of the work of the genre. This means, then, that the visual arrangements can be analyzed in terms of the genre work they do. We can ask, then (for example), why the visual presentation of an academic or literary page is generally supposed to efface itself or how it is that we have come to expect 'professional looking' webpages not to look like plain white double-spaced paper pages.

The visual elements and arrangements of a text perform persuasive work.

Someone designing a logo for a company considers very carefully how the color and shape and images in the logo will persuade those who see the logo to think of the company. A designer hopes, for example, that using a mountain in a logo for an insurance company will suggest that the company is solid and reliable but also big and likely to be around for a long time.

A writer constructing a logical argument on paper might break her text into four sections that have numbered headers. The visual presentation of the headers signal to a reader that these sections contain the four most important points of the argument; on the page, they construct the logical arrangement of the argument for the reader.

Attitudes toward the visual aspects of texts change over time.

Think of illuminated manuscript pages of the Middle Ages, where one person would spend months hand-lettering the pages and another person would spend months painting elaborate illustrations in the margins and illuminating the letters that began each chapter. The amount of time spent on these pages was a result of the technologies of the time as well as a result of societal structures in which only the very rich could pay for the lengthy time of hand production—but the amount of time spent on these pages was also a result of the educated believing that the visual presentations of pages were to make for a reading process where readers moved slowly through pages, contemplating the words and paintings and using the visual presentation of the pages as an aid to memory.

In our century, reading is different. We often place value on the quick and efficient transmission of information. In many of our texts—textbooks as well as fix-it manuals—we expect layouts that help us get to what we need with no distraction or slowing down.

But reading in our time is changing. Computer-based technologies of communication have been designed so as to make possible new texts—such as webpages, email, interactive multimedia, MOOs and MUDs[1]—which are being shaped by computer scientists, hackers, students, and interface designers as well as by those in book publishing and academia. Desktop publishing allows writers more visual control over their own texts than the structures of book publishing have. These various technologies offer perspectives for considering and changing the approaches we have inherited to composing and interpreting pages: What kinds of new arguments are possible (for example) if writers of academic pages take more responsibility in choosing the visual presentations of their arguments? What sorts of relationships can writers establish with readers through different visual presentations? Is it appropriate to speak of 'writers' and 'readers' when writers are doing more visual layout and readers are interpreting texts that require other kinds of actions than decoding letter- and word-shapes?

---

[1]MOOs and MUDs are interactive, text-based applications in which users 'talk' with each other online, over networks, as they move onscreen within and between common rooms and spaces that have been designed to encourage interaction. MOOs have been widely used in writing (and other) classrooms; to learn more, see Haynes and Holmevik (1998).

The visual aspects of text are (therefore) to be understood not simply in terms of physiology but also in terms of social context.

The size of our hands certainly has something to do with the size of our books, for example, and our eyes' abilities to distinguish fine detail certainly have something to do with the appearance of type on a page. But reasons for the size of our books and the typefaces we use, as with other visual aspects of our texts, are also tied to other, social, practices.

When books were rested on lecterns so that someone could read aloud while others worked (which was the practice in the scriptoria of medieval monasteries), the books tended to be larger and considerably heavier than the ones we carry now.

Typefaces have also varied widely over time. At the beginning of the Renaissance, for example, most books in Europe were lettered in what we now call **blackletter** typefaces, which were relatively new; self-consciously, the Italian Humanists wanted their books to look classical rather than modern, and so they studied Imperial Roman inscriptions and designed typefaces emulating the shapes of those inscriptions. It took several centuries for these Roman typefaces (the predecessors to Times New Roman or other typefaces with "Roman" in their names) to catch on across Europe, but printers—and scholarly readers—used these new typefaces to signal their attachments to the classical: These typefaces were originally designed to call attention to themselves on a page. Now, however, designers use these typefaces precisely because they no longer stand out; through practice and use these faces have become familiar and "invisible." **If the Humanists had not desired to re-create what had disappeared from European pages, our pages now might be printed in type like this—and you would** (probably) **have no trouble reading it.**

In doing analysis of the visual aspects of pages and screens, then, we need to keep in mind the social circumstances in which a text is composed and into which its author or authors hope it will fit and do its work.

Composing a visual text (thus) involves choosing strategies for shaping what is on a page or screen to direct a reader/viewer/browser's attentions, within the context of other texts.

Someone composing a text that has visual materiality has to pick and choose among available strategies to build a text that attracts a desired audience, is understandable to that audience, and moves it toward the ends desired by the composer. What (for example) should a reader notice first on a page, and what second? What mood should the text create?

Categories and Terminology to Use in Analysis

Here is one possible way to categorize what we see when we look at a text:

- The page or screen itself.
- What is on a page or screen.
- What helps readers make connections among the parts of a multi-paged or multi-screened text.
- What "contains" the page/screen.

Three of these categories are explicated shortly in the Approach section. The second category—What Is on a Page or Screen—requires terminology with which you might not be familiar, so it is unpacked here.

What is on a page or screen: TYPE

When a letter or word or sentence or paragraph is placed on a page or screen, it is given visual materiality and hence must be given a particular *lettershape, style, size*, and *overall shape*.

Lettershapes: Typefaces. Letters have shape because of their typefaces. Because typefaces are a major visual strategy for a text's composers to signal the genre into which the text is to fit, and because the choice of different typefaces can signal argumentative moves in a text, it is worth giving typefaces—their categories and histories—some attention.

One possible first step in categorizing a typeface is to ask whether it is most often used in short, quickly read phrases—such as in headers or in advertising catchlines—or in longer blocks or paragraphs for more engaged reading. In the practices we have inherited, designers use the first category when they want a typeface to call attention to itself on the page; designers use the second category when the typeface is supposed to attract no attention to itself. The first category is often named **DECORATIVE** (although such typefaces function in ways other than decorative); the second, **FOR EXTENDED READING**. Here is a further breakdown of the two categories (and notice that some typefaces could be placed in more than one category):

Decorative Typefaces

Script typefaces
These look as though they were drawn by hand with (a more or less controlled) pen. Examples: *Avalon*, **Caflisch**, *Cézanne*, **Erik**, *Ex Ponto*, *Monoline Script*, *Nuptial*, *Soda Script*

Novelty faces
Examples: ALMONTE SNOW, DIABLOS DISTRIBUTIONS, ⊙⊙⊙⊙⊙⊙⊙⊙, KARLOFF

Blackletter or gothic

Examples: Notre Dame, Formal Text hand

Grunge or Postmodern

Examples: Acidic, Contrivance, Crud, DYSpLaSLa, fragile, Not Caslon

Typefaces attached to a particular arts movement or person

Examples: Alphonse Mucha, ART AND CRAFTS, Isadora

Other decorative faces

Examples: Baby Jeepers, BERMUDA SQUIGGLE, BUDMO JIGGLER, Comic Sans, Journal

Typefaces for Extended Reading

Roman typefaces

As described earlier, these faces have their origins in the desire of the Renaissance Humanists to give their writing classical weight. These typefaces are to look as though drawn with quill and ink, and have lines—called *serifs*—at the end of the main strokes (see Fig. 6.1); serifs are supposed to look like the finishing touches a stone carver would give to a letter to clean up its edges. Examples: Garamond, **Minion**, Baskerville, Times New Roman

Modern typefaces

These are typefaces that were modern when they were first designed, in the 18th century. Type designers wanted new typefaces to reflect the rationality of the Enlightenment, and new printing technologies allowed them to design faces using very thin strokes. Examples: Bodoni, **Ellington, Fenice**

Slab serif or Egyptian typefaces

When Napoleon set out to conquer Egypt as the 18th century turned into the 19th, he sent artists and historians as well as the army; although the army ended up surrendering to Britain, the artists and historians brought samples of Egyptian art to France, starting a craze for all things Egyptian, in-

serifs   FIG. 6.1.

cluding typefaces that looked Egyptian. In the typefaces that have grown out of the original designs, there are no curving transitions into the serifs. Unlike the two previous categories of serifed faces, slab serif faces generally have strokes that are all the same weight. Examples: Caecilia, Courier

Sans serif typefaces

Type designers, in tune to the industrialization of Europe and the United States in the latter half of the 19th and into the early 20th century, wanted typefaces that functioned rationally, like machines. They streamlined the typefaces with which they had grown up, removing everything they saw as extraneous, such as serifs. ("Sans" is French for "without.") Examples: Avant Garde, **Futura**, Helvetica

NOTE how most academic and literary texts use only one or two typefaces throughout, although there are writers experimenting with the argumentative possibilities of mixing multiple typefaces, as one of the examples for analysis shows.

NOTE also that, although I have divided all typefaces into two large categories based on function, these categories grow out of social use and practice. As practices change, these typefaces can take on different functions and new typefaces appear.

Styles of Type. The typefaces I have categorized "for reading" can have different styles attached to them. Designers use these styles for different purposes: When applied to only a few words or lines, they call visual and hence conceptual attention to words or phrases; they can mark text that is supposed to represent spoken words.

This **Garamond** typeface, for example, has regular, *italic*, **semibold**, *semibold italic*, **bold**, and ***bold italic*** styles. When working with texts that are to have a harmonious appearance, designers often choose a typeface family with multiple styles, such as the Garamond, because the letter-shapes of the different styles derive from each other, giving the styles a unified—and hence harmonious—appearance.

The Size of Type.

What do you think when you see type this size?

The different genres of pages we see have different sizes—and mixes of sizes—associated with them. This page is (mostly) set in a size you expect to see in an academic text. Children's books often have very large faces, which are then scaled down somewhat for young adult books, which are then scaled down again for adult texts. How do you think these size conventions developed?

NOTE how most academic or literary texts, on paper or screen, use the same size of type throughout, although—as with mixing typefaces on a page—some writers are experimenting with the argumentative possibilities of widely varying sizes, on paper and on the web.

The Overall Shape of Type. The shape of type on a page—or screen—can suggest many things to us; compare, for example, the pages shown in Figure 6.2.

Do these layouts suggest different kinds of texts? How difficult do you judge the texts to be, based on the overall shape of the type? (The first and third pages have what is called "left alignment"; the middle page has "fully justified alignment.")

Early Greek and Roman papyruses do not have lower- and uppercase letters, and most often do not have spaces between words or contain the blocks of type we now call "paragraphs"; these features of type on pages (and now on screens) came to be over many centuries, often accidentally. (The indented paragraph, for example, may have come to be when, in the early days of the printing press, printers would leave a space at the beginning of text blocks for painters to add the large capital letters we associate with early texts; in the rush to get books to market, printers often never got books to the painters, and soon readers came to expect the open—indented—space at the beginning of each block of text.)

Because we have come to associate different kinds of texts—and different kinds of appropriateness—with different shapes of type on a page (and hence on a screen), page composers can arrange the shape of text to achieve different ends.

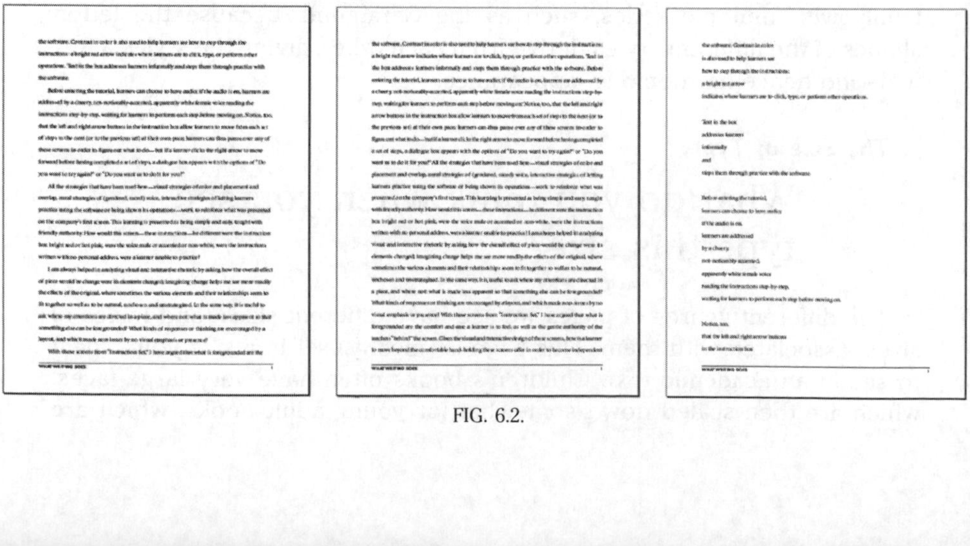

FIG. 6.2.

What Is on a Page or Screen: Other Visual Elements

In addition to type, page and screen composers can make their arguments with *shapes, color, photographs, drawings and paintings, charts and graphs, animations, visual transitions, video*, and *sound*.

Shapes. Look how the authors of the web page shown in Figure 6.3 have used solid-colored shapes not only to differentiate what is clickable or background information from what is 'content,' but also how the shapes—rectangles with curved edges, like a 1950s car fin—signal that this site is supposed to appeal to those who think such techno-nostalgia is hip.

Think also of what the shape of a bullet in text can signal:

- It can be as visually unobtrusive as possible but still perform its function of indicating a point.
- It can echo the overall shape of text on a page or screen, emphasizing the geometric organization and order of a text.
- It can suggest another time period or the physical presence of an author.

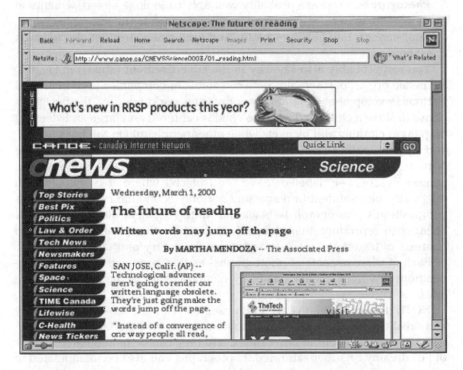

FIG. 6.3.

Color. You've grown up with and into uses of color, and can probably easily describe the colors that would most likely be used in children's books or a website promoting health through relaxation—as long as the book or website was designed and intended to be read in your country.

NOTE, however, that color uses you take for granted do not carry across cultural lines: In China, for example, the traditional color of a bride's clothing was scarlet and the color of mourning was white.

NOTE also that, when you are analyzing a text, the amount of color is something to note alongside what colors are used. You do not generally expect to see anything but black and white in academic or literary paper-based texts, except on the covers of books. Websites that want to give the appearance of being serious tend to use muted colors and a limited number.

In addition, consider the range of black through grey to white as a range of colors. Some typefaces form blocks that are very dark, and some light, in overall tone. Some pages or screens are designed to present a very evenly toned surface (like the pages in this book, for the most part) while others use different typefaces and other graphic elements to create a variable surface that can look playful or create a sense of geometric order.

Photographs. You are probably well able to look at advertisements in magazines to analyze why a model in a photograph is (for example) White, female, slender, tall, healthy-looking, and gazing at a product she holds at chest-level.

You can probably also say why in the advertisement (shown in Fig. 6.4) for netaid.org, a "partnership" between software companies and the United Nations Development Program for addressing world poverty, the designers chose to show a child, and why the child is centered and large and sleeping on piles of clothing and blankets while other people mill in the background, and why the child's arm reaches out as it does, down toward and off the bottom of the page. You can probably also say why the button—as on a computer screen—is labeled "Save" and placed where it is. Finally, you might also be confident in discussing not only economic reasons why this composition's photograph is black-and-white (because black-and-white is cheaper to reproduce than color), but also how this photograph calls to contexts of traditional black-and-white documentary photography.

Each of these aspects of photographs—as they are used in various compositions—involves choices made by composers for achieving persuasive ends.

NOTE that photographs are often used to bring an sense of immediacy and "reality" to a layout—but photographs can also be fading black-and-white presentations from other times, and they can be manipulated to look old or dreamy or super-saturated. Photographs can also be manipulated in other ways: Pyramids can be moved to emphasize what an author/designer

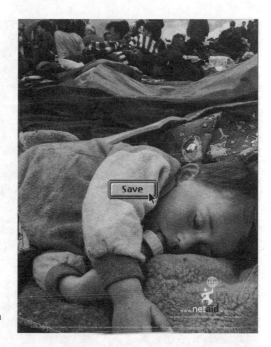

FIG. 6.4. Reproduced with permission of the NetAid Foundation.

wants (as happened recently with a *National Geographic* cover), a model's face can be made completely and unhumanly blemish free, or people who would or could never be in the same room can be seamlessly aligned. Photographs have never been 'caught moments of reality' (they have always been the result of a photographer's attentions, choice of framing, and technological knowledge), but because of changes in technology photographers now have many more choices available to them for constructing their work.

NOTE how easy it is to focus almost exclusively on the photograph(s) when you analyze a text composed mostly of photograph and type. Be sure to attend to how the photograph(s) and the type have been designed to interact, and how the typeface, its size, and alignment also work in the whole layout.

Drawings and Paintings. A drawing or painting—an illustration that is not supposed to look as though it were made with a camera—can look quickly sketched or minutely observed; it can be a technical illustration that seems never to have been touched by a hand; it can be the central focus of a page or a background pattern.

The appearance of an illustration is a composer's choice—as is whether to use an illustration or a textual description in a text.

In the screen shown in Figure 6.5, from a multimedia CD-ROM about the Beat Generation, the central illustration—the parts of which can be clicked

FIG. 6.5.

to learn about movies or music or writing of the time—suggests what a living space from that time could have looked like, but it is also a hard-edged
though loose sketch in a limited range of dark colors. The illustration provides a darkly playful frame for looking at the work of the Beats. Imagine,
also, how different your experience of this piece would be if this screen
were simply a list of words to click—Movies, Texts, Recordings, Art, Pornog-
raphy—rather than an illustration where to see excerpts from films made by
the Beats you click the Super-8 projector in the illustration.

In Figure 6.6, notice how the composers use technical illustrations rather
than words or photographs to demonstrate a process. Such illustrations allow a page's composer to present objects more abstractly than in photographs, and so to present only what in an object is relevant to the purposes
of the page. Notice here, though, how hands are part of the drawing, to
lessen any potential coldness that can accompany technical illustrations;
the illustrations are also softened—and hence the instructions made more
inviting—by the use of gray shading.

Charts and Graphs. Charts and graphs are sometimes referred to as
"data visualizations," which indicates how—when they are used on a page
or screen—they are intended to bring a scientific or technical tone to a text.

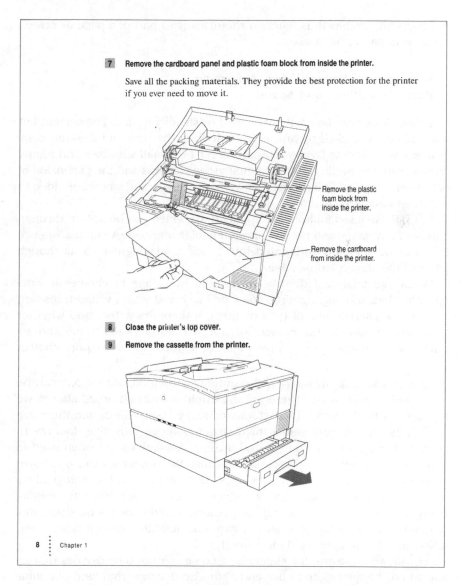

7 Remove the cardboard panel and plastic foam block from inside the printer.

Save all the packing materials. They provide the best protection for the printer if you ever need to move it.

Remove the plastic foam block from inside the printer.

Remove the cardboard from inside the printer.

8 Close the printer's top cover.

9 Remove the cassette from the printer.

8 Chapter 1

FIG. 6.6.

There is no one chart or graph that perfectly represents or encapsulates a dataset: Any chart or graph is the result of its maker's decisions about what data to foreground and what not. Someone designing a chart or graph also has to decide what kind of chart or graph (scatterplot vs. pie chart, for example), what typefaces and colors to use, the weights of lines, and whether to include illustrations (as in the charts and graphs of *USA Today*).

Charts and graphs thus function rhetorically as part of a page or screen but also in and of themselves.

What Is on a Screen: Video, Animation, Visual Transitions, and Sound

Video. Video can be edgily hand-held or steadily formal. The current but always-being-stretched technical limitations of the web and desktop computers have restricted video on our screens to small windows and jumpy frames; with the proliferation of digital video cameras and the expansion of computer power we will probably have more, larger, and smoother video to watch and analyze on screen.

In CD-ROM-based multimedia applications, video can be shown through masks of any shape and not just in rectangular windows. A video sequence can thus be smoothly integrated into a scene, making it look as though parts of the screen "come alive."

When you analyze video, keep in mind the range of choices a videographer has: framing, lighting, color or black and white, visual transition between sequences, use of type or titles, if there are actors and whether those actors address the camera or not, and so on. Each frame and sequence contributes to the overall effect of a video, and so require choice.

Animation. Like drawings and paintings and video, animations can be presented in many ways: There are the bright colors and broad shapes we associate with children's TV cartoons or many Disney films, and there are finely rendered 3D animations of dinosaurs woven into 'live' footage to seem as though we are transported in time. Animations are often used in explanations of technical processes because the processes can be shown abstractly, with direct focus on the important details. The technological capabilities of the web and various software packages are also encouraging many people to experiment with animations inspired by poetic structures (and sometimes by the practices of experimental film), mixing type, color, drawings, photographs, and movement.

As with all these graphic elements, a composer not only decides that an animation is appropriate to her ends but also decides what kind of animation, its colors, and so on.

Visual Transition. At present, when you click a regular link on most web pages, the current page disappears from screen to be replaced, bit-by-bit, by a new page; this is close to a jump cut in video or film. Certain software allows developers to incorporate visual transitions in onscreen files; most software for developing CD-ROM-based multimedia applications gives developers choices for how one screen will change into the next.

A dissolve between two screens, for example, can make it look as though what is on one screen morphs slowly into what is on the other, implying a relation of similarity between the screens. A push transition can make it look as though you are seeing one long page moving behind the onscreen window, as though what is on the two pages is in one, united, place.

Because transitions establish visual relationships between different screens, they are important choices for composers—and analyzers—to consider in arguments.

Sound. There is no small speaker embedded in this page to suggest how hip-hop or Bach playing while you read affects your sense of my arguments—but you ought to be able to imagine the differences.

Sound on screen can be a voiceover, repeating or expanding upon what is onscreen. Designers choose this strategy sometimes for educational reasons—helping children with difficult words or supplying additional modes of presentation for those who learn in different ways—and sometimes for commercial ends, enthusiastically pitching a product.

Sound can also be ambient, suggesting a mood or place. This strategy can make a text seem more present and real because it encourages us to experience the text similarly to how we experience our day-to-day actions in spaces where sound and movement (and smell) are mixed.

Try watching MTV without the music to hone your sense of what sound and visual strategies bring to texts together and separately.

AN APPROACH FOR ANALYZING THE VISUAL ASPECTS OF TEXTS

In this section I list and discuss questions for considering how the visual elements and contexts of a text contribute to our overall experience of the text. The questions are not exhaustive of what we can ask of the visual elements of a text, certainly, but they provide an initial framework that can be modified and expanded; these questions ask us to:

1. Name the visual elements in a text.
2. Name the designed relationships among those elements.
3. Consider how the elements and relations connect with different audiences, contexts, and arguments.

The questions thus help us define the objects of analysis and they encourage preliminary interpretations of what we see.

Below are the questions, tied to the categories I named before; the Analysis section that follows shows how the kinds of observations generated by these questions can be connected and composed into interpretation.

Questions for Looking at a Screen or Page Itself

- *Naming the elements:* What is the size of this page/screen? What is its shape? Its texture? How is it colored?

- *Naming relationships among elements:* Do the visual elements on the page look small and centered and swallowed up by the page, or do they take over the whole page? Does the shape of words on the page fit and echo the shape of the page, or suggest geometric order, or is there incongruence? Is the page/screen designed so that you are not supposed to notice it but only the elements on it?

- *Contextualizing the elements:* How would your experience of this page/screen be different if it were a different size or shape or color or texture? What does this tell you about the expectations about the visual you bring to this text, expectations of which the author/designer is taking advantage?

Questions for Looking at What Is on a Single Page/Screen

- *Naming the elements:* What are the visual elements of this page/screen? What kinds of typefaces have been used—or are there any visual words at all? Are there photographs, illustrations, charts or graphs? What are the sizes of the different elements? Is there color? What colors, and how much?

- *Naming relationships among elements:* How does your attention move over this page/screen, that is, what catches your eye first, what second, what third—and why? (The size and color of something, and its placement at top or left or bottom or right, or what it presents (photographs, drawings) help answer this question—although it is also important to notice when your attention is directed evenly across and down a page). This tells you the order the author/designer wants you to see and hence think about what is on the page/screen, the hierarchical relation between elements. (For example, a block of text that has been made the exact same size and shape as a photograph perhaps tells you that the photograph is just as important in this text as the block of text.)

- *Contextualizing the elements:* With what sorts of audiences do you associate the elements—and the relationships between them—you have named? How would this page/screen be different if one of its elements were different, or if elements were added/removed? (How would this page be different if the type were purple or larger or the page were twice as tall? How would this screen be different if the photograph of Barbie were replaced by GI Joe or Toni Morrison or Rosie O'Donnell? How would this screen be different if its video clip were replaced by a drawing?) Sometimes imagining a page with a replacement or change helps us see much more clearly what the page is intended to achieve, because it helps us denaturalize the page and see its elements as choices that could have been otherwise. What do the author/designer's choices of visual strategies tell you about her/his conception of the audience for this page/screen?

Questions for Looking at What Helps Readers Make Connections Among the Parts of a Multi-Paged or Multi-Screened Text

- *Naming the elements:* What visual strategies did the designer use to tell you that these various pages or screen are to be understood as one text? (Are the pages bound together? Do the different screens/pages use similar colors or typefaces or graphical elements? Did the writer-designer compose this to look like one text?)

- *Naming relationships among elements:* How are you introduced to this text? What does the opening page or screen lead you to expect about the rest of the text?

- *Naming relationships among elements:* What tells you that this text continues on other pages or screens? How have you come to recognize this visual strategy? (That is, you have been explicitly taught that the lines of text on a book page continue on the next page or have some explanation of how they continue on a later page—but how have you learned about the workings of links on web pages? How have you learned to recognize what is clickable in texts like video games or exploratory multimedia like *Myst?*) How do the contexts of your learning affect your attitude toward these texts and their pages/screens?

- *Naming relationships among elements:* How do the acts you must take to move through this text affect your sense of the relationships among the different parts of the text? How do the visual relationships between the different pages/screens of this text contribute to your sense of the text? (When you go to the next screen of a web page by clicking a text link, what sort of relationship do you think exists between the two pages? How is this different from the relationship you imagine between successive pages of a book? How is a graphic link different from a text link? How is a vertical 'listing' of onscreen buttons/icons different from listing of words that are clickable? How is a web page that ends with multiple links different from a web or book page that offers no such set of choices?)

(How would a set of screens be different if instead of being linked by a dissolve they were linked by a wipe or scroll? What if a set of pages were stapled rather than bound, or were in a box rather than a cloth wrapping? What if a magazine article about the literacy practices of rural third-graders were opposite an ad for weight-reduction pills rather than an article about computer use in elementary schools?)

- *Contextualizing the elements:* What do your observations tell you about how the designer hoped the audience would approach and move through this text? Does the way this text has been composed for you to move through it suggest other kinds of practices? (For example, do you move through this website as though through a deck of cards, or are you supposed to feel as though you are having a conversation with someone? Do these paper pages look mass-produced or have they been designed to make you think of handwork?) What sort of relationship with the text does the structure of this text ask its audience to have? What sort of relationship with other people?

Questions for Looking at What "Contains" the Page/Screen

- *Naming the elements:* If you close your eyes and 'picture' this text as a whole, what do you see? Is it a rectangular shape with cloth covers, or . . . ? Is it a round shiny plastic thing in a clear plastic box with a paper wrapper? How is the cover/wrapper labeled?
- *Naming relationships among elements:* What expectations do you develop in response to the specific visual presentation of this text as a whole object? (With what is shown on its cover, or its size? With the packaging of the CD on which this piece of interactive multimedia arrived? With the window through which I am viewing this web page? With this computer?)
- *Contextualizing the elements:* With what sort of context do you associate this object and its visual appearance? What kind of people do you think will carry and use this object?

Finally . . .

- The preceding questions ask you to approach a text as a discrete object with distinct visual organization (what is on a page/screen, the page/ screen itself, relations between the pages/screens, the "container" for the pages/screens). Does this organization work for the text you are analyzing? What is left out of this organization, or excluded?

APPLIED ANALYSES

For the sake of space, I do not apply all the questions from the Approach section to each text I analyze below (nor do I apply them always in order), but the following analyses should give you ideas about how the questions can help you identify and relate the elements of a text so as to construct understandings of why texts have been given their particular visual arrangements.

Analysis of a Page From a Magazine

The page I analyze (shown in Fig. 6.7) comes from the March 2000 issue of *WIRED* magazine. An issue from a previous year carried the subtitle "The Business of Change" on the its cover, and the magazine's articles cover technological developments—primarily dealing with computers and all things digital—and their economic and social connections. Because this is a magazine devoted to high tech and money, areas where being up-to-date and attentive to future possibilities are important, the pages of this magazine—advertisements and articles—are designed to persuade readers that any information they take from these pages is as close to the moment (or the coming moments) as possible. Given, however, that the business of technology is so much caught up with technological objects like computers and music appliances, the border between knowledge about technological objects and wanting those objects can be thin; the "business of change" can only continue if business—which means consumption—holds a steady course.

This analysis examines one page that I think works to create such a steady course by not only informing readers about new technologies but also by shaping desire for those technologies.

The "Fetish" page (shown in Fig. 6.7) is a regular feature in recent years of *WIRED*. It shows new technological tools (and toys) that might interest the magazine's readers. While the word-title "FETISH" is certainly an indication of the relationship the authors/designers hope readers will establish with what is on this page, the word is not the only strategy employed to encourage that relationship: The layout of the page is also very much strategized.

■

The "Fetish" page is on the right side of a two-page spread, and—like all pages in the magazine—is made of a thick, white, semigloss, smooth paper; the paper feels slick to my touch but substantial. The page is in a usual size for magazines. There are no consistent margins anywhere on the page, and the objects shown on the page fill the page and even overflow its edges.

At the top of the page is the word "FETISH," in a blue and light green sans serif typeface; the individual letters look three-dimensional, as though

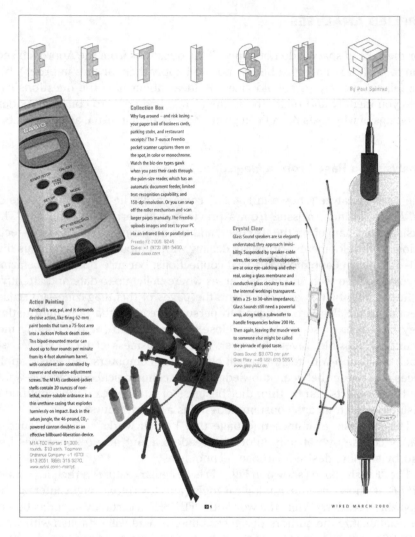

FIG. 6.7. Wired/Condé Nast Publications, Inc. Photos by William Faulkner. Reprinted with permission.

constructed out of sheets of aluminum. There are photographs of three objects on the page: a pocket-size scanner (for scanning business cards or receipts), a mortar (for playing paintball), and see-through loudspeakers; the objects range in price (I learn if I read about them) from $250 to $3,100. The three objects are shown in muted colors against the white of the page; they have been cut out from any thing that was around them so that there is nothing to distract my eyes from them. There are also three small columns of text: These columns describe the objects, give pricing and contact information, and are in a sans serif typeface—like "FETISH"—and in a uniform small size in light blue and black ink; they do not overlap or in anyway visually interfere with my view of the objects. At the bottom of the page is the name of the magazine, the issue information, and a page number—as on most other pages of the magazine.

There is an overall balance and harmony to this page: All the elements are muted in color, and the text blocks are close in size to the photographs; there is only one kind of typeface used on this page, and most of the type is in the same size; there is a lot of white space left around all the elements, giving the page an open feeling. The photographs and columns of descriptive text are given an informal but nonetheless careful arrangement: On the left of the page are two objects, each with a column of text aligned evenly to it, creating a solid and balanced shape; to the right, centered to the left side of the page, is the third object, with its corresponding text (in turn) centrally aligned to it. The photograph of the third object, the speakers, is also sized to extend exactly to the top of the scanner and to the bottom of the mortar, so that the objects have an orderly and aligned visual relationship to each other.

Because there is a harmonious arrangement to the page's elements, however, does not mean that some elements aren't emphasized. Although the columns of text and the objects are roughly the same size, the text has been shaped into columns that make even, uneventful patterns, with no particular visual emphasis of style or size given them. It is the objects that have been given emphasis: They are differently shaped than the repeated even columns of type, they have been cut off from whatever 'reality' surrounded them in their original photographs, and they have been made to extend off the page, so that we have to use our imaginations—bring them into our heads—to complete them. They are not shown in use, but rather stilled, objects to observe and consider—and desire.

And because there are only the objects and a few pieces of unemphasized text on this page, arranged as they are, my eyes move around the objects circularly. I see first what is at the top of the page (I have, after all, been taught to read starting at the top), and then move down the left column of objects, up and over to the right object, back to the top, and around again; notice how the objects have been arranged so that their edges and legs point into each other, keeping my eyes moving over them.

I think, then, that the visual strategies used to arrange this page are aimed at catching me up in a circle of desire: I may not have known these objects existed before I came to this page, but now I am presented with them arranged to keep my eyes on them, moving over them, seeing little else but them. The harmonious overall arrangement of the page keeps the desire from seeming irrational or out of control; instead, in the world of this magazine, to desire these objects is in order.

Analysis of an Interactive Multimedia Piece on CD-ROM

To many, "computer game" equates with *Super Mario Brothers* or *Diablo II*, which are usually wordless but not soundless and which require players to figure out increasingly complex problems in order to advance to new and more difficult levels of play; the challenge is to keep advancing so as to end with more points than anyone else, to have found all that was hidden, or to be the last one standing.

The multimedia piece I analyze, *Eve*—by Peter Gabriel and his Real World Multimedia studios along with Starwave Corporation—has those baseline features: There is almost no text (although there is plenty of sound and some speaking), there are four levels of play reached by figuring out puzzles, and the challenge is to work your way to the end. But you don't 'win' at *Eve*: You don't accumulate points or annihilate enemies. Instead, solving the puzzles returns you to an onscreen garden (see Fig. 6.8) that you lost at the beginning; at the end, the garden is richer, fuller, and more mature than it was. You also achieve overlapping worlds of music and art for exploration, play, and creation.

The name of the piece—*Eve*—suggests the initial, Biblical, garden state and its loss. The name is also apiece, however, with aspects of *Eve* that are unlike other computer games: As you move through *Eve*, untangling its challenges, you encounter screens where you can watch visual artists at work; you can hear various speakers—people off the street as well as geneticists, priests, social anthropologists, music therapists, and writers like Kathy Acker or artists like Orlan—who talk of the stages of human romance and attraction. In *Eve*, it is as though you, the player, through concentration, wits, and play, work through the piece's challenges to learn about creation, reproduction, and loss so that you can regain what has been lost. And so *Eve* aspires, I think, to give you a sort of heroic mythical experience: By "playing" *Eve*, you lose the initial garden but you also—through overcom-

FIG. 6.8.   © Real World Multimedia Ltd.

ing challenges and acquiring knowledge—rebuild the garden. In the analysis that follows I suggest how the visual presentations and interactivities of *Eve* come together to give a player such experiences.

■

Eve's screens are sized for the most commonly available computer monitors. When you open the piece, it takes over the entire screen; although some other multimedia pieces allow you to see your computer's desktop behind them, *Eve* blocks all that from sight: It is as though the piece becomes your whole world. In addition, you play *Eve* as though you were in that world. For example, the main screens of the piece—of the initial garden, of that garden built over and become a sodden grey industrial site, of twisted and flattened grey nothingness after a nuclear explosion, of the regained garden—are 360° panoramas; these give you the sense of being in the place, of being able to look around and see it all. In addition, you decide where to move on screen; you are not controlling a character or asked to choose attributes as though you have to become someone else, as in some games. You work this piece as yourself.

Eve's screens have been made to look not quite real, as though you were hovering in a place that doesn't quite exist or that exists in dreams. The various screens have been built out of photographs, but the photographs have been treated to look less glossy and less hard-edged than usual, with more saturated color than usual to suggest the not-quite-real. All the screens have been given similar presentation, so that they clearly belong together and so create a sense of a unified world. This sense of a unified world is also built by the way the various puzzle screens are visually linked: These screens, to which you come as you move in and out of the panoramas I mentioned earlier, are visually connected through a strategy like the literary figure of synecdoche (where a part of something stands in for the whole, as when "sails" means "boats"). For example, one puzzle screen (Fig. 6.9) shows a country cemetery with a steepled church in the background; on screens linked to this one, the steeple of the church appears in the background for you to click, to go to the cemetery screen, as in Figure 6.10.

It may seem, from my description, that the screens of *Eve* are cartoon-like, as though aimed at children, but this is not at all the case; instead, the screens have a high level of visual detail that encourages close observation. And observation is required: The challenges of the piece require you to figure out what you can click or otherwise control with your mouse.

As with other games, what you are required to figure out and do—how you can interact—becomes increasingly complex. When the world is just mud, you simply click and hold the mouse down to uncover (for example) fish at the bottom of puddles. As your actions bring more and more green and other life to the screen, as the world becomes more built and human-

FIG. 6.9. © Real World Multimedia Ltd.

FIG. 6.10. © Real World Multimedia Ltd.

ized, you have to drag the words of a poem into proper order or adjust a radar dish so it can track a satellite. What appears on screen, then, and your actions, give the sense of a world become more complex, a world shaped and working by human convention.

As you continue working with *Eve*, then, it is your actions that cause both the blooming of the initial garden and its eventual over-crusting with buildings. If you become caught up in the ever more complex challenges, it is your actions that lead to a grey industrial-wasteland world and eventual nuclear annihilation—but then it is also your actions, your continued puzzle-solving and interactions with art and music and listening to various thinkers, that lead to the garden being reestablished.

In the visual structures and interactions of *Eve*, then, there are arguments about the role of human action and thought in shaping the world. There is also, perhaps, a kind of learning-by-doing-and-interacting that is very different from learning by book-reading. A reader might question the profundity of the presentation and play, but might also see possibilities—in this sort of interactive visual work—for different kinds of learning and different kinds of arguments than are usually possible on a page.

Analysis of Pages From Books

The page shown in Figure 6.11 could be in almost any academic journal or book. The page uses one typeface—an oldstyle—in a single size, in even black lines that, interspersed with the spaces between the lines, build a grey rectangle on the page. All this book's pages look the same, and were you to hold this page up to a light, you would see how the text rectangle on the back aligns perfectly with the text rectangle on the side facing you. If I consider the relationship between the pages of this text, the effect is of visual sameness and evenness. Just as spelling and punctuation are consistent, so is there is no change of typeface or size or page texture to encourage my eyes to note anything particular as I move over these pages. There is nothing on these pages to encourage me to be attentive to the materiality of the pages, their context of particular time and place. Instead, what is emphasized by this visual presentation is what is not on the page but rather what is beyond the page—the thinking, the 'content.'

This sort of visual presentation creates, then, an unremarkable even pattern so that my reading attentions are on—or in?—immaterial thoughts which exist independently of any particular visualization. This presentation works so that I can ignore the materiality and temporality of a text in order that I might range freely and deeply in thought, as though thinking itself is unbound by time and place. What might then be the effect of the time we spend with books like this, the books that fill our libraries, the books whose pages all look, unremarkably, the same?

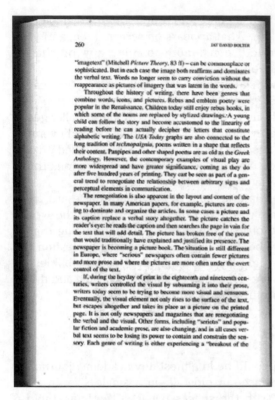

FIG. 6.11.

The visual presentation of these pages suggest that visual sameness rather than visual difference is valued. Such standardization is not limited to book pages, obviously: I think here of the aisles of evenly stacked goods in supermarkets, of cars coming off assembly lines, of the rows of desks in my elementary school classrooms. Might it be possible to argue that pages like the one I have shown here—when we connect them to the larger contexts in which we see and experience them, when we connect them to the times in which they are produced—align with industrial and educational processes that encourage standardization and evenness?

If that is possible, then if authors/designers wanted to question those other processes, and to question their connections to academic work,
would it be sensible of them
to make a composition
that followed the visual conventions of the standard academic page?

Figure 6.12 shows the final pages (before the notes) of *Hiding* by Mark C. Taylor (who teaches philosophy and religion at Williams College) in collaboration with the designers Michael Rock, Susan Sellers, and Chin-Lien Chen. These pages call attention to themselves as different from the usual aca-

To err live an
amidst irreducible
shifty enigma :
interfaces nothing
that know is
no end is to hiding.

FIG. 6.12.

demic page. There is a single sentence, in a bolded slab serif typeface much larger than what we usually find in an academic text, in a small white space—that has the rough proportions of two side-by-side 8½″ by 11″ pages—surrounded by bright red on a semigloss paper. Only the physical size of this book fits into usual academic possibilities.

The book's closing pages are not the only pages that have been designed differently from academic expectation. The book has five chapters, each of which has its own overall patterning and color scheme; one of which is printed on different paper from the rest.

The first chapter, "Skinsc(r)apes," has black and white type on red paper printed with blurry images of diseased skin, as though the bumps and blotches of the disease were on the paper itself. In the chapter, Taylor discusses Dennis Potter's *Singing Detective* television drama, which is about, sort of, a man who is in the hospital being treated for psoriatic arthritis who is also writing a detective novel—except that the man's hands are so affected by his disease that he cannot write; it is unclear then where the detective novel is taking shape. Taylor writes that

Potter's programs fold back on themselves not once but at least twice to examine questions that televisual and telephonic media raise about the relation between fact and fiction, reality and illusion, truth and appearance, history and story, and surface and depth. When read in the context of contemporary technology and media culture, The Singing Detective *becomes a story about the possibility or impos-*

sibility of detection in a world where all "reality" is rapidly becoming virtual real-ity. (pp. 24–25)

These then are also Taylor's concerns in the book, the relation (or even ex-istence) of surface and depth, the possibility of anything hiding and need-ing us to perform detective work to find and understand it.

And so the first chapter, both in its writing and in the look of its pages, makes us look at skin, at what it covers—or doesn't—and about what hap-pens when we try to peel away at skins, as with detective or psychoanalytic work: There is only more skin, more layers, more clues, "but no solutions" (p. 71).

Chapter 2, "Dermagraphics," is printed on vellum, a thin translucent pa-per that allows me to see, somewhat, what is on the pages underneath. Tay-lor and the designers with whom he worked lay out a history of tattoo and body decoration in this chapter, with—printed in green—illustrations and photographs of tattoos and piercings taking up the full left-hand page of each spread and even columns of fully justified oldstyle type (printed in black) on the right. This chapter then moves our attentions out from the skin and diseases that seem to erupt from within to the things humans have done and now do to their skins in the hopes of making meaning—but, as all the elements of this text argue, the meaning can only come from referring to other things we have made, to other signs, not to anything hiding behind or underneath a representation.

In chapter 3, "De-Signing," Taylor moves us out again, from skin to what we put over our skin (but which acts like another layer of skin): fashion. The chapter opens with a series of full-color page spreads. These full-color spreads show photographs from fashion magazines, which are overprinted with phrases like "Falling Apart at the Seems" or "Transparency." The full-color spreads are followed by pages like the one shown in Figure 6.13, where columns of black type (in a modern typeface) make a continual fully justified column at the top and bottom of the pages as various texts in a pale blue sans serif face run through the middle of the pages, sometimes in the expected vertical format and sometimes in a horizontal format. The blue texts take their titles from the phrases printed over the color photo-graphs at the chapter opening, and are made to look like fashion magazine layouts. In these blue texts Taylor spreads out his considerations of fash-ion, using excerpts from fashion magazines that speak about specific fash-ion trends to show how those trends echo and repeat ideas in other areas—philosophy, literature, architecture; for example, Taylor connects fashion that reveals the seams and linings of clothing to the intellectual habits of deconstruction. In the black text, Taylor links fashion to the overall prac-tices of modernism, the desire to be up to date and current, as well as to in-tellectual habits of dichotomizing, as with the concepts of *being/becoming,*

FIG. 6.13.

masculine/feminine, profound/superficial, and so on. As in the preceding chapters, he questions those divisions through all the strategies available to him on pages, arguing that

> *Through its wily de-signs, fashion conspires to extend life by perpetually engendering desire. To embrace fashion is to affirm life—"not the life that shrinks from death and keeps itself untouched by devastation, but rather the life that endures it and maintains itself in it."* (p. 214; quoted words are from Nietzsche)

Chapter 4, "Ground Zero," then takes on what might seem to be the next layer we build around ourselves, architecture. As in chapter 3, the pages in chapter 4 have two texts on them, but these two texts both continue throughout all the pages, one at the top in an oldstyle typeface printed on light green, the other at the bottom of the page, printed in a sans serif face. In both texts Taylor considers what we might consider to be the central problem for architecture, that of space; the top text considers space as something with (economic) value; the bottom text considers space in its relations to time. Occasional sentences in either text are outlined and printed in green and then linked to the other text by a line. On the penultimate page of the chapter, the two texts break in mid-sentence, and—when a reader turns the page—there is present only one text, which can be read as the ending to either of the two preceding texts, where "proliferating signs immerse us in a superficial flux that never ends ... the substance of our dreams is stripped away to expose the inescapability of time and the unavoidability of death" (pp. 266–267).

In the last pages of chapter 4, chapter 5—"Interfacing"—has been erupting from the middle of the page, which Figure 6.14 shows: The new chapter starts on a small white page-shape in the middle of the pages of chapter 4, and grows progressively larger as the book proceeds, until chapter 5 finally fills the whole page of the book and takes over. In this final chapter, which is printed in a black oldstyle of varying sizes with various red lines and boxes and photographs and illustrations interspersed, Taylor gives a history of the notion of virtual reality, whose origins he argues develop out of questions about society and culture that are similar to those that shaped Kant's thinking at the end of the 18th and beginning of the 19th centuries. Taylor steps us through Kant and Hegel and Nietzsche, and through the development of cinema and robotics and molecular biology and neurology to lead us back to the concerns of virtual reality and postmodernity. To the matters of surface and depth, of inner and outer and proper division and boundary, Taylor now adds questions about the divisions between human and machine, biology and machine, information and biology.

As the title of the final chapter together with all the strategies of the preceding pages suggest, Taylor has been building an argument that we need to reconceive the relationships we believe exist between terms like surface and depth or real and unreal. Rather than relations of opposition, Taylor would rather we work with the notion he develops of interfaces, where boundaries are not fences or walls or barriers but are instead chancy and

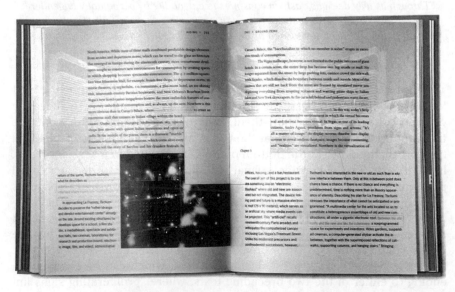

FIG. 6.14.

permeable membranes. Such a conception, he argues, not only addresses the shortcomings of much thinking of our time but also is appropriate for the situations of our time.

■

The book has thus followed only a baseline of expected visual and structural academic conventions: It is a size that fits on bookstore and office shelves, its text is primarily in fully justified columns of black oldstyle type, it contains chapters (which build out from an introductory idea), its quotations are made visually clear. But the book breaks most other academic conventions in its incorporation of multiple typefaces, chapters that do not look alike, multiple texts on a page, photographs that go underneath columns of text, different texts that end with the exact same words on a page, different kinds of paper, bright colors, and so on. In other words, the pages of this book call attention to themselves.

The pages of the book call attention to the page as a surface to be looked at and used and not as a surface that exists merely to indicate some depth of thought hidden somewhere else. The pages call attention to their construction and temporal fashionability (in their use of tattoos and virtual reality, for example). The pages call us to be attentive to surfaces and their temporality as what we have to work with, as what there is.

No matter your tendency to lean toward or away from the arguments of this book, you ought to be able to see that such arguments would be undermined had Taylor and his collaborator-designers produced a book that followed strict academic conventions. You ought to be able to see how, by breaking visual conventions, they have been able to call into question other—less visible—conventions.

Analysis of Pages From a Technical Instruction Website

People learn software differently: Some are independent and confident, wanting only to play with new stuff on screen; others want handholding and guidance, not wanting to get themselves into situations they can't get out of. If you were designing web-based software instruction for someone in the latter category, how would you proceed?

You'd want, probably, to make webpages that seemed inviting but not strident, pages that would give readers confidence in the technical knowledge of the people who made the pages and confidence that those people can help readers learn, at a reasonable pace. Look at the screen shown in Figure 6.15, the first page for the website of "Instruction Set," an "Education Solutions Provider".

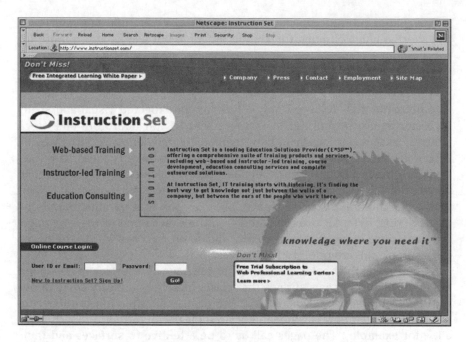

FIG. 6.15.

You cannot see color in this illustration, but the webpage is almost completely green, a toned-down green that to my eyes is a mix of what catalogue clothing companies call "sage" and the color of doctors' scrubs. This color use, then, suggests both the natural and the medicinal, and so the page's green performs several functions: The audience for these pages is made comfortable—colorfully promised that what these pages deliver will not be hard-edged, coldly, and only technical—at the same time "Instruction Set" is aligned with the gently, naturally therapeutic.

Although you cannot see the color here, you can probably tell that there is not a lot of visual contrast on the screen: The elements have been lightly toned; nothing pops out or calls strong attention to itself. The element given the most visual attention is the company name, which stands out by its placement toward the top left, its size, the size of the rounded-edge white box around it, and its darkness and boldness in comparison to the other elements on screen. The company name is presented in a no-nonsense, straightforward but rounded sans serif typeface, with the word "Instruction" made darker than "Set." The company's logo, to the left, is also simple: It is two rounded shapes placed on top of each other, implying gentle circular movement or integration, almost like two cupped hands. Notice, too, how many of the shapes on this page are rounded, so that the straight edges of crisp organization are softened but not erased.

There is not much text on this page. After I see the company name, my eyes are pulled by the line coming down out of it to the paragraphs on the right; these paragraphs, in the same blue as the company name, describe what the company does and emphasize that this company "listens." To the top right is a listing of links where it is clear I can learn more about the background of the company; to the left of the two paragraphs there is a listing of categories of educational services offered; to the bottom left I can log into online courses. With the exception of the company name, there is no piece of text on this page that does not align horizontally with another piece of text. The overall effect for me of the amount of text and the careful alignment is of careful, uncluttered order, of simplicity and a company that is to-the-point but friendly.

There is a piece of text I have not yet described, the company's trademarked phrase "knowledge where you need it." I see this phrase when my eyes follow the green line that comes out of the company name, parallels and underlines "SOLUTIONS" as it helps visually link the descriptive paragraphs and the company's services, and then runs into the head at lower right, where the phrase is placed over the forehead. The phrase creates a visual pun, implying both that the company's instructions are easily accessible and that the company can deliver instruction sets directly to your thinking facilities—and showing, I imagine the designers of this page hope, that the company has a sense of humor.

And then, finally, there is the face at lower right, peeking up playfully from behind the text. The face is a young man's, whose haircut and glasses and age place him, for us in the early 21st century, in the world of the hip techno-geek. His expression is not hard-edged or demanding; instead, he seems relaxed and amused as he looks directly at whoever is there on the other side of the screen: He has, perhaps, the expression of someone who has just opened the door for us, peeked around to see who we are, and is about to let us in. It is unclear to me whether he is a student or a teacher here: Imagine how differently this screen would be were he replaced by the stereotyped older female English teacher or older leather-elbow-patched tweed-jacketed professorial male, or by a worried- and harried-looking administrative assistant; it might be clearer then whether he was to represent someone coming to this site to learn or the person who is to teach. Instead, because (to me) his youth suggests he is a learner but his visual alliance with the techno-geek suggests he is a teacher, his presence and position give a welcoming ambiguity to the page: Perhaps I am meant to understand that there are no strict hierarchies here but that teachers and learners move comfortably together.

Every element of this page, then, works with every other to create a sense of simplicity, invitation, ease, and comfortable confidence for a potential learner—as well as a sense that there is a friendly someone there behind the screen, ready to help.

The visual, auditory, and interactive presentation of the tutorials them-selves work to create similar appeal for a learner. Figure 6.16 shows a screen from the "Introduction to Word" tutorial offered by "Instruction Set"; this screen opens in a separate window over the page where a learner has logged in to "Instruction Set" in a standard Web browser window.

This screen is necessarily more complex than the opening screen, be-cause here the company is showing, explaining, and teaching the workings of an application that has been designed to stand functionally and visually on its own. By making this tutorial appear in its own window, the designers avoid the increased visual complexity that would come if, at the top of this window, were the usual browser software's usual row of buttons; instead, this screen is presented in the plainest window possible.

In order to differentiate instructions from the software being taught, the instructions are placed in a saturated, middle-valued blue box at lower right. Because the software being taught has been designed in primarily light grey and white, the blue of the instruction box stands out by contrast, and the box looks as though it rests on top of—separate from—the software. Contrast in color is also used to help learners see how to step through the instructions: A bright red arrow indicates where learners are to click, type, or perform other operations. Text in the box addresses learners informally and steps them through practice with the software.

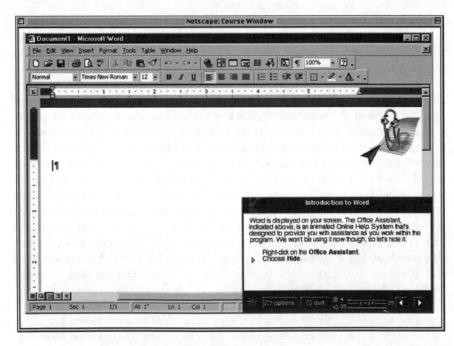

FIG. 6.16.

Before entering the tutorial, learners can choose to have audio; if the audio is on, learners are addressed by a cheery, not-noticeably-accented, apparently White female voice reading the instructions step-by-step, waiting for learners to perform each step before moving on. Notice, too, that the left and right arrow buttons in the instruction box allow learners to move from each set of steps to the next (or to the previous set) at their own pace; learners can thus pause over any of these screens in order to figure out what to do—but if a learner clicks the right arrow to move forward before having completed a set of steps, a dialogue box appears with the options of "Do you want to try again?" or "Do you want us to do it for you?"

All the strategies that have been used here—visual strategies of color and placement and overlap, aural strategies of (gendered, raced) voice, interactive strategies of letting learners practice using the software or being shown its operations—work to reinforce what was presented on the company's first screen. This learning is presented as being simple and easy, taught with friendly authority. How would this screen—these instructions— be different were the instruction box bright red or hot pink, were the voice male or accented or non-White, were the instructions written with no personal address, were a learner unable to practice?

I am always helped in analyzing visual and interactive rhetoric by asking how the overall effect of piece would be change were its elements changed; imagining change helps me see more readily the effects of the original, where sometimes the various elements and their relationships seem to fit together so well as to be natural, unchosen and unstrategized. In the same way, it is useful to ask where my attentions are directed in a piece, and where not: What is made less apparent so that something else can be foregrounded? What kinds of responses or thinking are encouraged by a layout, and which made non-issues by no visual emphasis or presence?

With these screens from "Instruction Set," I have argued that what is foregrounded are the comfort and ease a learner is to feel, as well as the gentle authority of the teachers 'behind' the screen. Given the visual and interactive design of these screens, how is a learner to move beyond the comfortable hand-holding these screens offer in order to become independent and active in using the software or in learning other software? How could this software be designed so as to encourage the learner to push against the instructions in order to see what might happen if she were to make other choices, try other options?

On the interactive learning screen, my attentions are, necessarily, directed to learning specific tasks, to the instructions but also and primarily to the white space in the middle of the screen, where I learn by typing a memo. The space where I write the memo has the most contrast in light-to-dark value: I write in black on white, while all around are shades of grey and the dark blue of the instruction box; visually, as with the instructions, my attentions are directed to the center and to the writing, and not to the edges. What then can I see if I shift my focus to the edges? What options are offered, and what not? I cannot write in anything but straight lines, although I can choose other colors for my type. I can only write on a white screen, and only as though the screen were flat, like a piece of paper; I cannot write three-dimensionally. I cannot make marginal comments. I cannot write over a line with handwritten corrections. These might seem odd observations about what is allowed here, given that the observations imply that I want to do some things almost no one does when writing. But my observations get at the shapes on the page that seem natural when we write—and there has been considerable thinking and argument in the last century about how those shapes, aligned with other cultural practices and the materiality of our communications, necessarily constrain what we can think and how we perceive and interact with others. The receding grey edges of this software show that it—like most technologies—has been designed to help me do my work easily, efficiently, and without needing to think much about the technology and its design. But what might be consequences of design that asks me to use it unquestioningly, to acquire through what I see and do the values of efficiency and transparency?

Can software—any piece of design—be shaped to question itself, to help audiences question what is hidden or backgrounded or assumed? What would screens (or pages) look like that encouraged their audiences to ponder the assumptions about work-life and worker-status that are implied (for example) in the choice of an anthropomorphized paperclip as an assistant? How could this instructional website have been designed so that its users asked why the face shown on the first screen is male rather than female, white rather than not, or so that learners asked, similarly, why it is a cheerful, unaccented (to White, middle-class people) female voice guiding them? What in this design could help learners ask about the choice to teach—as though it were the most natural use of this software—a business memo? In other words, is it possible to make designs that ask us to see and to question the cultural and economic assumptions and values guiding the designs, so that we might make designs that help us support and encourage other values if we so wanted?

Ought software—and the other screens and pages we make for each other—be designed to encourage audiences to question in these ways?

CONCLUSION: ON MOVING FROM ANALYSIS TO COMPOSITION

To anyone wanting to compose texts employing communication modes in addition to or other than the alphabetic-on-a-page, it should be comforting to notice how reified are (in general) the existing genres for alphabet-only-on-a-page texts. To anyone believing that we see each other more generously and thoughtfully when we learn to see—as much as is possible—in unreified manners, the safe repetitions of strategies within genres can be both saddening and an invitation.

Learning to compose pages or screens that fit effectively into a reader/viewer's expectations can be, then, a matter of learning to observe well. Apply the analytic questions of this chapter to a collection of generic pages (magazine pages that advertise liquor or watches, or pages from online newspapers or one discipline's academic journals), list what you see in common, and you will see how much repetition of strategy there is. You will see some differences of composition related to particular audiences, but you will also see crisply delimited similarities in choices of color, of kind of typeface, of width of margin, of use of photograph or drawing, of alignment of elements, of placement of specific elements, of expectation of how a reader/user/viewer will interact with the composition, and of strategies peculiar to each type of composition (notice the time on the watches in watch ads, for example). To build your own compositions can thus be a matter of looking hard at and analyzing the genre that is most appropriate for your ends and then copying what you observe, modifying it to fit the particular rhetorical situation. This is not as easy as it sounds, however, because the level of detail on pages and screens is fine: It is one thing to build pages or screens that roughly match what is expected, it is quite another to build a composition that can flawlessly insert itself into the ongoing conversations and expectations to which our eyes and ears have become so subtly accustomed through long and usually undiscussed exposure. With that last sentence I do not intend to dissuade you from the attempt, but rather to interest you in the fine workings of detail and in the value of showing what you make to others and learning from their responses just how practiced our eyes and ears are at knowing what fits—or not. In addition, I have listed below resources that, although they might not describe their tasks this way, can be understood as summaries of different genre conventions for paper and onscreen texts.

But what about making visual and interactive compositions that do not so readily fit audiences' expectations, compositions that ask audiences to question, first, how they came to have their expectations and, then, the limitations and constraints of those expectations? What about making compositions that ask their audiences, in other words, to see and interact differently with texts, to consider arguments outside their usual experience? How do you persuade your readers/viewers that your composition is serious, worth reading, and, in fact, can be read? Two texts I have analyzed here—*Hiding* and *Eve*—can be problematic or overlooked by their intended audiences because they do not look or act like "serious" texts, no matter their potential value: The first violates a tremendous number of the expectations most academic readers have for how academic pages should look and behave; as for the second, few academics have, undoubtedly, ever seen it because it looks like a video game—and unlike *Hiding*, *Eve* isn't found in bookstore Philosophy sections.

If it seems valuable to you to create compositions that push against and question our expectations, then you will need to augment the list of analytic questions I have included in this chapter by questioning some specific expectations we have about how texts circulate and are consumed. You will need to question not only what happens on pages and screens and how what is on pages or screens asks readers to respond, but also how audiences come to consider certain texts as worth reading, how audiences learn and use the interpretative strategies (such as reading) that make some texts seem readily accessible and others not, and how texts are published and circulate so that we know of their existence in the first place. The pleasures of visual composition and rhetoric are many, and are of particular use when they help us see and consider how we have become and continue to be who we are.

ACTIVITIES

Analysis

1. Go to the bookstore and to a section where you usually don't: Go to the comics or graphic novel or children's section, or to math or physics, or romance or cultural studies. Find a book that attracts you: What in the visual presentation attracts you, or helps you feel confident about approaching the book? How could you apply these visual strategies in your own work?

2. Watch a friend move through a piece of interactive multimedia she or he has never seen before. At each new screen, ask your friend how she or he knows what to click, and why. What assumptions about the visual elements on screen is your friend making? What do you think is the origin of those assumptions?

3. Choose 4 or 5 categories of screen- or paper-based texts (entertainment or education for small children, personal web pages, poetry, manuals for using small home appliances, regional guides, college level textbooks in economics, etc.), and then look at 8 to 10 examples from each category. What strategies of visual presentation unite the examples within each category? What do these similarities tell you about our expectations of the visual presentations of this kind of thinking or information? How are the texts visually different? How do these visual differences help the different texts appeal to different kinds of people within a larger audience?

4. Interview someone who designs texts for a living. Ask after the considerations that person has in mind as she or he lays out a particular kind of
text. Ask both about how the person thinks about the specific text as well as
about the constraints that come along with the particular kind of publishing
(i.e., what design considerations exist because of budget or deadline or com-
puter-platform).
  OR:
  Interview someone who has written a text that was then handed over to
a designer to be given its visual presentation. How did the writer respond
to the text after it had been designed? Would the writer have designed the
text differently? Why?

5. This chapter makes uneasy use of the terms *writer, reader, text, user*,
and *designer*, because sometimes these terms don't seem to catch appropriately the actions taken by or the position of those who 'consume' and those
who compose various of the texts considered in this chapter. Choose several
web pages or CD-ROM pieces on a related topic, and consider how you move
through the pieces, and how as a result you perceive the maker(s) of the
pieces. What name (reader? interactor? participant? user? or . . . ?) seems
most appropriate for the actions you take as you move through the texts?
What name best describes the actions taken by the text's maker to put these
pieces together? Why do you choose these names? Do you give yourself different names for different kinds of or differently designed texts?

Analysis Leading to Composition

1. Sketch out several versions of a website that informs about something
of interest to you. Design a version for children, for a college-level audience,
for people who are blind, for an audience that does not have native fluency
with your language. What different visual strategies do you use in the different versions? Why?

2. Look closely at a textbook or piece of educational software you hate or
that you think gets in the way of you learning what the book is supposed to
teach (grammar and thermodynamics texts are often helpful choices). Try
sketching out a redesign of the text so that the visual presentation of the text
better supports your learning. What typefaces or kinds of illustrations or size
of page or kinds of headings will make the text seem more inviting and encouraging to you? Use any visual strategies you know to redesign the text,
and then defend your choices.

3. Choose a paper you have written for a class. Justify every visual design
decision: Describe why you chose the size and color of paper, why you used
the typefaces and typeface sizes and styles you did, why you indicated paragraphs as you did, why you put the page numbers where they are, how you
chose the margin size, and so on.

Redesign the paper so that your choices of visual strategy are insepara-
ble from the overall arguments and intentions of your paper. (It might help
you if you imagine you are redesigning this paper for a different audience;
imagine a popular magazine where this composition might appear.) In addition to considering typefaces, margins, paper size, how paragraphs are indicated, and so on, consider whether some of your concepts or arguments
might be better presented in drawings or photographs.

4. Pick any one-page design you see around you, and redesign it so that
its visual presentation encourages its audience toward generosity or slow
and careful thinking or intellectual playfulness or somber reflection or ...

FOR FURTHER READING

Here are questions tied to further research you can do; below are various
sources keyed to the questions.

1. Why do we consider texts that are composed of black letters in straight
   lines on white paper to be more serious than texts that contain more
   overtly visual elements?
2. How do semioticians/linguists approach the visual aspects of texts?
3. How do rhetoricians approach the visual aspects of texts?
4. How are the visual aspects of texts tied to our bodily experiences?
5. What other relationships have existed/exist between readers and the
   visual aspects of texts, between words and images?
6. Where can I learn more about creating visual design for page and
   screen?

Sources, Keyed to the Above Questions

4   Arnheim, Rudolf. (1982). *The power of the center: A study of composition in the visual arts.*
        Berkeley: University of California Press.
4   Bang, Molly. (1991). *Picture this: Perception & composition.* Boston: Little Brown.
3   Blair, Carole, & Neil Michel. (2000). Reproducing Civil Rights tactics: The rhetorical per-
        formances of the Civil Rights Memorial. *Rhetoric Society Quarterly, 30*(2), 31–55.
1, 5   Bolter, Jay David. (1998). Hypertext and the question of visual literacy. In *Handbook of liter-
        acy and technology: Transformations in a post-typographic world* (pp. 3–14). Edited by David
        Reinking, Michael C. McKenna, Linda D. Labbo, & Ronald D. Kieffer. Mahwah, NJ: Lawrence
        Erlbaum Associates.
5   Bolter, Jay David. (1991). *Writing space: The computer, hypertext, and the history of writing.*
        Hillsdale, NJ: Lawrence Erlbaum Associates.
3, 5   Carruthers, Mary. (1990). *The book of memory: A study of memory in medieval culture.* Cam-
        bridge, England: Cambridge University Press.
3, 5   Carruthers, Mary. (1998). *The craft of thought: Meditation, rhetoric, and the making of images,
        400–1200.* Cambridge, England: Cambridge University Press.

3   Foss, Sonja K. (1993). The construction of appeal in visual images: A hypothesis. In David Zarefsky (Ed.), *Rhetorical movement* (pp. 210–224). Evanston, IL: Northwestern University Press.

3, 6   Kostelnick, Charles, & David O. Roberts. (1998). *Designing visual language: Strategies for professional communicators*. Boston: Allyn & Bacon.

1, 2, 4 Kress, Gunther, & Theo van Leeuwen. (1996). *Reading images: The grammar of visual design*. London: Routledge.

1   Lanham, Richard. (1993). *The electronic word: Democracy, technology, and the arts*. Chicago: University of Chicago Press.

1, 5   Mitchell, W. J. T. (1986). *Iconology: Images, texts, ideology*. Chicago: University of Chicago Press.

1, 5   Mitchell, W. J. T. (1994). *Picture theory*. Chicago: University of Chicago Press.

6   Mullet, Kevin, & Darrell Sano. (1995). *Designing visual interfaces: Communication-oriented techniques*. Mountain View, CA: Sun Microsystems.

5   Nunberg, Geoffrey. (Ed.). (1996). *The future of the book*. Berkeley: University of California Press.

3, 6   Schriver, Karen A. (1997). *Dynamics in document design: Creating texts for readers*. New York: Wiley.

5   Smith, Keith A. (1989). *Text in the book format*. Rochester: Keith A. Smith Books.

1, 5   Stafford, Barbara Maria. (1996). *Good looking: Essays on the virtue of images*. Cambridge: MIT Press.

6   Williams, Robin. (1994). *The non-designer's design book: Design and typographic principles for the visual novice*. Berkeley, CA: Peachpit.

ANALYZING TEXTUAL PRACTICES

7

Tracing Process: How Texts Come Into Being

Paul Prior
University of Illinois at Urbana-Champaign

PREVIEW

Why is it important to study writing processes? The first and central reason is that writing processes are where texts come from. If you want to understand why a text is written as it is, how it might have been written differently, how it came to meet some goals but not others, how it could have been written better, then it makes sense to look not just at the text itself, but at the history of work and the varied materials from which the text was produced. In the 1970s, a number of researchers and teachers came to the conclusion that processes of writing are fundamental to understanding, teaching, and learning writing, that writing is not about learning and applying formulas for making fixed kinds of texts, but about ways of working— ways of acting—that align writers, readers, texts, and contexts.

In this chapter, we take up the central issue of how to study writing processes, the actual activities that people engage in to produce texts. As was discussed in the book's Introduction, the process of writing obviously includes the immediate acts of putting words on paper (or some other medium) and the material text or series of texts thus produced. However, the words have to come from somewhere. Thus, tracing the writing process also means tracing the inner thoughts, perceptions, feelings, and motives of the writer(s) as well as tracing exchanges (spoken or written) between people, exchanges in which the content and purposes of a text may be imagined and planned, in which specific language may even be "drafted" out in talk as we see in chapters 8 and 9. Thinking and interaction about a text may happen at any point, may be fleeting rather than sustained, may be planned or unplanned, recognized at the time or made relevant only later. A text may be drafted and written in less than a minute (as in a quick email response) or may represent the work of an entire lifetime. Many writers describe ideas arising when they are jogging, riding on a bus, watching TV, taking a shower, in the midst of an apparently unrelated conversation, waking up from a dream, and so on. A key issue in tracing the process is how a text gets initiated. Many accounts of writing processes bracket off the task, taking it as a given—perhaps because the researcher often gives it. However, all the elements of initiation and motivation—the emergence of some text as write-able in some context—are central to tracing the process. Finally, writers do not make texts up out of thin air. As chapter 4 emphasizes, writers must always draw on other texts, most obviously through quotation and citation, but also as models (direct and indirect) and dialogic partners. The role of these other texts must be considered as central parts of the process. When we understand the writing process in this way, there is clearly no single way to study writing processes and certainly no way of actually capturing everything that goes into producing even a single text. In this chapter, **we will consider a toolkit of methods for tracing writing, including intertextual analysis, think-aloud protocols, different types of interviews, use of existing accounts, and observation**.

BASIC CONCEPTS

Inscription, Composing, and Text. In everyday usage, "writing" signifies two distinct acts, **inscription** and **composing**, that are treated as one. Writing is a process of inscription, of inscribing text onto or into some medium. We usually think first of writing on paper, but in fact the **media** can be diverse. People also inscribe text on t-shirts, on electronic media, in stone, into tree trunks, on or in metal, in the dirt, and so on. **Tools of inscription** include pens, brushes, and pencils, computers and printing presses, lithographs and keyboards, knives and sticks. In any case, when we think of writing, our first image is probably of an act of inscription, of writing with pen in hand on paper or typing with keyboard on an electronic screen. In tracing the history of a text, it may be that we are tracing a series of material inscriptions, using several tools, sometimes layered together. For example, I first wrote parts of this text in pencil on unlined paper in a spiral notebook. I then used a keyboard to enter the text, revising as I typed, onto an electronic disk displayed on a screen. I printed that text and revised by editing and writing with a pen onto the printed page (sometimes writing longer revisions on the blank back surface).

In general, we may think of a writer as a person who is composing the text as she is inscribing it. However, **composing and inscription are sepa-**

rable. For example, a photocopy machine, a machine pressing words into a piece of metal, and a secretary typing up a hand-written manuscript without editing it are involved in inscription but not composing. Likewise, composing can, and often does happen, without inscription of a text, as when a person plans a text or even drafts out language mentally or in conversation with others.

When people talk about "**text**," there are several different senses that we should be aware of to avoid confusion. *Text* sometimes means a unique material inscription. In this sense, tracing the writing process might involve tracing a series of, perhaps diverse, texts that are linked together from the perspective of some final product. Writing a paper for a class then might involve many texts, not only drafts, but also notes of many kinds (including marginal notes in readings), raw and transformed data that will be discussed, written responses to drafts, the assignment itself, and so on. *Text* is sometimes taken more expansively, to refer as well to the various mental and oral representations of the material texts, regardless of whether they are ever written out. For example, what if a writer formulates a sentence verbally, either when writing alone or when composing collaboratively with other people, and then rejects that sentence? Is this moment of composing and revision fundamentally different because the sentence wasn't inscribed and erased? Sometimes, all of these material inscriptions (and perhaps the ideational representations) are idealized in retrospect as "the text," uniting all moments in the production under a unified label. It is common to say that I read a book, say *Harry Potter and the Philosopher's Stone*, regardless of which copy of it I read, whether in hardback or paper, on the Web or as a handwritten manuscript, whether in English, Spanish, or Arabic. Likewise, I might say "I spent a month writing that paper" meaning not that I slowly wrote a *single* document over a month, but that I worked toward the final product for a month, during which period I produced a whole series of texts in the first sense (drafts, notes, editorial marginalia, revisions, email messages to friends about the ideas, summaries of key readings). How we understand text—as a unique material object, as a representation regardless of medium (including thought and speech), as the ideal that unifies varied acts and objects in a process—is not the issue; the issue is being aware of the different senses, not shifting from one to the other unconsciously.[1]

Authorship. When we see that tracing the composing of a text, what classical rhetoric termed **invention**, involves the contributions of multiple people, it becomes clear that tracing the writing process also implicates

---

[1] In some technical uses, a text is understood as any specific semiotic object that we might reflect on and analyze. Thus, people can also talk about the text of a film, of the body, of clothing, of a conversation, of a cityscape, and so on.

tracing authorship. Goffman (1981) analyzed the everyday notion of the speaker/writer, suggesting that three roles are typically collapsed within that term: the **animator**, who actually utters/inscribes the words; the **author**, who selects the sentiments and words; and the **principal**, whose positions are being represented in the words. In many instances of situated discourse, however, these roles are divided, not fused. For example, a presidential press secretary (the animator) might make an announcement of an environmental initiative that the President (the principal) intends to enact, reading words written by an EPA speech writer (author). This simple division suggests that tracing the writing process also means tracing a **structure of participation**, of examining who is involved in making the text and in what ways.

Even Goffman's analysis of authorship, however, oversimplifies the complexities of the participation structure. If we return to the hypothetical example of the press secretary's announcement of an environmental initiative, it is unlikely that a lone speech writer in the EPA would produce such a text. Studies of writing in institutions have routinely found complex processes of collaborative planning and writing. Documents are cycled to various parties in the organization for comment, revision, and/or review. This chain of participants may also include editors who alter the text and word processors who inscribe written or taped drafts. In these chains, the history of a single text (in the idealized sense) is likely to involve multiple writers.

Even this more typical scenario, with authorship distributed among a number of people, oversimplifies, for we also need to consider **intertextuality** (see Bazerman, chap. 4, this volume) and the **dialogic influences** of real and imagined audiences. Each participant involved in making the text is recalling, anticipating, presupposing, or actually sounding out others (in this case, perhaps the president, the press, the public, special interests). In the government, public hearings of various sorts are often required parts of the process. In other domains (advertising, politics, public relations, marketing), focus groups and experiments are often used to test out ideas and products as they are in development. Each participant in the writing process also consults, draws on, takes text from, responds to, and argues with other texts. These complex structures of participation in authorship also complicate the notion of the principal (the one whose views are represented). Our hypothetical announcement may explicitly represent the president's position. However, through its history of production and intertextual influences, it will have come to represent the voices of many people. And, of course, whenever a government announcement of this type is made, it is read and analyzed in terms of whose voices, interests, ideas, and influences it reveals.

From this perspective, some form of **co-authorship** is unavoidable. To take another familiar example, in this view, every teacher is very actively co-authoring her students' texts, taking up key roles in the production of the text through initiating and motivating it, setting important parameters (the type of text to write, the length, what kinds of sources to use, the timing of the process), and often contributing to content (whether through class discussion or specific response). This role is not diminished because our cultural models of authorship do not acknowledge that teachers co-author their students' texts or because the quality of the text and problems with the text are usually attributed, especially in grades, solely to the student's knowledge or effort. Understanding how people represent the process and authorship and understanding how a text is actually produced in practice are related but distinct issues; it is important to explore both.

Writing as Practice.   When we look closely at situated composing, we do not find a smooth easy activity. Writing moves forward (and backward) in fits and starts, with pauses and flurries, discontinuities and conflicts. Situated **acts of composing/inscription** are themselves complex composites. Writers are not only **inscribing text**. They are also repeatedly **rereading** text that they've written, **revising** text as they write as well going back later to revise, pausing **to read other texts** (their own notes, texts they have written, source materials, inspirations), pausing **to think and plan**. In fact, if we look at actual **embodied activity**, we also see that writers are doing many other things as well—drinking coffee, eating snacks, smoking, listening to music, tapping their fingers, pacing around rooms talking to themselves, and so on. Many of these behaviors seem related to the writing, to managing the emotions as well as the creative process. Writers may also be engaged in **selecting text**—using boilerplate, drawing on prior texts, choosing quotations, and paraphrasing a source. And, of course, in many cases, composing also involves talking to other people while doing all these things—whether continuously at the time of inscribing the text as when people compose collaboratively or periodically as when writers seek input or feedback on what they are writing.

A text does not fully or unambiguously display its history—even the most insightful of interpretations and analyses are only likely to recover some elements of its fuller history, to notice some textual features that allow for uncertain guesses about their origins. Many texts (but not all) are produced across multiple moments of composing and inscription and involve a trail of related texts. Many (but not all) texts involve the active participation of two or more people. All texts build on and respond to other texts, which means that the history of any text is linked to histories of others. All writing draws on writers' knowledge, beliefs, and practices, built up through experiences of socially and historically situated life events. Writers themselves are only very partially aware of the many debts they owe to these intertextual and intercontextual influences. To understand how a text comes into being requires looking broadly at contexts as well as closely at specific situated activity. There is, it should be clear, no way to get the whole story of any text. However, there are ways to get much more of the story than the text itself can offer, and there is much to be learned from these additional insights.

METHODS AND APPLIED ANALYSES

This section discusses methods of analysis and presents a number of examples. Its headings, subheadings, and particular analyses can serve as a map of some of the kinds of analyses you might find it productive to pursue. Not incidentally, the examples also suggest some ways of displaying data, of making analysis visible.

Collecting and Keeping Track of Texts

One of the key steps for researchers in tracing writing processes is collecting and keeping track of the textual inscriptions themselves. In many cases, it is not possible to collect every text produced. Some are thrown out or get lost. Electronic texts may be deleted.[2] Marginal notes on readings are forgotten. However, the more relevant texts you are able to collect, the fuller the view you can develop of the process and its contexts. You might ask participants in a research study to maintain and make available not just drafts, but also drafts that they or others have written on, separate responses, notes or doodling, other texts that they have written and used or that were closely related, and so on.

As a practical matter, it is important to ask participants what the texts are and to add explanatory labels for yourself that include when the text was given to you, what it is, who wrote it, perhaps who wrote on it (it is not unusual for writing in different ink or pencil on a text to mark different writers—different respondents and authors—or different episodes of composing). These kinds of details may seem obvious when you get the text, but weeks, months, or years later when you are analyzing the data, it is easy to

---

[2]Some researchers have used programs that provide a full record of keyboard typing. Bridwell-Bowles, Parker, and Brehe (1987) offered a detailed analysis of keystroke data. Tracking periods of pauses, forward text production, cursor movements, revisions, editing, and various combined operations, they captured some of the fine-grained differences between the writers they were studying, both in terms of total time spent in each type of activity and the distribution of the activities over the episode of text production. Even in controlling settings, it is a challenging task to read and interpret such data. Movie screen capture programs can provide a more readable view of the changing electronic screen and the actions it indexes. Geisler (2001, 2003) has extended this method to naturalistic research on writing and reading with a PDA.

find yourself mystified when you pick up a text without this kind of **contextual record** attached.

For teachers interested in tracing the process for pedagogical reasons, many of the same concerns apply. A student's final draft often makes more sense if you have available a clear record of the texts that were produced along the way, by you and other respondents as well as the student. The student's own story of the process, the text, and the contexts written at the end of the process and/or along the way (e.g., as a series of memos reporting thoughts, questions, and progress) can aid a teacher's reading and response.

Intertextual Analysis

One of the central ways of tracing writing processes is to analyze how the text itself is related to other written texts or to instances of talk. In many cases, intertextual analysis reveals much about the structure of participation as well as about the sources of a text.

Relating Text to an Initiating Text. A classroom assignment leads to a student's text. An organization's call for conference paper proposals prompts and shapes an abstract that is submitted. A company's request for a proposal leads to a proposal tightly linked to the request. A client's request for information leads first to a letter and eventually to a change in a product's instructional manual. A letter to a senator leads—through complex channels—to a bill sponsored by the senator. Texts often respond to other texts that may be treated as initiators.

An initiating text does not simply control what follows. It has to go through processes of interpretation and negotiation. For example, in an education seminar, Professor Mead made the following assignment on the syllabus:

1. A proposal for a study, with bibliography. The proposal should contain a tentative title, statement of the problem, background to the study, statement of research questions or hypotheses, method (to include procedures for data collection and data analysis), and significance of the study as major headings. The details will get worked out as the proposal is adapted to the individual problem. The proposal should be no longer than four to six pages, exclusive of bibliography.

In a seminar session, Mead discussed this assignment, elaborating on the content and goals of each section of the research proposal. As he talked through the "method" section, he suggested a somewhat different, more specific set of topics and outlined them on the blackboard as follows:

5. Methodology
   —population
   —instruments
   —procedures
   —data analysis

All 12 students whose research proposals I received followed the outline Mead had given, using headings identical or nearly identical to those given in the syllabus or written on the board in the second week of class. Of course, assignments do not automatically lead to matching texts. In fact, Mead provided equally explicit directions for the organization of a second assignment, a critique of a research article, and the students did not closely follow that outline.

   Relating Text to Source Texts.   Sometimes "writing" is simply using others' texts, what we call either boilerplate or plagiarism depending on the context. As Hendrickson (1989) noted, accountants writing a proposal to audit a company are expected to simply fill in the names and dates and make no other changes because any change would create legal uncertainties. In academic settings, there may also be boilerplate. For example, a sociology student (Moira) in a research seminar was writing a report based on a common data set from a research project. Professor West, who had designed the research, had already written a careful description of the data collected. When Moira asked West in an early draft if she could just use that description in her report, West said it would be fine. Moira then simply pasted the $3\frac{1}{2}$ page description into her paper.
   In other cases, writers may copy text in ways that would not be so readily sanctioned. For example, when I analyzed use of sources in the master's thesis of an education student (Mai), I found a number of examples of source use that looked like the following (the bold print marks the text that Mai copied into her thesis from a book):

Besides the assumption of distinguishable underlying abilities, **advocates of a communicative competence approach make** <u>assumptions</u> **about** <u>language</u> **that have been largely ignored in traditional approaches to language assessment.** Joan Good **Erickson (1981)** argued that an appropriate <u>model of language assessment</u> **assumes**:

- **Language is a symbolic, generative process that does not lend itself easily to formal assessment.**

- **Language is synergistic, so that any measure of the part does not give a picture of the whole**.

- <u>**Language is a part of the total experience of a child and is difficult to assess as an isolated part of development**</u>.
- <u>**Language use**</u> (<u>**quality and quantity**</u>) <u>var</u>ies <u>**according to the setting, interactors, and topic**</u>.

Erickson maintained that <u>**language assessment should reflect the nature of the communication process and evaluate the major use of language—that of a verbal/social communicative interaction in a natural setting**</u>.

As you can see, Mai copied a lot and made few changes. Had the professors on her thesis committee realized that she was using source text this way, I am fairly sure they would have identified it as a problematic use of sources, possibly plagiarism, and required her to revise it. Oh, and by the way, the underlined text above is language that the author of the book Mai copied from—it wasn't Erickson's book—had copied from Erickson's book. Here too, I suspect that Erickson and her publisher would not have considered such copying appropriate.

Tracing a Series of Texts. I mentioned earlier the case of Moira and her writing in the sociology seminar. When I asked Moira for copies of texts related to her work in the seminar, she provided me with 12 separate documents produced over a period of 10 months. Three were drafts of her preliminary examination. Seven were drafts of a conference paper (which I refer to as *Arenas*). One was a memo Professor West had written in response to Moira's first draft of the conference paper (*Arenas 1*). The final text, put together to share with the seminar, included a different draft of her preliminary examination and a part of one of the seven drafts of her conference paper. In addition, eight of the texts included handwritten editing, comments and suggested revisions (in seven cases, this response text was written by West, in one case by a professor at another university whose theories Moira was employing in her research). Finally, some of the texts also included handwritten notes, editing, and revisions that Moira had added.[3]

Tracing language across multiple drafts requires a careful and close comparison of texts. Figure 7.1 displays an example of one way that West's

---

[3]This kind of complexity does not appear to be unusual. Geoffrey Cross (1994) describes how eight primary writers and several other contributors took 77 days to complete an eight-paragraph executive letter for an insurance company's annual report. The letter was signed by the CEO and the President, two of the eight primary participants, though their contributions were primarily oral planning and final approval of the text. In this period, the writers produced two conceptual outlines and seven primary drafts. Late in the process, earlier drafts were rejected and an entirely new draft was written more or less from scratch. Altogether, Cross collected 18 documents, six of which had handwritten comments and editing on them, including one document with the handwritten editing and comments of three different individuals.

Extract from West's memo of March 7

You need to be more specific about what is being tested. As I understand it, the arena of comfort hypothesis suggests the following model:

objective change $\xrightarrow{a}$ subjective discomfort (dissatisfaction? low self-esteem? lack of control?)

b

c

behavioral maladjustment

arena of comfort may possibly act as a moderator of a, b, c (c is the direct path from objective change to behavioral maladjustment)

In other words, you are investigating
a) Whether objective change leads to subjective discomfort (dissatisfaction)
b) Whether subjective discomfort leads to behavioral maladjustment
c) Whether objective change influences behavioral maladjustment directly (without mediation by discomfort or dissatisfaction with respect to the changing domain).
d) Whether the presence of an arena of comfort (where there is no change and satisfaction) moderates (decreases) the effect of objective change on subjective dissatisfaction
e) Whether the arena of comfort moderates (decreases) the effect of subjective dissatisfaction on behavioral maladjustment
f) Whether the arena of comfort moderates (decreases) the effect of objective change on behavioral maladjustment
g) You could also test whether a context constitutes an arena of comfort merely by satisfaction, or the absence of objective change, or whether both conditions are necessary.

*Arrows between columns added to clarify intertextual borrowing.

Moira's AN INTERCONTEXT MODEL OF RISK from Arenas 2 dated March 11

The general model, diagrammed below (Figure 1), investigates (1) whether objective change leads to subjective discomfort, represented by path A, (2) whether subjective discomfort leads to behavioral and psychological maladjustment, represented by path B, (3) whether the presence of an arena of comfort moderates (decreases) the effect of objective change on subjective dissatisfaction, (4) whether the arena of comfort moderates (decreases) the effect of subjective discomfort on behavioral and psychological maladjustment, and finally, (5) whether a context constitutes an arena of comfort merely by lack of discomfort, or the absence of objective change, or whether both conditions are necessary.

(Figure 1.) General Intercontext Model of Risk

Arena of Comfort

objective change $\xrightarrow{a}$ subjective change

b

Maladjustment

Arena of Comfort

FIG. 7.1. Professor West's memo as intertextual resource for the second draft of Moira's conference paper.*

words ended up in Moira's conference paper. In addition to responses written on the text of *Arenas 1*, West also responded with a separate 2-page memo. Moira incorporated parts of that memo fairly directly into her next draft, *Arenas 2*. In Figure 7.1 the arrows between the two columns point to how closely Moira's text echoes West's. For example, in Point A on the left West says "whether objective change leads to subjective discomfort (dissatisfaction)" and in Point 1 in *Arenas 2* on the right, Moira says "whether objective change leads to subjective discomfort, represented by path A." If you compare B to 2, D to 3, E to 4, and G to 5, you will see additional examples of this borrowing. While these comparisons do reveal some deviations from West's words, those deviations seem relatively minor and one case, the addition of "and psychological" after "behavioral" in Points 2 and 5 of *Arenas 2*, could be traced to West's responses in other parts of the text. A fuller analysis (Prior, 1998) of the ways that Moira did *not* take up West's memo suggested that she was resisting West's argument, as in Points c and f, that objective change in social environments had a direct effect on adolescents' behavior (without mediation of the adolescent's subjective response to that change).

In some cases, such **intertextual tracing** was less straightforward. For example, in responding to *Arenas 1*, West only crossed out the "s" in "adolescents" in the second sentence of Moira's abstract; however, in *Arenas 2*, that sentence was extensively revised.

Arenas 1 (Abstract, sentence 2)

> It is hypothesized that objectively measured transitions in multiple contexts will have an adverse impact on adolescents adjustment, and this response will depend on the actor's subjective perceptions and interpretation of the changes as negative.

Arenas 2 (Abstract, sentence 2; underlining added to mark changes)

> It is hypothesized that change in any given life arena will have less adverse psychological and behavioral consequences if the adolescent has an "arena of comfort" in another domain, characterized by lack of change and satisfaction.

Had Moira initiated the major revision of this sentence? At first, I thought so. However, West's response to another sentence—from page 3 of *Arenas 1*—suggested a different story. That response is represented at the top of Figure 7.2. West's revision was incorporated without change in *Arenas 2*, as shown in the bottom left of Figure 7.2—the bold print indicating West's words. The sentence on the bottom right of Figure 7.2 is the second sentence from the abstract again, the same as the one above, only now the bold print and underlining highlight the borrowing from the page 3 sentence, revealing a complex blend of Moira's and West's words. This exam-

The bold print represents words inserted from West's written response to Moira's sentence 5 on page 3 of *Arenas 1*. The double-underlined text represents words inserted from the original language of Moira's sentence 5 on page 3 of *Arenas 1*.

Arenas 1 **(p. 3, sentence 5)**

The revised hypothesis is that simultaneous change in all life arenas will have adverse [any given] [less] psych & behavioral consequences if the adolescent perceives the changes to be undesirable and has an arena of comfort in another

domain, characterized by lack of change and satisfaction. disruptive.

Arenas 2 **(p. 3, sentence 11)**	*Arenas 2* **(Abstract, sentence 2)**
The revised hypothesis is that change in **any given** life arena will have **less** adverse **psychological and behavioral** consequences if the adolescent **has an "arena of comfort" in another domain, characterized by lack of change and satisfaction.**	It is hypothesized that change in **any given** life arena will have **less** adverse **psychological and behavioral** consequences if the adolescent **has an "arena of comfort" in another domain, characterized by lack of change and satisfaction**

FIG. 7.2. From text to text—Tracing West's words in Moira's texts.

ple makes it clear that changes at one textual site sometimes triggered changes at another site. It also reveals the apparently seamless and uniform abstract of *Arenas 2* as a textured, dialogic, historic construction, something directly crafted by at least two people.[4]

Another crucial lesson for analysis from this example is that some of the language that ended up in Moira's final draft of the preliminary examination was actually written by West in response to early drafts of the conference paper, then copied by Moira into that paper, then later pasted by Moira into drafts of her preliminary examination. For example, the following sentence (compare to Fig. 7.2) appeared in the last draft of Moira's preliminary examination:

Following Simmons' formulation, it may be hypothesized that change in any given life arena will have less adverse psychological and behavioral conse-

---

[4]The problem of who is talking in sentences like this one is similar to the problem Wittgenstein (1958) noted with regard to recognizing the diverse functions of language: "Of course, what confuses us is the uniform appearance of words when we hear them spoken or meet them in script and print" (p. 6).

quences if the adolescent has an "arena of comfort" in another domain, characterized by stability (lack of change) and satisfaction.

This example points to the potential limits of looking only at successive drafts of *one* text. Consider how my analysis would have been limited, and likely misleading, had I looked only at the four drafts of the preliminary examination and treated sentences like the one above as new composing by Moira.

Relating Text to Talk. It is also possible to **trace intertextual relations between talk and text**. These relations are explored in greater depth in the next chapter. In some cases, those relations are very close indeed, as in the examples of Sean's hypotheses and Tony's arguments against Huck Finn that are described in chapter 8. In other cases, the effects may be less direct. For example, Lilah, a graduate student in American Studies was doing research on ethnicity in the United States for several courses, focusing especially on a study of local Cinco de Mayo celebrations in a northern city. Lilah noted that her choice for one paper came from watching a Bill Moyers' interview of Sam Keen on TV. She also noted in her own reflections, and displayed in her papers, that her analysis of the local history of Cinco de Mayo was strongly influenced by interviews with community activists. The activists' talk appeared not only in specific quotes in her paper, but in her rejection of an argument that the centrality of food, especially tacos, represented the commodification and hence diminishment of Chicano/a culture. Instead, with the activists, she focused on the visibility of the event and its economic benefits to the neighborhood.

Phelps (1990) observed that writing researchers had been caught up in "the textual and the psychologized rhetorics where abstractions like the fictive audience (textual representation) and the cognitive audience (mental representation) are more salient than the actual exchanges of talk and text by which people more or less publicly draft and negotiate textual meanings" (p. 158). Intertextual analysis of such exchanges of talk and text can provide much data on writing processes and on the structure of participation, the varied forms of co-authorship realized through the exchanges.

Eliciting Writers' Accounts

Intertextual analysis can provide much data on the writing process; however, there is much that cannot be captured by these methods: exchanges that are missed; the writer's thoughts, feelings, and sense-making; contexts that do not appear in the text. In particular, it useful to elicit writers' accounts of their goals, their contexts, their processes, their feelings, the meanings they see in their texts, the influences they are aware of or can reflectively construct for what they've written and done. Broadly, **participant**

accounts can be divided into concurrent accounts, those that are made immediately with the writing, and retrospective accounts made after the fact.

Concurrent Accounts (Think-Aloud Protocols). When you look at writers composing and inscribing text alone, it is difficult to see what is happening because much of it is locked up in the silent thinking, reading, and composing the writer engages in. Early researchers (e.g., Emig, 1971; Flower & Hayes, 1981) faced with this problem drew on a technique developed by psychologists to study other cognitive processes: the use of **concurrent, or think-aloud, protocols**. The use of think-aloud protocols was particularly central to writing research in the 1970s and 1980s when this methodology was the key way researchers explored the writing process. The methodology has been less central in the last decade for several reasons. There are questions about how thinking aloud affects the writing process. There also have been questions about the value of the cognitive models typically associated with this line of inquiry. In addition, think-aloud protocols have usually been attempted only in laboratory conditions while there has been an intense interest in studies of writing in naturalistic conditions. And finally, attention to composing in naturalistic conditions also suggested that many of the key processes were social as well as cognitive. These questions are real and important (see Smagorinsky, 1994, for more on these issues). However, it is also important to recognize that concurrent protocols for the first time began to crack open the notion of "writing," to reveal the complex, fine-grained, and diverse nature of the acts that are combined under that label. There is a wide gap between an everyday representation of writing, as in "I wrote a paper last night," and the image of writing that a think-aloud protocol makes available, and filling that gap remains a critical project for writing research.

The following is an example of instructions for a reading-to-write task.[5]

For this assignment, you should do the reading–writing task described in the envelope, talking aloud and recording your thoughts from the time the envelope is opened. Do not open the envelope until you are ready to do and record this exercise. You should be able to do the exercise in about 30 minutes.

Talking aloud means:

1. **reading aloud** whenever you read anything (including the task instructions) inside the envelope as well as your own text
2. **vocalizing the words you write** down as you write them
3. **saying aloud what you are thinking about**, remembering, imagining, visualizing, hearing—questions that come to mind, plans you are making,

---

[5]For another example of think-aloud instructions see Appendix A in Penrose and Sitko (1993).

> expectations, reactions, memories, images you see, conversations you
> recall or imagine, internal dialogues, etc.

Try to provide as complete a description of your thoughts as possible <u>while</u>
you are doing the writing task. The idea is to provide a kind of stream-of-
consciousness commentary on your thinking, not an explanation or account of
your thinking. Obviously, you should not say aloud anything that will be em-
barrassing or uncomfortable for yourself or others.

In a seminar I taught in 1993, we all produced think-aloud protocols on a
reading-to-write task (see Flower et al., 1990). I will present three brief segments out of the 21-page transcript that came out of my engagement with
this 30-minute task and consider the varied ways this kind of data might be
analyzed. In the first segment below, I am reading aloud (ALL CAPITALS) a
paragraph on literacy from Hunter and Harmen and I begin commenting
(plain text), questioning their definition by asking *which* texts one must be
able read, write, and understand to be literate. The stress when reading the
word "whatever" continued that line of doubt and the final comment
shown, "like physics," was said ironically, as an example of a kind of text
that many highly-educated people could *not* understand.

> . . . WITHIN THE GENERAL TERM LITERACY [clearing my throat], WE SUG-
> GEST THE FOLLOWING DISTINCTIONS, ONE CONVENTIONAL LITERACY, THE
> ABILITY TO READ, WRITE, AND COMPREHEND TEXTS, // it's like what texts
> are you talking about? // ON FAMILIAR SUBJECTS, AND TO UNDERSTAND
> **WHATEVER** SIGNS, LABELS, INSTRUCTION, //like physics, //AND DIRECTIONS
> ARE NECESSARY TO GET ALONG WITH ONE'S ENVIRONMENT .. // that
> seems like a . . . //it seems like it means something, //but (I do) have questions
> there, //TWO. FUNCTIONAL LITERACY,

After reading brief passages from five different texts, I reread the directions
and began to ask how I was going to "summarize and synthesize the ideas."
In the following segment, I am moving from a plan to look for themes to considering Hunter and Harmen's passage, labeling it for the first time as a "traditional" view and again questioning their lack of specification and
contextualization for understanding signs.

> . . . I could summarize and synthesize the ideas presented in the quotations //
> so I could be looking here for themes in terms of um, what, literacy is and
> what- what themes are there here, // drinking some coffee — //hmm — //what
> theme would I like to pull out? // I mean conventional and functional literacy,
> Hunter and Harmen is just the — // it's- hm, it's the least interesting, // it's just
> the very traditional kind of — discussion // and and, I read it as being very
> empty, //you know, UNDERSTAND SIGNS, // which signs? // in which contexts?
> // at what level of understanding? // um, either conventional or functional
> literac— // and and there- there's an interesting ideological thing going on

here, // where the functional literacy is is, um, stated in terms of what people, want for themselves, // but what people want for themselves is shaped by their social environment too

After more thinking and reading, and jotting down a few brief notes, I began writing. Here is the transcript where I compose the second sentence. I begin writing (the underlined words), thinking (plain text), rereading what I had written (UNDERLINED, ALL CAPITALS), and orally composing (quotes).

Literacy is a highly contested ....politically charged[7 second pause] // CHARGED term //ok [13 second pause] //um Traditional notions of literacy [8 second pause] whether...conventional..or..functional [7 second pause] // hm, I'm looking for a word here //"tend to" //"ought to" // right // TRADITIONAL NOTIONS OF LITERACY WHETHER CONVENTIONAL OR FUNCTIONAL, //um . . aw. I had a word in my head, which I didn't say aloud, // LITERACY IS A HIGHLY CONTESTED POLITICALLY CHARGED TERM // TRADITIONAL NOTIONS OF LITERACY WHETHER CONVENTIONAL OR FUNCTIONAL . .//. . "tend to be framed" // tend to be framed, // ok, I'm write-// framed in terms of // TEND TO BE FRAMED OF IN TERMS OF // skills and competence often. .viewing . . . .competence. . .as a. . .binary trait // ok // "something you have or don't have" //yeah, // thinking about treating this [as] a draft // something you have or don't have, //ok

Text produced: Literacy is a highly contested, politically charged term. Traditional notions of literacy, whether conventional or functional, tend to be framed in terms of skills and competence, often viewing competence as a binary trait, something you have or don't have.

To date, concurrent protocols have primarily been analyzed in categorical and quantitative terms. Thus for example, I would take the transcribed protocol and divide it into units. (Units are typically some kind of phrasal or clausal utterance as opposed to sentences, for reasons that should be obvious when you look at the preceding transcripts. I have roughly **parsed** these transcripts, using double back slashes // to mark the divisions.) I would then begin **coding** these units. The most basic codes are already indicated in the transcript, which distinguishes **reading the sources** (all capitals), **thinking** (plain text), **inscribing text** (underlined), **rereading the text written** (all capitals and underlined), and **orally composing text** (quotes). (**Pauses** could also be measured precisely, though they aren't in these transcripts.)

A basic analysis might consist of simply counting up the number of units (or the size of the units in terms of number of words, for example) for each of these categories. Typically analysts will want to go beyond these very basic classifications of the protocol, to identify more specific activities. For example, thinking may be subdivided into categories like **setting goals**, **generating ideas**, and **responding to other texts**. And these categories might be further subdivided. Setting goals might be divided into goals for content, procedure, style, organization, and rhetorical situation. Responding to texts may be divided in terms of how close the comment is staying to the text (e.g., summary vs. transformation), stance toward the text (e.g., agreement vs. rejection), or some other feature that seems salient in the data. Geisler (1994), for example, noticed that Ph.D. students in philosophy were regularly responding to texts in terms of what the authors were arguing while freshmen writing in response to the same texts rarely did so, focusing mainly on the ideas. Thus, she coded her transcripts for **author mentions**, which became a key element of her analysis.

With the think-aloud transcript divided into units and classified in these ways, analyses might focus on the overall activity, especially on comparisons between individuals or groups, between tasks, between conditions, and so on. This kind of coding and counting can provide a sense of what proportion of time is spent in each type of activity. It might also focus on the sequential pattern of the activity, addressing such questions as at what points in the process the writers read texts or how goal-setting is distributed across the process. It might identify sequential patterns over the session (as in the shift seen in the three extracts above from early reading with limited commentary, to mid-session thinking and planning, to late session composing and inscribing) or types of repeated sequences (e.g., write-evaluate-write or write-reread-comment-write as seen in the last extract).[6]

However, these think-aloud transcripts could be analyzed from other discourse perspectives. For example, drawing on Bakhtin's (1981, 1986) theories of language as dialogic and intertextual and Vygotsky's (1987) understanding of development as fundamentally social, I might instead look for traces of, and responses to, others. The underlying notion of internalization was articulated by Vygotsky (1987): "An operation that initially represents an external activity is reconstructed and begins to occur internally . . . Every function in the child's cultural development appears twice: first, on the social level, and later on the individual level; first, *between* people (*interpsychological*) and then *inside* the child (*intrapsychological*). . . ." (pp. 56–57). Wertsch (1991) emphasizes the contribution of Bakhtin's notion of **hidden dialogue** (dialogue with the second voice missing) to understanding internalized speech. Analyzing parent–child interactions around a puzzle, he traced the shift from the parent's verbal and nonverbal scaffolding to the child's own self-regulation of the activity. **Inner speech**, like intertextuality, can involve **repetition** and **presupposition**. In general, it does not involve full inner dialogue (e.g., a person mentally asking herself "What does that piece look like?" and then answering "It looks like the

---

[6]Flower et al. (1990) would suggest ways of linking an analysis of the text I wrote (classified in terms of how I used sources and added in other ideas), the strategies displayed in the text and protocol, and the think-aloud protocol comments.

bus"). Inner dialogue will typically appear as the answer that presupposes a question or even the shift to regulated attention without words (just looking at the pieces with a particular puzzle-making orientation).

> Bakhtin's account of dialogicality . . . suggests that what comes to be incorporated into, or presupposed by, an utterance are voices that were formerly represented explicitly in intermental functioning. The issue is how one voice comes into contact with another, thereby changing the meaning of what it is saying by becoming increasingly dialogical, or multivoiced. (Wertsch, 1991, pp. 90–91)

The notion of inner speech and hidden dialogicality, of inner speech as incorporating iteration and presupposition, could be used as a framework for analyzing think-aloud protocols.

For example, in the extracts I have presented from my think-aloud, I am directly adopting (without quotation or citation) a categorical scheme (conventional vs. functional literacy) from Hunter and Harmen, a clear example of intertextual uptake. In the second segment, I identify Hunter and Harmen's views as traditional, setting up a contrast between traditional and other (modern) views of literacy. In making this contrast, I am not echoing any particular text, but am acting in response to many texts I have encountered that tell a metanarrative of progress. In other words, this contrast and the organizational structuring it affords is another trace of intertextual influence. When I question Hunter and Harmen in the first two segments, I am echoing a repeated experience, a request for specifics, that I have experienced in school and out, directed at others' texts and my own. The form of this practice—that incessant questioning of what, how, where, when, and why, that demand for precision and detail—is again intertextual. However, it is also a presuppositional stance taken up in relation to texts: At no point in the transcript did I consider what stance I should take to these texts. (And, of course, there are other stances. I might have approached the text as a poem, perhaps saying the words aloud to savor their sounds and rhythms or working to learn them by heart.) Finally, there is my use of "tend to." Here I see hidden dialogicality (presupposition), a response to the repeated questioning from teachers and readers, "Always?" that has crystallized into the kind of carefully qualified stance toward claims typical of many academic texts. With this brief analysis, I mean to suggest that other forms of discourse analysis could be employed when looking at think-aloud protocols. These kinds of analysis would be particularly useful when accompanied by other intertextual analysis and by interviews.

Retrospective Accounts of Writing. Retrospective accounts of writing rely on people's memory, and it appears clear that people remember relatively little of the moment-to-moment thinking and action they have engaged in. Retrospective accounts must also be considered as reflections and constructions tuned to the social situation and time in which they are produced. The farther the separation between the event and the recall, the more likely that the account will contain the familiar **conventionalization** and **simplification** that Bartlett (1932) first described. Details drop out and new ones are added.

Using Naturalistic Accounts. Some of the earlier theories and research on writing were inspired by writers', typically professional writers', accounts of their processes. Such accounts might appear in **autobiographical or biographical narratives or in interviews**. The series of *Paris Review* interviews with literary authors represented one key source, often presenting images of manuscript texts in progress as well as close accounts of writers' habits. Ernest Hemingway, for example, reported (see Plimpton, 1963) writing in the morning, standing up at a reading board, writing in pencil on onionskin paper. His interview begins with an image of one of his handwritten manuscript pages. In some cases, people have set out to document in great detail institutional processes of writing. For example, a publicist, Terry Erdman, wrote a book on the production of Star Trek TV shows and films, *Star Trek Action* (1998). The book includes richly detailed observations of writers at work, including recorded dialogue and texts from writers' brainstorming meetings, sample scripts and storyboards, and examinations of transformations that occur during production and post-production. Here again, naturalistic accounts can provide valuable information.

Process Logs. You can also ask writers to keep a log on a daily basis (or so many times a week) of the activities they engage in and their thoughts on the writing process. See Figure 7.3 for an example of instructions for a **process log** in relation to a study of writing in a class. The instructions could be modified in varied ways to fit other settings, to vary the regularity or form of the log (e.g., entries could be sent as emails), to address other kinds of participants (e.g., instructions for a 10-year-old would need to be quite different), and to highlight different questions. Nelson (1993) reported on process logs as a window into undergraduate students' research processes. Log entries varied from longish discussions of sources and writing activities on days of intense activity (usually close to deadlines) to brief, telegraphic, somewhat whimsical entries such as the following:

November 2: Thought about my paper with a feeling of dread. Decided I had to go to the library that day. Didn't. (p. 107)

In a research project I conducted (see Prior, 1998), one graduate student (Lilah) agreed to keep a log (out of some 60 who were invited to do so). Dur-

A process log is a journal in which you discuss what you are writing, what you are reading in relation to your written work, and how writing for this class relates to other writing you are doing or have done. I ask that you spend about 15 minutes four times a week writing in your process log. I also ask that you maintain copies of notes and drafts of your writing that I can collect from you.

What should I write about in my logs?

1) Keep track of any **writing** you have done for this course since your last entry. If you have not done any writing, say so. (By writing, I mean not only substantial work on a draft of a paper or other assignment, but also notes you write to yourself about what you need to do, email exchanges about course writing tasks, fragments of ideas or neat sentences that you scribble on a scrap of paper, whatever....) I am interested in the stories and scenes of your writing: in what you wrote, how long, when and where.

2) Keep track of what you are **reading that relates to your writing**. I am interested in how you approach and read texts in your field. I am particularly interested in hearing about instances where reading something triggers thoughts about your writing, even if the reading was not obviously related, even if the reading was not academic (e.g., reading a newspaper, a novel for pleasure, surfing the web).

3) Keep track of **discussions** you have with professors, other students, friends, family, co-workers, or whoever that relate to your writing. These discussions may be anything from a conference with a professor to a casual conversation on a bus. You may include lectures you attend, discussion in this or other classes.

4) I am interested in **what you think and how you feel** about the writing you are doing, how you are understanding the task, imagining the text, facing particular problems, feeling frustrated or excited.

5) If you do not have much to write about some days, I would be interested in ways the writing you do for this class relates to past writing you have done as well as to future projects or work, in your writing processes (e.g., How do you write? Where? Who reads your writing? How do you get ideas? Do you think about your writing during other activities? How do you experience ideas when you write—as words in your heads, voices, images or pictures? What are your attitudes toward writing? How do you evaluate your writing?)

What texts should I keep track of? As #1 above suggests, I am interested in <u>any</u> writing you do in relation to this course. I would also be interested in papers you have written in the past that relate to your writing here, anything you are writing that relates but is not for this course. I am interested in scribbled notes, outlines, lists of things to do, ideas you write in the margins of books or articles, data that you are using, email exchanges, list serve discussions, and, of course, drafts you print out (including ones with handwritten editing or responses from your instructor). The more you provide me, the better. Please do not be concerned about issues of correctness, clarity, neatness. I will show you my early drafts of papers, which have many misspellings, typos, errors, incomplete ideas. For many people, myself included, writing is a messy process. We tend to keep the messy pieces to ourselves, but I hope you will be willing to share them because they are essential to the process. (Of course, if you are one of those people who sit down and write a single final draft, that is fine too.) If you are writing on a computer, keeping electronic copies of your work in a separate folder for this research might be easiest. You could photocopy paper texts or give them to me temporarily so that I can photocopy them.

FIG. 7.3. Sample instructions for a process log.

ing a 10-week quarter, Lilah provided 23 entries of varying length and format (from essay-like, paragraphs on focused topics to telegraphic lists of ideas for papers), totaling 73 handwritten pages of text. In an early log entry, after she has decided to study the history of the local Cinco de Mayo celebration, Lilah recounts a conversation from another seminar:

One woman is writing her paper on Tex-Mex cuisine. As it happens, the year Tex-Mex became big was also the year when illegal aliens and cracking down on border control was the hot political issue. She thinks it has something to do with imperialist nostalgia—desire for cultural artifacts of destroyed or subjugated peoples. It's also a commodification of culture—a way of getting "goods" from another culture without the people.

Someone mentioned that she should go to the International Festival and look at how that is commodified. Suddenly, ethnicity=food, i.e., something consumable. This is what I'm wondering about with Cinco de Mayo. What's used to present ethnicity? And is the festival really about ethnicity or more about commodification of an ethnic community that makes it more palatable to the larger American community? I've always felt a little disappointed with these events that claim to be international and end up just featuring different dances, clothes, foods. But until today I didn't know why. Really, they lose their cultural differentness by putting it into a shape Americans can buy.

In both cases, the logs display key points in the history of the text, reveal much about affect and motivation, and facilitate interviewing. A question about the class where Tex-Mex food and imperialism were discussed is more likely to trigger a rich response than an open-ended question about whether class discussions influenced the paper (especially weeks or months after the event).

Semi-Structured Interviewing. Semi-structured interviewing essentially consists of asking questions that have been worked out to some degree in advance, but also involves leaving the script behind to follow up on the interview. For example, when I first interviewed Sean, a sociology graduate student whose dissertation prospectus is discussed in chapter 8, I asked a standard question—whether his papers were related to personal interests:

Paul: um, is this related to personal interests at all? is this something you expect, something that that you might have been interested in four years ago, before you got involved in the project?

Sean: no, no, definitely not, no, it was more of looking at the five variables and deciding what I was going to do, basically the three biggies as far as I could see were self-esteen, self-efficacy, and depression, self-esteen I know first hand was just a very complicated literature, it's gigantic, and there are some very serious complications with the whole idea of self-esteem, so I didn't want to get into that, and um the, and also there's a lot of good work that's been done on self-esteem, so if it would be difficult for me to make a contribution in that area, not only in terms of getting on top of the huge literature, trying to cirumvent the fundamental problems, but also in trying to come up with something new and that you know people would be interested in, very difficult variable to work with I think, self-efficacy was actually a very good variable, but someone already took it

Sean quickly responded "no" to the question of whether he was personally interested in his topic (depressive affect). However, he immediately went on, beyond the question, to talk about the five variables in the data set and how he judged which one would be the best for him. This information provided insights about the research project he was working on and about the rhetorical character of topic selection. When he mentioned (in the last line of the quote) that "someone" had already taken his first choice, I followed up with another (unplanned) question:

Paul: somebody else here or . . . ?

Sean: well, Dave Lynch, the, Professor Lynch, he already had self-esteem, er self-efficacy, and so I felt as though depression would be my best shot, so that's what I {I laugh} I but you know I've thought about this often, you're supposed to, like an author, you're supposed to write what you know right? well, I don't know any depressed teen-agers {I laugh}, this has all been a very library oriented thing

Paul: yeah, not a personal experience

Sean: not at all {he laughs, I laugh}

The follow-up told me more about how different members of the research team had carved out personal niches and about Sean's motivations for his research. Discursively, his shift in interpersonal representations—from "someone" to "Dave Lynch" to "Professor Lynch" (perhaps after starting to say "the professor")—was also interesting, perhaps a sign of the multiple social footings for graduate students working on the sociology research project, perhaps also a sign of his negotiating my status as researcher in relation to the group. In the end, Sean returned to my initial question, with a sense of irony.

These exchanges illustrate the way **semi-structured interviews move between scripted questions and open-ended conversations**. The initial questions can be fairly generic (like the question I asked Sean at first) or grounded in specific knowledge you have built up through earlier research. As an example of the latter, in an interview with Lilah (the American Studies student who did the process log), I drew on several comments she had made in the process log about her efforts for the three professors she was writing papers for that quarter and asked if she had a sense of why she had put more effort into her paper for Nash than for Marini, and more for Marini than Kohl.

Stimulated Elicitation Interviewing. When asking a question in typical semi-structured interviews, you are depending on the person's memory as the basis for a response. Many researchers have found that an interviewee's responses become richer when the person interviewed has some

external stimulus, some object that can trigger and support memory as well as serving as a source for new reflection. The specific props and directions can be varied. The prop might be a text or specific highlighted parts of a text (in original form or transformed), photographs of certain scenes, an audiotape of some interaction, or a videotape of some action. The directions for how to respond to the prop can also be quite varied. Let me give several examples here of ways that texts might be used as props in text-based interviewing.

In interviewing a NNES sociology student who had provided only a single draft of one paper with the professor's responses on it, I went through the text and highlighted a number of the editorial marks, corrections, and marginal comments the professor had made and asked the student in the interview to read the comment aloud, explain what it meant, and state what action if any he had taken in response to the comment. From this interview, I learned much about which comments the student seemed to understand and which he didn't. It also became clear that, although he was supposed to be revising the document, he had not thought through the responses and had not begun revision at the point of the interview.

In an early interview with West (the sociology professor), I asked her to look at each student's text and tell me a bit about the history of that text and the student. She would glance through the texts as she was talking, sometimes stopping to read bits of text and especially any of her own written responses.

In another study (Prior, Hawisher, Gruber, & MacLaughlin, 1997), we were interviewing teaching assistants and faculty on how they had implemented writing-across-the-curriculum practices in their courses. We would ask them to talk through their syllabi and explain specific assignments. In some cases, when instructors had brought copies of the assignments, their talking from those assignments combined with questions by the interviewer (who also could use the assignment text to form new questions) resulted in very detailed discussion of the instructor's motivations and expectations for the assignment.

One form of **text-based interviewing** that has been used often in writing research is called **discourse-based interviewing**. Discourse-based interviewing (Odell, Goswami, & Herrington, 1983) was developed to help uncover writers' tacit knowledge of, and motivations for, texts. It is a method that involves some transformations to the original texts. This technique typically involves: (1) presenting one or more alternatives for some passage(s) of a text to the writer (or possibly someone else), (2) asking if she would accept the alternative(s), and (3) asking her to explain why or why not. For example, in a discourse-based interview on an email message, I might cross out the salutation "Dear Professor Hujwiri," and write in a proposed alternative salutation "Anisa." Of course, alternatives could involve any transformation: deleting text, adding new text, moving text around, changing the font or the medium (e.g., from handwriting to print). It is important to make it clear to the writer that the alternative is *not* intended to be a correction or a proposed improvement, that it might be better, worse, or no different.

Here again, this basic method can be varied.[7] In some cases, I made similar transformations to a professor's written comments and then asked the student whether she would prefer the original comment or the alternative and why. In a case study of Moira and West, I made extensive use of parallel discourse-based interviews on Moira's texts with both Moira and West. I chose this approach because I wanted to gauge whether Moira had accepted West's revisions because West was the authority and to see whether Moira and West would agree on the reasons for and against specific alternatives—in other words, to see if Moira was just making the changes or if she was learning from them.

In this case, I included alternatives taken from Moira's earlier drafts that had been revised. Most of these prior draft alternatives were ones that Moira had authored, West had rewritten in her response, and Moira had accepted in her revision. I prepared three texts for the discourse-based interviews. Using clean copies of the three texts (*Arenas 4* and *7* and *Prelim 4*), I introduced 36 alternatives (in some cases two alternatives in a single sentence). Moira responded to the full set of alternatives in her interview. However, because I was interviewing West about other students' texts and her time was limited, I only presented 21 of those alternatives to West. In this interview, I offered Moira 16 opportunities to replace revisions West had written and she had copied with her original language. In seven of the 16 cases, Moira chose to return to her original language, not realizing that that was what she was doing. In five cases, she chose to retain West's revisions. She expressed no preference in two cases and rejected both in two others. Evidently, when West's authority was removed from the revisions, some became much less compelling, while others appeared to have become internally persuasive. In a separate interview, West was offered nine of the same alternatives (changes that placed Moira's original texts against West's revisions). West chose to keep her own revisions seven times, to return to Moira's wording once, and to reject both once.

Although the quantitative data were suggestive, I was especially interested in comparing the reasons they offered and the extent to which those reasons matched. That analysis revealed complex patterns of convergence and divergence. Figure 7.4 displays an example. The sentence at the top represents the prompt I constructed. The proposed alternative, "operationalized, this becomes a bit tricky," is actually Moira's language from

---

[7]Although she does not name the technique, Nancie Atwell (1987) describes using discourse-based interview questions during her "evaluation conferences" with middle-school students.

        `operationalized, this becomes tricky.`
However, ~~[the relationship between objective change and subjective discomfort, and their~~

~~implications for psychological and behavioral adjustment, remain problematic]~~.

Moira	West
...ok, hm, I like the change, because this was so wordy, but I don't know if it gets at it ( ) because I don't know if it was necessarily in her operationalization I mean because it- the article I was reading was more theoretical argument than an operationalization, so er uh, or empirical work, so since she's never tested it herself, I don't think that "operationalize" would be the right word but I would definitely accept revamping this sentence and simplifying it, I like this because of the "tricky" but "operationalize" is probably not the right word...	...here I would think that the new wording is simpler, so that's a benefit of it, but the referent to "this" is unclear because uh, and I think that the revision changes the meaning of the sentence, because what you're initially talking about here are the relationships among variables, a theoretical connection whereas the new wording introduces the issue of measurement, and uh, and and it's a- it's ano- it's another issue, so I think I would reject that alternative...

FIG. 7.4. Moira and West reply to a proposed change in *Arenas 4*.

Arenas 1; the printed, crossed-out text is a substitution West had written in and Moira then included in all subsequent drafts of *Arenas*. Moira rejected both the alternative and West's revised language, whereas West rejected the alternative and kept her wording. However, Moira made it clear that she no longer felt comfortable describing the issue as one of "operationalization," as she had in *Arenas 1*, seeing it instead as "theoretical." In fact, in spite of their different decisions, comparing the transcripts from West's and Moira's interviews made it clear that both agreed that the real issue was theory, not operationalization. Thus, on that issue, we see clear convergence. Both Moira and West also mentioned some benefits to "simplifying" the language. However, Moira seemed more attached to her original tone, particularly preferring the word "tricky" to "problematic." In other words, Moira had found the content of West's words persuasive, but was resisting the kind of language and style that West employed.

Another way to elicit accounts is to **ask writers to draw their writing processes and contexts** (and then describe that drawing). In a current research project that Jody Shipka and I are conducting (see Prior & Shipka, 2003), we ask writers to draw two pictures of their processes for a specific writing project. The drawing of the first image is prompted by something like the following directions:

> The first picture should represent how you actually engaged in writing this particular piece. That picture might show a place or places where you wrote, a kind of sustained espisode of writing, what resources you use, other people who are involved, how you vary your activities as you engage in a specific episode of writing, how you feel during the writing, and so on.

In addition, we show the participant examples of several other writers' drawings produced in response to this prompt (intentionally choosing drawings that are quite different in detail and style). The second image is elicited with something like the following directions, aided once again by several examples of other writers' drawings:

> The second picture should represent the whole writing process for this project from start to finish (or to the current stage). The picture might show how this writing project got started, interactions with other people and other texts, experiences that have shaped the project over time, the history of drafts and responses to drafts, your evaluations of and emotions about this project at different times, and so forth.

For the first image, writers typically draw rooms in their homes where they write and some of the objects and people they interact with there. For the second, they typically draw a chain of events across a variety of sites. (One drew the continent of Africa with a small village hut in the middle because that was where her field research occurred.) In both drawings, participants often produce visual metaphors to depict thought processes and emotions. The task of doing these drawings in response to our prompts and examples seems to encourage participants to provide detailed descriptions of the scenes and resources of their writing, of the "procrastinating" downtime behaviors they engage in as well as the focused work, and of the emotions they experience (and how they manage those emotions). While participants are doing the drawing, we also have an opportunity to look at the text or texts that they have brought in. We ask them to bring to the interview whatever would help us to understand their writing on this task. Participants have brought draft and final texts (sometimes with written comments from others, such as instructors), notes, assignments, personal journals, photocopies of articles marked up by the writer, and so on. While the participants are drawing, we look over the texts. The interview then is semi-structured, with some general questions about writing, a request to talk through (and possibly amend) the drawing, and questions prompted by our reading of the texts.

Figure 7.5 presents two drawings that an undergraduate student, Laura, produced as we talked about a paper she wrote for a non-fiction writing class. The scene of writing at the bottom of the figure represents her apartment. With the drawing as prop, Laura described her movements between her upstairs bedroom, where the computer was, and the downstairs couch, where the TV was (for breaks). She explained why she normally wrote at night because of her class schedule and talked about a number of the conditions of her typical writing: eating pizza, listening to instrumental jazz, being interrupted by telephone calls, reading texts that lay around the room, and so on. In talking through the drawing of the overall process, Laura began with reading the book that she would write about, getting an idea (a light bulb in the drawing) and then going to the main library stacks. She went on to represent her process over the next 7 weeks as she researched and wrote the paper, turned it in, got back her draft with a grade of C, and then went through a process of working through her sadness over the grade, revising the paper, and finally turning it in and getting a better grade. (Laura also brought the final paper with the instructor's handwritten response and the draft she had turned in, with her instructor's comments as well as some extensive handwritten notes and drafting she later added to it.) What is critical here again is not the specific images on the drawing, but the ways that the drawing is described and elaborated on in the interview and the follow-up questions that those descriptions support.

Using videotaped or audiotaped records of composing as a basis for interviewing is another type of stimulated elicitation. Rose (1984), in his study of writer's block, asked people to write in a laboratory session. He used two cameras, one focused tightly on the page so that it would display what was being written and the second on the person. Immediately after the writing was over, Rose presented the images on split-screen TV and asked the writers to talk through what they were seeing on the tape, stopping it sometimes to explain in more detail. DiPardo (1994) describes a similar use of audiotaped records of peer response groups.

Observation of Writing

Participant observation of sites of writing offers researchers additional resources that support data collection. Being at sites of composing can result in getting greater access to basic data (e.g., texts that are being produced), in building a knowledge of the histories and typical processes of writing and review, and it can allow direct observation of interactions. Of course,

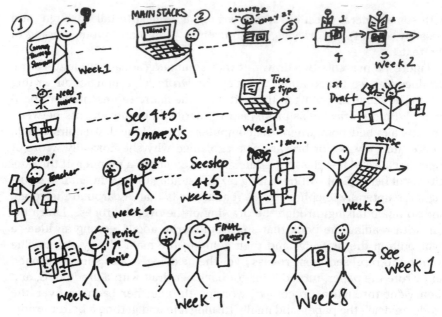

Drawing of the overall process

Drawing of the scene of writing

FIG. 7.5. Drawings of the writing process.

some of these benefits can also be achieved by asking participants to audio-tape or videotape themselves (or perhaps to turn on their Web cameras).

Field Notes on Writing Processes. Latour and Woolgar (1986) describe an ethnographic field study of a biochemistry lab at the Salk Institute. Although their focus was on science, much of their data looked at processes of inscription. Through **field notes and photographs** of the lab, they developed a fine-grained account of the ways that data were produced (which involved much labeling of samples, the keeping of meticulously detailed laboratory notebooks, and computer printouts), the ways that raw data were transformed into table and graphs, the ways that those tables and graphs then became the data and were moved to the biochemists' offices where they were used, along with articles, books, grant proposals, and already written articles, to produce new articles, which were circulated to colleagues, submitted to journals, revised, sometimes becoming publications which were then resources for new publications and citations to add to articles, grant proposals, and vitae. Their study suggests some of the key values of participant observation.

Recording Events Related to Writing. Matsuhashi (1987a) provides close analysis of revising based on **videotaped recording of participants writing** in a research setting. With the videotaped record, she was able to examine pauses, noting the quite diverse temporal patterns of inscription, and also to trace the precise details of revision during the process. In her data, she focused entirely on what was happening on the page; however, videotaped records could provide for detailed analyses of writing practices more broadly.

A number of researchers have used or created **settings where people have to collaborate on their writing** and then recorded those interactions. (For example, see Kamberelis and de la Luna's example of the owl pellet report in chapter 9.) Although such recording could be used for stimulated elicitation interviewing, it can also be used for direct analysis. Syverson (1999) describes a study in which she asked a collaborative group in her class to audiotape their meetings. By listening to the discussion in the dorm rooms, Syverson learns much about the conditions of composing (e.g., late nights, regular interruptions) as well as about the details of collaborative planning and composing of the text.

Integrating Data From Multiple Sources

Dyson (1997) suggests the richness of mixing participant observation, interviewing, text collection, and recording in her accounts of elementary students planning, writing, and performing story-plays for writers' theatre. She is able to trace individual and group patterns over weeks and even across years and to explore in detail ways that students incorporated mass media in their texts.

Through participant-observation, text analysis, and interviewing, Kamberelis and Scott (1992) analyzed the complex origins of two elementary students' texts. One fourth-grade student, Lisa, wrote "Living in the Black Life," which read in part:

> Its nice living in the black life. I haven't been harmed in Detroit. Back then black was treated bad and beaten and spat at. . . . We communicate with each other but it is a wonderful life that my life being black. And I don't hate for being black and other blacks shouldn't hate being black. They should be happy who they are. And no matter what whites do to blacks we are good people still. So love who you are don't hate yourself and thank God for making you a person.

Kamberelis and Scott found that, given the opportunity, Lisa had creatively adopted the utterances and ideologies of many others.

> . . . for example, Lisa told members of a peer editing group that "it's [the title] from a song I like called "Back in the High Life Again" [by Steve Winwood] that's about having a good life after some down times." Similarly, Lisa noted in an interview that "I got the idea to say 'it's a wonderful life' from a movie I saw at Christmas about a guy who wanted to kill his self 'cause his life was really a mess and how an angel told him he should like himself and go back and be with his family." (p. 377)

In interviews about her writing, Lisa describes what Jesse Jackson said on TV, a guest from a local university (Professor L.) said in class, and her mother and people in her church said regularly about the need for Blacks to be proud even if they face hatred or mistreatment from Whites. Kamberelis and Scott note: "This message is re-envoiced in *Living in the Black Life* in a way that seems to preserve both the urgency of the message and the ministerial cant in which it was originally delivered by Jackson and Professor L." (p. 378). Here again, Kamberelis and Scott (1992) were able to unpack many specific intertextual influences because of the intense longitudinal collection of multiple types of data (see also Kamberelis & de la Luna, chap. 9).

CONCLUSION

The naturalistic study of writing processes is complex; however, it is also critical. **We can only understand where texts come from—in terms of their authorship and social contexts as well as their content and textual**

organization—by careful tracing of their histories. The richest histories will emerge from multiple methods, with intertextual analysis, participant accounts, and observation of activity working together to produce a fuller portrait of the process. When we trace such histories, we are studying not cognition alone or social context alone, but rather the intersection of the cognitive and the social in activity that is distributed across individual acts, collaborative interactions, and many socially and historically developed tools (from technologies of inscription and distribution to discourse genres for communication). Research on writing processes has already led to major shifts, not only in our understanding of how writing gets done, but also in our practical sense of how to manage our own writing and how to teach others to write. Various process-influenced pedagogies of writing have become the dominant model for teaching writing at all levels, though many older practices not informed by process research certainly remain in place. Much remains to be learned in this field. We have, for example, just begun to explore writers' everyday practices—the embodied, situated, mediated, and dispersed processes out of which specific texts emerge. There is every reason to suppose that what we find through this line of research will continue to contribute to our practical work as writers—and, for some of us, as teachers of writing—just as it will continue to enlarge our understanding and propel our theories of people's literate practices.

ACTIVITIES

This section presents some activities you might engage in to begin exploring methodologies for tracing the writing process.

1. Consider a paper you have recently written. Make a drawing that represents the key concrete activities you engaged in as part of this writing process. Be sure to include activities involved in invention (like reading, talking to others, coming up with ideas about the paper—wherever that might happen) as well as inscription (like the actual production of the text, your drafts and notes). Then draw another visual representation in which you create a visual metaphor (or metaphors) that represents key elements of your process of writing the paper. Compare the two representations. Do they tell you different things about the process? What does each include? What does each exclude?

2. First, write a general account, based on your memory, of how you write summaries. Second, do a think-aloud protocol, following the instructions presented earlier in this chapter in the section on concurrent protocols. Your task will be to summarize and respond to the discussions of the nature of "texts" found in the following passages of this book: Wysocki's discussion

of the visual nature of text in the second section of *Basic Concepts*, p. 124; the first two paragraphs of Kamberelis and de la Luna's *Texts: Forms of Writing and Formal Characteristics of Written Language*, pp. 240–241; and the second paragraph of *Three critical issues* in the Introduction by Bazerman and Prior, pp. 6–7. Immediately after the protocol, sit down and write about the experience. Pay attention to the relationship between what you said aloud and what you experienced in your head. Also note how thinking aloud affected the way you read and wrote. Then transcribe the protocol (using the conventions discussed in chap. 8). Now compare your initial account of writing with the think-aloud protocol and the immediate account. Note differences as well as similarities across these accounts.

3. Using the instructions for process logs provided in Figure 7.3, keep a process log of your writing in relation to a class assignment or some other writing project. (While you are doing the writing project, don't begin to review and study your log.) When the writing is completed, first write up an account from your memory of your process for this project and then begin to look through your log and materials (any drafts, notes, email, etc.) you maintained. Consider the following questions.

- Compare the account of the process you wrote up with the log and materials? Are there differences? (I would expect the log and materials to include evidence of specific events and decisions that would not appear in the final account, though the opposite is also possible. You may also find points on which the two accounts disagree about what happened.)
- How complete do you feel the record is? Are there important events, certain types of information, or certain types of materials that are not included in your process log? Also, are there log entries or materials that you have kept that you might not be comfortable sharing with a researcher?
- Examine the development of a few selected passages from your text. Using any drafts or notes, try to trace the precise changes that occurred in the texts through the writing process. Then consider what evidence you have *in the process log* (entries and materials) for why these changes happened. (You probably have memories that go beyond what it is the process log, but as a researcher of others' writing, memories would only be available through additional participant accounts, e.g., from interviewing.)
- Finally, from these comparisons, what do you see as the benefits of process logs and their limits or problems?

4. Look at writing in a specific site (a school classroom, at home, at a workplace). Using observation, intertextual analysis, and interview meth-

ods, examine where, when, and how writing is typically done in that site, who participates in writing and at what points in the process, why people engage in writing, how texts (including drafts and notes) are produced and kept (or discarded), who reads the texts produced and why they do, and how texts draw on other texts.

FOR FURTHER READING

Early research on writing processes continues to be of value. Janet Emig's (1971) study is a seminal work in the field and introduced think-aloud methodologies. It also points to earlier literatures, such as the *Writers at Work* series of interviews from *Paris Review* (e.g., Plimpton, 1963). Donald Graves' (1983) collection features several early studies of the composing processes of young children. A series of studies (see, e.g., Flower & Hayes, 1981, 1984) that was associated with the Rhetoric program at Carnegie Mellon pursued writing processes in laboratory-like conditions (i.e., writers writing in an institutional space, like a classroom, for short periods of time on assigned research tasks). Analyses in this line of research drew heavily on cognitive processing models for studying differences in expert and novice knowledge.

Rymer (1989) attempted to extend the think-aloud design to naturalistic composing processes in a study of biologists writing (but found few were willing to engage in this approach while doing their actual work). Geisler (1994) extended the think-aloud design by asking paid participants to write more extensive texts over multiple episodes and by assigning tasks that sought to simulate typical academic writing tasks. Various later studies have employed other methodologies aimed at getting writers to externalize their thinking, either by setting up and recording peer group or collaborative writing situations in relation to course assignments (e.g., Flower et al., 1990; Syverson, 1999) or by taking advantage of naturally occurring discussions of texts in progress (e.g., Cross, 1994; Prior, 1998).

Matsuhashi's (1987b) collection brought together a variety of early observational studies of writing processes. This type of research seemed to recede in the late 1980s as researchers shifted to studying social contexts of writing and talk about texts. However, studies of workplace cognition, communication, and action have begun to present very close observational analyses of the functions and temporal character of writing. Goodwin and Goodwin (1996), Heath and Luff (2000) and several studies presented in Luff, Hindmarsh, and Heath (2000) offer detailed observations and recording of operations centers, tracing the complex interplay of talk and text across multiple channels and media.

A number of ethnographic and historical accounts of scientific knowledge have included rich observations of writing processes. Latour and

Woolgar's (1986) account of experimental practices in biochemistry at the Salk Institute focuses on the ways chains of inscription are produced and transformed in laboratories. In another biochemistry laboratory, Amann and Knorr-Cetina (1990) offer a more detailed look at ways that talk mediates the reading and interpretation of raw data and how interpretations are then transformed in writing. Gooding (1990) offers detailed mapping of experimental practice and writing. Bazerman (1999) offers close accounts of the ways laboratory notebooks mediated invention and led to other genres, including patents and publicity. Myers (1990) traces chains of genres in scientific work, especially the move from grant proposals to technical articles to popular reports.

Over the last decade, research on writing processes has shifted toward naturalistic studies of writing processes in diverse settings: communities (e.g., Kalman, 1999), schools (e.g., Dyson, 1997; Finders, 1997; Kamberelis, 2001), and workplaces (e.g., Beaufort, 1999; Cross, 1994). Most of these studies rely heavily on externalized collaborative activity as a window into the process. Some have also provided detailed tracing of series of texts. Finally, I would note that Kress (1997) offers a fascinating view of, and theoretical framework for, literacy development as part of a general multimodal, multimedia development of sign-using and sign-making. Several of his observations bear on processes by which children make semiotic objects, including texts.

8

Speaking and Writing: How Talk and Text Interact in Situated Practices

Kevin Leander
Vanderbilt University

Paul Prior
University of Illinois at Urbana-Champaign

PREVIEW

For a variety of cultural and disciplinary reasons, talk and text, the oral and the written, have typically been represented as very different and very separate phenomena. However, as chapter 7 suggested, studies of writing (and reading) processes—in schools, workplaces, and the community—quickly found that writing is often initiated and planned in talk, that readers often talk through texts they are reading with others (sometimes reading all or part of a text aloud), that readers' responses to writers' in-progress texts often involve talk, and that many texts (such as scripts for plays and movies, speeches, advertisements, and religious rituals) are written to be spoken. A political speech, for example, may be talked through in a series of meetings, written and rewritten, orally performed and critiqued, rewritten again, and finally memorized or read aloud with a teleprompter. A note to a friend that two students write during lunch at school may be interactively composed in talk as it is written ("tell her about the fight," "say that she was really kickin' it at the dance"). In terms of content, not only do people often talk about texts, but texts often represent people talking: Either the note or the political speech may report on other people's conversations (so and so said . . .). In short, through processes of production and reception, talk and writing are often jumbled together. In this chapter, we explore the important and complex relationships that link talk and text, mapping some of the ways that talk is transformed into, shapes, and occasions texts as well as some of the ways that text is transformed into, shapes, and occasions talk.

In taking this approach, we are challenging some of the common stereotypes of how writing and reading are done. Writing is often imagined as private activity, and authorship is often imagined as singular (see chap. 7). At the same time, talk is typically imagined as just plain talk, everyday conversation, not linked to texts. Moreover and paradoxically, many of our images of how people talk come from written representations of talk in novels, journalistic reporting, and so on. As we will see, actual talk often is quite different from those written representations. Finally, the talk–text binary is itself misleading. Talk, for example, normally includes gestures. The communicative import of talk and writing often depends on drawings, pictures, diagrams, and even physical objects. In other words, writing and speaking typically interact with other sign systems. The word **semiotic** is often used to refer to signs in multiple systems: talk, text, gesture, graphic, sound, mathematical, symbolic, plastic, etc. Such multi-semiotic processes are not exotic. They are, for example, routinely seen in the earliest writing of children at home and at school; in the work of architects, industrial designers, and engineers; on the production sets of TV shows and film; in the design of the millions of product labels and containers that now fill our world; and in the construction of monuments (from the individual grave to the national monument).

Once we have recognized the ubiquity of these relations between talk, text, and other sign systems, it becomes clear that we also need methods of research that are capable of capturing and analyzing such complex activity. In this chapter, we first review some key concepts and then examine how transcripts represent talk as well as exploring the new problems encountered if we want transcripts (or other kinds of texts) to represent not only talk, but also the ways texts are being read and written, and the ways gestures and other sign systems come into play. Finally, we work through several analyses of relations between speaking, writing, and other semiotic activity. How to transcribe talk remains an unsettled and complex issue. How to capture the role of texts in talk and how to capture other sign processes are even newer, and hence even more unsettled, areas of research. Nevertheless, if we wish to study textual practices—the processes of reading and writing—as they are found in many settings, it is critical to understand these issues.

BASIC CONCEPTS

Orality, Literacy, and Semiotics. There is a growing recognition that orality and literacy are more complex and more intertwined than initial theories imagined them to be. Biber (1994), for example, offers a framework for analyzing varieties (registers) of language in use. His framework is oriented to looking for patterns of co-occurrence, clusters of situational and linguistic characteristics (see also Barton's discussion in this volume, chap. 3). In his delineation of situational characteristics, **mode** ("written/spoken/ signed/mixed/other") is just one of seven possible parameters for distinguishing forms of language. Mode is not, for example, equated with **permanence**, thus allowing for recorded talk and transitory writing (like on a fogged mirror or a beach as the waves roll in). Nor is spoken discourse collapsed with **shared space and time**, allowing for face-to-face writing (as in writing on a whiteboard in an office or classroom) as well as for distant audiences for talk, as is common with radio, TV, film, telephone, and now the Web. In his analyses, Biber finds that bundles of linguistic features vary with the whole range of situational features, not just mode. Although some linguistic features may correlate fairly strongly with a particular mode, others do not. When looked at carefully, it is not surprising that oral language and written language vary on a continuum of multiple dimensions, that everyday spoken conversation and instant messaging on the Internet may share a number of features, as will a formal lecture on population genetics and an essay on that same subject.

Ong (1982) offered an interesting classification of orality and literacy. He suggested that **primary orality** be reserved as a classification for cultures (notice, not individuals) with no literacy. Ong saw the orality of literate cultures as quite different because forms of language and thought developed in writing come to saturate the forms and content of oral language. He labeled this orality as **secondary orality**. He further classified literacy according to its basic technologies. **Chirographic literacy** is marked by use of pen, brush, or pencil; texts are written in a hand and each copy of a text has to be made individually. **Typographic or print literacy** creates texts of uniform appearance and allows for mass reproduction. **Electracy**, which Ong saw as much in terms of the mass media of television and radio as in terms of electronically encoded written texts, creates new configurations, especially as the mass distribution of scripted oral language extends and transforms the domain of secondary orality. As Wysocki makes clear in the form and content of chapter 6, electracy is also altering the appearance of text (e.g., creating new typographic flexibility), producing new multimedia hybrids, and changing the nature of reproduction and distribution in significant ways. In the broadest sense, semiotics challenges language-centric views of communication and thought and calls attention to the simple fact of multiple media, modes, channels, and sign systems.

Conversation Analysis and the Social Organization of Talk

In the 1960s, a group of sociologists became very interested in everyday talk. Instead of seeing such face-to-face interaction as the product of social norms, roles, and rules—with society as the equivalent of a computer program generating individuals and events, they came to see everyday interactions as the forge where social order, social identities, and social relations get made, as the source of social life rather than a pale, neoplatonic reflection of some underlying macrosocial structure. (The central criticism these microsociologists have faced is that they grant too much freedom and agency to individuals and situations.) One group of these microsociologists developed what has come to be known as **Conversation Analysis** (CA).[1] Because of the importance they placed on situation, CA researchers began to audio- or video-tape people interacting and to provide detailed analyses. They were especially interested in **understanding talk as a temporal, sequential phenomenon**, as something that participants must constantly understand and produce as it unfolds in real time. In part, this orientation led them to focus especially on the complex ways that participants accomplish **turn-taking** (the ways they move from turn to turn). Central to these approaches is a very careful analysis of situated interaction itself, an analysis that examines the practices of talk and does not bypass them to address content or presumed rationales.

Goffman (1974, 1981), as a microsociologist but not a follower of CA, argued that **the participation structure of talk** is often much more complex than the idealized model of a speaker and listener. He began to imagine participation in public places (like talk on a bus where others might overhear), identifying a broad range of structural positions for speakers and hearers, which may be traced at rather gross levels of analysis or by subtle shifts in tone and stance. Goffman was concerned with tracing how interactants continually shift their alignments vis-à-vis one another and their stances in relation to an emergent interaction. Goffman termed these shifting alignments and stances conversational **footings**. For example, among the many possible alignments, the role of speaker/writer may be split into those of **animator**, **author**, and **principal**, as described in chapter 7. Goffman also notes that we often represent others' words and voices in talk (**speaking *as* and *for* others**). These phenomena are often talked about in terms of represented speech, constructed dialogue (Tannen, 1989), or voicing. Goffman differentiated the role of hearer as well; a hearer might be **addressed or unaddressed**, a **ratified or unratified** (e.g., overhearing, eavesdropping, or even just viewing) participant in the event.

Yet, tracing footings is more complex than simply charting the relations among co-present interactants within readily visible settings. Goffman (1981) notes that a structural account misses the "essential fancifulness of

---

[1]Conversation Analysis (CA) is usually, and somewhat confusingly, a term that names one specific, though influential school (founded in the 1960s and 1970s by Harold Garfinkel, Harvey Sacks, and Emmanual Schegeloff) rather than naming the general activity of analyzing a conversation. Deborah Tannen and Erving Goffman, for example, analyze conversations but are not followers of CA.

talk" (p. 147), or our creative ability to represent or "figure" ourselves as agents in a narrated scene. That is, in telling a story to a friend about being chased by a menacing neighborhood dog, one inhabits the (narrated) world of the neighborhood, and also the current social situation of the storytelling. Participation frameworks belonging to narrated worlds come to be embedded, if only figuratively, within the current social situation. Moreover, Goffman argued that general structural accounts of forms of participation must be further specified by particular cultural practices. For example, consider the very different practices of audiences in a Black Baptist church service versus an Anglican church service or at a classical music concert versus a rave. Combining the structural possibilities, the figurative gymnastics, and the cultural elaborations, Goffman (1981) argues that people do not simply move from footing to footing, but maintain multiple footings: "In truth, in talk it seems routine that, while firmly standing on two feet, we jump up and down on another" (p. 155).

Methods of Studying and Recording Talk and Writing

Selecting a Research Site. Although it is difficult to predict in advance whether a research site will yield rich data for the types of questions you are raising, a few broad questions can help you make some important distinctions. First, what types of writing-related activities are present at a potential research site, and how visible are they to you as a researcher? This question involves looking beyond first impressions. Some of the most interesting settings (such as workplaces, scientific laboratories, and community centers) or events (such as lunch meetings, talk in hallways, or work done at home) are those that may be difficult to see or at which writing may not initially appear to be important. Second, to what degree and in what ways is writing related to talk or other textual practices in the proposed research site? A common problem, for instance, in studying the relations of talk and writing in classrooms, is that classrooms tend to be filled with teacher talk. Classroom "discussions" are often little more than teacher recitations (at least in terms of talk in the common public floor). Besides thinking of the sheer amount and type of talk in the setting, you might consider the ways in which talk and mundane textual practices are interwoven in the course of activity. For instance, note taking during classroom lectures, restaurant work, police activity, medical consultations, and even in places of worship is a very common, but understudied interaction of talk and writing. Third, how is the particular setting at a research site related to the multiple writing situations in which members participate? Although it is tempting to make "setting" and "situation" equivalent, you will find that writing situations multiply and divide. For instance, in many university and public school classrooms, writing is simply assigned and then later submitted for evaluation. In these cases, student writing processes are situated in many non-classroom settings: in dorm rooms and at family kitchen tables, in coffee shops and in Internet chat sessions. Even within a classroom, "the situation" can rapidly divide into response group work, individual drafting, and side-sequences of talk and writing. Approaching a potential research setting as a complex assemblage of situations will help you make decisions about research sites and the scope of your project.[2]

Making a Record by Taking Fieldnotes. The first step to analyzing talk and activity is to produce a record. **Fieldnotes** can provide some record of talk and activity, although most researchers find that fieldnotes alone fail to capture the rich and rapid dynamics of interaction. The means of recording data is itself a movement toward analysis and theory-building about what is going on; the world "looks" much more dynamic and multiple through the lens of a video camera than through fieldnote etchings. At the same time, fieldnotes can permit you to focus and freeze your vision, whereas raw video data may later overwhelm you with unmediated representation of activity. We have found, when possible, that simultaneous and multiple means of data collection (e.g., audio, video, and fieldnotes) provide optimal data sources for both focusing and complicating the analysis of communication across various modes and media.

Making a Record by Audiotaping. Although it is beyond the scope of this chapter to discuss the complete range of technical issues involved in obtaining good audio and video recordings of interactions,[3] we offer some initial suggestions, based in part upon the mistakes we have made in our own research experiences. One of the most basic principles in audio recording is getting the microphone close to the speaker or speakers. The placement of microphones is not simply a technical issue, but is rather a methodological decision about the kinds of data deemed important. If the primary data source of interest in a classroom is the teacher and her talk, then a single lapel microphone will suffice. However, if you want to capture both the officially ratified and backchannel talk of students, then you will need multiple and carefully placed microphones. For instance, in extended

---

[2]Once you have shaped your research goals and have initially selected your research site(s), in the United States you will likely need to pursue written consent to conduct your research from an Institutional Review Board (IRB), which is a university-wide committee whose purpose is to protect the rights of research subjects. Local institutional regulations vary significantly, so you should check with the IRB at your institution and especially with researchers who have successfully submitted proposals in the past. In our experience, securing IRB approval may take a significant period of time, from weeks to months (in complex cases).

[3]For example, see chapters 4 and 5 in Duranti (1997), Goodwin (1994), Heath (1997), and chapter 4 in ten Have (1999).

classroom research, one of us (Leander) normally used three microphones (PZM, see below) to capture large group interactions, connecting these microphones to the cassette recorder through a small portable mixer. (The mixer allows the added advantage of gaining one microphone up and another down, in order to follow the shifting dynamics of interaction. Stereo recorders, with two microphone jacks, are also available.) Two of the microphones were placed at the sides of the classroom (one closer to the front) and one was placed at the back. For capturing audio data in a given space, omni-directional microphones are a good choice, while directional microphones are useful when trying to single out a speaker from other sound sources. A popular type of an omni-directional microphone, which lays flat on a surface, is called a PZM microphone. To avoid unwanted sound, a microphone should not lay on a surface that will be vibrated or moved, such as a floor or classroom desk. Microphones should also be kept away from sources of noise, like air conditioners, heaters, computers, or a window outside of which there is traffic or other noise. These sources often produce much more sound than you perceive because your perception filters out constant noise.

As discussed earlier, situations involving writing and talk often split apart and become widely dispersed. One flexible means of recording simultaneous and distributed activity is to use multiple mini-cassette recorders with built-in condenser microphones. These recorders can quickly be placed at the center of group activities. Although the recording quality in these cases would be better with an external microphone, you might elect to sacrifice a bit of quality for the rapid distribution of fairly unobtrusive recording devices as groups begin working. Because writing and talking practices may be widely distributed, you may ask writers or writing groups to record themselves in settings that you do not have access to for reasons of convenience or privacy. For instance, in one study, one of us (Leander) had groups of engineering students self-record their discussions of a group writing project. The discussions they recorded were situated in a pizza restaurant and a dorm room. (As a bonus, the students also regularly recorded non-solicited messages for the researcher!) As in any research, particularly important in this kind of recording practice is to make sure that all participants have given consent. Finally, in any process of recording, it is critical to keep careful written records—on tape labels and in research fieldnotes—about who is involved in which recording and on what occasion.

Making a Record by Videotaping. Many of the issues discussed concerning audiotaping are also relevant for videotaping. In fact, a common problem in videotaping is poor sound quality. A carefully placed external microphone or two will greatly help remedy this problem. We have found it best to audiotape and videotape simultaneously. This practice has the added advantages of giving you a choice of data format during analysis and of reducing the chance of losing data completely when equipment fails (and you should anticipate failure). When videotaping, it is best to have an inexpensive headset connected to the camera in order to periodically monitor sound quality. Digital video cameras are becoming more affordable and the standard for research. Digital cameras capture high quality images, and digital videotapes can be copied with little or no loss and eliminate lengthy processes of digitization for analysis and editing. Perhaps the most basic suggestions for improving video quality are to stabilize the image by setting the camera up on a tripod, and avoiding frequent zooms. Because literacy activity moves, however, you will sometimes want to take the camera off of the tripod. Many tripods have a quick-release feature, allowing you to leave an attachment plate on the camera such that it can be rapidly mounted or dismounted. As with audiotaping, video recording involves complex decisions about what kind of data you wish to capture. If you want to follow, for example, a general discussion in a classroom or meeting (say, to understand the social dynamics of planning), you will want to position the camera to capture the widest possible scene. If you want, however, to trace how one individual takes notes, you will want a relative close shot of the paper or computer screen where the notes are appearing. Multiple cameras are also an option in some settings. One final issue to consider when filming is when to start the camera and when to shut it off. Because it is often the case that important forms of activity happen in the boundaries between communities and activity systems, you might try starting the camera before an activity begins and leaving it running after the activity is said to be officially over. Such "transition zone" data can be surprising and illuminating.

Methods of Transcribing and Representing Talk and Writing

Tools for Transcription and Analysis. If you are collecting more than a very minimal amount of audio data, you will want to use a transcription machine. Transcription machines typically allow you to slow the speech to a desired speed. More importantly, the foot pedal of such machines allows you to start, stop, and rewind the tape, while you keep your hands (oh so patiently) on the keyboard. For the analysis of video data, new computer programs (e.g., Transana, CLAN editor) are emerging that permit a researcher to create a written transcript in one window of the computer while watching a (digitized) video segment in another window. Once created, the transcript from such programs is typically "live," such that clicking on any part of it will cue up the video to the parallel moment. These developing transcription and analysis programs allow researchers new analytic tools, including archiving specific segments of (digitized) video data, linking these segments to other forms of ethnographic data, and coding video segments for qualitative and quantitative analysis.

Current Challenges and Limitations of Transcription

There is always a challenge when you attempt to represent one modality in terms of another. A musical score provides only a rough representation of how a group of musicians should play the music. Much of the score needs to be fleshed out through conventions of practice and through the innovative and idiosyncratic performances of musicians. In the same way, a transcript of talk (a written version of oral language) offers only a partial representation of talk. Variations in loudness, pitch, and speed are ignored or represented in quite limited ways. What gets represented is also varied. Notes on a class lecture may record certain key points, the rough order of topics, perhaps a few quotations—more likely phrases than full quotes. Taking dictation for a letter on the other hand involves producing a word-for-word record of what the speaker says. (Actually, taking dictation is even more complex because only the foregrounded "text" is written down: the speaker's asides, false starts, laughs, requests to reread a sentence, comments on the temperature in the room, phone conversations, and other immediacies are all filtered out and ignored.) Attempting to represent in a written transcript the continuous spatial signs of gesture, posture, and movement is an additional challenge. Even the most detailed transcription systems capture only small portions of any behavior. At present, many transcription systems exist and researchers routinely adapt existing systems and create new conventions to best suit their needs.

The most commonly used transcription conventions, however, ignore the presence of texts in interactions. They do not include ways of representing that talk is being read out of a book, off a computer page, or from some visible sign. Nor do these systems provide ways of representing the writing participants do in a situation, even in such commonplace examples as teachers writing text on the board in the midst of a lecture or a class discussion, much less the "private" writing of notes during a lecture that are not made publicly available. More generally, these systems typically assume a single common **floor** dominated by a speaker and tend to ignore all activities of hearers (including writing), even co-existing conversations (e.g., two students talking to each other during a lecture).[4] These limitations have remained in spite of the fact that many conversation analysts have studied classrooms where such behaviors are routine.

---

[4]For an interesting exception, see Gutierrez, Rymes, and Larson (1995), who make a point of analyzing student interactions during teacher lecture or teacher-led discussion. They represent these parallel and interwoven floors through multiple columns.

Conversation Analytic Transcription. CA transcription uses many literary devices to represent recorded talk. Conversation analysts follow the practice of representing dialogue by breaking paragraphs with each change of speaker. They have often used **eye dialect** as one means of representing the sound of talk (e.g., "dje'eat yet?" in place of "did you eat yet?").[5] However, CA has also extended literary devices in several key ways to capture the details of talk as a temporal and multiparty act. In particular, CA transcripts routinely include pause times and a fuller record of talk (with its repetitions, false starts, laughter, sighs). Because of an interest in **turn-taking** as a sign of the on-going creation of social order, CA transcripts also have developed conventions to represent phenomena like **overtalk** (simultaneous talk). Since early CA systems were developed (see in particular Jefferson, 1989), various conventions have been used by analysts of talk. The following is an example of a set of transcription conventions that owe much to CA systems.[6]

Speaker A: I woke up=	*The equal signs indicated*
Speaker B: =in the morning?	*latching (no perceptible pause*
	across turns).
Speaker A: I thought // he was //	*Overtalk, simultaneous talk*
Speaker B: //No //	*of two or more speakers can*
	be signaled by double slashes.

---

[5]The problem with using eye dialect is that it is not a tool designed to produce accurate representation of sound. For example, consider the following excerpt from a transcript of Schegeloff (1996, p. 57):

> Bee: Eh-yih have anybuddy: thet uh:? (1.2) I would <u>k</u>now from the <u>E</u>nglish depar'mint there?
> Ava: <u>Mm-mh</u>. Tch! I don't think so.

This transcript displays the ad hoc and inconsistent nature of eye dialect. Why, for example, is the second syllable of anybody represented as "buddy" and the last syllable of department as "mint," while standard spelling is used for "would know" instead of something like "wood 'no"? Likewise, based on typical phonological processes it seems unlikely that Ava clearly enunciated the 't' in "don't think." Why not "don' think"? The problem of inconsistency is potentially intensified by the fact that eye dialect is a device typically used to represent a speaker as non-standard, often in ways that are socially marked for class, ethnicity, or region. There are systems of full phonetic transcription (e.g., that of the International Phonetics Association), which in this case might realize Bee's utterance as something like the following:

> Bee: ə ɹɪ hæv ɛnɪbʌdɪ ꞉ ðæt ə aɪ wʊd noʊ frʌm ðə ɪŋglɪʃ dɪpartʔmɪnt ðer

However, such systems have the drawback that they require readers to know the specialized alphabet and perhaps to understand certain phonetic processes.

[6]For a summary and analysis of transcription conventions used in research literature, drawing heavily on earlier CA conventions, see Dressler and Kreuz (2000).

Speaker A: I wasn't think-	*Hyphen at the end of a word can mark an abrupt self inter- ruption.*
Speaker A: So she says "Go ahead"	*Quotation marks can mark*
Speaker B: Yeah, "Go ahead and fail."	*represented speech or constructed dialogue.*

- Empty parentheses ( ) mark an unintelligible strip of talk. Parentheses enclosing a word or words (just forget it) mark an uncertain transcription.
- Square brackets [laughing] can be used to enclose an explanatory note. A square bracket with a number inside it [1.5] marks a pause in seconds.
- . . . . Material deleted from transcript.
- *Italics* Emphatic utterances or syllables.
- hhh Aspiration (like a sigh or laugh). Also within parentheses inside a word, it can indicate laughter: I (h)wouldn(h)'t.

Think Aloud Transcription. In order to capture more of what people are thinking about and doing as they write and read, some writing researchers have used think-aloud methods. These methods ask participants to say aloud anything that they are thinking, reading, and writing down (see chap. 7 for more details about this method of research). This research has led to the development of a number of useful conventions for representing literate practices in transcripts. The following are extracted from sample guidelines for preparing a written transcript of a recorded think-aloud protocol.

- Indicate **READING ALOUD** by placing all words in CAPS.
- Indicate the vocalizing of **what is being written** by <u>underlining</u> the words.
- Indicate if the writer is **REREADING HER OWN TEXT** by writing all words in <u>CAPS AND UNDERLINING</u>.
- Indicate if *PARAPHRASING WHILE READING ONE'S OWN TEXT* or *PARAPHRASING WHILE READING ANOTHER'S TEXT* by adding italics.
- Indicate the **deleting of written text** by using ~~strike-through~~.
- Indicate the "**drafting out of possible text but not writing it**" by using "quotations."

These conventions could extend the more established conversational transcription conventions so that transcriptions could represent on-line literate activity as well as talk. We use several of them below in looking at two students giving a speech in a classroom. However, in typical activity, participants might seldom vocalize their writing or reading. (At the same time, this convention could be used to represent writing as captured on video.)

Other Approaches to Transcription. Transcription systems are always theoretical (Ochs, 1979). Hengst (2001; Hengst & Miller, 1999) has developed a transcription system (see Fig. 8.1) designed to enact some of Goffman's key notions of interaction. Analyzing two children and an adult playing an imaginary game, Hengst and Prior (1998) worked to capture the way participants shift footings by speaking as others.[7] For example, they distinguished between talk in which the participants were talking normally as themselves (signaled by placement within curly brackets), in which they were talking as characters (signaled by regular font), and in which they were talking *sotto voce*, in a kind of conspiratorial whisper often used to propose or negotiate the game activity outside of the game frame (signaled by use of italics). Taking up Goffman's argument that face-to-face communication is continuous for speakers *and* hearers, Hengst's transcripts display all the participants co-present, whether talking or not.

Goffman (1981) also argued that it was critical to understand the nonverbal and material activity of participants (a point Hengst took up by noting key activities). For example, Goffman noted that everyday service encounters at stores can take place without any talk on the part of the customer especially. Likewise, a mechanic who says "Wrench" and is handed a wrench by an assistant does not need that assistant to offer any verbal answer. On the other hand, a nonverbal action, like reaching for a remote control to turn on a television, may prompt a verbal response, "No, I need quiet." These simple examples point to the need in many settings to incorporate **embodied practices**[8] as well as talk into transcripts in order to produce an intelligible record of an event.

---

[7]The animation of other voices appears in many transcripts as speakers attempt to project the talk of other people (real, imagined, stereotyped). Here again, typical transcription systems largely ignore this dimension of talk, yet imagine transcribing a comedy routine of Robin Williams without any way of displaying animated voices.

[8]By "embodied practices," we mean the movements of bodies through space and their alignments in relation to one another (**proxemics**, e.g. Hall, 1959) as well as bodily movements and gestures (**kinesics**, Birdwhistell, 1970). One concern among studies of embodied practices is how bodies are used to construct or "frame" social contexts. In this vein, Kendon (1990) noted the importance of the **F-formation (face formation)** in face-to-face interaction. An F-formation is described as arising "whenever two or more people sustain a spatial and orientational relationship in which the space between them is one to which they have equal, direct, and exclusive access" (p. 209). If you think about people at a party and the way there are shifting, flowing groupings over time, or about a large dinner table where a conversation splits into subconversations and then regroups, you can get a sense of how important such formations are. One of us (Leander, 2002) has traced the very dynamic flow of F-formations that appeared in a high school classroom during large group discussion.

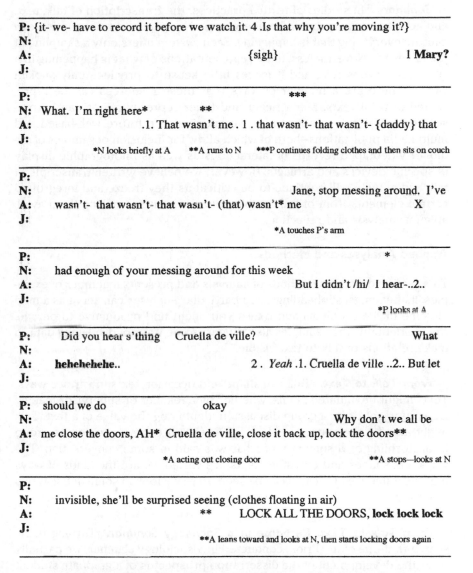

P: {it- we- have to record it before we watch it. 4 .Is that why you're moving it?}
N:
A: {sigh}   1 **Mary?**
J:

P: ***
N: What. I'm right here*   **
A: .1. That wasn't me . 1 . that wasn't- that wasn't- {daddy} that
J:

        *N looks briefly at A   **A runs to N   ***P continues folding clothes and then sits on couch

---

P:
N: Jane, stop messing around. I've
A: wasn't- that wasn't- that wasn't- (that) wasn't* me   X
J:

                                        *A touches P's arm

P: *
N: had enough of your messing around for this week
A: But I didn't /hi/ I hear-..2..
J:

                                                    *P looks at A

P: Did you hear s'thing   Cruella de ville?   What
N:
A: **hehehehehe..**   2 . *Yeah* .1. Cruella de ville ..2.. But let
J:

P: should we do   okay
N: Why don't we all be
A: me close the doors, AH* Cruella de ville, close it back up, lock the doors**
J:

        *A acting out closing door   **A stops—looks at N

P:
N: invisible, she'll be surprised seeing (clothes floating in air)
A: **   LOCK ALL THE DOORS, **lock lock lock**
J:

                    **A leans toward and looks at N, then starts locking doors again

---

FIG. 8.1. Playing with voices: Cindy Magic Episode.* Adapted from Hengst and Prior (1998). Standard print, bold print, italics, and brackets all indicated particular registers. Respectively, they represent speaking in main character (e.g., Anna as Jane), in secondary character (e.g., Anna as a cheetah), in a conspiratorial register, and as everyday self (e.g., Anna as Anna). This transcript has been simplified in several ways (e.g., proxemic boxes have been dropped).

Summary. In studies of textual practices, the transcription of talk, text, and activity can and should be interwoven. No system of transcription can capture everything that is happening. Each system offers only a sampling of the full event. Nevertheless, fuller representations of what is happening in a situation are possible, and it makes little sense to privilege only spoken words. There are a number of ways that these resources can be represented in print texts. Much richer and fuller representations can be presented in oral presentations and, we anticipate, in future web-based and multimedia publications—both of which allow for inclusion of samples of audio- or videotaped records of interactions as well as photographic display of specific devices and artifacts. However, we believe written transcripts of talk and activity will continue to be critical as they freeze and foreground certain elements from of the complex buzz of activity, making them available for analysis and reflection.

Applied Analyses and Methods

This section discusses methods of analysis and presents a number of examples. Its headings, subheadings, and particular analyses can serve as a map of some of the problems and issues you might find productive to pursue. Not incidentally, the examples also suggest some ways of displaying data to make relations of talk to text visible.

From Talk to Text. Talk can shape and occasion texts in various ways. Texts might be initiated in talk, whether by a teacher or supervisor making an assignment or by a group discussion identifying the value of a text. Talk might also be the source of ideas for a text, in cases as varied as group brainstorming or a summary of what was said in some conversation. The ways talk shapes and occasions texts are varied, as are the kinds of ways that the influence of the talk can be seen. Here we look in some detail at two examples.

From Talk to Text: Response in a Sociology Seminar. Turning to research that one of us (Prior) conducted in a sociology seminar, we partially track the development of the dissertation prospectus of a graduate student (Sean). In one seminar meeting, Sean presented a draft of his dissertation prospectus (in effect, a proposal that mapped out why and how he would do his dissertation research). Professor West and another professor (Lynch) attending the seminar that day were leading the research project that Sean intended to draw his data from, and both of them would sit on the committee charged with approving or disapproving the prospectus in a meeting the following week. Sean's proposal involved reviewing the literature, stating the hypotheses he would test, and detailing the methods. After two very intense hours of seminar talk focused especially on Sean's seven hypotheses and their rationales, only the first three of his hypotheses emerged intact. Hypotheses 4 and 5 had undergone major revisions, and 6 and 7 had been dropped. The changes in these hypotheses and their support illustrate the kind of relations that exist between talk and text.

In the seminar discussion, Sean first stated his key research question as the following: Why do adolescent girls (and women) suffer from greater depressed mood than adolescent boys (and men)? Sean wanted to argue that differences in depressed mood might come from gender-related differences in the contents of thought and forms of social interaction. Figure 8.2 presents the core of Sean's argument for Hypothesis 4, a series of **truncated**

Introducing the hypothesis

...hypothesis 4 is the most controversial one, um,

and it's based on some speculation about uh what happens when girls get together

and they engage in social support, expressive social support,

Sean's first premise on girl talk

and it-it's thought that-it's argued that, there's a lot of evidence that

girls ruminate more than boys do,

and that if they get together and engage in expressive social support,

then the content of that is going to be, it's going to be like vocal rumination,

it's going to be very negative,

Sean's second premise on depression

and then there's um also an interpersonal theory of depression

that says that when someone expresses negativity,

the other person is much more apt to deny its legitimacy,

which increases the seriousness of the person's negativity

Sean's narrative conclusion

and so, when you get two girls together engaging in expressive social support, uh

one is going to express some negative things, they're going to ruminate out loud,

the other one is likely to deny that, that those feelings are legitimate in some way,

and that could increase the negativity of that person, but...

FIG. 8.2. Episode 1. Sean explaining his hypothesis in the seminar.

narratives (see Eubanks, chap. 2, on narrative). (The text is boxed to high-light its structure. The talk was continuous.) He introduced the topic as "what happens when girls get together and engage in social support," a double-voiced construction, combining everyday discourse—*girls getting to-gether*—and disciplinary discourse—*engaging in social support*. He then pre-sented the first premise of his argument, his basic story of girl talk. He next offered the second premise, a *someone* story depicting the interpersonal theory of depression. Finally Sean made a narrative conclusion, drawn from the two narrative premises, laying out his combined tale of how girls' talk leads to girls' depression.

Sean's hypothetical tale of girl talk was immediately challenged by Thomas, who suggested that if girls get together and talk over their trou-bles, he would expect them to listen and be supportive. Later in the ses-sion, he more bluntly challenged Sean, asking: "Are you saying that that, uh, the ways that girls support each other is dysfunctional, the ways boys sup-port each other is more functional?" At that point, West (the principal in-vestigator and Sean's advisor) entered the conversation to say:

West: =it seems like the critical issue is what's happening in these inter-changes and if in fact it does generate kind of, you know, mutual gloom and //negativity//

Sean: //umhm//

West: you know, you tell me about your problems and that makes me more depressed, and I'll tell you about mine, and you'll get more depressed, and then I'll say "I'm depressed" and you'll say [laughing] "There's no reason to be you know." [8 seconds of West and others laughing; multi-ple voices]

With her decidedly non-technical term "mutual gloom," strengthened by the sing-song prosody of her "you tell me" and "I'll tell you" and finally cli-maxing in a **constructed dialogue** carried on laughter, West's ironic retell-ing of Sean's story was punctuated with 8 seconds of loud laughter and mul-tiple voices as the common conversational floor dissolved. West then concluded that Hypothesis 4 was "the most controversial" and the "least amenable to test in the kinds of data" the study had collected.

Later in the talk, West began to reformulate Hypothesis 4, suggesting that support is beneficial for boys *and* girls, but is somewhat *less* beneficial for girls because *some* girls are enacting Sean's story of mutually reinforc-ing rumination:

West: now maybe you (could) state this in a somewhat weaker form, and to just say that you would expect that the uh positive implications of so-cial support or uh (effect) would be weaker- would be less for girls than for boys because some girls may be engaging in these processes that you don't- you don't expect so much for boys

Sean: how do you- "the positive aspects of expressive support will be greater"

West: no /what you say is/=

Sean: /"will be less for"/

West: =is that- is that, you know, you're expecting (that) social support will have a negative effect on depressive affect, you could say that that negative effect would be stronger for boys than for girls

At this point, the focus of the talk shifted for the first time in the seminar response to **joint textual production** as Sean sought to capture West's precise wording. Sean started to ask how to state this hypothesis and then tried to verbalize it, prompting West to restate it. As she formulated for Sean what to say, West also shifted from the everyday use of "negative" as "bad" that Sean had employed in his draft hypothesis to a more technical, mathematical phrasing in which "negative" means "quantitatively lower"— which in the case of depression would be good. As can be seen in the final revision of Hypothesis 4 (Fig. 8.3, *Final*, lines 27–29), a somewhat elaborated version of West's reformulation became the final word in Sean's prospectus. After Sean had accepted West's reformulation of his hypotheses, however, another issue was raised that shaped the final hypothesis: how to conceptualize the relationship between another hypothesis (girls get *more* support) and Hypothesis 4 (expressive support is *less effective* for girls) so that the result (girls being *more* depressed) still obtained.

The talk of the seminar session bears a complex relation to Sean's final revision of his prospectus. Figure 8.3 provides a side-by-side display of relevant sections of the draft and final versions of Sean's dissertation prospectus. The bold-printed text, indicating areas of revision, shows that little remains of the draft text. The most obvious and direct effect seen in Figure 8.3 is the reversal of Hypothesis 4 (compare lines 1–3 with 27–29). Sean's original hypothesis suggested that expressive support was bad, increasing girls' depressive affect; the revised hypothesis suggests that it is good, decreasing their depressive affect, although this decrease is less than the decrease instrumental support provides for boys (the formulation West offered). The complex language about magnitudes in Hypothesis 5 (lines 30–34) reflects the puzzle over how to reconcile more support with less efficient support so that the result is still more depression. Specifically, the use of "negative" in a numerical sense (lines 27, 29, 31, and 33) and "stronger" (line 28) as well as the overall meaning and syntax echoes West's precise wording in the seminar talk, as seen earlier (". . . social support will have a negative effect on depressive affect . . . that would be stronger for boys than girls . . .").

In some cases, as in the two hypotheses that were dropped entirely, the effect of the talk can only be seen in the absence of text. In Sean's case, this absence is visible to us because the hypotheses appeared in an earlier draft and the participants explicitly decided to delete them as they talked

Draft: *[Hypotheses 4 and 5 from page 8 of Sean's draft prospectus, excerpted from a paragraph in which all seven were listed.]*

1 (4) Expressive social support will have negative implications
2 for depressed mood, especially among girls; among females,
3 these effects will be more pronounced among same-sex
4 dyads. (5) Instrumental support will have positive
5 implications for negative mood, especially for boys.

[Support for hypotheses 4 and 5 was found on pages 5 and 6 of the draft prospectus]

6 These relationships could explain gender differences in
7 the process by which adolescent depressed mood is
8 determined. Research suggests that females internalize their
9 problems and ruminate more than males, who engage in
10 distractions and externalizing behaviors (Nolen-Hoeksema,
11 1987; Conway et al., 1990; Patterson and McCubbin, 1987; and
12 see fn. #7 in preliminary). For females the affective quality of
13 expressive social support will be negative, reflecting this
14 rumination. Coyne's (1976) interpersonal theory of depression
15 further suggests that expressions of negative affect will tend
16 to be rebuffed, as not legitimate feelings. This denial
17 enhances negative mood.[1]

[footnote at the bottom of same page]

18 (1) Thus, ego (seeking support) expresses negative feelings.
19 Expressive social support becomes a forum for further
20 rumination. Yet alter, from whom support is elicited,
21 disconfirms ego's feelings. This denial leads to greater
22 negativity. This dynamic is most pronounced in a female
23 dyad engaged in expressive social support. In such cases,
24 alter not only negates ego's expressions, but imbues the
25 exchange with her own negativity as well.

[page break to page 6]

26

Final: *[Hypotheses 4 and 5 with accompanying support as presented on pages 4 to 6 in Sean's final prospectus.]*

27 4) The negative, causal relationship between instrumental
28 support and depressed mood for boys will be stronger than the
29 negative, causal relationship between expressive social support
30 and depressed mood for girls. (5) The difference between the
31 magnitude of the negative causal relationship between expressive
32 social support and depressed mood for boys and the magnitude of
33 the negative, causal relationship between instrumental social
34 support and depressed mood will be negligible.

[In Sean's final prospectus, support for hypotheses 4 and 5 was presented in two paragraphs immediately following the two hypotheses.]

35 These hypotheses acknowledge the often observed, negative
36 relationship between social support and depressed mood (e.g.,
37 Friedrich et al., 1988; Cohen et al., 1985; Dean and Ensel, 1983).
38 However, the salutary effect is greater for boys than girls.
39 Research suggests that females tend to be negative, reflecting this
40 rumination, internalize their problems and ruminate more than
41 males, who engage in distractions and externalizing behaviors
42 (Nolen-Hoeksema, 1987; Conway et al., 1990; Patterson and
43 McCubbin, 1987; and seen fn. #7 in preliminary). For females the
44 affective quality of expressive social support will sometimes be
45 negative, reflecting this rumination. While such rumination could
46 be beneficial, operating as a catharitic release, it could also
47 contribute to further rumination, which would detract from its
48 beneficial effect. The instrumental support received by boys
49 assists them in changing or reacting to their stressful
50 circumstances. Hypothesis 5 reflects the speculation that the less-
51 salient type of social support will have roughly the same effect
52 between the genders.

FIG. 8.3. Comparison of Hypotheses 4 and 5 in Sean's draft and final prospectus.

through the session. If there had been no draft, the absence might only be visible by comparing the text projected in talk with the subsequent written text. Other consequences of the talk were indirect and involved a complex mix of **deletions, additions, and changes**. With the revised Hypothesis 4, Sean's support for his argument has also changed. Coyne's interpersonal theory of depression, with its tale of denial, is gone (*Draft*, lines 14–17 and 19–26). Coyne (1976), a key source in the draft, is not even cited in the final. There are also additions. The first sentence (*Final*, lines 35–37), with its three new citations, highlights the beneficial effect of social support, a point West repeatedly stressed in the seminar discussion. Finally, there are revisions. The central issue of gender and depression, foregrounded in the first sentence of the draft support (lines 6–7), appears (in more specific, but weakened terms) in the second sentence of the final (line 38–39). These changes resulted from the seminar talk and were clearly linked to the content of that talk. However, none of these textual changes were explicitly discussed.

This example displays the complex pathways between talk and text. Sean sounded out key audiences about the specifics of his draft, and Sean's revision was jointly motivated, thought out, and partially drafted in talk. Yet Sean's text displays no explicit acknowledgment of the role of this seminar response, which only becomes apparent when we can see the relations between the draft, the seminar talk, and the revision.

From Talk to Text: The Huck Finn Discussion. Our second example comes from a longitudinal study one of us (Leander) conducted in a secondary school. In this event drawn from the research, students in a secondary English classroom were to write an essay on whether or not Mark Twain's novel *Huckleberry Finn* should be banned from the school district. The essay was to be written as a letter to the school board, was to state a clear thesis and develop an argument, and was to use specific examples from the novel and related readings. The essay writing followed extensive classroom discussions on the text; one class discussion in particular was devoted to the essay topic. In this case, unlike Sean's case, the students had not yet drafted their texts.

Tony, an African American student, wrote an essay that begins as follows:

> Dear Unit 4 school board members, By your request I'm writing this letter about why you shouldn't ban the book The adventures of Huck Finn. I feel that the book shouldn't be banned but not be required for some students to read it if they don't want to read the book.
>
> Some people say and feel that this book is a good book since it tells of a black man in slavery days and shows how life was for black people. Some also feel that the book is educational, i disagree with this because the book doesn't

stand out to me as being a good book except that they use the word nigger over 200 times an that is ridiculous. Class mates of mine and that i know who have read this book fall out like 50/50 on this situation some feel that the book itself isn't racist but there is no need to have the word nigger in there almost 200 times. Others feel that to take the word nigger out would almost change history. But I don't agree with that statement because slaves didn't have to be called nigger and even still that wont mean we will forget all the deaths of many blacks just because one word is taken out.

Comments from the teacher included: "your ideas are not well organized . . . you jump from idea to idea without really explaining what you mean." While Tony was graded as a marginal writer (earning 48/75 points), he was centrally engaged as a speaker in the classroom discussion of this issue. Tony made more utterances (20) than any other participant, some of them quite extensive, and had the topics he introduced taken up by others. How do we make sense of this apparent disconnect between Tony's speaking and writing? Or, should we frame the problem as one of the complex relationships between Tony's speaking and writing?

In fact, we will illustrate how the classroom discussion prior to Tony's essay writing was far more than simply interesting "background" to his text. Instead, the classroom discussion and his essay writing were related in at least two key ways. First, in the discussion, classroom participants produced arguments that Tony borrowed from in his essay (intertextual relations). Second, Tony's written argument was at least partially pre-structured by the lines of argument and counterargument that were produced within that classroom talk. Through tracing intertextual relations and the pre-structuring of Tony's argument, it appears to be more accurate to think of Tony's "writing" as beginning during the discussion, and not when Tony inscribed (or to a certain extent, "transcribed") words onto a page.

The first part of Tony's second paragraph can be summarized as deploying, coordinating, and critiquing the following arguments, numbered for the analysis of a discussion excerpt that follows:

Argument #1: *Huck Finn* has historical value;

Argument #2: *Huck Finn* has moral and educational value; and

Argument #3: *Huck Finn* is a bad/racist book for its use of derogatory language.

We can make the structuring of Tony's argument more available for comparison with the classroom discourse by parsing the text into responsive utterances. (The numbers after each utterance refer to the three arguments identified earlier.)

- Some people say and feel that this book is a good book (#2)
- since it tells of a black man in slavery days and shows how life was for black people (#1).
- Some also feel that the book is educational (#2),
- i disagree with this because the book doesn't stand out to me as being a good book (#2)
- except that they use the word nigger over 200 times (#3) an that is ridiculous

A brief examination of the classroom discussion illustrates how the foregoing arguments are pre-"written" and coordinated in talk. At one critical point, Tony argues that the book is not morally educational (opposed to #2), claiming that Huck Finn fails to give any "guidance or knowledge of some sort." Shortly afterward, Marie (another student) makes a claim for the text's historical (#1) and educational (#2) value, which Maureen (the teacher) relates to Tony's earlier argument, positing Marie's contribution as the text's "moral lesson" (#2).

Marie: I don't think we should ban it because, in the book it deals with racism, like, in a really harsh way and how some of us might have to deal with it later on? And it shows a way for him to overcome like Huck overcomes his racism throughout the book and he *helps* Jim and I think that helps us see that we need to overcome ours and that we *can* be equal and be (united).

Maureen: So is that an answer to Tony's question—what's the point of the book? like, so maybe the moral lesson it's trying //to teach is//

Tony: //It uses the// word nigger over 200 times

Just as Maureen raises the possibility of the text offering a moral lesson (#2), Tony responds with an argument about language (#3). His point about language (#3) challenges the moral value argument (#2) and is counterposed to the history argument (#1). The specific structuring of Tony's text as argument and counterargument is at least partially developed through the specific dialogues of the classroom; Tony was not creating imaginary rhetorical concessions to some imagined audience, but was, in effect, reanimating the classroom discussion even as he wrote his text.

While Tony drew on the discussion intertextually and displayed his positionings relative to others in the class, his written text was not simply a replay of the classroom talk. In fact, his general conclusions conflict with arguments he made in talk and at other points in his text. For example, Tony claimed that *Huckleberry Finn* was "trash" in the classroom discussion, while the opening paragraph of his essay argues that the book "shouldn't be banned, but not be required for some students to read it." Moreover, Tony's final written conclusion conflicts with both of these positions:

> I feel that this is not a recommended book for younger kids or even older ones but should be discussed just so that many know that many people are twisted mentally and should be watched and can make anything a book.

We might read the possible contradictions as evidence that Tony simply did not know how to support his thesis. However, the evidence within the text indicates otherwise. Through a chain of topic-associated reasoning that drew upon the discussion, Tony clearly argued in the body of his essay that *Huckleberry Finn* was a racist text and had little moral or educational value. Alternatively, we might consider how Tony's written text had different audiences from those of the classroom discussion. Tony's writing is not only dialogically drawing on the class discussions, but also anticipating future discussions and audiences, including that imagined school board and certainly Maureen, as his teacher, acting now in the capacity of grading his writing. In this sense, Tony's written text accumulates and attempts to coordinate audiences and positions that extend well beyond those of the classroom discussion. Since Maureen (and perhaps even the school board) selected this text for him to read, the position that *Huckleberry Finn* is "trash" may not be as readily available within the essay. In these contexts, a reasonable strategy might be to take strong issue with the text (as Tony does in the body of his essay), but also to support its reading for limited audiences who choose to read it (as Tony generally argues in his introduction and conclusion).

This example displays the ways a text may be jointly, even if unintentionally, "drafted" in talk and how textual relations may index face-to-face interactions and relations. Unlike Sean's text, Tony's explicitly (if not precisely) points to the conversations that stood behind it (e.g., "Some say . . ."). It certainly points to the limits of any notion of audience as an element that only comes into play *after* a text is produced. In this case, the audience co-authored key elements of the text in talk: Their contributions to the discussion, along with Tony's immediate responses, are re-played and transformed in the text. Thus, the audience's responses preceded the text more powerfully than they followed it. The example also displays how, in analyzing a piece of writing, highly diverse audiences accumulate, becoming laminated and even hybridized with one another. Tracing the co-presence of ongoing dialogues—with past, present, and imagined audiences—can build important evidence about the work a particular text is attempting to do, and also about the real rhetorical complexities writers must sometimes navigate.

From Text to Talk. Text can shape and occasion talk in various ways. When people speak from notes or actually read a text aloud, the relationship is clear, even if the words spoken don't exactly reflect the text written. In other cases, however, the influence of text may be more subtle, as when a speaker draws on some written text—in genre, organization, or specific wording—as she talks. In other cases, a text may structure the order of talk, as written court procedures order the organization of courtroom events or a lesson plan guides a teacher in a classroom. Ong's (1982) notion of secondary orality encompasses all of these kinds of influences of written texts on spoken language. The ways texts shape and occasion talk are varied, as are the ways that the influence of the text can be seen. Here we look in some detail at one example.

Text to Talk in a High School Classroom Presentation. A common form of writing-to-speak activity in public school classrooms is the "oral presentation." In the following, we consider an oral presentation that involved response to Upton Sinclair's novel *The Jungle* by two students in a secondary English class. Students (and teachers) construct the task of oral presentation in diverse ways, which involve varying uses of print texts (e.g., notecards, scripts) and graphic texts (e.g., posters, scenery backdrops). For Marie and her partner Catherine, oral presentation was closely knit to the activities of writing and group reading.

In Figure 8.4, we have represented part of a whiteboard that Marie and Catherine stood in front of during their *Jungle* presentation. The white board was divided up into eight boxes, each of which were labeled with a character name (e.g., Jurgis, Dede Antanas, etc.) and contained textual information about that character. In the margin around these eight boxes, as well as within them, additional notes were added after the main text was complete with a green marker (bolded in Fig. 8.4), with arrows pointing to the referents of the notes.

The following transcript segment represents Marie's introduction and first segment of the presentation. It has been transcribed following the conventions we presented earlier for think-aloud transcription.

This is Jurgis' family. And this is just showing you, like, the characters, and in the green is, how they are related to Jurgis, or, what they are in the family. And, this is all their jobs they've had. Um [sigh], the first job JURGIS has is he GETS HIRED TO SHOVEL GUTS AT BROWNS FOR 171/2 CENTS AN HOUR. And then, he WORKS AT—and that's when, um, he shovels guts into this trap door, and they take the guts later and make them into meat, or something. And then, he WORKS AT DURHAM'S FERTILIZER PLANT and he SHOVELS FERTIL-IZER INTO CARTS WHEN IT COMES FROM THE GRINDING MILL. And them, um, after he gets out of jail he goes to, um, the JONES and he *GETS HIRED TO PUSH* A TRUCK BUT he NEVER GETS TO WORK BECAUSE HE IS BLACKLISTED and the boss finds out that he beat up on his boss. And then he <u>GETS A JOB AT A STEEL MILL MAKING STEEL RAILS FOR RAILROADS</u>. And then he <u>JOINS A HARVEST CREW WHERE THEY MAKE COMBINES TO HARVEST WHEAT</u>. And then, um, the grandfather <u>ANTANAS</u>, he is <u>JURGIS' FATHER</u>, and he <u>TAKES</u> a <u>JOB FOR 1/3 JURGIS' WAGES, HANDLING UNCLEAN MEAT</u> and standing in the pickle juice.

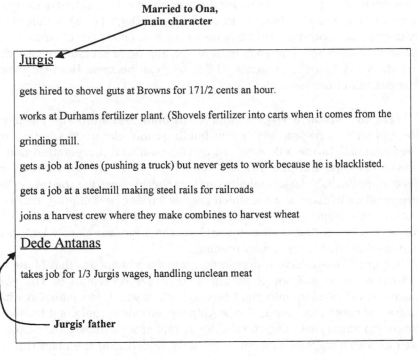

FIG. 8.4. An extract from Marie and Catherine's whiteboard text.

What is Marie doing when she is giving an oral presentation, and what does writing have to do with it? A number of issues are highlighted by the transcript, while the transcript also glosses a number of problems. First of all, although in some sense Marie is reading her "own" script, the text has been produced, ahead of time, by Marie and Catherine working together, and is a summary of information garnered from the novel, study guides, group discussion, and other possible participants. Thus, a more complete picture of what Marie is doing and how she is orienting to this text and event may include a tracing of such intertextual processes (see Bazerman, chap. 4, Prior, chap. 7, and Kamberelis and de la Luna, chap. 9). Here we are directing our attention not to the history of the text but to this particular social-interactional scene. Unlike reading from a paper that one is writing (upon which the earlier transcript conventions are based), Marie is reading from white board, where text is prominently displayed for the class. Marie's reading does not communicate something out of view or hidden to other participants, as reading a paper may. Rather, the text is prominently displayed for others' readings. Thus, Marie may be considered to be engaged as a "reading leader" for the class's (silent) reading.

Interpreting Marie's presentation as an activity of reading-in-common is also supported by the form and content of Marie's speech. Although some "juicy" facts are added (e.g., Jurgis shoveling guts through a trap door), Marie's verbal text stays very close to the white board text. Aside from the introduction, spoken additions to the written text were typically added as modifications or expansions, and followed, grammatically, the main (written) ideas that they modify. Thus, Marie matches the gerund phrase "HANDLING UNCLEAN MEAT" in her expansion, "and standing in the pickle juice." The transcript also shows only one clear instance where Marie paraphrases as she reads, transforming "gets a job at Jones (pushing a truck)" into "gets hired to push a truck." The other possible paraphrase is when Marie introduces Antanas as "the grandfather," which might be a paraphrase of the written text she reads that identifies Antanas as Jurgis' father.

In addition to asking what type of task Marie and Catherine are constructing out of the oral presentation, we might consider how the talk of their presentation is organized through their writing. The script that Marie and Catherine have prepared does not simply give them content for their speaking; rather, it structures a particular form of speaking. This structuring is particularly evident in the repeated transitions of the form "And then, he . . ." Whereas the written list displays its list-like quality by beginning a new line for each idea within the boxes, and by separating characters in diagrammed boxes, Marie needs to accomplish, orally, some other means of marking shifts in ideas while also making the ideas cohere to a central character. She elects to mark these ideas temporally with prepositions (chiefly "then"). Although her talk is strongly organized by the text, in her talk Marie improvises an enhanced coherence to the flow of information that moves beyond that produced in the white board text, with its late additions and arrows marked in green. In particular, note how Marie seamlessly weaves in the (green) text that was added late in her writing process, and is spatially outside of the flow of her print text, with "And then, um, the grandfather ANTANAS, he is JURGIS' FATHER."

Finally, what the oral presentation is doing in this instance is made more evident in how the presentation is brought to a close. After Marie presents the first half of the whiteboard and Catherine the second half, Marie adds one comment to expand Catherine's description of a particular character. Then Marie looks out at the audience:

Marie: Any questions?

Students: [few seconds of silence]

Teacher: Good.

We might analyze this interaction as an instantiation of the genre of asking for questions and not receiving response, something repeated often in classrooms, complete with a teacher's evaluation ("good"). Yet, we might also argue that the lack of questions is related to the organization of the presentation as a text on the whiteboard, and the manner in which that text was followed by Marie and Catherine: Questions are structured as being outside of the event. Once the character chart on the whiteboard has been completely accounted for, further modification of it would be reaching well beyond the bounds of the event as a form of guided reading. Additionally, the content information within the character boxes on the board does not seem oriented to raising questions, but to fact-finding. In sum, this example displays some of the ways that text may script and structure talk. It also suggests that folk descriptions of literacy events (e.g., "oral presentation, classroom discussion, and writing response group") may be misleading when we inquire into how such events structure and are structured by texts.

   Interaction of Text, Talk, and Activity in Face-to-Face Communication. In the foregoing analyses, we have primarily traced writing and speaking as unidirectional processes, considering how one form of activity shapes the other. We have also focused on situations where the text (or talk) was an end in itself. However, we have not yet considered the ways that writing, speaking, and embodied activity co-evolve and interact in a specific strip of interaction. Nor have we looked at instances where writing serves an instrumental function in support of some other ends. Such multi-modal relations are critical for understanding how writing operates in human activity, how written texts are used, and how they come to point to certain meanings rather than others.

   In this section, we focus our attention upon data gathered from studying a group of individuals involved in a school-based construction project. Through this data we illustrate, first of all, how writing may be used as a resource in task definition, planning, and coordinating perspectives. The example illustrates ways writing serves cognition, helping to move a thinking process forward. Cognition is realized here as a social act, distributed among the individuals present, their communication processes, the various texts they are producing, and other available tools and processes. Secondly, this example illustrates how written texts may be connected to other semiotic resources in the flow of activity. The example makes clear that interpreting how writing comes to mean one thing rather than another, in activity, involves tracing the articulation of written texts with other present "texts," including gestures, speech, and even silence. Finally, this analysis illustrates the continuing challenge of integrating representations of talk, text, gesture, and action.

Designing the Beam. One of us (Leander) followed a group of high school students and their teachers as they worked to build a replica of Thoreau's cabin. This project was set in an innovative program—in a school within a school—that strove to integrate the curriculum and also to develop valuable workplace skills (see Leander, 2003). Here we consider some data from a videotape of a teacher ("Sid"), a school social worker ("Steve"), and two students ("Elizabeth" and "Trisha"), who were working on the cabin-building project. In this episode, the group is planning to construct a supporting top beam for the cabin. During the discussion, Steve holds a long wooden board, upon which he sketches diagrams. Steve draws the diagrams sequentially across the board, as separate pieces of text from left to right. These texts—the written diagrams—form the basis of our discussion. That these diagrams are inscribed on a piece of wood suggests the close relations between written texts, material objects, and talk, which is further illustrated in our later discussion. Moreover, the presence of the drawings on the wooden board suggests the importance of using different media for data collection during research. We need to have ways to capture writing that does not occur on paper but on surfaces that are not easily transported, borrowed, and photocopied. Examples might range from instant messaging systems on computers to writing on chalkboards, on the ground, on buildings and other surfaces (as with graffiti), on paper napkins, on the body, on stone monuments, on glass, on beaches or in the dirt, on sidewalks, and so on. Such writing can become as fleeting as unrecorded talk. **Videotaping** is one option, but it very often does not record high quality images of texts (as a still photograph might). On the other hand, **photography** might capture finished writing, but cannot capture the processes of inscription. In the present case, the diagrams were recorded as **fieldnotes**, which were then copied, electronically, as the diagrams embedded below. We also present a still image taken from a videotape to capture the intersection of gesture and drawn text.

Contexts of This Transcript. Before considering some of the details of the interaction, we should provide some context on the construction process. Essentially, two different designs for constructing the beam were being presented in this segment: an alternating design, involving four pieces of 2 × 4 of alternating lengths, positioned so as to overlap one another (Fig. 8.7, top) and a parallel design, involving six pieces of 2 × 4 of relatively equal length, stacked atop one another in two rows (Fig. 8.7, bottom). In both designs, the 2×4 boards are layered on either side of a $1/2''$ thick board, which the group refers to as the "sandwich" piece. At times, the parallel and the alternating designs are simultaneously in play in the transcript, and are worked out in the different conversational footings between Sid and Elizabeth on the one hand and Sid and Steve on the other.

Task Definition, Planning, and Coordinating Perspectives. A folk theory of creating and working from a written plan might suggest a kind of stage model, in which individuals move from defining a task to planning their activity, and finally to carrying it out. A folk theory might also assume that a written plan points clearly to particular objects or activities in the world. Yet, anyone who has attempted to follow a written plan—whether it be a road map, a recipe, or directions for operating a computer—realizes that the relations of a written text to activity, objects, and other texts is not nearly so linear and transparent. Planning, defining, and carrying out tasks are often tightly interwoven with writing; understanding writing as situated activity pushes us to consider how moments where people actually inscribe texts are surrounded by a range of activities rarely described as "writing." Such relations are made all the more complex when we consider how planning evolves among individuals working as a group, coordinating their multiple footings and perspectives. Figure 8.5 presents a brief segment of the participants' planning. The central column represents talk and includes letters that refer to the far-right column, where certain gestures, writing, and other activity are described. The far-left column lists figures that present graphics of texts/drawings or photographs of gestures relevant to the talk and activity in the other two columns.

In this sequence, Steve frames the task initially as manufacturing the beam so that its seams align with the supporting posts (line 1). The placement of the beam on two supporting posts is illustrated in Diagram 2 (Fig. 8.6). In response to Steve, Sid (lines 2–4) begins to calculate measurements to rest the seams on the posts, developing a parallel design and suggesting that the "sandwich" piece of wood might overlap the three 2×4 sections (line 4). Note that the design of the beam is only partially suggested in Diagram 2—neither the separate segments of 2×4 pieces nor the $1/2''$ "sandwich" board are represented. Rather, a joint understanding of the parallel design is constructed between Sid and Elizabeth (lines 2–10) through multiple semiotic resources, as discussed below.

The interaction between Sid and Elizabeth seems to be played out on a different conversational footing than that of Sid and Steve, or the footing of Steve's silent interaction following it. Although the transcript displays verbal participation and turn-taking, this information is not sufficient evidence for interpreting the multiple footings at play. Orientations toward different written texts are one key resource in interpreting different footings at hand:

Graphic Text	Speaking	Gesture, Writing, and Other Activity
Diagram 2 (Fig. 8.6)	1. Steve: But the se-the seam would actually not be right over that post, [a.] but would in that opening a little bit. 2. Sid: Hm:. (. .) So--for that end we need—this is, when we're going to build it we're going to have the seams over, so, we need two, 3 foot 2 by 4's [b.], and a sandwich 3. Elizabeth: Uh-huh. 4. Sid: But the sandwich needs to be longer [c.], and over here [d.]--two 3 foot 2 by 4's. And then here [e.], three--two, three—what's that, four and a half? [f.]	a. Pointing with pencil to space above post in drawing, indicated by dashed line. b. Indicating span with index finger and thumb of left hand. Span is far left top section of drawing. c.Waves right hand parallel to board. d. Moves finger span to top right section of drawing. e. Moves finger span to middle top of drawing. f. Points with finger to written numbers below drawing.
Diagram 2 Diagram 3 (Fig. 8.7)	5. Steve: Yeah. [g.] [6. Elizabeth: Two of em? 7. Sid: Yeah, cause they'll be on either side. [h.] And then, a long piece of this sandwich will need to go, so that its seams are (. .) [ɪ.] either there and there? [j.] Which would probably make more sense so why don't we do that. 8. Elizabeth. M-hm.	g. Beginning to draw diagram 3 (Fig. 8.7) h. Presses palms of hands together in sandwich shape. i. Shows span in middle of top beam with finger and thumb, Photo 1. (Fig. 8.8) j. Moves finger span to left top and next to right top of drawing.
Diagram 2	9. Sid: So exactly there [k.] and there. [l.] 10. Elizabeth: Okay. (. . .)	k. Moves finger span to left top of diagram. l. Shifts finger span to right top, then back to left top. m. Waving pencil tip above diagram 3a (top sketch in diagram 3).
Diagram 3a Diagram 3b Diagram 3a	11. Steve: Now, I wonder, Sid, that whether we're [m.] 12. Sid: Or, just make a long one? [n.]= 13. Steve: Wonder if we're better off, just, instead of, having that many seams [o.], just [p.]= 14. Sid: Cause we have, we have six foot four inch two by fours already cut [q.]= 15. Steve: Yeah.	n. Waves finger above diagram 3a. o. Spans entire diagram 3b with finger and thumb. p. Moves pencil point up and down diag. 3b. q. Pointing toward diagram 3a.

FIG. 8.5. Segment 1: Designing the Beam.

Steve is quietly drawing Diagram 3 (Fig. 8.7) during several lines of Sid and Elizabeth's discussion (approximately lines 6–10). The talk and gestures of Sid and Elizabeth indicate that their interaction is focused around Diagram 2. Yet, Diagrams 2 and 3 bear an important relation to one another; the parallel design of Diagram 3b (bottom) is largely a selection and reduction of information from Diagram 2 (discussed following). Thus, like the transcribed talk, the diagrams raise a number of questions about the developing footings among Steve, Sid, and Elizabeth. Is Steve an overhearer to Sid and Elizabeth's conversation, merely catching bits of it along the way as he

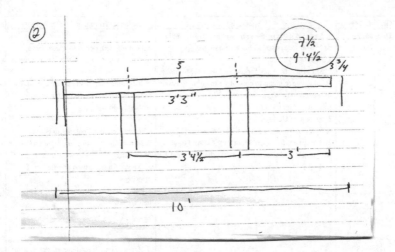

FIG. 8.6. Diagram 2.

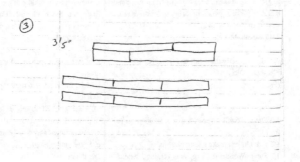

FIG. 8.7. Diagram 3.

works toward his own purposes in drawing? Or, is he more of an active eavesdropper, laminating his own drawing activity with their interaction, gathering as much verbal information as he can in order to summarize it and expand upon it?

Even while this transcript displays a series of drawings in relation to emergent talk, drawing and writing processes are not transcribed here, as in the thinking-aloud conventions. Thus, here we see (at letter g in Fig. 8.5) where Steve begins drawing, but we don't see the precise relation of his drawing to the talk or even when the drawing is completed. This absence is related to both data collection and transcription procedures. Because Sid and Elizabeth were talking, the researcher (Leander) focused on their activity at the time, rather than upon Steve's silent drawing, missing his writing processes. Moreover, in terms of transcription, the conventions that have been developed for think-aloud protocols have no way to represent the online emergence of a drawing. By not recording and transcribing the temporal emergence of Steve's drawing, we risk treating it as a fully formed object which the talk simply "references"—outside of the time and space of the evolving footings and meanings of the interaction.

As noted earlier, Diagrams 2 and 3 bear an important relation to one another. This relationship raises questions about conversational footings, but is also suggestive of how texts are used to define and redefine tasks in activity. Diagram 2 (Fig. 8.6) and the associated discussion (lines 1–10) focuses on placing the seams of the top beam directly over supporting posts. However, this problem is no longer represented in Diagram 3 (Fig. 8.7) and associated discussion (lines 11–15). In fact, the supporting posts are eliminated from Diagram 3 altogether. Treating the supporting posts as extraneous information helps to focus the planning around a new task in the emergent activity. Diagram 3 redefines the task as reducing the total number of seams in the beam, accomplished by replacing the parallel design with the alternating design (also, line 13). Across the interaction, task redefinition is supported by selecting, deselecting, and expanding particular texts in the stream of ongoing talk.

Relating Writing to Other Semiotic Resources in the Flow of Activity

No researcher can ever capture all of the forms of evident or potential communication in an interaction. (A slight breeze, a twitch, or a quick glance may all be highly meaningful.) At the same time, we must examine writing in relation to other salient semiotic resources; failing to do so risks overstating or otherwise misunderstanding what writing does. Many instances of the multi-modal nature of activity involving writing are illustrated in this episode. For instance, although Sid and Elizabeth's planning refers to the same written text (Diagram 2, Fig. 8.6), they strongly rely upon talk and gesture to make this text a "common" text and hence to develop a joint understanding. A striking instance of the simultaneous multi-modality of interaction occurs in line 7 when Sid pauses for two seconds after saying "so that its seams are," and then, so to speak, finishes his sentence with a gesture (seen in Fig. 8.8). And his gesture, which indicates a span in the middle of the top beam (a three-piece plan for cutting the "sandwich" piece) is dependent upon Diagram 2 (Fig. 8.6) as a referent. We have provided a photo (Fig. 8.8) of the hand gesture, as this significant "text" in the interaction is entirely absent in the talk. Thus, speaking (and silence), gesturing and the text work together in Sid's meaning-making; it is impossible to interpret meaning from any one of these modalities alone. The relations developing among different modalities of interaction are also richly evident in lines 11–15. Note how Steve and Sid's talk appears telegraphic, intertwined with

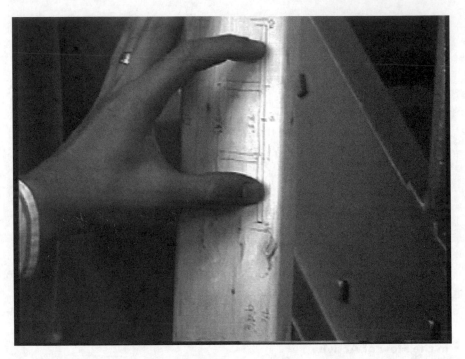

FIG. 8.8. Photo 1.

text (Diagram 3) and also with gesture (e.g., Steve in line 13: "Wonder if we're better off, just, instead of, having that many seams [o.], just [p.]").

Not only do people relate talk, writing, and gesture in interaction, they also work through lived space to produce relationships among these semiotic resources. Although diagrams in academic papers—with arrows, geometric shapes, and charts—might suggest two-dimensional relations among texts and textualizing processes, this example illustrates how diverse texts are arrayed, produced, and "entered into" across three-dimensional space. Sid's hand gestures, variants of which are repeated (e.g., lines 2, 4, 7, 9, letters b, d, e, f) latch onto the drawing, producing a combined sign, spatially overlaying his gesture with the written signs of the drawing. The "text" itself is produced as a composite of hand, writing surface, and graphic marks (accompanied by talk). The timing and precise location of these different signs is critical for interpreting them as a unified text. Another striking example of spatial relations occurred later within the interaction (not represented here) during a moment in which Trisha actually takes a wooden board (the same type of wood planned for the "sandwich" piece) and physically places it over Diagram 2, parallel to the lines that represent the sandwich piece. In other words, she aligns the material board in spatial relation to the sketched boards in order to construct and confirm her understanding of the plan. "Acting into" the space of the text, and producing spatial alignments among texts, bodies, and objects, is an important process to consider in the joint production of meaning, a process that has also been noted in some analyses of the use of diagrams by scientists (Ochs, Jacoby, & Gonzales, 1994; Suchman & Trigg, 1993). Among other issues, such analysis illustrates how the materiality of written texts is an important means by which they become spatially and symbolically connected to other texts and to bodies in activity.

We recognize that it is difficult to follow such detailed analysis across the multiple representations we have presented—the three columns of Figure 8.5, the multiple representations of the drawings in Figures 8.6 and 8.7, the photograph in Figure 8.8, and our own written descriptions of what was happening. Multimedia representation (on Web pages or on CD or DVD disks) could allow for a more integrated image of the activity. However, such technologies will not solve the challenges of analysis. Without a written representation that freezes the action and foregrounds particular elements, making it available for analysis, it would be difficult to catch what is happening so quickly. In any case, this example should make clear both the potential value of, and the significant challenges facing, a fuller semiotic representation of situated literate activity.

CONCLUSION

In this chapter, we have illustrated three ways that relations between talk and text might be explored. First, we looked at cases where talk shapes texts. The sociology seminar's response to Sean's text is perhaps the most familiar. Here we see oral response to a draft text, response that is subsequently visible in the revised version of the text. For over twenty years, writing researchers have been looking at these kinds of relations in studies of the ways teachers, tutors, and peers orally respond to writing in schools and, more recently, in looking at ways that supervisors, colleagues, clients, and customers respond in workplaces. In contrast, the way Tony drew on a class discussion as he structured a paper is less familiar. In this case, Tony had not yet written a text. Here the discussion in class was clearly intended to serve the purpose it did—to prepare students for the writing; however, the specific ways that Tony drew on his and others' contributions to structure his argument, and the close association between specific oral utterances and later written text, were not planned by the teacher and were difficult to trace. Moreover, this analysis points to the possibility that any conversation can be recruited into some later text (e.g., as when we later decide to narrate an event we experienced). For researchers interested in tracing relations between talk and text, that possibility presents real challenges. The second type of relation, the way texts script talk, is certainly a recognized phenomenon; however, it has been little studied and, as we note, conventional transcription systems do not provide ways to distinguish among utterances that are being read, paraphrased as read, and spoken extemporaneously. The third type of relation we illustrated is more complex because it asks us to capture the literate acts (the writing and perhaps reading) that participants engage in during activity. Here again, we have suggested some resources to pursue this emerging area of research.

To study any of these kinds of relations between talk, text, and other semiotic modes requires the capture of a rich record of interaction. It also requires the use of a system of transcription that makes visible and represents the talk and activity. These requirements carry writing researchers into areas that have developed significantly over the last several decades, that face continuing challenges, but also that ultimately promise exciting new insights into literate practices and their complex roles in our lives.

ACTIVITIES

In this section, we present several activities that you might engage in to begin exploring the methodologies or to extend them into other areas:

1. Record a conversation among three or more participants and transcribe it, using two different systems of transcription. Consider what each system makes visible and what it tends to hide.

2. Videotape people who are collaborating on writing a document. Transcribe their talk, writing, and activity using some conventions suggested in this chapter.

3. Make at least one audio or video recording of naturally occurring interaction that involves participants writing (as in #2). Write an extended reflection on your data recording practices. Consider, among other issues, the nature of your involvement in the situation, the selection and placement of recording devices, the quality of the recording, the perspective of the recording, and how your data collection shifted with the evolving activity.

4. Record a speech that is memorized or based on notes and compare the written version to the spoken. How would you represent differences in a transcript?

5. Select a transcript of naturally occurring talk from this chapter or elsewhere and prepare a dramatic reenactment of the text with a small group of others. In class, discuss how the dramatic interpretation of the text draws upon the transcript and how it moves well beyond the written transcript.

You might compare different interpretations of the same transcript in order to explore the interpretive range of the text.

6. Studies of interaction and gender have tended to find that males talk more than females in settings like classrooms and institutional meetings. One obvious way to measure such dominance is **total number of words**. Conversation analysis (CA), with its focus on turn taking, suggests several other ways of measuring conversational dominance. In classrooms, with multiple participants, **number of turns** might be an important measure. (This measure would work less well in a dyadic conversation.) And, of course, **words per turn** might provide another view. Yet, these measures might not tell the whole story. For example, think of a teacher in a classroom, a Senator in a committee meeting, or a CEO meeting with employees. In these cases, the person in power may say little but run the show. CA has noted the importance of who get to nominate the next speaker (e.g., "George" or "George, can you comment on this?") and who gets to nominate topics (e.g., "What about the server?" or "I think we need a dedicated server."). Actually, of course, a nomination of speaker or topic might be taken up (ratified) or not. Thus, another dimension of talk to analyze would include measure of **next speaker nomination, ratified vs. unratified nominations, topic nominations**, and **ratified vs. non ratified topic nominations ratified**. (Because of their interactive structure, electronic chat spaces may also be analyzed in these terms.) Take a conversational transcript and use each of the measures above to analyze conversational dominance. Consider where the measures converge and where they diverge.

FOR FURTHER READING

There are several excellent collections that serve to introduce readers to a range of approaches to analyzing discourse. *The Discourse Reader*, edited by Jaworski and Coupland (1999), offers a collection of original writings from scholars representing a number of different traditions in discourse analysis, including speech act theory, conversation analysis, narrative analysis, and critical discourse analysis. Through its collection of 34 original texts, the reader provides a substantive introduction to ongoing methodological problems (e.g., transcription, context, intertextuality) and theoretical issues (e.g., social structure, identity, power relations) in discourse studies. Another valuable edited collection that purposes to bring together various traditions of discourse study (e.g., rhetoric, narrative, genre analysis, and cognitive analysis) into an accessible introduction is Teun van Dijk's two volume *Discourse Studies: A Multidisciplinary Introduction*. Yrjö Engeström and David Middleton's collection, *Cognition and Communication at Work*, documents how communication is deeply situated in workplace practices and material settings, considering spoken, written, embodied, and visual texts in airline terminals, hospital corridors, courtrooms, and other locales. Chapters by Charles Goodwin and Marjorie Goodwin and Christian Heath link still images to transcripts of talk to capture material and nonverbal contexts and actions as well as to capture ways that participants interact with media (television screens displaying remote activity, telephones, computer terminals). Transcripts may represent computer keystrokes, computer screens, face-to-face talk, and telephone or radio communication all together. Alessandro Duranti and Charles Goodwin, in their edited collection *Rethinking Context* (1992), bring together analysts from diverse traditions who are interested in understanding the ways talk and gesture interactionally produce, and are produced by, social realities. Finally, Elinor Ochs, Emmanuel Schegeloff, and Sandra Thompson's (1996) collection, *Interaction and Grammar*, offers a range of sociolinguistic approaches to interaction.

For a practical introduction to collecting, transcribing, and analyzing data, Paul ten Have (1999) offers a useful guide based on the traditions of conversation analysis. Unlike many other introductions to discourse analysis, ten Have addresses basic "field" concerns, such as selecting between audio and video recording, gaining consent, and building up rich transcripts from recorded data. Another classic CA book is Atkinson and Heritage's *Structures of Social Interaction: Studies in Conversational Analysis*. Whereas ten Have's introduction is clearly conversation analytic, James Paul Gee's (1999) *Introduction to Discourse Analysis* is located at an intersection of critical discourse analysis, sociocultural theory, and sociolinguistics. The strength of Gee's text is in providing tools for the analysis of discourse data, including practical tools (e.g., breaking up discourse into lines and stanzas) and theoretical tools (e.g., situated meanings and cultural models). Deborah Tannen's *Talking voices: Repetition, Dialogue, and Imagery in Conversational Discourse* offers an accessible and interesting introduction to the analysis of conversation. Her chapters on repetition and constructed dialogue are particularly effective at making mundane and unnoticed features of talk visible and interesting. Her work is also of interest as she draws on literary rhetorical traditions for analysis of tropes in her analyses of every talk.

Adam Kendon's *Conducting Interaction* brings together five key studies that consider talk, eye gaze, movements, and bodily orientations in space as they relate to conversational organization and behavior. Kendon's studies, drawing upon Goffman, Bateson, Birdwhistell and others, generously open up a range of insights that may be realized by shifting from audio-based to video-based analyses of interaction, including how various semiotic resources are coordinated.

For the ethnography of communication, a highly accessible introduction is provided in *The Ethnography of Communication: An Introduction* by Muriel Saville-Troike. Classic works include Dell Hymes' *Foundations in Sociolin-*

guistics: An Ethnographic Approach and John Gumperz's *Discourse Strategies.* Penelope Eckert's *Linguistic Variation as Social Practice* (2001) offers a social network approach.

A number of journals routinely publish studies of spoken interaction. Among them, *Discourse Processes* is an interdisciplinary journal with psychological leanings, whereas *Discourse and Society* is invested in critical discourse analysis and theory. *Written Communication* and *Research in the Teaching of English* occasionally publish papers that relate written and spoken texts. *Mind, Culture, and Activity* publishes theoretical papers that are at times connected to interaction in workplace and other naturalistic settings (particularly noteworthy examples for communication study include Vol. *4* No. 4 on writing and activity, and Vol. *7*, No. 1–2 on vision and communication). For interdisciplinary analyses of interaction in schools and other educational contexts, two significant venues are *Linguistics and Education*, published in the United States, and *Language and Education*, published in the United Kingdom.

CHAPTER

9

Children's Writing: How Textual Forms, Contextual Forces, and Textual Politics Co-Emerge

George Kamberelis
University at Albany

Lenora de la Luna
Skidmore College

In this chapter we focus on the writing practices and products of relatively young children (preschool through grade 5). Like the authors of some other chapters in this book, we argue for a multidimensional and situated approach to understanding and interpreting writing. Thus, this chapter is grounded in a theoretical orientation to writing that we might call psycho-linguistic-social-cultural-historical wherein writing is understood as occurring at the intersection of textual knowledges and practices (e.g., Huckin, chap. 1, this volume; Barton, chap. 3, this volume), a variety of contextual forces (e.g., Prior, chap. 7, this volume; Leander & Prior, chap. 8, this volume), and textual politics (e.g., Clark & Ivanic, 1997; Kamberelis & Scott, 1992; McGinley & Kamberelis, 1996). Given this theoretical orientation, we try to keep in view the idea that writing is situated activity and that it also entails the historical durability and significance of linguistic, rhetorical, and text-level conventions. Finally, when we use the term **writing** we refer simultaneously to products, processes, practices, contexts, and politics. When we want to refer more specifically to one of these dimensions of writing, we do so explicitly.

Deciding on an approach (and concomitant units of analysis) to study children's writing is difficult for several reasons. First, *everything* is relevant to understanding complex and highly situated activities such as children's writing. Yet, one needs to draw boundary lines around any object of study to say anything meaningful about it. Second, complex activity systems are difficult to parse. Each level or dimension of the system interacts with other levels or dimensions in co-constitutive ways. A writer's decision-making processes, for example, are thoroughly embedded within historically constituted sets of writing practices. Similarly, choices about how to organize text at various levels of organization (word choice, sentence, genre) are influenced by various contextual forces such as the ostensible task and the imagined audience. A third difficulty involved in studying children's writing is choosing or creating a unit of analysis that allows one to manage and reduce one's data without eliding too much complexity and nuance. In this regard, we agree with Cole (1992), Wertsch (1991), Kamberelis (1995), Russell (1997a), and others who argue that understanding situated social activity requires focusing simultaneously on persons working with social and cultural resources on specific tasks within specific activities with definable (if not clearly defined) goals within activity systems that are almost always linked in constitutive ways to other activity systems. By insisting on such a complex unit of analysis we are not suggesting that each of its dimensions must be attended to equally and systematically in every research endeavor. We simply want to emphasize that complex units of analysis are required for understanding complex social phenomena.

With these ideas in mind, we organized our approach to studying children's writing around three co-constitutive dimensions: **text**, the formal semiotic features of writing products, **context**, the forces (both proximal and distal) that exert effects on writing practices and products, and **politics**, the situated power relations involved in writing.

We devote approximately the first third of this chapter to defining and describing the key constructs that constitute these dimensions, along with various sets of research strategies useful for understanding, interpreting, and explaining each of these dimensions. In the second section of the chapter, we discuss methods of data collection and analysis typically used to understand children's writing. The final section of the chapter contains multi-leveled analyses of two texts written by different children. The first text is a science/information report written by a kindergarten girl in the context of a life science unit. The second text is a science report written by a pair of fifth-grade boys, also in the context of a life science unit. We conclude the chapter with some final comments about the relative purchase of our approach to analyzing, interpreting, and explaining children's writing.

GUIDING CONSTRUCTS

Texts: Forms of Writing and Formal Characteristics of Written Language

One dimension of children's writing that demands more attention and analysis than the writing of older, more experienced writers is the physical, formal, and functional characteristics of the texts they produce. Following Derrida (1974), Hodge and Kress (1988), and especially Bakhtin (1986), we use the term **text** to refer to any coherent constellation of signs that constitute a structure of meaning for some audience. Examples of texts include conversations, lectures, drawings, songs, mathematical equations, telephone numbers, bird calls, multimedia installations, and so on. In this chapter, we restrict our discussions and analyses to texts that have some graphic form.

Importantly, texts are traces of activity—sedimented objects produced in specific social situations and for specific purposes. Although the origins of textual meanings derive from discourses and discursive practices external to texts, these meanings find their expression in texts, and they are negotiated in and through texts in concrete situations of social exchange. The notions of discourses and discursive practices foreground the social and ideological dimensions of language and language use. This emphasis radically alters structuralist notions of semiotic systems (e.g., natural language, photography) as transparent media that record externally present things-in-themselves. Texts are not simply denotative devices that stand for and correspond to "real-world" referents that lend them meaning. Instead, they give shape to the reality they implicate as much as they present or represent it. Because texts are indexical—pointing to the contexts in which they have concrete meanings and functions—paying careful attention to the formal (semiotic) properties of texts can tell us a lot not only about the internal organization of the texts themselves but also about their authors, contexts of use, audiences, and so on. For example, even in the absence of much context data, careful textual analyses (especially of multiple drafts) can often provide material evidence about discourse choices a writer made from the range of discursive options available to him or her. In turn, knowing about these choices can help researchers make inferences about the writer's stance, imagined audience, positioning within a material/ideological context, and rhetorical intent.

Carefully analyzing children's texts can also provide certain kinds of knowledge that are harder to come by in studies that focus almost exclusively on context (e.g., specific scaffolding experiences within highly circumscribed activities and activity settings). This does not mean that what is most important about children's writing has little to do with context. On the contrary, because children's writing is influenced by so many contextual forces beyond their immediate situations (e.g., recreational reading, family literacy activities, media viewing, peer activities), it is preposterous to assume that only documented aspects of writing activity are relevant. Again, texts often index relevant but undocumented contextual forces.

Given that texts are such complicated, multilayered, and indexical phenomena, it is important to realize that the meaning of the terms **write, writing, text**, and the like can differ considerably between adults and children and between children of different ages and levels of development. Especially for very young children, writing may be a term used to designate many different semiotic forms or sign systems such as drawing, scribble, strings of letters or letter-like units, numbers, equations, graphs, various kinds of invented spellings, and conventional orthography (Sulzby, Barnhart, & Hieshima, 1989). As information technologies become more accessible and more sophisticated, children's texts will doubtlessly also embody an increasing variety of aural, visual, and even synesthetic semiotic resources available within them.

Also important to consider is the fact that children's responses to writing tasks suggest that they may not necessarily operate with distinctions commonly used by adults such as oral language/written language or drawing/writing. More often than adult writers, child writers may also assume that their audiences know everything that they know and thus may be quite glib in their efforts to construct and convey meaning and achieve particular rhetorical effects. Additionally, because children have only nascent control over the tools and strategies for graphically representing their messages, their writing may actually be shorthand for richer, longer, and more complex messages than meets the eye (e.g., Clay, 1975; Kamberelis, 1993, 1999; Luria, 1983; Sulzby, Barnhart, & Hieshima, 1989; Vygotsky, 1978). Finally, prior to using more or less conventional orthography, the purposes and content of children's written texts may be less stable and more variable than those of more experienced writers. In other words, what they intend to write may transmogrify as they write, and what they claim their writing "says" may also vary over time. Therefore, researchers need to find ways to make visible the sometimes invisible richness, complexity, and variability that are often embodied in children's texts. We discuss some of the strategies most commonly used for making such aspects of children's writing visible later on in the section on research methods.

In addition to attending to the multiple semiotic resources that children bring to bear within writing activities, researchers need to attend to the linguistic and discursive textures and structures of children's texts. Although there are seldom if ever completely homologous relations between these textures and structures and the accomplishment of specific rhetorical, generic, or stylistic goals (see Bazerman, chap. 11, this volume), formal and functional dimensions of writing do vary in reasonably systematic ways. Alisdair McIntyre's (1981) brilliantly insightful observation that a queen's gambit is seldom followed by a lob over the net is as equally applicable to children's writing as to social life in general. Although children may write many different stories, each story typically bears a stronger family resemblance to other stories they write than to their science reports, sonnets, or wish lists. There are exceptions to this social fact, of course. All writers, including child writers, sometimes violate conventions to achieve particular rhetorical effects. However, because children have only nascent understandings of conventions and systems of conventions, violations in their writing may or may not have been intentional. Thus, determining whether nonconventional features within children's texts were "unintentional," is a difficult (and sometimes impossible) task that researchers of children's writing often face.

Contextual Forces and Effects

As we have already noted, texts are indexical sign complexes. Although some of their meaning resides within the texts themselves, much of their meaning is provided by the contexts within which the texts are produced, distributed, and consumed. As several other authors in this volume have already pointed out, the term **context** is an elusive and often oversimplified construct. Contexts are not simply containers within which actions, practices, and activities occur. Instead, they are dynamic streams of overlapping and integrated discourses, spaces, sociocultural practices, and power relations. Although for analytic purposes we persist in using the term **context** in this chapter, a more ecologically apt term might be something like **text-context-activity relations**.

Contexts exert effects on children's writing in both proximal and distal ways. **Proximal resources and constraints** might include an open text in front of the writer or an audience to which one is directly and immediately answerable. More **distal resources and constraints** might include a socialized and embodied predisposition toward particular discursive acts and activities such as those that commonly occur between parents and children, teachers and students, doctors and patients, lawyers and clients. As contextual forces become more distal, the constructs we use to describe them become more abstract, and thus the forces themselves become more elusive and less visible. Therefore, understanding more distal contextual forces and their effects often requires greater efforts at making them more visible through careful observation and interviewing, as well as more inferential analytic work.

There are many proximal contextual forces that operate on children as they write. These include knowledge of particular books or television shows, conversations with parents, and suggestions from peers. Children's perceptions of what teachers want may influence the topics they choose to write about and the texts they eventually produce. How teachers or peers respond to children's writing may influence what children write and how they write it. Children's writing may also be influenced by how they imagine their audiences will react to their writing.

Writing tasks (and how they are construed by writers) are also important proximal contextual forces that exert effects on children's writing, especially in school. For example, a fifth-grader writing an argument as part of a project-based social science unit might compose over several weeks, seek input from others, revise her text several times, and proofread it. In contrast, if this same child were asked to write an argumentative essay on the same general topic in 45 minutes for a state-mandated writing exam, she would likely proceed quite differently. It should be obvious that you could multiply this comparison exponentially.

A complex set of contextual forces that seems midway between the proximal and the distal and that affects children's writing in powerful and pervasive ways are **social practices**. As a theoretical construct, "practice" is conceptually ambiguous, referring simultaneously to particular actions done by particular people at particular times for particular purposes and also to habituated forms of action sedimented over time. Social life is produced through practices—the constant interaction between historically produced and durable "permanencies" that tend to reproduce social life and all situated, improvisational instantiations of these **permanencies** that can produce social change.

Three specific kinds of writing practices are especially important for understanding children's writing: **intertextual practices**, **interdiscursive practices**, and **intercontextual practices**. **Intertextual practices** involve the heterogeneous production of texts out of other specific texts or text fragments. Sometimes the sources of these texts or partial texts can be traced to their sources, and sometimes they cannot be. For example, faced with the task of writing a get-well card to a classmate, a child might incorporate phrases such as "get well soon," "you are in my prayers," or even "just do it." In each case, the phrases come to a speaker or writer with particular histories of meaning and use; these meanings and uses are at least partially shared by writers and their audiences; and a given writer laminates a new meaning onto this history to achieve a new and quite specific rhetorical goal.

Interdiscursive practices involve adhering to abstract conventional ways of organizing language at the level of the sentence, paragraph, or text. Interdiscursive practices are thus predicated on knowledge of the basic shapes or structures of texts common to particular discursive formations and involve composing new texts that share those shapes or structures. Interdiscursive practices thus function to accomplish specific rhetorical goals within definable discursive formations and to mark writers as "insiders" or "outsiders" with respect to those formations. For example, faced with the task of writing a science report about cats, a young child might draw on her experience with published informational texts about cats and compose a text that bears some family resemblance to those texts. Although the child's text may not embody any specific intertextual poachings and while its similarity with published exemplars may be nascent and fuzzy, it nevertheless is often more similar in shape and structure to informational texts than to narrative, poetic, or procedural ones.

Interdiscursive practices usually pivot on two global aspects of discourse organization: **genres** and **social languages**. As Bazerman (chap. 11, this volume) discusses, **genres** are organized at the level of the whole text and function as discursive frames that organize discourse into typified or durable text structures and social practices that accomplish specific purposes within typical communicative activities. **Social languages**, however, organize discourse practice at more local levels of text organization (e.g., sentence, paragraph). Although durable, social languages are also dynamic and fluid. Most people learn and deploy many different social languages, switch among them as they move across different social contexts, and develop their own hybrid versions.

Intercontextual practices (e.g., Floriani, 1993) involve the invocation or partial reenactment of prior contexts, situations, or situated activities because people recognize that the practices and activity structures required in current contexts are similar to or the same as practices and activity structures that were required in previously experienced (or relevant but different) contexts. The practices and activity structures from previous (or relevant but different) contexts thus become resources for imagining, negotiating, and enacting practices and activities in the new contexts. When social actors (including writers) invoke previous or relevantly different contexts, they do so to figure out what to do in the new context, how to do it, why one might do it, and what products or outcomes will or should result from their actions and practices. For example, faced with the task of staging a mock trial and in the absence of much explicit instruction or experience with such a task, a group of children might invoke knowledge of similar activities such as an argument, a debate, a television talk show, and a television drama series such as *Law and Order*. Collectively, they might pool their knowledge of and experience with such contexts/activities and negotiate the ways in which the structures and practices of these contexts/activities could be imported into the new context/activity of writing and producing a mock trial.

Intertextual, interdiscursive, and intercontextual practices are thus particularly relevant constructs for understanding how children become more proficient writers because they are fundamental scaffolds for learning and development. As legitimate peripheral participants within ongoing activity systems, children construct texts that are "like" the texts that they perceive to be common currency within these systems. They do this by borrowing from and building upon prior texts, text fragments, text shapes, and textualizing practices across multiple contexts, which they also perceive to be "alike" in relevant ways. Over time, the texts of young writers come to more closely approximate the kinds of texts that are valuable and valued within the collective or discipline. Because young writers typically operate in multiple activity systems at once, however, these valued and valuable texts are never archetypes but continually changing (albeit usually quite slowly) typifications of ongoing social–rhetorical activity within particular systems, which are themselves continually changing. In sum, texts, text-making practices, and contexts, then, are all dynamic, flexible, and changing due to the variety of individual, social, cultural, and historical forces that operate within and across them. Thus, members of a particular community of practice never learn to write once and for all but must continually learn the ways of making meaning with texts that evolve within streams of ongoing social–rhetorical activity both within and across various cross-pollinating activity systems.

Politics of Writing: The Positioning of Young Writers In and Through Discourse

Much like speaking, writing is a kind of micro-political activity in which people position themselves in relation to other people and groups in strategic ways. Three specific constructs are useful in understanding how this happens—**Discourses**, **subject positions**, and **subjectivities**—all of which are inextricably related. We begin with **Discourses**. According to Gee (1996), **Discourses** are "identity kit[s]" comprised of

> socially acceptable association[s] among ways of using language, other symbolic expressions, and 'artifacts', of thinking, feeling, believing, valuing, and acting that can be used to identify [people] as [members] of . . . socially meaningful group[s] or 'social network[s]', or to signal (that [people are] playing) . . . socially meaningful 'role[s]'. (p. 143)

Discourses make certain **subject positions** visible and available to us, and they render others relatively invisible or undesirable. The subject positions that Discourses make visible and available to us seem natural and good because everyone around us seems to occupy them. The subject positions rendered less visible by our Discourses seem weird, even wrong.

As we participate within various Discourses, we have some limited agency in the ways in which we "take up" the subject positions they make visible and available. We use the term position-taking strategies as a way to talk about our limited agency in this regard. We say limited because the Discourses that made the subject positions available in the first place have already predisposed us to think they are normal and good and that others are less normal and less good. We can occupy available subject positions without question; we can challenge them as many "new" fairy tales do by making females heroines and less dependent on outer beauty; or we can resist them entirely and look for other subject positions to occupy. Re-appropriating and redefining (with a celebratory spin) the term "queer" within the gay and lesbian community might be an example of such resistance.

Finally, our **subjectivities** are the sedimented outcomes of the processes of being positioned by Discourses and engaging in position-taking strategies in relation to these Discourses. As we live more complex lives and are constructed within multiple Discourses (some of which are similar to others; some complementary; some contradictory), then we are engaged in multiple processes of being positioned and taking up those positions in particular ways. We thus develop and exist as multiple, complex, and contradictory subjectivities, which we continually juggle, balance, reconcile, compartmentalize, and so on through our daily practices. Finally, these ongoing streams of positioning/position-taking practices become part of the set of collective cultural resources that we draw upon as we fashion new texts and thus new, renewed, and newly inflected subjectivities.

METHODS OF DATA COLLECTION AND ANALYSIS

Introductory Remarks

Some aspects of children's writing practices, products, and competencies are revealed in their everyday experiences in various "natural" social contexts—in their self-selected writing, in their imaginative play, in their attempts to negotiate power and to get things done, and even in their responses to specific writing tasks. Thus, qualitative (basically ethnographic) case studies of children's writing are quite useful for understanding what they know about and can do with written language. As the name suggests, the unit of analysis for qualitative case studies is the "case," which is typically defined as a "bounded system" (Smith, 1978) or an "integrated system" (Stake, 1995). The case might be a student, a peer group, a writing workshop, or a classroom. In general, qualitative case studies of children's writing involve observing children writing in relevant settings, asking them questions about their texts and text-making practices, and documenting as many contextual forces as possible (see Prior, chap. 7, this volume, for descriptions of different kinds of interviews). The reports generated from qualitative case studies are particularistic, richly descriptive, heuristic, and interpretive.

To capture a more targeted (and sometimes fuller) range of children's writing processes, products, and competencies, however, it is sometimes necessary to conduct ethnographically informed experimental simulations—to create situations for children that allow them to demonstrate skills that they might not reveal if we just waited for them to occur spontaneously. To avoid limiting markers of systematic variation to some preconceived set, however, writing tasks used within experimental simulations should satisfy several criteria. They should be ones that children find familiar and comfortable (i.e., ones that fit with their past experiences and the parameters of ongoing activities). They should be relatively open-ended so as not to constrain the children's creativity and imagination. Yet they should be structured enough to allow for reasonable comparisons across different children or groups of children. Satisfying this criterion is especially important if quantitative linguistic analyses are to be conducted. Finally, some tasks should be designed to capture children's actual writing practices, and others should be designed to capture their abilities to talk about their knowledge of writing practices and products.

Despite the current preference for case study research methods and the descriptive power they afford, some research questions may be better answered using ethnographically informed experimental simulation designs. Such designs are particularly powerful—even essential—when a researcher is interested in learning about patterns of performance across relatively large samples of children. Indeed, several recent studies of children's genre learning (e.g., Donovan, 2001; Kamberelis, 1999) were conducted using ethnographically informed experimental simulation designs, without which their authors may not have been able to offer the kinds of multilayered accounts that they offered. Additionally, even in the context of case study research designs, the use of some more constrained tasks and some descriptive and inferential statistical analyses can be both useful and telling.

Collecting Data on Children's Texts and the Contexts and Politics of Their Production

As we have already mentioned, depending upon the research questions of a particular study, a researcher may want to collect texts that are "naturally" produced within particular activities or activity settings (e.g., a folktale writing task, a thematic curriculum unit, a science project). Or the researcher may want to constrain the activities and tasks a bit more by asking children to produce particular kinds of texts on particular topics within particular situations with particular production constraints.

A variety of data collection strategies are used to understand the contextual forces and textual politics involved in children's writing. Conducting various kinds of observations and interviews and collecting relevant artifacts are essential practices for the researcher interested in reconstructing even the most partial history of processes, practices, contexts, and politics involved in children's writing.

Observing and taking rich fieldnotes is one strategy for capturing and understanding writing processes and practices. Because only so much can be captured in fieldnotes, recording children's composing practices with audiotape or videotape often results in a particularly rich record of various influences and effects of writing processes, practices, contexts, and politics. Moreover, this strategy is essential if the researcher plans to conduct discourse analyses of the processes and politics of talk or to try to map relations between talk and text.

Interviewing children about their texts, their audiences, their purposes, their decision-making processes, and the aspects of context salient to them is another strategy commonly practiced by researchers (see Prior, chap. 7, this volume, for a fuller discussion of interviews and interviewing). With respect to interviews, Sawkins (1971) reported that 10- and 11-year-old children are quite able to talk about their composing goals, processes, and products in sophisticated ways and with a high degree of validity and reliability. Yet, developmental research has suggested that more inference and speculation may be required to interpret the self-reports of younger children (e.g., Kamberelis, 1999; Langer, 1986; Zecker, 1996).

Finally, collecting various kinds of relevant artifacts can provide very useful information about the processes, practices, contexts, and politics of children's writing. Such artifacts may include "found objects" such as task assignments, lesson plans, preliminary drafts, and copies of cultural tools used (e.g., encyclopedias, books, etc.). Researchers sometimes also choose to "stage" the collection of contextual data relevant to children's learning environments and experiences. For example, for 4 months prior to collecting writing samples for one study that one of us conducted, children, teachers, and parents were asked to keep records of all assigned and self-selected reading done by children in the classroom, at home, and at school. These data proved very useful in constructing partial and preliminary maps of the possible (and likely) intertextual, interdiscursive, and intercontextual streams of influence embodied in children's texts. They also provided information that could be used for generating interview questions to probe (and sometimes verify) hunches about traces in children's texts that we thought were there.

Analyzing and Interpreting Children's Textual Products

Once a corpus of texts has been collected, a researcher must select tools for parsing the texts, choose relevant features to analyze, and conduct quantitative or descriptive analyses of the texts. Many of these tools and procedures are discussed in detail by Huckin (chap. 1, this volume). Nevertheless, we offer a general synopsis of these processes.

As a first step in the process, the researcher needs to decide exactly what counts as a text. For older children whose texts are composed in alphabetic writing with reasonable approximations to English orthography, this is seldom a problem. However, if children use multiple forms of writing or compose multimedia texts, some thought has to be given to what will be parsed, coded, and analyzed. For example, if children inscribe their texts using nonphonetic writing systems (e.g., pictures, scribble, nonphonetic letter strings, equations, etc.) or if they produce difficult to decipher inventive spellings, what does one do? Because researchers will most often be interested in the text's intended meanings and functions, they typically try to recover/reconstruct these meanings and functions. There are a variety of strategies for doing this. For example, children may be asked to read what they wrote—a relatively simple means for linking text form to text content (Sulzby, Barnhart, & Hieshima, 1989). Interviews of various kinds may also be helpful in reconstructing the intended meanings and purposes of children's texts. Finally, if the child has been audiotaped or videotaped, his or her verbal commentary during composing may provide invaluable information about the meanings and functions of his or her texts.

Once texts (and their meanings) have been established, they need to be parsed or segmented in some way. A number of segmenting units have been proposed by various researchers (e.g., T-units, idea units, clauses, and utterances). Next, text segments need to be coded for discursive features relevant to the research questions being asked. In a study of genre learning, for example, these features would be ones that tend to vary systematically as a function of genre. Once coded, text features may then be analyzed using relevant inferential statistical procedures (e.g., chi square analyses, t-tests, ANOVAs, MANOVAs) that reveal systematic patterns of similarity or difference as a function of relevant independent variables (e.g., genre, grade, task, gender).

Finally, because most quantitative analyses answer "what" questions much better than "how" or "why" or "under what conditions" questions, it is often a very good idea also to augment quantitative analyses with descriptive/interpretive analyses of at least a subset of the texts in any given corpus. These descriptive/interpretive analyses provide a better sense of the variation and richness of the texts produced, suggest text-context-politics relations worthy of further study, and facilitate the interpretation of findings from statistical analyses.

Analyzing and Interpreting the Contextual Forces and Textual Politics of Children's Writing Practices

As we mentioned earlier, various kinds of qualitative analyses are typically conducted on the diverse and complex data sets often collected in studies of children's writing. Although there are many kinds of qualitative analysis, some form of inductive analysis and some form of discourse analysis are the kinds most often used to understand children's writing. Moreover, they complement each other quite well.

Inductive Analysis. In general, inductive analysis (e.g., Bogden & Biklin, 1998; Glaser & Strauss, 1967; Merriam, 2001) involves analyzing multiple forms of data (e.g., texts, observations, interviews) to discover recurrent themes and thematic relations. Most forms of inductive analysis involve several recursive and interdependent phases, along with various forms of preliminary analysis and cross-checking. Coding and analyzing data begin almost as soon as data collection begins, and the process continues throughout the final write-up. The first phase of analysis involves segmenting and organizing one's data into meaningful (yet preliminary) themes or categories from which more in-depth analysis can occur. Some of these themes or categories may derive from previous theory and research (e.g., intertextual, interdiscursive, and intercontextual relations); others emerge from the data themselves. As categories are generated, they are constantly compared, refined, deleted, added, merged, and so on until a relatively small, manageable, and maximally relevant set of categories are settled upon. This process of data collection and comparison continues until a **saturation** point is reached—a point where no new categories emerge and continued data collection and analysis is unlikely to provide additional information that will really amplify one's understanding of focal issues or concerns.

As researchers continue to generate categories that help them understand patterns in their data, they also begin to break categories down into subcategories and to search for relations among categories and subcategories (e.g., many possible relations may exist between and among categories; some categories may constitute conditions for others; two or more categories may interact in systematic ways; some categories may seem like consequences of others).

While engaged in trying to discover and describe systematic relations among categories in the data, researchers typically end up refining the categories and category relations being developed/produced quite a few times. They also try to determine which category or categories are most central to the questions that drive their research. As all categories are not equally important, this phase is particularly important for developing in-depth and grounded explanations or models of the phenomenon under study.

Throughout any study, categories, category relations, and emergent interpretations are repeatedly linked back to the data from which they are produced. This process assures that the content from which categories and category relations are developed are not stripped from the analysis process, so as not to lose the original texture of the data that have been collected (Maxwell, 1996).

As Strauss (1987), Wolcott (1994), and others have noted, the processes just described, including data collection and description, analysis and interpretation, are neither mutually exclusive, nor do they occur sequentially. Rather, these processes almost always occur simultaneously; they are recursive; and they are interwoven. Finally, all of these processes continue together until saturation has occurred. Again, saturation is the point at which little in the way of new categories, insights, interpretations, or explanations seem forthcoming. Saturation is particularly important for achieving confidence in your interpretations and explanations and thus producing a "trustworthy" account of the phenomena under study.

Discourse Analysis. Whereas inductive analysis is used to discover and map recurrent "macro" patterns that characterize writing practices, contexts, and politics, discourse analysis is used to examine the "micro" patterns embodied in specific verbal-visual interactions (usually represented in transcripts) to understand both the forms and functions of these interactions and the ways in which they both index and sustain recurrent macro patterns. Thus, discourse analysis often yields powerful exemplars of the various macro patterns found in any study. Conversely, these macro patterns can be used to understand and explain the micro patterns found within and across individual interactions.

There are many kinds of discourse analysis ranging from conversational analysis (e.g., Atkinson & Heritage, 1984) to narrative analysis (e.g., Cortazzi, 1993; Wortham, 2001) to critical discourse analysis (e.g., Fairclough, 1989, 1992). Many researchers mix and match techniques and procedures from these different kinds of analysis, and, indeed, the foregoing description reflects this eclecticism. As we mentioned, a primary goal of discourse analysis is to show how specific verbal–visual actions and interactions both index and sustain general and durable patterns of action and interaction common to a given social formation. As a first step in this process, verbatim transcripts are coded and analyzed for a variety of linguistic and interactional features such as turn-taking strategies, markers of interactional control, politeness markers, the use of modal verbs to assert relative degrees of authority, shifts in social language use that mark affiliation, solidarity, or resistance, key words or metaphors, and salient intertextual, interdiscursive, and intercontextual patterns. Such information is crucial for understanding how individuals position themselves in relation to each other through specific discourse practices.

Once transcripts have been carefully analyzed for relevant linguistic and interactional features, they are examined to determine how specific interactions and interactional patterns might be related to larger discursive practices and social practices. As noted earlier, **discursive practices** refer to specific patterns of producing, distributing, and consuming knowledges and artifacts within specific fields of action (e.g., domain-related genres, behavioral protocols, conventional routines). **Social practices** refer to the often taken-for-granted worldviews and dispositions that motivate certain discursive practices (e.g., the ideologies, politics, and everyday practices of elementary education). Because residues from discursive and social practices exist in textual products and specific verbal–visual interactions, this second level of analysis can be quite useful in interpreting (and even explaining) how writers produce, reproduce, and transform their subjectivities, their alignments with contextual forces, and their social relations—often in complex and contradictory ways—within particular writing activities and settings.

Combining Inductive Analyses and Discourse Analyses. Before moving on to our own analyses of children's writing, we would like to underscore the fact that combining inductive analysis with discourse analysis is a particularly powerful way to map the complex set of relations among the texts, contexts, and politics of situated writing activities. Discourse analysis is especially useful for critically examining the often opaque relations between and among categories generated through inductive analysis. Good inductive analyses are enormously useful for conducting systematic and compelling accounts of the durable discursive and social practices that influence the emergence of specific texts and interactions.

With respect to reporting practices, findings and interpretations generated from each type of analysis are usually used to amplify, support, and complement each other. In most case-study accounts of children's writing (or other social-material phenomena), multiple analyses and resulting interpretations are usually integrated more or less seamlessly into coherent, compelling, well argued, and adequately supported accounts. We present two such accounts next. Although we used both inductive analysis and discourse analysis to construct them, the exact analytic work involved is not presented in a transparent, step-by-step fashion.

ANALYSES OF EXEMPLARY CHILDREN'S TEXTS

In this section we offer two examples of case-study analyses of children's writing. In each example, we introduce the case and then analyze it at three levels—text, context, and politics. Both cases are notable for the many and various ways in which their authors drew upon available social, material, and environmental resources to compose complex texts. Both texts are also notable for the ways in which the "official" tasks within which the texts were produced were rearticulated by the child authors to meet what seemed to be multiple rhetorical goals.

**Example 1: Tensions Between Everyday and School
Discourse in "Please Call This Toll-Free Number"**

The first case we analyze pivots around a text written by a 5-year-old African American girl (whom we call Denise).[1] This text, which is shown in Figure 9.1, was elicited in the context of an ethnographically informed experimental simulation, where Denise was asked to write a story related to but outside of the writing practices that typically occurred in her classroom. One of us met with Denise individually and asked her to write a "science report" about an animal or animal group that she knew a lot about. This writing task occurred toward the end of a 6-week thematic unit on animals, animal lifestyles, and animal habitats. During the unit, children experienced many shared readings of mostly narrative but also some nonnarrative texts about these topics. They explored many books and other resources on these topics on their own. And they wrote about these topics in their journals on a daily basis. Sometimes, children were given props or questions to write about. Sometimes they could choose what to write about and how to write it. Additionally, the children had several pets in their classroom and were sometimes encouraged to observe and to write about these pets during journal writing time. Finally, the children and their teacher hatched chicken eggs and conducted a naturalistic experiment in which they observed real caterpillars turn into butterflies in their classroom. Importantly, both the processes/practices involved in producing the text and the text itself might have been very different had the writing situation and its enabling and constraining conditions been different.

In many ways, Denise's text was similar to the science reports produced by many kindergarten children (and some first-grade children) in the larger study from which the text was culled. Many of their science reports, for example, were composed using multiple semiotic forms. Many were **hybrid constructions** (Bakhtin, 1981), embodying characteristic features from several different genres (especially narrative genres and popular cultural genres). And many seemed to index ambiguous uptake with respect to understanding the nature, purpose, and audience of the task.

    Text. First, let us look at the physical characteristics of Denise's "composed" text. This text is deceptively simple and wonderfully indexical as we see as our analysis unfolds. This text was composed from multiple semiotic resources (oral annotation, pictures, numbers, letter-like figures, scribbles, etc.). More specifically, it includes two simple addition equations, two local telephone numbers, and a picture of a cat and a dog on the lawn in front of a tree or a house. Denise placed her cat and dog at a significant distance

---

[1] All proper names of research participants are pseudonyms.

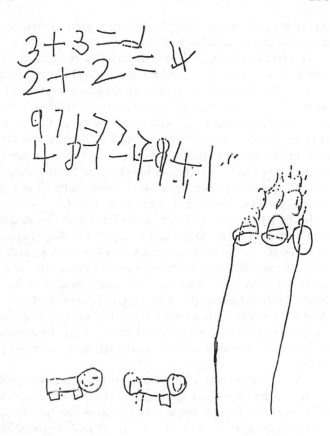

Child's Reading of Original Manuscript

There's a cat and a dog out chasing each other on the lawn.

Call collect.

Start calling now if your cat and dog ever do this.

And please call this toll-free number.

FIG. 9.1. Denise's science report (kindergarten).

from the equations and telephone numbers and between the lower center and lower left limits of the page. From a semiotic perspective, this placement is interesting for a couple of reasons. The separation of text and illustration is a trademark of children's storybooks, and separating text and illustration is often physically mandated in children's writing by paper that is unlined at the top and lined at the bottom. That this logic is reversed here is interesting but not entirely explainable. The most plausible explanation has to do with the fact that Denise composed the illustration first, perhaps orienting the ground/lawn at the bottom of the page.

The bodies of Denise's animals have been constructed from simple geometric shapes (e.g., rectangles, squares, and circles) and without depth or perspective. Abstract, geometric minimalism is quite common in children's writing. It is also a central feature of some children's books, comic books, and animated film, all of which are likely to inform children's interdiscursive practices in powerful ways. Additionally, the faces of Denise's cat and dog seem incongruous in relation to her text's message content. Both animals have smiling faces, and both seem to be gazing out at us from the text. In contrast, in her "read" text, these animals are chasing each other around the lawn causing all sorts of mischief.

Directly to the right of the cat and dog is a very prominent figure—a tall thin rectangle with circles and complex curving shapes at its top. Sometimes Denise referred to this figure as a tree, and sometimes she referred to it as a house. Whether this figure represents a tree or a house seems less important, however, than the fact that it seems to function to mark the whole bottom two-thirds of the page as lawn and sky, perhaps indexing Denise's emerging knowledge about the organization and use of space in written texts. More specifically, Denise seems to demonstrate knowledge here of the separation of text and illustration common to many children's texts.

Denise placed two addition equations and two telephone numbers together in the upper left quadrant of the paper, a position that is visually prominent for English readers (i.e., where one begins to read each page). Orthographically, most of the numbers and symbols are written conventionally. Additionally, these symbol strings follow the left to right orientation typical of written English, and they follow the syntactic conventions typical of addition equations and telephone numbers. Besides providing evidence that Denise has mastered these conventions of written English, the addition equations and the telephone numbers suggest that she is also developing a firm grasp of the **sign concept**, the **message concept**, **rules of syntax**, and perhaps a nascent sense of the **alphabetic principle**. When children understand the **sign concept**, they realize that signs (e.g., pictures, words, numbers, strings of words and numbers) represent or stand for ideas and objects. When children understand the **message concept**, they realize that print encodes messages that are also carried by speech. When children understand the **rules of syntax**, they realize that strings of signs must be assembled in specific ways. When children understand the **alphabetic principle**, they realize that sounds are represented by letters, numbers, or more complex graphemes.

Also of interest here is the fact that Denise's equations slant up slightly while the telephone numbers slant down considerably, suggesting they

might function in different ways. Perhaps the equations stand in for the
"problem" at the heart of the text in some way. And perhaps the telephone
numbers slanting downward toward the house might intimate a certain
kind of addressivity on the way toward a solution: "Go into the house and
call the toll-free number." However, because we were not particularly vigi-
lant in collecting contextual data in this study, we do not know, for sure,
what her intentions were.

The suffix of one telephone number overwrites the other, rendering both
partially obscure. Whether intentional or not (and we suspect not), this violates the **directionality** and **line structure conventions** of English writing
and makes the text's ostensible message difficult to decode. Additionally,
one 6 is reversed and the line directionality of at least one 8 is unconventional. These reversals and other deviations of **shape** and **orientation conventions** are not unusual in children's texts, and they provide evidence for
how children's writing differs from, approximates, and eventually emerges
into conventional or "adult" writing.

Now let us look at the characteristics of Denise's "read" text which
seems to hold her intended meaning and thus embodies at least some of
the knowledge she has about science reports, related genres, and their
functions. The report begins much like an online event cast (Hicks, 1990), in
which a narrator is telling an audience about an event that she is witness-
ing. Perhaps implicitly, an initiating event or a problem is stated. Such a feature is one of the few obligatory structural (or at least conventionally expected) elements of narrative texts. Next, Denise provides a solution to the
problem (another obligatory structural element of narrative texts), but this
element is clearly cast in a style and social language more common to popular informational genres such as media advertisements, infomercials, or
public service announcements. A final structural element embodied in
Denise's text is the imperative sentence construction. Three of the four
clauses in her report are imperatives. Importantly, imperatives are much
more common to popular informational genres than school-based informational genres or many other kinds of genres for that matter. To be sure,
Denise's report contains information that is useful for dealing with a particular sort of problem. However, neither this information nor the linguistic
and discursive conventions embedded within it are typical of school-based
science reports or even school-based information reports more broadly
conceived. Instead, they bear a strong family resemblance to popular informational genres, which, quite interestingly, are quite wonderful analogs to
the school-based science genre that Denise was asked to write. In addition
to containing these various structural elements from various genres,
Denise's report contains a variety of telling textural (or sentence-level) features. Her report is about both specific participants (a cat and a dog on the
lawn) and generalized participants (anyone's cat or dog). Importantly, spe-

cific participants are more common to narrative texts and generalized participants are more common to scientific and informational texts. Additionally, Denise's entire report (even its narrative elements) is cast in the present tense, a grammatical choice much more common to informational genres than narrative genres and designed to foreground the timelessness and universality of generalized characteristics and activities.

Context. A variety of forces from the various places and practices that constituted Denise's home and school life seemed to exert powerful effects on her writing. The physical formatting of her text adheres to conventions typical of children's storybooks and the kind of writing paper children often use in school—half lined, half unlined. The pervasiveness and instrumental function of numbers in the human environment seems to have influenced her interdiscursive and intercontextual practices considerably. When asked, for example, to justify classifying her text as a science report rather than some other kind of text, Denise's first response was " 'Cause it's got numbers in it." Additionally, in a variety of interviews and conversations around this text and other texts she wrote (reports, stories, poems, biographies, letters), she repeatedly emphasized the central importance of numbers in science and information reports. For example, she noted that "an information book has numbers, the places where people go, and where people live, and their phone numbers." She also claimed that "information books are different from a story by numbers and the things that tell you how to get things or how to call people." Finally, Denise repeatedly referred to the telephone book as a prototypic informational text. Among other things, she said: "You can look for information in the phone book." "You can learn from it about writing and numbers." "You can learn how to call numbers, how to read something, and find something." Clearly, she seemed to think that many informational texts, and phone books in particular, are valuable resources for finding specific types of information, especially relevant numerical information.

The basic frame for Denise's writing seemed to derive from her knowledge of information genres from popular culture (e.g., infomercials, public service announcements). Not a bad strategy, really, since we already noted they are close cousins to the informational genres more typical of school-based discourses. Not surprisingly, as Denise appropriated and deployed popular speech genres to accomplish this "school-based" task, she deployed both the social languages of popular culture/advertising and those of school. This is particularly apparent when you look across her actual written text and what she read from her writing. For example, note that her written text begins with horizontally displayed addition problems—semiotic forms much more common to elementary school classrooms than most other social spaces. Note also the drawings that are so typical of the texts kindergartners compose in both school and nonschool contexts. Additionally, the intonation Denise used when reading her text definitely betrayed the social language of school discourse. For example, it was much more monotonic than we expected and embodied intonational contours much more characteristic of round robin reading than either face-to-face talk or good oral interpretation. Finally, when asked who might want to read and use her report, Denise mentioned her teacher and some of her classmates as target audiences. Indeed, the opening sentence of her report resembles the "setting" of a typical kindergartner's story that would most likely be addressed to teachers and peers.

In addition to features that index school tasks, spaces, and practices, Denise's report contains many features more common to the tasks, spaces, and practices of everyday life. For example, the problem posed by the text is a common everyday problem. Additionally, the central trope around which the text pivots is the telephone number, two of which are prominently displayed in the middle of her written text. Although few children make telephone calls in school, telephone calls constitute an important and pervasive part of everyday life. Additionally, the specific telephone practices inscribed in Denise's text are practices used to solve everyday problems by enlisting the advice or the assistance of experts who may be reached by calling 911 or whose telephone numbers are contained in the yellow pages, infomercials, and public service announcements. Finally, although Denise mentioned her teacher and some classmates as the target audience of her report, the last three clauses of her "read" text seem to be addressed to a more generalized and everyday audience—any citizen who might experience such a problem.

Ironically, many intertextual, interdiscursive, and intercontextual forces that would be relevant to a science-writing task are ostensibly absent in Denise's writing. Despite having experienced many science books and other kinds of information books in "read-aloud" activities and "shared reading" activities, little of the texture and structure of these kinds of books is present in her report. This is all the more peculiar given that, in interviews and conversations, Denise could readily remember and talk about these kinds of books. For example, she noted having read books about food, rainbows, cats, and dogs, and she was able to relay some of the features of these texts, features that, in fact, are considered obligatory to science/informational texts. For example, when describing the contents of a book she had recently read or had read to her, she noted that "fish can swim in water, and fish can breathe in water." When pressed about the kind of book from which she learned these things, however, Denise was adamant that it was a storybook and *not* a science or information book.

Denise's comments about the functions of science reports and information reports were equally interesting and complicated things even more. When asked what science reports and information reports are used for, she noted that they help you learn "about writing," "about parrots, cats, and dogs," and "about numbers." Among other things, these various indices of contextual influences seem to indicate that Denise's understandings of different text types and their relations to different contexts and practices were just beginning to emerge and were still quite inchoate. Even so, the almost total absence of intertextual, interdiscursive, and intercontextual influences from school-like informational texts and textual practices seemed odd to us, given her complex and contradictory responses to our queries. However, some other things that Denise said—or rather insisted upon—began to help us understand the possible reasons for these salient absences.

Politics.   Despite its ostensible simplicity, Denise's text embodies and indexes a very complicated set of textual politics. Let us begin by discussing the ways in which Denise positioned herself by appropriating and deploying the particular forms of language embodied in her text. To invoke Goffman's useful "footings" construct (see Prior, chap. 7, for a description of this construct), Denise seems to begin as both the author and the animator of her text in the sense that she both created and delivered the message contained in its first clause ("There's a cat and dog out chasing each other on the lawn."). After this first clause, however, she continues only as the animator of the text and the author becomes a kind of ubiquitous "agency" to which calls of distress may be addressed. Similarly, in the first clause, the participant framework (or audience) seems to be specific people who are ratified to hear the message—her teacher and classmates. However, the remaining clauses seem to address a much broader and more complex range of her possible participant framework—a ubiquitous "you" who might include all sorts of ratified and nonratified hearers. These particular ways in which Denise is positioned in relation to the discursive resources she appropriated and deployed (as well as how she deployed them) are very important for understanding how her subjectivities and social relations were being constructed within multiple streams of discursive practice. Among other things, the preponderance of the "ubiquitous" that characterizes her positioning within the language of the text seems to index the very strong effects exerted by the discursive practices of everyday life on her own text-making practices. Yet, the first clause of her report also indicates her efforts to locate herself within the tasks, languages, and discursive practices of school.

In addition to how Denise positioned herself in and through her language choices, she positioned herself in less visible ways in relation to a particular social field (school-based scientific literacies) and a particular set of relationships with other people (both particular people and people in general). For example, based on the immediate task requirements of Denise's writing, the most immediate and particular audience for her science report was a university researcher. That she addressed this audience earnestly was apparent in our data. For example, when one of us approached Denise to work on her report, she said, "Am I going to write another story for you?" Along with many other students, she also asked the researchers in her classroom when it was going to be her turn to write again. Additionally, in the context of interviews about her knowledge of science and science writing, Denise shared a considerable amount of accurate and eloquently articulated scientific information with us about parrots, dogs, cats, fish, and rainbows.

Because Denise's composing work was also embedded within the multiple streams of activity that constituted the 6-week thematic unit on animals, her audience also included her teacher. Indeed, she was often excited to share her texts with her teacher, and she participated regularly in the "author's chair" activities that her teacher staged. Denise and other children also "published" their work in bulletin board displays and in small volumes produced for the classroom library.

Because Denise was specifically asked to write a text that her peers would enjoy, find interesting, and learn something from, she was also writing for them. Although we have little direct evidence for the extent to which her peers were a focal audience for the particular science report we discuss in this chapter, we watched Denise and her peers interact with enthusiasm and interest around their writing throughout the school year. Moreover, in their imaginative play, Denise and her friends frequently staged everyday dramas like the one featured in her science report.

Finally, Denise also seemed to imagine a yet larger audience that included her family and other people in her community for whom practices related to everyday problems, their solutions, and the role of popular information genres in these problems and solutions were a salient part of everyday life. That this audience was relevant and "real" is indexed by the setting, content, and tone of the report itself, which is clearly located within the social practice of collectively engaging in/with the popular media common to everyday life among African American families (Heath, 1983; Taylor & Dorsey-Gaines, 1988). Indeed, in interviews about the forms and functions of science and informational genres, Denise shared stories about looking through the telephone book with her mother "with a pen in hand" to find friends' telephone numbers, the telephone numbers of people who "do her hair" and "fix her car," and the telephone numbers "for the police and fire."

Example 2: Textual Poaching and Streams of Activity in the "Owl Pellet" Report

In this section, we present a multilevel analysis of another case of children's science writing. This example comes from a naturalistic observation of a fifth-grade science unit on barn owls, owl pellets, and dissection practices. Although this example was chosen strategically for illustrative purposes, it is "representative" in the sense that many, if not most, of the texts written by other dyads were similar to this one, both in their development and their compositional structure, and thus could have functioned equally well as examples here.

The science-writing event (and the text produced within it) that we analyze was the capstone assignment of a several-week life science unit. Children studied the characteristics, habits, habitats, and life cycles of barn owls; they dissected owl pellets and reconstructed the skeletons of the animals contained within them; and they wrote science reports. The unit began with students viewing an educational video, *Ecology and the Barn Owl* (Carter & Maligian-Odle, 1994), which provided an abundance of information about the physical features and habits of the barn owl, including a long section on owl pellets. The students were asked to take careful notes on the video, which some but not all did. While viewing the video, most students were active audience members, often oohing and aahing at what they saw. Their teacher followed up this video with a *very* traditional Initiation-Response-Evaluation/Initiation-Response-Follow-Up set of questions about the content of the video. For example, she asked: "What is an owl pellet?" "What do barn owls eat?" "What's another word for field mouse?" "Has anyone ever seen a live barn owl?"

Next, the classroom teacher explained that she was going to distribute owl pellets and dissection tools and that students were going to begin dissecting owl pellets and reconstructing the skeletons found within them. She also told them they would make annotated posters of their skeletons and would write reports on what they had done and learned within the dissection activity and the larger unit in which it was embedded. The teacher also referred students to relevant informational resources in the classroom that they could use to learn about barn owls, including books she had placed in their classroom library and posters of various animal skeletons (e.g., mouse, vole) that students could use when attempting to identify the animals eaten by owls. As the teacher talked, the students became increasingly active, expressing both their excitement and apprehension about this new activity. Several side conversations broke out around the room. A few students made faces that mimicked what a barn owl might look like as it readies itself to purge a pellet. What appeared chaotic at first blush was actually a highly productive anticipatory activity for the work that would follow.

Next, the teacher began a long cautionary diatribe about the care required to carry out a successful dissection, and she warned them to dissect their pellets very carefully: "Be gentle. Don't slam with your tools like this (slams a tool on the desk). Don't pull too hard with your tweezers 'cause you'll break the bones." She then paired up students for the dissection activity and distributed their dissection trays and tools, which included an owl pellet, scalpels, tweezers, teasing needles, and paper towels. Once they had their tools, each dyad worked independently for the most part, and the teacher (and some researchers) circulated around the room observing, consulting, and keeping order.

Most dyads finished dissecting their owl pellet and assembling the skeleton of the animal within it in a few sessions. Toward the end of the first dissection session, the teacher elaborated for the students what the science report assignment entailed. She specified that these reports should have factual information about the barn owl and that "they had to include something about their personal experiences" dissecting owl pellets and reconstructing the skeletons within them. This task assignment, which we elaborate on next, is very important for understanding the processes and products of composing engaged in by the children, as we demonstrate later.

After assigning the report writing task linked to studying barn owls and dissecting owl pellets, their teacher reminded them they had already learned a lot about barn owls and owl pellets from the *Ecology of the Barn Owl* video. She reminded students that many of them had notes from the video, and she provided them with an information sheet that had accompanied the video. She also reminded them that she had assembled a collection of books and other resources for them to use in writing their reports. Finally, she brought the students to the library later that day so they could gather additional resources.

While students were dissecting their owl pellets and writing their reports, we tape-recorded much of the talk of several of the dyads. Because there was so much noise in the room and because some children moved around a great deal, the recordings from various dyads vary in quality—both from moment-to-moment and session-to-session. Nevertheless, our recorded data contain a rich, if partial, account of much of the talk and text-making work engaged in by the children.

The written text that we analyze in detail is the final draft of the science report written by two boys—Kyle and Max. This text is displayed in Figure 9.2.

Because the histories and positionings of social actors are critical for understanding their practices, it is important that we say a bit about Kyle and Max. Both boys were from working class European American families. Kyle's family had lived on the East Coast or in the Midwest for many generations. Max's family had migrated to the Midwest from the Appalachian

"The Amazing Barn Owl"

by Kyle & Max

1. As it swoops down from the sky, it grabs a little shrew in its talons.
2. Shrews are like small feasts to these huge owls.
3. If you see one swoop down out of the dark, you shouldn't be surprised.
4. These animals are nocturnal. ¶
5. Barn owls live almost anywhere.
6. They live in trees, barns, steeples, old houses, and silos.
7. I bet you thought barn owls only live in the midwest, huh?
8. Wrong.
9. They actually live in many different parts of the world. ¶
10. The barn owl's face is shaped like a disc.
11. This disc pulls noises from the ground into its ears.
12. So the barn owl has very good hearing.
13. It has good eyesight too.
14. It needs these senses to catch its prey. ¶
15. Barn owls are huge.
16. A full grown barn owl is about 14 inches tall and has a wing span of about 44 inches.
17. They weigh about 20 ounces.
18. They have four talons.
19. They eat shrews, mice, birds, gophers, and other things.
20. Barn owl pairs can eat as many as 1000 small rodents during mating season. ¶
21. What the owl cannot digest, they regurgitate and hurl up as a huge hairball called an owl pellet.
22. Beavis, he said "hurl."
23. We dissected owl pellets in biology.
24. It made me feel like I was really being a biologist or a surgeon.
25. There are a couple of things you should know about owl pellets.
26. They smell like a dentist's office because of how they're preserved.
27. You might find a vole or a bird or a field mouse in them.
28. You have to dissect them very carefully so you don't break any bones.
29. You can't act like you're the terminator.
30. If you are careful, you will get a nice, maybe even complete, skeleton.
31. But figuring out which bone goes with which other bone is hard work. ¶
32. When we finally put our skeleton together, we think we had a vole or a field mouse.
33. We also think voles and field mice are part Vulcan because they have such big ears.
34. Our skeleton has a big skull, about one inch long.
35. It also has a huge jawbone, about 1½ inches long.
36. We think we found every bone except for one neck bone. ¶
37. Before I knew it, I was writing this report, something scientists also do.
38. Now you know something about the amazing life of the barn owl.
39. We hope you get to dissect owl pellets some day.
40. At first I thought it was really sick, but it's actually very interesting.

FIG. 9.2. Kyle and Max's science report (fifth grade).

South a couple of generations ago. When the owl pellet activity occurred in early October, both Kyle and Max had already been relegated to quasi-outsider status in the classroom. With the death of Kyle's father, earlier in the year, Kyle became even more of a social enigma than he had been earlier, turning to television and movies as an emotional escape. A bright child, Kyle had a very sophisticated sense of humor, and made links across the media and society that were much more advanced than many of his peers. Kyle was perceived as quirky, flighty, unpredictable, and irresponsible, which in some ways he was. Classmates typically considered him interesting, but a liability in small-group activities. Max had been marked as a kid from "the wrong side of the tracks" who was rough around the edges, a bit dull witted, socially intrusive, and a kid with exciting but undesirable avocations such as collecting weapons and hunting.

Text. Having given some sense of the writers, the writing task, and the setting in which the writing was located, we turn to the formal features of the text Kyle and Max produced. Unlike Denise's text, their text is reasonably conventional both in terms of English orthography and in that it has many of the features typical of the science report genre. However, understanding its production, its functions, and its audiences involves much more than meets the eye. First, note the pastiche-like quality of their text. Basically, it is a **"narrative of nature"** (Myers, 1990), within which are embedded an expository report about the barn owl, an instruction manual or "how-to" text about dissecting owl pellets, and elements of a personal recount. This is not surprising since, according to Myers (1990), **narratives of nature** are the kinds of scientific texts commonly found in more popular science publications, which are written for the general public. Although embodying many features of scientific discourse, they often include everyday/popular language; they have less dense and complex syntax than more academic scientific texts; they are usually organized temporally/chronologically rather than logically and hierarchically as in more academic science texts; and they tend to foreground scientific content and activity rather than theoretical concepts and experimental procedures, as in academic texts. Parenthetically, many of the texts written by other students in this class were similar in that they blended features from expository science reports, narratives of nature, and other genres. As mentioned earlier, the teacher's directions were ambiguous, even confusing. For example, she told them that they could write about barn owls, owl pellets, dissecting owl pellets, or some combination of topics. She referred to the texts they would write as "reports," but she emphasized writing about what they learned from the experience of dissecting owl pellets. In short, the genre requested of the students was a hybrid science report/personal narrative. However, hybrid compositional structures like Max and Kyle's are also quite common in media texts on scientific topics such as documentaries about animals produced by *National Geographic* and the *Discovery Channel*, which many of the students in this class often watched.

Although it is not organized as conventionally as it might be, much of the texture and structure of Max and Kyle's text is predictably school scientific. This is especially true of the first half of the text, which, except for its opening lines, is constructed as a fairly prototypical expository report of the sort one might find in an encyclopedia or a science book published for educational purposes. The first half of this text contains statements about characteristic activities (e.g., lines 5, 6). It also contains descriptions of attributes (e.g., lines 10, 15, 29). However, there are other features of this part of the text that seem rhetorically unconventional, even out of place. For example, the text begins more like a narrative of nature of the sort common to popular television science programs (e.g., line 1). The text also contains apparent asides to an apparently intimate audience (e.g., lines 7, 8, 22).

The second half of Kyle and Max's text, which begins with the statement, "We dissected owl pellets in biology" (line 23), is equally interesting. Stylistically and compositionally, it is a hybrid text composed primarily of elements of a narrative of nature (e.g., line 34), a personal recount (e.g., line 32), and an instruction manual or "how-to" text (e.g., lines 28, 39). It also seems to include elements more common to everyday conversation (e.g., line 26). Besides being written in a more intimate and colloquial style than the first half of the text, this half seems more explicitly "owned" by its authors. It is about a specific event they participated in, and it is addressed to a specific reader (i.e., those who might also dissect owl pellets some day) rather than a more general audience. Finally, although there are fewer odd or out of place utterances in the second half of this text, there are some unpredictable and surprising comments (e.g., lines 26, 33). We discuss these apparent oddities later in the chapter.

Context. Understanding both the conventional and unconventional features in this text, as well as something about the text's production, functions, and politics, requires analyzing the contextual forces/effects at work during the text's production. Although we cannot map all of these forces/effects—because only some of them were visible to us and because of the space limitations of this chapter—we map enough of them to provide a nuanced sense of how context analyses contribute to understanding Kyle and Max's writing practices and products.

Much of the content of the text could be traced back to talk that the boys engaged in while dissecting their owl pellet and reconstructing the skeleton within it. In addition to embodying specific intertextual fragments and interdiscursive tropes, their text embodied aspects of the general discursive hybridity that often characterized their interactions while doing their dissection work and in many other classroom activities as well. As they worked, Kyle and Max drew together discursive and material strategies and artifacts from a wide range of contexts and activities.

Significantly, the opening utterance of the final draft of their text (lines 1, 2) was not included in earlier drafts. As it turns out, Kyle and Max overheard another dyad reading their text during a writing conference, and they virtually copied it verbatim. Importantly, textual poaching was common practice in this classroom. In fact, in speaking with the students who originally included these lines in their report, we learned that they had paraphrased it from a nature show they had watched on television. This fact partially explains why the social languages and genre structures embodied in this text fragment are typical of narratives of nature, such as the voice-over narratives that are often part of television science programs.

The next sentence in the text (line 3) bears a strong resemblance to the opening lines in terms of its style and compositional structure. However, although it also draws heavily from the video, it was intentionally crafted by Kyle and Max to form a transition between the narrative material they poached from their peers and the more scientific material that constitutes the second, third, fourth, and beginning of the fifth paragraphs of their text. As already noted, most of material in these paragraphs is cast in language typical of expository science reports, especially ones written for children. For example, it is composed primarily of short indicative sentences that contain attribute descriptions and statements about characteristic activities typical of taxonomic descriptions. Its social language is distinctively biological. This is not surprising given that most of the material in these paragraphs seems to have been appropriated and copied almost verbatim from various classroom resources, especially Kyle and Max's notes on the barn owl video and the information sheet that accompanied it.

However, a closer look at these paragraphs reveals some interesting bumpiness. Although Kyle and Max re-voiced almost verbatim much of the material they poached, they rendered some material in more colloquial terms (e.g., lines 13, 21). The coupling of more scientific language with more colloquial language in a single utterance is what Bakhtin (1981) called a **hybrid construction**. Hybrid constructions involve the mixing together in a single utterance of two styles of speech (or two different social languages) that are widely separated in terms of history or social space. Among other things, they often indicate a speaker or writer's efforts to gain some ownership of a new and unfamiliar set of language practices. Indeed, there was evidence in our fieldnotes to suggest that the boys were doing just this. They spent a considerable amount of time looking through various books and other resources while composing this portion of their text. While doing so, they also engaged in a lot of verbal play and laughter around the phrases we have suggested are more colloquial. Finally, they pondered and negotiated the final wordings of these hybrid constructions longer and more contentiously than many other text segments.

Lines 7 and 8 constitute an easily isolatable segment of text that seems especially odd or out of place. Although we are not completely sure where this segment came from or why Kyle and Max placed it where they did, the segment's content, compositional structure, and function seem remarkably similar to a segment of the *Ecology and the Barn Owl* video, wherein the narrator forges a transition from talking about the immediate habitats of barn owls to their regional distribution. Indeed, such vernacular utterances are also tropes found in many narratives of nature, especially ones produced for video or television. Additionally, during the question and answer period following the viewing of the videotape, the teacher posed similar questions to the students, asking them, for instance, if and where they had seen barn owls. She also explained that they could be found in various parts of the country. Whatever the precise source, Kyle and Max seem to have rewritten this transition (or transition type) to recontextualize it within the task at hand and the culture of their classroom, positioning their Midwestern peers and teacher as the target audience.

Following this unexpected utterance is another hybrid construction (line 9). Stylistically, the word "actually" embedded within this sentence seems more like everyday talk while the rest of the sentence seems more like the language of scientific discourse. However, whereas the previous hybrid constructions we discussed seemed to function as bootstrapping devices in Kyle and Max's efforts to assume scientist identities, this one seems to provide a transition back into the substantial and coherent expository science report within their text. Given its transitional function, this utterance's hybridity does not seem surprising. In a sense, the medium is the message.

Another odd and surprising utterance in Kyle and Max's report is line 22. Although this is the only discursive trope in their text that explicitly indexes the *Beavis and Butthead* television show, Kyle and Max invoked this and other popular cultural contexts and artifacts almost constantly as they worked to dissect their owl pellet. A couple of examples of such activity appear below:

(1) Kyle: This smells like my dentist, heh heh, heh heh. *((Kyle seems to be impersonating Beavis of the* Beavis and Butthead *cartoon.))*
     Max: You're weird, Beavis, heh heh *((Max seems to be impersonating Butthead.))*
(2) Kyle: I'm going in. *((He makes a sound as if he were using a saw or drill.))*
     Max: Cool. *((one element of the binary "cool–that sucks" that seems to characterize how Beavis and Butthead organize every aspect of their social world))*

Inserting the Beavis utterance where they did in their text resulted in a drastic frame break. It was also an action about which the boys seemed quite ambivalent. For example, this utterance was not included in early drafts of the text but appeared only in the final draft. Additionally, Kyle and Max deleted it when they read their text aloud to the class—a performance that was evaluated by their teacher and peers for a grade. Importantly, as they were rehearsing their oral presentation, Kyle and Max debated about whether to include this utterance. They also debated about the inclusion of two other utterances (lines 26, 29). However, they ultimately decided to leave these two utterances in their oral presentation.

These debates and the decisions that resulted in them are interesting for several reasons. They surrounded the most obvious frame breaks, which were all excursions into popular cultural terrain, from the task at hand, namely, writing a science report. As such, the social languages and generic forms of these frame breaks marked significant departures from the social languages and generic forms of the majority of utterances that constituted the bulk of their text. To eliminate these outliers from their oral presentation seemed to constitute good common sense. Although eliminating all such outliers from their presentation may have constituted even more common sense, the fact that they did not do so was not particularly surprising given their expert knowledge of and extreme investments in the contexts and artifacts of popular culture, as well as the social capital that accrued to them because of these investments. What we mean here will become clearer when we discuss the politics of their writing.

Approximately one third of the second half of Kyle and Max's text, beginning with line 23 and ending with line 37, is a cross between a narrative of nature and personal recount in which Kyle and Max narrate the experience of dissecting their owl pellet replete with what they did and found, and some evaluative commentary, a required component of their report, which is an important component of a compelling narrative (Labov, 1972). Note the shift back and forth between singular and plural first person narration. This feature was constitutively related to the practices involved in the production of the text. Because Kyle was both more knowledgeable about science and popular culture than Max and because he was also more proficient and responsible, he took the lead in composing it. Most of the time, Kyle and Max worked on the text together, but Kyle always wielded the pencil or keyboard; he usually contributed much more information than Max; and he made more decisions than Max did. Occasionally, Kyle composed alone and then showed Max what he had written. Max usually neither questioned nor responded to what Kyle had written. When he did, Kyle resisted and Max backed down. Even though Kyle and Max tried to revise and proofread their text to smooth out some of its rough edges (including its narrative voice), they did not completely succeed, and their final draft reflects this.

The last two thirds of the fifth paragraph (beginning with line 25) and the final sentence of Kyle and Max's text are interesting for the ways in which they seem to blend elements of a narrative of nature with those of instruction manuals or a television "how-to" shows. Most utterances within these segments are addressed to a ubiquitous "you." They include mainly material process verbs cast in a timeless present tense. They are filled with factual descriptions of attributes and processes. And they focus on the *how, where,* and *when* of the dissection process. Additionally and importantly, most of these utterances seem to be ventriloquized versions of instructions contained in the video they watched, the information sheet that accompanied it, and the teacher's various lectures, minilessons, and modeling activities.

Several utterances in these segments, however, represent interesting examples of hybridizing intertextuality, interdiscursivity, and intercontextuality that can be partially traced back to interactions between Kyle and Max that occurred while they were dissecting their owl pellet and reconstructing the skeleton within it. Most of these utterances also index the boys' compelling investment in popular culture and their propensity to bring this investment to bear in their writing (lines 22, 26, 29, 33). For example, when they first began to dissect their owl pellet, the following interchange occurred:

Kyle: Scalpel. *((Kyle extends his hand.))*
Max: Scalpel. *((Max places scalpel in Kyle's hand.))*
Kyle: This smells like my dentist, heh heh, heh heh. *((Kyle seems to be impersonating Beavis of the* Beavis and Butthead *cartoon.))*
Max: You're weird, Beavis, heh heh *((Max seems to be impersonating Butthead.))*

The idea that owl pellets smell like a dentist's office was repeated by Kyle several times during the dissection activity. Other students overheard him and began to echo his comment in their own talk. Eventually, this "factoid" ended up in Kyle and Max's text as part of the hybrid construction (line 26) we analyzed earlier. Like other hybrid constructions we have discussed, this one seems to index the "mangle of practice" (Pickering, 1995) that seemed to constitute Kyle and Max's writing—an unruly mix of their knowledge of scientific discourse, their abiding investments in popular culture, their constant language play, sedimented traces from their dissection activity talk and other talk, and a host of other contextual and political pushes and pulls.

Another interesting utterance within these segments is "You can't act like you're the terminator." Like a stone on water, this utterance seems to have skipped from the teacher's instructions to Kyle and Max's talk during the dissection activity to their written text. This path is visible in the following transcript of a segment of interaction that occurred while Kyle and Max were dissecting their owl pellet:

Kyle: I think we got a skull, Max.

Max: Yeah, that's a skull all right.

Kyle: I'm going in. *((Kyle makes a sound as if using an electric drill or saw.))*

Max: Cool. *((Max seems to enact a Butthead voice.))*

Kyle: I could easily crush these bones. *((Spoken with an accent and delivery style reminiscent of Arnold Schwarzenegger in* The Terminator. *He confirmed that he was re-voicing Terminator- speak. His utterance also seems to reach back to the warning given by the teacher at the outset of the dissection activity, "Be gentle. . . . Don't pull too hard with your tweezers 'cause you'll break the bones. And the skull is the most fragile part."))*

In connection with this interaction, Kyle was constantly embodying/ventriloquizing the speech of his favorite media icons (e.g., Beavis and Butthead, Schwarzenegger, *Star Trek* characters). The particular utterance in question (line 29) seems to have been born in the context of the teacher's instruction, to have been dramatically transformed when re-voiced by Kyle acting as the Terminator, and to have been re-domesticated as a deontic modal construction among other such constructions in the context of Kyle and Max's written text. As they had done many times before and would do many times again, Kyle and Max built on and extended the intertextual, interdiscursive, and intercontextual streams that circulated within their classroom, often laminating media and popular cultural accents onto school and scientific discourses.

Politics. The politics of writing associated with Kyle and Max's "science report" seemed to function in at least three ways: (a) to help them boot-strap themselves toward becoming competent scientists and science writers, (b) to help them gain some recognition and legitimacy as competent students in the classroom, and (c) to help them forge solidarity relations with peers. Moreover, their actions and activities often seemed to embody two or more of these functions at once.

As we mentioned earlier, the students in the class were set loose to engage in dissection activities and to write science reports with very little explicit instruction, modeling, or guidance. In the absence of these support structures, they had to figure out for themselves what to do and how to do it. Different students developed different strategies for doing this. Kyle and Max tended to engage heavily in intertextual, interdiscursive, and intercontextual practices related to the media. For example, they invoked the context of television dramas such as *ER*, and they adapted its medical discourse to accomplish their laboratory work. This was quite astute since the medical discourse common to such shows is a close cousin to the discourse of the laboratory, even if it is more dialogic and more sensationalized. When writing their text, Kyle and Max seemed to enact similar tactics. They poached heavily from classroom materials, television nature shows, and their peers' poachings from similar resources. In forging various intertextual, interdiscursive, and intercontextual connections with these various discourses, the boys seemed to become more conversant with the social languages and genres of science and scientific work, thus bootstrapping themselves toward more legitimate identities as scientists/science writers. This discursive work also positioned them as good students within the classroom. Their hybrid constructions (e.g., lines 9, 26) seem particularly telling in this regard. Specifically, these constructions seem to betray the awkwardness with which Kyle and Max positioned themselves betwixt and between the worlds of everyday life, school, and science. Yet, it is precisely this awkward positioning that seemed to function as the bootstrapping device that allowed them to feel more "at home" both in the world of science and the world of school.[2]

Another odd and apparently out of place utterance that seems particularly important to the politics of writing in Kyle and Max's complex and multiple social worlds are lines 7 and 8. The colloquial and fully "owned" character of this utterance makes it fit only so well with the narrative of nature utterances that precede and follow it. However, it seems to function powerfully to position Kyle and Max as not only animators but also as authors and principals of their discourse, perhaps for the first time in this text. More specifically, it seems to afford them legitimate positions as "narrative of nature" narrators, which also functions to position them as serious students (and teachers) within the classroom. Additionally, along with many other utterances we have already discussed, this utterance contributes to reconstructing the space of the classroom as a space within which everyday, popular, academic, and scientific discourses and practices may cohabit and interanimate each other.

The various intrusions of media and popular cultural discourse that pepper Kyle and Max's text are important for other reasons as well. Besides functioning as scaffolds for developing scientific identities and practices, they functioned crucially to position Kyle and Max more favorably within the society of their peers, a very important function if you recall that both boys desired more legitimacy and respect within the micropolitics of classroom life. In fact, being acknowledged as equals among their peers was at least, if not more, important to them than being acknowledged as good students and scientists. In the contexts of the owl pellet dissection activity, the writing activity, and the public presentation of their text, both boys were able to leverage their rich funds of popular cultural knowledge to social advantage.

---

[2]This kind of discourse was called "mushfake" by Gee (1996), and he argued that it serves precisely this function. Bartholomae (1985) suggested that such loose fitting language functions as a bootstrapping device as well.

Somewhat to our surprise, Kyle and Max's work within this life science unit also yielded positive long-term political effects for these boys—both in terms of their positioning as students and scientists and in terms of their positioning among their peers. In fact, this activity seemed to mark a turning point in how they were perceived and responded to by their teacher and classmates. From this point on, Kyle and Max experienced increasingly less social marginalization. Although students had already recognized Kyle's rich knowledge of popular culture, his artsy antics began to be read less by others as signs of his "oddness" and more as signs of his competence as a student and social desirability as a peer. As the year unfolded, he was increasingly enlisted to contribute his pop culture expertise in both academic and social activities. Similarly, those things about Max that children initially found "unsavory" became less important to his classroom identity than his diligence and talent for teamwork.

Not only were Kyle and Max repositioned within the social dynamics of the classroom, their nonconventional approach to classroom work exerted powerful effects on their peers and on the activity system of the classroom. For example, their report drew high praise from their teacher, who told us she "had no idea they could write so well." Some of their classmates echoed these sentiments, and Kyle and Max's report became an interdiscursive resource for many students' future work. In fact, we would argue that this report became a benchmark for the hybrid discourse potential that all children were now sanctioned to exploit in their own work. Indeed, as the school year progressed, more and more students adopted experimental approaches to their academic work, often consulting Kyle, Max, and several other particularly inventive children in the classroom about what they were doing. For instance, as the students were engaged in a study of the 1996 presidential election, one child created a one-man-show mock presidential debate, role-playing each of the year's three presidential candidates. His videotaped performance was replete with caricatures of the candidates' speech styles and body language, as well as poignant statements about their stances on various political and economic issues.

Also important to the micropolitics surrounding Kyle and Max's text were changes in the teacher's stance toward them and their inventive hybridizing practices. Early in the year, she tended to sanction only authoritative discourses and to silence internally persuasive discourses such as discursive detours into the landscape of popular culture. As the year progressed, however, she allowed and even encouraged such detours. When we called her attention to this change, she told us that she had come to realize not only that the children's hybrid discourse practices were often productively task related, but that they also allowed children to "show off" their knowledge, creativity, and prowess. She also mentioned that, for some children, allowing their investments in popular culture to become part of classroom life opened up opportunities for "social acceptance" and "social growth."

Although the year was marked by a progressive reconstruction of the discursive space of the classroom, this process was neither linear nor straightforward. Approval and sanction coexisted with disapproval and censorship in ways that were not always predictable. Although opportunities increased for Kyle, Max, and the other students in the classroom to go public with their internally persuasive discourses, these same discourses were sometimes challenged or silenced. These various findings suggest that both official and unofficial practices are seldom clean, systematic, and straightforward. Rather, as Foucault (1977, 1984) convincingly argued, they are constituted within a discursive/material topology with many contours and gaps, nodal outcroppings and invisibilities, and local articulations within wider streams of practical and political discourses and practices.

CONCLUSIONS AND IMPLICATIONS

Why are these data and these analyses important for understanding children's writing and the role of their writing in becoming school learners, increasingly legitimate members of various communities of practice, and complex social/political subjects? There seem to be several reasons. First, our analyses seem to suggest the value of developing and maintaining complex and holistic units of analysis for our analytic work. Together, our analyses of texts, contextual forces/effects, and textual politics seem to yield richer, more complex, and more nuanced accounts of Denise, Kyle, and Max's writing than analyses of any one (or even two) of these dimensions might have yielded. Although extremely difficult, navigating one's way between the Charybdis of reduction and the Scylla of expansion is fundamental to understanding texts and how they work.

Second, we would like to argue that understanding the texts, contexts, and politics of Denise, Kyle, and Max's writing activity was fundamental to understanding that (and how) they were "bootstrapping" their ways toward understanding science and science writing, however nascent these understandings may have been. If we are correct here, their complex hybrid discourse practices functioned much like Vygotsky claimed that *play* functions to propel development. In play, children often "behave beyond [their] average age[s], above [their] daily behavior; in play it is as though [they] were a head taller than [themselves]. As in the focus of a magnifying glass, play contains all the developmental tendencies in a condensed form and is itself a major source of development" (Vygotsky, 1978, p. 102). As children engage in discursive play in the context of school writing activities, they experiment with scientific texts and identities, cobbling together discursive strategies that resemble but are not homologous with the scientific "real thing." They enact "as if" modes of scientific being and acting. Importantly, however, these "as if" modes become more genuinely lived modes over time. As they inhabit these tentative and temporary modes of being, children bootstrap their own progress toward fuller understanding and participation in particular communities of practice and toward richer, more practiced, and more transparent identities within those communities.

ACTIVITIES

1. Tape record social activity in different contexts (e.g., a classroom, playground, the counter of a fast food restaurant, a place of worship). Transcribe the tape recordings of each event. For each sample, ask three questions: What is happening or being accomplished? Who are the participants and what are their relations with each other? What roles or functions is language playing in these interactions? Analyze each language sample for recurrent linguistic and discursive patterns and compare the patterns present in the samples. How are the patterns the same? Different? What kind of communicative work do various patterns do in terms of defining the communicative event, accomplishing particular communicative goals, and forging particular kinds of social relations among participants?

2. Collect a set of different kinds of texts written by or for children (e.g., stories, information reports, instruction manuals, poems, letters, advertisements, etc.) culled from different activity settings either in or out of school. Analyze these texts in ways similar to how you analyzed the oral texts from the previous activity.

3. Collect a range of texts representing different genres typical of different contexts (e.g., academic articles, children's stories, editorials, "how-to" manuals). Sort each text into piles according to their relative prototypicality. Analyze the texts to the extent that you can explain why some are more or less prototypical. Speculate about how more and less prototypical texts might function to reproduce or disrupt the social (including writing) practices that occur in the different contexts.

4. Select a child who interests you with respect to his or her apparent interest and investment in language and writing. Spend as much time as you can observing the child in multiple social and institutional contexts for several weeks. Collect relevant artifacts. Document and analyze the different ways in which literacy (especially writing) is involved in the varied activities. Interview the child about things that interest or puzzle you. Document and analyze as many of the intertextual, interdiscursive, and intercontextual relations as you can between the child's writing practices and products and the

texts, text types, practices, and contexts that seemed to influence his/her writing processes and products.

5. Select a child with whom you can conduct a case study. Find out what the child is interested in (e.g., rap music, the internet, hockey, ballet, magic cards). Ask the child to decide upon and complete a significant writing project that he or she is interested in doing. This project should be substantive and carried out over an extended period of time (e.g., biography of a cultural icon, instructions about how to play a favorite game). Help the child find and use relevant resources to complete the writing project. Provide response and scaffolding if the child requests them. Analyze the texts, contextual forces, and politics involved in the development of the final text.

6. Spend some time in a kindergarten or first-grade classroom during language arts activities. While there, document the activities that children are asked to engage in. Observe, take fieldnotes, and perhaps videotape children as they write. Ask the children to read their texts to you. Ask them questions about their writing processes, practices, and products. When relevant, such questions may include: What kinds of writing did you use in your text (e.g., drawing, scribble, letter strings, inventive spelling)? Is this text just the way you want it or do you want to change it or add things to it? Is this text the kind of text your teacher asked you to write and why? Where did you get your ideas for this text? Who would enjoy reading this text?

FOR FURTHER READING

In this section, we offer suggestions for further reading in three areas of theory and research indexed by our work in this chapter: (a) children's development and use of multiple graphic sign systems, (b) rich, descriptive, case-study accounts of individual child writers, and (c) cross-sectional and longitudinal accounts of children's writing development over time. Although our suggestions are selective, we do not think they are idiosyncratic. Finally, we apologize to the scholars whose work is not represented here either because of space limitations or accidental omission.

Given how interesting this topic is, surprisingly little sustained research has been conducted on children's development, use, and integration of multiple graphic sign systems. What research has been conducted has focused primarily on the textual dimension and secondarily on the contextual and political dimensions. Probably the most compelling and theoretically sophisticated work in this area has been done by Gunther Kress and his colleagues (e.g., Kress, 1993, 1997, 2000; Kress & van Leeuwen, 1996). All of this work is predicated on the ideas that (a) more than ever, the present globalized fast-capitalist, media saturated world demands that people be competent at using multiple, interanimating sign systems and that (b) children do use (and probably always have used) whatever semiotic means necessary to communicate graphically with others. In addition to Kress' work, several other theorists and researchers have contributed in significant ways to this domain of inquiry. These include Clay (1975), Dyson (1986), Ferreiro and Teberosky (1982), Gallas (1994), Golomb (1974), Harste, Woodward, and Burke (1984), Luria (1983), Rowe (1994), Siegel (1984), Sulzby, Barnhart, and Hieshima (1989), Temple, Nathan, and Burris (1983), and Vygotsky (1978).

As we mentioned earlier, most recent research on children's writing has involved highly contextualized case studies of various kinds. Bissex (1980), Calkins (1983), and Schickedanz (1990) are book-length treatments of case studies of individual child writers that are likely to become classics. Perhaps the most sustained program of case-study research on children's writing has been done by Dyson (e.g., 1989, 1993, 1997). Her work has focused variously on children's coordination of multiple sign systems, the social worlds of child writers, and how children's writing is related to their investments in the media. All of Dyson's work is theoretically sophisticated, methodologically rigorous, and highly readable. Besides Dyson, many researchers have conducted particularly interesting case studies that foreground various social, cultural, and political dimensions of children's writing. These include but are not limited to Lensmire (1994), Taylor and Dorsey Gaines (1988), Schaafsma (1994), Lofty (1992), MacGillivray (1994), McCarthy (1994), Kamberelis and Scott (1992), McGinley and Kamberelis (1996), and Mulhern (forthcoming).

There are many published articles, monographs, and books devoted to describing and explaining children's writing development over time. Some of these reports are based on studies that employed cross-sectional designs; others are based on studies that employed longitudinal designs. Particularly important here is the work of Martin and his colleagues (e.g., Martin, 1984, 1989; Martin & Rothery, 1980, 1981), which reports on a longitudinal study of the writing of a large number of kindergarten through sixth-grade children. Other particularly important studies of children's writing development over time include Britton, Burgess, McLeod, and Rosen (1975), Chapman (1994, 1995), Donovan (2001), Harste, Woodward, and Burke (1984), Kamberelis (1993, 1999), Langer (1986), Newkirk (1989), Sulzby, Barnhart and Hieshima (1989), and Zecker (1991, 1996).

10

Rhetorical Analysis: Understanding How Texts Persuade Readers

Jack Selzer
Penn State University

Suppose you want to understand better some piece of writing that you are interested in or find important. Maybe it is an environmental impact statement, or a piece of fiction set during World War II, or a magazine article about the death penalty, or a proposal under consideration by the local school board, or even a routine thing that you see on a daily basis, such as the comics or advertisements in your local newspaper. The previous chapters in this book have given you several approaches for analyzing such documents. But especially if those pieces of writing have a persuasive intent, especially if (in other words) they have designs on your beliefs and attitudes (and nearly all writing does have that purpose, to some extent), the activity known as rhetorical analysis can offer you additional perspective and understanding. This chapter is designed to give you a good understanding of the key concepts involved in rhetorical analysis and to make you comfortable conducting instructive rhetorical analyses on your own.

SOME BASIC CONCEPTS

Let's begin with some basic terms and concepts, beginning with the phrase **rhetorical analysis** itself.

There is no generally accepted definition of rhetorical analysis (or **rhetorical criticism**, as it is also called), probably because there is really no generally accepted definition of *rhetoric*. The various people who have written about rhetorical analysis (see the list of Further Readings at the end of this chapter) inevitably differ on its meaning because they hold to different ideas about the nature of their subject. To the general public *rhetoric* most commonly seems to denote highly ornamental or deceptive or even manipulative speech or writing: "That politician is just using a bunch of rhetoric," you hear people say; or, "the rhetoric of that advertisement is highly deceptive." But the term rhetoric is also commonly used as a synonym for speaking or writing in general or for any other kind of communication: "*Silent Spring* is one of the most influential pieces of environmental rhetoric ever written," someone might say. As an academic subject (and that gets at another important meaning of the term, for rhetoric has a long association with education—Aristotle wrote an educational treatise *On Rhetoric*, for example), the word is often associated with the means of producing effective discursive acts. Rhetoric textbooks are usually how-to books therefore—advice manuals for how to produce effective pieces of communication: "the art of discovering in any given case the available means of persuasion" (as Aristotle put it). But in recent years rhetoric has also taken on an interpretive function; rhetoric has come to be used not just as a means of producing effective communications, but also as a way of understanding communication.[1] In short, **rhetoric can be understood as both a productive and interpretive enterprise:** "the study of language—and the study of how to use it."

Aristotle's emphasis on persuasion, evident in the quotation from him that I just offered, has been influential in the history of rhetoric. And so it is now common to understand rhetoric as fundamentally involved in the study of **persuasion**. But "persuasion" as used here must be persuasion very broadly defined, because recently the realm of rhetoric has come to include a great deal of territory—written and oral language used to persuade, to be sure, but also a great many other kinds of communications that have general designs on people's values and actions, attitudes and beliefs. Speeches and writing usually have such persuasive designs, and so rhetoricians attempt to understand how to produce effective acts of verbal and written persuasion. By extension, **rhetorical analysis or rhetorical**

---

[1]Jeffrey Walker of Emory University, responding to an earlier draft of this essay, offered the following observations on Aristotle's definition of rhetoric: "Aristotle's definition actually calls rhetoric a 'faculty' (*dunamis*) of 'observing' (*theorein*): hence the phrase, 'faculty of observing the available means of persuasion in any given case.' Note further that 'available means of persuasion' comes from Greek words that can also mean 'possible' and 'permissible' means of persuasion. . . . That is, rhetoric is a trained faculty or capacity for analytically observing what is both possible to say in a given situation (an inventory of all possible arguments) and what is allowable (what lines of argument ought to be persuasive; what one can get away with; what one should assent to or not; etc.). What I find interesting about this analysis of Aristotle's definition is the suggestion that he is mainly thinking of rhetoric as a critical faculty, and that rhetorical theory as he begins to outline it is a terminology for rhetorical analysis." I am grateful to Professor Walker for that commentary and for a number of other comments that helped me to improve this essay.

criticism can be understood as an effort to understand how people within specific social situations attempt to influence others through language.

But not *just* through language: Rhetoricians today attempt to understand better every kind of important symbolic action—speeches and articles, yes, but also architecture (isn't it clear that the U.S. Capitol Building in Washington makes an argument?), movies, and television shows (doesn't "Ally McBeal" offer an implicit argument about the appropriate conduct of young professional women? doesn't "Friends" have designs on viewers' values and attitudes?), memorials (don't the AIDS quilt and the Vietnam Veterans Memorial make arguments about AIDS and about our national understanding of the Vietnam war?), as well as visual art, Web sites, advertisements, photos and other images, dance, popular songs, and so forth. (Anne Francis Wysocki's chapter in this book attends to visual rhetoric, and Gunther Kress and Theo van Leeuwen (1996), John Berger (1972), Alan Trachtenberg (1989), Charles Kostelnick and David Roberts (1998), and any number of others have also directed people on how to analyze visual images.) Recently a group of scholars together demonstrated that even physical bodies of various kinds make arguments too—through hair styles, clothing, musculature, make up, prosthetics, and piercings of various kinds (see Selzer and Crowley's, 1999, *Rhetorical Bodies*). Doesn't a woman who undertakes cosmetic surgery in order to appear like a living Barbie doll (as a young woman named Cindy Jackson has recently done[2]) embody arguments about the importance to our culture of a particular version of beauty?

Rhetorical analysis as it is discussed in this chapter is applicable to all these persuasive uses of symbolic words and acts (although I deal here mainly with written texts in line with the central focus of this book). Through rhetorical analysis, people strive to understand better how particular rhetorical episodes are persuasive. They get a better sense of the values and beliefs and attitudes that are conveyed in specific rhetorical moments. It might be helpful to think of **rhetorical analysis as a kind of critical reading**: Whereas "normal" (i.e., "uncritical" or "reactive") reading involves experiencing first-hand a speech or text or TV show or advertisement and then reacting (or not reacting) to it, critical reading—rhetorical analysis, that is—involves studying carefully some kind of symbolic action, often after the fact of its delivery and irrespective of whether it was actually directed to you or not, so that you might understand it better and appreciate its tactics. The result is a heightened awareness of the message under rhetorical consideration, and an appreciation for the ways people manipulate language and other symbols for persuasive purposes. Although normally people read as a member of a speaker's or writer's intended or actual audience and as a person very interested in the subject at hand, when they read rhetorically they may or may not be a member of the audience and

---

[2]Aimee Agresti, "Addicted to Perfection," *Mademoiselle*, January 2001, pp. 38–40.

may or may not care much about the issue; all that is necessary is that a rhetorical analyst try to get some distance and perspective on the reading experience. It's almost as if rhetorical analysts are eavesdropping on what someone is saying or writing to someone else, with the purpose of understanding better how it is said or written. When people read rhetorically, in any event, when they engage in rhetorical analysis, they not only react to the message, but they appreciate *how* the producer of that message is conveying the message to a particular audience too, whether that intended audience includes the analyst or not.

For example, as a citizen you may have experienced George W. Bush's inaugural address firsthand; you may have been swept up in the moment and carried away by his words. But as a rhetorical analyst, after the speech you might try to understand and appreciate how President Bush marshaled his rhetorical resources—ideas, phrases, cultural symbols, even gestures and clothing and intonation—in order to begin to achieve the aims of his administration, especially given the fact that he was elected without a majority of the popular vote and after a controversial court battle. A second example: As a reader you might respond very forcefully even today to the words of Abraham Lincoln at Gettysburg or to Martin Luther King's 1963 "I Have a Dream" speech or to Abigail Adams's famous letters to her husband—rhetorical performances never intended for you at all. But as a rhetorical analyst your job is not so much to react to these rhetorical acts as to understand them better, to appreciate the **rhetorical situation** (i.e., the circumstances of subject, audience, occasion, and purpose) that Lincoln, King, and Adams found themselves in—and how they made choices to further their aims. A third example: For entertainment you might watch "Ally McBeal" (and its commercials); but as an analyst you would try to learn who watches "Ally McBeal" and what its creators are trying to teach those watchers, knowingly or not, and through what means.

I do not want to overemphasize the differences between these two kinds of reading, for even in the act of "normal" reading people usually read critically (to one degree or another) as well as for content; and the two activities of reading and reading critically aren't really separable. But you get the point of my comparison: Rhetorical analysis is an effort to read interpretively, with an eye toward understanding a message fully and how that message is crafted to earn a particular response.

METHODS OF RHETORICAL ANALYSIS— AND SOME EXAMPLES

Rhetorical analysts—readers who are committed to understanding how persuasion works—must attend to the same matters that persuaders themselves attend to: how an idea should be shaped and presented to an audience in a particular form for a specific purpose. There are many approaches indeed to rhetorical analysis, and no one "correct" way to do it; there is no simple recipe for it. But, generally, approaches to rhetorical analysis can be placed between two broad extremes—not mutually exclusive categories but extremes along a continuum. At the one end of the continuum are analyses that concentrate more on texts than contexts. They typically use one or another kind of rhetorical terminology as a means of careful analysis of a single symbolic act considered on its own discrete terms. Let me call this approach **textual analysis**. At the other extreme are approaches that emphasize context over text; these attempt to reconstruct a rhetorical moment within which a particular rhetorical event (the one under scrutiny) took place, to create a thick description of the (sometimes complex) cultural environment that existed when that rhetorical event took place, and then to depend on that recreation to produce clues about the persuasive tactics and appeals that are visible in the performance in question. Those who undertake **contextual analysis**—as I'll call this second approach—regard particular rhetorical acts as parts of larger communicative chains, or conversations. By understanding the larger conversations that surround a specific symbolic performance, an analyst can appreciate better what is going on within that performance. Let me discuss each approach in detail.

TEXTUAL RHETORICAL ANALYSIS: USING RHETORICAL TERMINOLOGY AS AN ANALYTICAL SCREEN

Over a period of many years, experts in rhetoric have developed sophisticated terminologies to help them teach their lessons. Just as expert teachers in every field of endeavor—from baseball to biology—devise specialized vocabularies to facilitate specialized study, rhetoricians too have developed a set of key concepts to permit them to describe and prescribe rhetorical activities. A fundamental concept in rhetoric, of course, is the concept of **audience**—that term used to denote any one of three general ideas: the actual listeners or readers of a rhetorical act, or images of those readers in the mind of one developing an argument, or (more recently) the presence of an audience within the text itself (as "Bill Bennett" is present in one of the example documents I discuss later). Aristotle was at pains to describe audience (understood as actual listeners) in his *Rhetoric*, where he detailed the kinds of strategies likely to compel particular types of auditors and readers, and he also classified the most common and vital rhetorical occasions faced by rhetors in ancient Athens: **forensic rhetoric**, characteristic of courtrooms, involved questions of guilt and innocence (concerning actions done in the *past*); **deliberative rhetoric**, characteristic of legislative forums, was organized around the kinds of decisions a civic or social organization must make (about a *future* course of action); and **epideictic rhetoric** was ceremonial discourse used to create and reinforce community values (at a given *present* moment). In forensic and deliberative discourse, audiences are asked to make judgments or decisions—guilt or innocence, this course of action or that one; in epideictic discourse, the audience is asked to reconsider beliefs and values.

Moreover, classical rhetoricians in the tradition of Aristotle, Quintilian, and Cicero developed a range of terms around what they called the "canons" of rhetoric in order to describe some of the actions of rhetors: *inventio* (i.e., the finding or creation of information for persuasive acts, and the planning of strategies), *dispostio* (or arrangement), *elocutio* (or style), *memoria* (the recollection of rhetorical resources that one might call upon, as well as the memorization of what has been invented and arranged), and *pronuntiatio* (or delivery). These **five canons** generally describe the actions of a rhetor, from preliminary planning to final delivery, although no specific sequence of events was envisioned by the ancients (especially since invention and memory are required throughout rhetorical preparation and action). Over the years, and especially as written discourse gained in prestige against oral, the first three and the last canons especially encouraged the development of concepts and terms useful for rhetorical analysis. Aristotelian terms like *ethos*, *pathos*, and *logos*, all of them associated with **invention**, account for features of texts related to the trustworthiness and credibility of the rhetor (*ethos*), for the persuasive reasons in an argument that derive from a community's mostly deeply and fervently held values (*pathos*), and for the sound reasons that emerge from intellectual reasoning (*logos*). Arrangement required terms like *exordium* (introduction), *narratio* (generally equivalent to what we refer to today as "forecasting"), *confirmatio* (proof), *refutatio*, and *peroration* (conclusion) to describe the organization of speeches. Delivery has given rise to a discussion of things like voice, gesture, and expression (in oral discourse) and to voice and visual impact (in written). And a whole series of technical terms developed over the years to describe effective stylistic maneuvers (*elocutio*)— many of them terms still in common use such as antithesis, irony, hyperbole, and metaphor, but also many others as well—arcane terms, such as epanalepsis, antimetabole, and anacoluthon, that are rarely mentioned today. Although all these terms seem to have been devised to guide rhetorical performance, they have also been used to help analysts understand better the tactics visible in specific instances of rhetoric.[3]

---

[3]Fundamental to the classical approach to rhetoric is the concept of decorum, or "appropriateness": that everything within a persuasive act can be understand as in keeping with a central rhetorical goal that the rhetor consistently keeps in mind and that governs consistent

Classical terminology is not the only rhetorical terminology, by any means. Many other terms, developed long after classical times (and sometimes quite recently, for rhetoric is a subject of particular interest in our culture today), have been used to help would-be persuaders and those who would understand those persuaders. My own favorite 20th-century rhetorician, Kenneth Burke, for example, developed a host of terms that he used to understand rhetorical performances, and his admirers have continued to employ Burkean terms like *act, agent, agency, scene, purpose, identification,* and *consubstantiality* (I will spare you a mention of many others) to understand better the rhetorical moves that exist in all sorts of rhetorical acts. Similarly, feminist critics for at least the past three decades have devised interpretive technologies that are especially attentive to gendered power relations as they are present in a text, and the philosopher Stephen Toulmin suggested a series of terms that would account for the conduct of arguments in particular fields. Recently cultural studies theorists have developed many terms to account for what happens in the act of persuasion, especially (but certainly not only) terms related to class conflict, ethnicity, and the distribution of power. Whereas most cultural studies practitioners concentrate on understanding phenomena against the frame of specific cultural events (and thus belong more to the next section of this chapter), after the methodological example of Roland Barthes' pioneering analyses of wrestling and toys in his *Mythologies* (1972), other semioticians today examine cultural signs pretty much on their own terms, apart from considerations of setting. In short, a great many powerful terminologies—interpretive screens, Kenneth Burke called them—have been devised to permit powerful and telling rhetorical analyses of various kinds. What is good as advice for would-be persuaders is also frequently useful for analysts of persuasion, and vice versa.

DOING TEXTUAL RHETORICAL ANALYSIS: AN EXAMPLE

A text-based rhetorical analysis considers the issue that is taken up, of course—what the writer has to offer on a given subject to a particular audience. But it also considers, more basically, things that rhetorical advice offers by way of invention, arrangement, style, and delivery. Let me offer an extended example of text-based rhetorical analysis, one that employs the terminologies associated with ancient rhetoric, because it should clarify what I am talking about and should illustrate one approach to rhetorical

---

choices according to occasion and audience. The concept of decorum lies behind rhetorical analysis in that decisions by a rhetor are understood as rational and consistent—and thus are available for analysis.

analysis. The reprint in Appendix A is E. B. White's (1944) well-known short essay, "Education." Let us use the terms of classical rhetoric (terms that continue to be very influential in rhetorical studies) to understand it better.

What is the purpose of E. B. White's essay? (If you haven't read "Education" before, take time to do so now; that way, you can more easily follow the rest of this analysis.) **Is it an argument—a piece of deliberative rhetoric or epideictic rhetoric or forensic rhetoric?** Is it meant to influence public policy or to reinforce or form community values or to offer a judgment? White wrote the essay a half century ago, but you probably find it to be interesting and readable still, in part at least because it concerns a perennial American question: What should our schools be like? Is education better carried out in large, fully equipped, but relatively impersonal settings, or in smaller but intensely personal, teacher-dominated schools? Which should count for more: the efficiencies of an educational system that is "progressive" (the word comes from paragraph two), or the personal traits of the individual classroom teacher? In other words, you might easily look at the essay as deliberative in nature. On the other hand, maybe you find the essay to be less deliberative than epideictic; maybe, in other words, you see it as designed to shape values more than to persuade about specific public policy. The essay is a personal one (as opposed to public), after all, in that it is the education of his own son that White is "worried about" and writing about. And yet it is public matter, too. White published it in *Harper*'s, a magazine with a readership wide and influential. *Harper*'s is a magazine that people read for enjoyment too; it accommodates both deliberative and epideictic rhetoric. Or maybe you even consider "Education" to be forensic in nature—to make a judgment between two alternatives, as in a courtroom. After all, the essay is a comparison, and comparisons often are offered to provide a judgment or preference. Does White, in short, have a position on the issue of education? Is he recommending support for one kind of school?

Or maybe it is not an argument at all. At first it might seem that the author takes no sides, that he simply wishes to describe objectively the two alternatives, to record his son's experiences in each circumstance, and to celebrate each as an expression of national values. He gives equal time to each school, he spends the same amount of space on concrete details about each, and he seems in firm control of his personal biases ("I have always rather favored public schools"). Through his light and comic tone White implies that all will be well for his son—and for our children too—in either circumstance, that the two schools each are to be neither favored nor feared by us. "All one can say is that the situation is different" (paragraph four), not better, in the two places.

Or is it? Many readers—I'm one of them—contend that "Education" is less an objective, neutral appraisal than it is a calculated, **deliberative argu-**

ment that subtly favors the country school and schools like it (with an **epideictic undertone** concerning the values that we want to sponsor through our education system). To such readers, White's objective pose is only that—a created pose, an attempt to create a genial, sympathetic, and trustworthy speaker. By caring so obviously for his son (final paragraph), by confessing his biases, and by treating both schools with distance and detachment and reliable detail, White creates effective *ethos*—**that quality of a piece of writing that persuades through the character and trustworthiness of the speaker or writer**. By poking gentle humor at just about everything—his son "the scholar"; his wife the prim graduate of Miss Winsor's private schools; himself "the victim of a young ceramist"; and, of course, both schools—White makes himself seem enormously sympathetic and trustworthy: fair-minded and unflappable, balanced and detached.

But is this reliable speaker arguing or merely describing? Those who see the essay as a deliberative argument supporting the ways of the country school can point to the **emotional aspects** of White's "Education"—to its *pathos*, in other words. The image of the one-room schoolhouse, for instance, is imprinted in positive terms on the American psyche, and White exploits that image for his argumentative purposes. The "scholar" walks miles through the snow to get his education; like the schoolhouse itself, he has the self-reliance and weather-resistance to care for himself and to fit into a class with children both younger and older; and he learns a practical curriculum—there is "no time at all for the esoteric"—"just as fast and as hard as he can." It is all Ben Franklin and "Little House on the Prairie," Abraham Lincoln and "The Waltons," isn't it? And the teacher who presides over the country school appeals to the reader's emotions as only The Ideal Mother can (at least the "ideal mother" as some would stereotype her). This teacher–mother is not only "a guardian of their health, their clothes, their habits . . . and their snowball engagements," but "she has been doing this sort of Augean task for twenty years, and is both kind and wise. She cooks for the children on the stove that heats the room, and she can cool their passions or warm their soup with equal competence."

No such individual Ideal Mother presides over the city school. Instead, that school is supervised by a staff of Educational Professionals—a bus driver, half a dozen anonymous teachers, a nurse, an athletic instructor, dietitians. The school itself is institutional, regimented, professionalized. There the scholar is "worked on," "supervised," "pulled." Like the one-room schoolhouse, the regimented institution is ingrained in the American psyche and in popular culture. But in this case **the emotional appeal** is negative, for The System is something that Americans instinctively resist. True, the city school is no prison; and true, the scholar in this school learns "to read with a gratifying discernment." But the accomplishments remain rather abstract. Faced with such an education, such a school, no wonder the students literally become ill. At least that is the implication of the end of paragraph three, where the description of the city school is concluded with an account of the networks of professional physicians that discuss diseases which never seem to appear in the country schools.

For all these reasons many readers see "Education" as an argument against the city school (and its "progressive" education) and an endorsement of the country one (and its "basics"). They see the essay as a comparison with an aim like most comparison essays: to show a preference. The evaluative aim is carried out by reference to specific criteria, namely that schools are better if they are less structured and if they make students want to attend (because motivated students learn better); a structured, supervised curriculum and facilities are inferior to a personalized, unstructured environment that makes students love school. Days at the country school pass "just like lightning"; to attend the country school the boy is literally willing to walk through snowdrifts, while to get to the city school he must be escorted to the bus stop—or be "pulled" to classes. The country school is full of "surprises" and "individual instruction," while the city school is full of supervision; there are no surprises in the "progressive" school. In a real sense, therefore, White persuades not only by the force of his personality or through emotional appeals (pathos) but also through hard evidence, or logos. "Education" amounts to an **argument by example** wherein the single case—the boy scholar—stands for many such cases. This case study persuades like other case studies: by being presented as representative. White creates through his unnamed son, who is described as typical in every way, a representative example that stands for the education of Everychild. The particular **details** provided in the essay are not mere "concrete description" but hard evidence summoned to support White's implicit thesis. The logic of the piece seems to go something like this: "Country schools are a bit superior to city ones because they generally make up for what they lack in facilities with a more personal, less authoritarian atmosphere that children readily respond to."

E. B. White, then, wins his reader's assent by means of *ethos, pathos*, and *logos*. But the country-school approach is also reinforced by the essay's **arrangement, or *dispositio***. Notice, for example, that the essay begins and ends with favorable accounts of the country school. In other words, the emphatic first and final positions of the essay are reserved for the virtues of country schools, while the account of the city school is buried in the unemphatic middle of the essay. The article could easily have begun with the second paragraph (wouldn't sentence two of paragraph two have made a successful opener?); but such a strategy would have promoted the value of the city school. By choosing to add the loving vignette of the Ideal Teacher in his opening paragraph, White disposes his readers to favor country schools from the very start. Notice too that the comparison of the two schools in the body of "Education" proceeds from city to country. Again, it didn't have to be so; White could have discussed the country school first, or he could have gone back and forth from city to country more often (adopting what some handbooks call an "alternating" method of comparison as opposed to the "divided" pattern that White actually did use). By choosing to deal first with the city school, all in one lump, and then to present the country school in another lump, White furthered his persuasive aim. After all, most writers of comparisons usually move from inferior to superior, from "this one is good" to "but this other one is even better," rather than vice versa. So when White opts to deal first with the city schools, he subtly reinforces his persuasive end through very indirect means.

A rhetorical analysis of "Education" that uses classical concepts must also consider **style, or** *elocutio*, those sentence and word choices that are sometimes equated with the style of a particular essay or author. Like most rhetoricians, I personally resist the idea that "style is the person"–that style is something inherent in a writer, that it amounts to a sort of genetic code or set of fingerprints that are idiosyncratic to each person, that it is possible to speak generically of Joan Didion's style or Martin Luther King's style or E. B. White's style. It has always seemed to rhetoricians more appropriate to think of style as characteristic of a particular occasion for writing, as something that is as appropriate to reader and subject and genre as it is to a particular author. In other words, stylistic analysis is often highly contextual, as opposed to textual: Words and sentences are typically chosen in response to rhetorical circumstances, and those words and sentences change as the occasion changes. If it is sometimes possible to characterize E. B. White's style or King's style or Faulkner's style in general (and I'm not even sure of that), then it is so only with respect to certain kinds of writing that they did again and again. For when those writers found themselves writing outside *Harper's* or *The New Yorker* (in White's case) or outside of fiction (in Hemingway's), they did indeed adopt different stylistic choices. It is probably wiser to focus not on the idiosyncrasies associated with a Didion or a King or a Faulkner or an E. B. White, but on the particular word and sentence choices at work in a particular rhetorical situation.

Nevertheless, textual analysis of style is still quite possible. White's sentences are certainly describable. They move in conventional ways–from subjects and verbs to objects and modifiers. There are absolutely no sentence inversions (i.e., violations of the normal subject/verb/object order– what classical rhetoricians called **anastrophe**), few distracting interrupters (what classical rhetoricians called **parenthesis**; the parentheses and the "I suspect" in that one long sentence in paragraph two are exceptions), and few lengthy opening sentence modifiers that keep readers too long from subjects and verbs. Not only that, the sentences are simple and unpretentious in another sense: White comparatively rarely uses subordinate (or modifying) clauses—clauses beginning with "who" or "although" or "that" or "because" or the like (what the ancients called *hypotaxis*). I count only two such modifying (or dependent) clauses in the first and third paragraphs, for instance, and just five in the second; if you don't think that is a low number, compare it to a 600-word sample of your own prose. When White does add length to a sentence, he does it not by adding complex clauses that modify other clauses, but by adding independent clauses (ones that begin with "and" or "but"—what classical rhetoricians called *parataxis*) and by adding modifiers and phrases in parallel series. Some examples? The teacher is a guardian "of their health, their clothes, their habits, their mothers, and their snowball engagements"; the boy "learned fast, kept well, and we were satisfied"; the bus "would sweep to a halt, open its mouth, suck the boy in, and spring away." And so forth. The "ands" make White's essay informal and conversational, never remote or scholarly.

White uses relatively simple sentence patterns in "Education," then, but his prose is still anything but simple. Some of his sentences are beautifully parallel: "she can cool their passions or warm their soup"; "she conceives their costumes, cleans up their noses, and shares their confidences"; "in a cinder court he played games supervised by an athletic instructor, and in a cafeteria he ate lunch worked out by a dietitian"; "when the snow is deep or the motor is dead"; "rose hips in fall, snowballs in winter." These precise, mirror-image parallel structures are known as *isocolons* to rhetoricians. White delights in them and in the artful informality they create. He uses parallelisms and relentless coordination—"and" after "and" after "and"—to make his prose accessible to a large audience of appreciative readers. And he uses those lists of specific items in parallel series to give his writing its remarkably concrete, remarkably vivid quality.

That brings us to White's word choices. They too contribute to White's purposes. Remember the sense of detachment and generosity in White's narrative voice, the ethos of involvement and detachment apparent in the speaker? In large measure that is the result of White's word choices. For instance, White has the ability to attach mock-heroic terminology to his descriptions so that he comes across as balanced and wise, as someone who doesn't take himself or his world too seriously. The boy is a "scholar" who "sallied forth" on a "journey" to school or to "make Indian weapons of a semi-deadly nature." The gentle *hyperbole* and *irony* (to use more terms from classical rhetoric) fit in well with the classical *allusion* inherent in the word "Augean" (one of Hercules' labors was to clean the Augean stables): there is a sophistication and worldly wisdom in the speaker's voice that qualifies him to speak on this subject. And remember the discussion of whether White's aim was purely descriptive or more argumentative in character? White's *metaphors* underscore his argumentative aim: The city school bus "was as punctual as death," a sort of macabre monster that "would sweep to a halt, open its mouth, suck the boy in, and spring away with an angry growl"; or it is "like a train picking up a bag of mail." At the country school, by contrast, the day passes "just like lightning." If the metaphors do not provide enough evidence of White's persuasive aim (see Eubanks, chap. 2, for more on metaphor and argument), consider the **connotations** of words—their emotional charges, that is—that are associated with the city school: "regimented," "supervised," "worked on," "uniforms," "fevers." And then compare these with the connotation of some words White associates with the country school: "surprises," a "bungalow," "weather-resistant," "individual instruction," "guardian," and so forth.

This analysis by no means exhausts the full measure of rhetorical sophistication that E. B. White brings to the composition of "Education." You may have noticed other tactics at work, or you might disagree with some of the generalizations presented here. And the use of terms from an approach to rhetoric outside classical rhetoric would have yielded different results. But the purpose of this discussion is not to detail every aspect of the rhetoric of White's "Education." It is merely to illustrate a method of rhetorical analysis, or critical reading, that you might employ yourself. The point has been to offer a method for permitting someone to read not just for what is said—although this is crucial—but for how it is said as well. For reading is as "rhetorical" an activity as writing. It depends on an appreciation of how writer, subject, and reader are all negotiated through a particular document. The precise terms of this negotiation are often uncovered by means of contextual analysis.

CONTEXTUAL RHETORICAL ANALYSIS: COMMUNICATION AS CONVERSATION

Notice that the fact that E. B. White's "Education" was originally published in *Harper's* magazine did not matter too much to the previous discussion. Nor did it matter what material conditions motivated White to write it or when the essay was written (1939) or who exactly read it or what their reaction was or what other people at the time were saying about education. Textual analysis, strictly speaking, need not attend to such matters; it can proceed as if the item under consideration "speaks for all time" somehow, as if it is a sort of museum piece unaffected by time and space just as surely as, say, an ancient altarpiece once housed in a church might be placed on a pedestal in a museum. Museums have their functions, and they certainly permit people to observe and appreciate objects in an important way. But just as certainly museums often fail to retain a vital sense of an art work's original context and cultural meaning; in that sense museums can diminish understanding as much as they contribute to it. Contextual rhetorical analysis, however, as an attempt to understand communications through the lens of their environments, does attend to the setting or scene out of which any communication emerges. It does strive to understand an object of analysis as an integral part of culture.

And, as in the case of textual analysis, contextual analysis may be conducted in any number of ways. "Contextual analysis," "frame analysis," "cultural studies," "reception analysis," "historical analysis," "ecocriticism," and so forth: all of these and other terms can be rough synonyms for a constellation of analytical methods that can give people a better sense of how the particular pieces of a rhetorical performance emerge from, are owing to, and speak to specific contexts. Contextual rhetorical analysis proceeds from a thick description of the rhetorical situation that motivated the item in question. It demands an appreciation of the social circumstances that call rhetorical events into being and that orchestrate the course of those events. It regards communications as anything but self-contained: Contextualists understand each communication as a response to other communications (and to other social practices), they appreciate how communications (and social practices more generally) reflect the attitudes and values of the communities that sustain them, and they search for evidence of how those other communications (and social practices) are reflected in texts. Rhetorical analysis from a contextualist perspective resists notions of the "bounded text" cut off from others; it understands individual pieces as parts of communication chains that work together to perform rhetorical work; it resists the notion of transhistorical or ahistorical texts. Contextualists are drawn to metaphors such as *dialogue, dialectic, debate,* and *conversation,* for those metaphors carry with them the values of contextual criticism. (Another term useful to contextualists is *intertextuality*—the concept you learned about earlier in Charles Bazerman's chapter 4.)

Here is a famous example of the conversation metaphor from Kenneth Burke's *The Philosophy of Literary Form* (1941/1973):

> Imagine that you enter a parlor. You come late. When you arrive, others have long preceded you, and they are engaged in a heated discussion, a discussion too heated for them to pause and tell you exactly what it is about. In fact, the discussion had already begun long before any of them got there, so no one present is qualified to retrace for you all the steps that had gone before. You listen for a while, until you decide that you have caught the tenor of the argument; then you put in your oar. Someone answers; you answer him; another comes to your defense. (p. 110)

Burke's metaphorical account of the dynamics of all discourse—every particular item should be understood as part of and in relation to a larger conversation—challenges analysts to immerse themselves in the details of cultural conversations as a means of understanding any particular discourse.

As the passage from Burke suggests, contextual analysis will turn up information about what is said and why (invention), about the order in which it is said (arrangement), and how it is said (style and tone). Rhetorical analysis, like writing, is a social activity. It involves not simply passively decoding a message but actively understanding the designs the message has for readers who are living and breathing within a given culture.

How can you recover the cultural conversation surrounding a specific piece of rhetorical action? Sometimes it is fairly easy to do so. If you are an expert on any subject, you probably read about that subject quite often—often enough to know quite well what people are saying about that topic. People who carefully followed the presidential campaign of 2000, for example, could recover pretty easily the dialogue about the issues that was carried on by the Democrats and Republicans and their supporters. People who have strong feelings about the environment or cloning (or about gay rights, affirmative action, school choice, the lack of competitive balance in major league baseball, or any number of other current issues) are very well informed about the arguments that are converging around those topics. (In that sense, textual analysis and contextual analysis often work together, for often the text itself will contain important clues about context. A careful look at the text of Lincoln's "Gettysburg Address"—not to mention texts written in ancient times, about which we may know little—tells us quite a bit about its context.)

But other times it takes some research in order to reconstruct the conversations and social practices related to a particular issue—research into how the debate manifests itself in cultural practices or how it is conducted in current magazines, newspapers, talk shows, Web sites, and so forth (if the issue concerns current events); or archival research into historical collections of newspapers, magazines, books, letters, and other documentary sources (if the item being analyzed was from an earlier time period). That research usually puts people into libraries, special research collections, or film and television archives where it is possible to learn quite a bit about context.

DOING CONTEXTUAL RHETORICAL ANALYSIS: AN EXAMPLE

Perhaps an example will clarify how contextual analysis works: It will take a while to reconstruct some of the "conversations" that a piece of discourse participates in, but the result will be an enhanced understanding—and an appreciation for how you might do a contextual rhetorical analysis yourself. This time take a look at Appendix B, Milton Friedman's (1989) essay "An Open Letter to Bill Bennett." (As you did for "Education," take time to read the article carefully before you read further.) You are probably able to follow Friedman's argument pretty well without the benefit of much background reading, because the possible decriminalization or legalization of drugs continues to be an issue in our society (witness the recent film "Traffic") and because the text-based ways of reading that I discussed earlier in this chapter permit you to appreciate some of the dynamics of Friedman's prose. You can certainly follow the basic thrust of Friedman's argument in favor of decriminalization and appreciate the supporting points that he makes, his overall arrangement, some of the ways he builds credibility, and his general stylistic choices. Textual analysis can supply all of that.

But a contextual analysis will give you even more appreciation for and understanding of this argument. For one thing, some research will tell you that Friedman (born in 1913), a well-known staunch conservative (even libertarian) whose "monetarist" approach to economics influenced the policies of Ronald Reagan and his successors, is a Nobel laureate in economics who taught for many years at the University of Chicago and who was later affiliated with the Hoover Institute at Stanford University. Thus his credibility, his ethos, is established not just by his textual moves but by his reputation, especially for *Wall Street Journal* readers who would recognize his accomplishment: the respected daily newspaper, which printed "Open Letter to Bill Bennett" on September 7, 1989, is published weekdays by Dow Jones and Company in order to disseminate news about financial affairs and some political affairs. Friedman in his essay was addressing not so much the "real" Bill Bennett, therefore—although Bennett, President George H. Bush's "drug czar" in 1989, certainly read the piece carefully, as I will indicate in a moment. (If he had really been addressing Bennett as his primary audience, Friedman would have written Bennett a personal letter.) Instead, "Bill Bennett" is mainly a textual construct, an implied audience who actually stands in for the host of conservative, mostly well-to-do people who read the *Wall Street Journal.*

Why does it matter when the essay was written? On September 5, 1989, President George H. Bush announced in a nationwide, televised address that he was proposing to launch a \$2.9 billion anti-drug campaign that he hoped would gain the support of congress. Declaring the moral equivalent of war, the President proposed to add \$719 million to his previous commitment, bringing the total to nearly \$3 billion, and he suggested that the funds might come from borrowing and/or from funds allocated from housing and juvenile-justice programs or pork-barrel projects. Democrats responded that they supported the initiative, but at the expense of military spending and certainly not at the expense of housing or juvenile justice; concerned about the budget deficits that were at historic highs, reluctant therefore to borrow money to support the initiative, and sensing that the war on drugs would give them an opportunity to leverage a reduction in military spending that they regarded as wasteful and unnecessary, Democrats were also loathe to appear soft on drugs. On the one hand, Bush and his supporters were concerned about the terrible social costs of drug abuse in America: A crack cocaine epidemic was ravaging the nation's cities and claiming the lives of citizens as prominent as University of Maryland basketball star Len Bias (who died in 1986); crack and other kinds of addictions were leading to serious crime, to serious illness, to lost work days, and to broken lives; many children were being introduced to illegal and potentially harmful drugs at a young age. On the other hand, other citizens were skeptical of the proposed initiative (even though many of them detested drug abuse as much as anyone) because its cost would contribute to a severe budget shortfall that was plaguing the federal government and the nation's economy; because they felt that the drug problem in America ought to be regarded as a medical problem more than a criminal one; because they were skeptical that the approach advocated by the President would be effective; because they feared that a crackdown on drug users might be a cure worse than the disease (if many otherwise law-abiding citizens were jailed as a result and if civil liberties were compromised by the drug war); and because they feared foreign policy difficulties would result from a drug war carried out beyond American borders. This national conversation about drugs was apparent in the magazines, books, newspapers, talk shows, barber shops, and hair salons of America in September, 1989. If I had more space, I would offer detailed examples of the scope and depth of that debate by quoting from some representative and influential articles and news programs in circulation at that time.

Nevertheless, I can still document here quite a good sense of the conversation surrounding the "Open Letter to Bill Bennett" simply by examining (with the help of my university library) the pages of the *Wall Street Journal* itself, in very rich detail, on that one very day—September 7, 1989. A front-page story in the *WSJ* that day entitled "In Columbia, the War on Drugs Is Producing Some Real-Life Heroes" lionized drug enforcement agents in South America who were doing their jobs under difficult, even life-threatening circumstances. Two other front-page items, both brief, mentioned that Congress was having trouble accommodating the anti-drug plan in its tight, debt-ridden budget and that Columbia a day before had extradited a reputed drug financier, Eduardo Martinez Romero, to the United States for prosecution. The Wall Street Marketplace page in the *WSJ* carried a story on September 7 about the dearth of evidence that drug testing plans work to curb drug abuse by employees. The Politics and Policy section that day carried two articles whose contents are fairly indicated by their headlines: an analysis entitled "Bush Drug Plan Sparks Scuffle Over Budget"; and a historical piece entitled "Bush's Get-Tough Drug Plan Shares Philosophy That Didn't Work for [New York Governor Nelson] Rockefeller 20 Years

Ago." The editorial page carried the essay by Milton Friedman that we are concerned with analyzing, but it also carried two related opinion pieces: an editorial expressing guarded support for the anti-drug plan (the writer was worried about Big Government and high taxes, and spoke of the need for personal responsibility); and a second editorial, "Only in America," that complained that the drug war was a result of a failure in American legal systems: The writer was especially incensed that three federal judges had recently overturned the convictions of four Colombian drug runners on a legal technicality. Following the editorial page, and next to the letters to the editor, was a sober, realistic column by Alexander Cockburn entitled "From Andes to Inner Cities, Cocaine Is a Good Career Choice": "A war on drugs has distinct political advantages" to President Bush and other Republicans, wrote Mr. Cockburn (a writer associated with the progressive magazine *The Nation*). "In the present drug war, long-cherished constitutional protections are being shunted aside with the same elan as [Police] Chief Darrell Gates's battering ram bashing in the doors of suspected crack houses in Los Angeles. In the end, the 'war' ends up as a boon in prison construction" that would especially affect minority citizens.

All of these articles are part of and representative of the larger national debate over drugs that was apparent in September, 1989. Although the *Wall Street Journal* is certainly a conservative newspaper, it still managed to offer a range of views on the subject—a surprisingly broad range, some might say, but in any event a reasonable representation of the conversation on the subject that one might have heard among informed American citizens at that moment. One could even argue that advertisements for beer, alcohol, and tobacco (in the *Wall Street Journal* and in so many other publications in September, 1989) were a part of that discussion—not to mention drug czar William Bennett's concurrent speeches and talk-show appearances on behalf of the President's plan during that week or in the months following (e.g., "Should Drugs Be Legalized," *Reader's Digest*, March 1990).

So of course was an earlier article on drugs that Friedman himself had written 17 years before for *Newsweek*—excerpts of which were carried in a sidebar to Friedman's 1989a *Wall Street Journal* essay. In that 1972 essay, which is worth summarizing at some length for reasons of comparison and because the 1989 piece accompanies and plays off it, Friedman had begun by quoting in a mocking way the evangelist Billy Sunday's predictions about the benefits he expected from "victory" in another "drug war" that had been waged in America at the turn of the last century: Because of Prohibition, predicted Sunday early in the 20th century, "Men will walk upright now, women will smile, and the children will laugh. Hell will be forever for rent." After that introduction, Friedman then developed this comparison of the war against drugs in 1972 to the days of Prohibition against alcohol—a period when a national social experiment in prohibiting a widely used and frequently harmful drug, alcohol, had so "undermined respect for the law, corrupted the minions of the law, [and] created a decadent moral climate" that Prohibition was repealed by a 1930 amendment to the constitution. Friedman did not even need to mention explicitly the gangsterism, police corruption, and other social ills that people routinely associated with the 1920s because those problems were understood by his readers, many of whom would have been devoted fans of the popular 1960s TV series "The Untouchables," which represented the heroism of Chicago police detective Eliot Ness against the hooliganism of rumrunning mobsters like Al Capone and which was still in popular syndication in 1972. Friedman then noted that "the individual addict would clearly be far better off if drugs were legal" and turned to benefits to the rest of society: Depending on the economic law of supply and demand—something Friedman believes is a natural force akin to gravity—he contended that legalization would eliminate pushers, drive down prices, and consequently reduce the crime rate since addicts would no longer be "driven to associate with criminals to get drugs, become criminals themselves to finance the habit, and risk constant danger of death and disease." And legalization would mean that other nations would no longer be corrupted by illegal drug manufacture. On that final note, and with a final allusion to Prohibition, Friedman closed his *Newsweek* essay: "We cannot end drug traffic. We may be able to cut off opium from Turkey—but there are innumerable other places where the opium poppy grows."

How are these discourses visible in—intertextual with—Friedman's 1989 article? How does all of this background make the "Open Letter to Bill Bennett" more understandable? This contextual study comes to fruition when it becomes apparent that a great many things indeed in Friedman's essay in fact derive from or speak directly to other discourses and social practices. To take the most obvious example first, consider Billy Sunday's predictions about the benefits that he expected from Prohibition, quoted obliquely in paragraph 7 (indeed, that paragraph cannot easily be understood without a knowledge of the Billy Sunday quotation in the 1972 essay). That allusion works far more strongly when it is read against the full text of Friedman's 1972 *Newsweek* essay, which begins by ridiculing Prohibition as the social experiment of buffoons like Sunday. In both cases, 1972 and 1989, the ridicule of Billy Sunday fits in well with the ideology of Friedman and the *Wall Street Journal*: Billy Sunday was poorly educated, low-church, and authoritative among the working-class Americans that *Wall Street Journal* readers often regard as beneath themselves. In that way the allusion allies Friedman with his readers' values, far better in fact than it had done in his *Newsweek* piece, since *Newsweek* reaches a more egalitarian set of readers. A second direct allusion in the 1989 essay, the unusual words from Oliver Cromwell that open the piece, performs very different and more complicated rhetorical work. Since Cromwell is associated with religious Puritanism, the sympathetic allusion actually seems to position Friedman as in league with a social stance, social "puritanism" (small p) as it is informally and broadly known, that actually seems counter to his own stance on drugs (since people normally associate puritans with an anti-drug stance). The allusion to Cromwell, in other words, builds identification with members of his audience who are highly skeptical about legalization of drugs. Moreover, Cromwell is also associated with the anti-aristocratic, radically revolutionary forces who beheaded English king Charles I in 1649, another fact that positions the well-to-do Friedman as unexpectedly egalitarian against the implied elitism of William Bennett and his *Wall Street Journal* fellows.[4] (That the allusion is quite obscure also reinforces Friedman's ethos as a scholarly and cosmopolitan genius.) In short, the allusions to Billy Sunday and to Oliver Cromwell help Friedman to have it both ways; they permit him to draw cultural capital from both right and left and to present himself, in this instance at least, as above partisan politics.

More important, Friedman depends in 1989 on the same extended comparison that he exploited so thoroughly in 1972 and that the *Wall Street Journal* article on Rockefeller used—between the war against drugs in the 1980s (and 1960s) and the disastrous Prohibition-era war against alcohol conducted in the 1920s. Paragraph three alludes directly to the days of Prohibition: Illegality "creates obscene profits that finance the tactics of the drug lords; illegality leads to the corruption of law enforcement officials; illegal-

---

[4]The Cromwell quote is from a letter he wrote to the Scottish clergy, or more precisely to the General Assembly of the Kirk of Scotland, on August 3, 1650. After the execution of Charles I, the new English republic faced opposition from Ireland and then Scotland. Appalled by England's unilateral execution of their king, the Scots immediately declared the late king's son, Charles II, king of great Britain and Ireland. On July 22, 1650, Cromwell led a preemptive military invasion of Scotland. The letter of August 3 was an attempt to set the various elements among his opponents (royalist, Scottish, Presbyterian) against each other. Unlike the case of his quite brutal massacre of the Irish papists, Cromwell treated the Scots as erring brethren and wanted to bring them back into the fold: hence the appeal to shared biblical language. Here is the first part of the paragraph that the quote comes from:

"Your own guilt is too much for you to bear: bring not therefore upon yourselves the blood of innocent men, deceived with pretences of King and Covenant, from whose eyes you hide a better knowledge. I am persuaded that divers of you, who lead the people, have laboured to build yourselves in these things wherein you have censured others, and established yourselves upon the Word of God. Is it therefore infallibly agreeable to the Word of God, all that you say? I beseech you, in the bowels of Christ, think it possible you may be mistaken. Precept may be upon precept, line may be upon line, and yet the Word of the Lord may be to some a Word of judgment, that they may fall backward, and be broken and be snared and be taken."

I thank my colleague Laura Knoppers for the information in this note.

ity monopolizes the efforts of honest law forces so they are starved for resources" to fight other crimes. The final sentence of paragraph four makes the comparison explicit: "Our experience with the prohibition of drugs is a replay of our experience with the prohibition of alcoholic beverages." And the quotation from Billy Sunday reinforces that analogy further. If Friedman's 1972 essay alluded obliquely to "The Untouchables" TV series, his 1989 essay conjures up the 1987 movie of that same title (starring Kevin Costner as Eliot Ness[5]). Friedman did not even need to emphasize further the gangsterism, corruption of police, and other social ills that people were routinely associating with the 1920s.

Other discourses, other pieces of contemporary cultural conversations, are apparent in Friedman's 1989 performance. His point that drug use in America had gotten worse in the previous two decades picks up on arguments articulated in the historical essay on Governor Rockefeller's drug war of the 1960s: One failed attempt ought to testify to the likely failure of other attempts. Friedman's emphatic conclusion to paragraph six—"Fewer people would be in jails, and fewer jails would have to be built"—recalls Cockburn's argument about how the drug war feeds incarceration. The commentary on Columbia, Bolivia, and Peru (paragraph seven) alludes directly to *Wall Street Journal* news coverage of the conduct of the drug war in other nations. The comparisons to alcohol and tobacco in paragraph nine are brought home by the prevalent, even ubiquitous advertising for both substances apparent in 1989 media. And so on.

Note that Friedman in his "Open Letter" plays down the argument for legalization that he personally finds most appealing—the libertarian position that government has no right to coerce an individual to adopt any moral or ethical position. He had done the same thing in 1972, limiting himself to a paragraph defending the notion that government has "no right to use force, directly or indirectly, to prevent a fellow man . . . from drinking alcohol or taking drugs," to a short repetition of the libertarian slogan popularized by Henry David Thoreau—"that government is best when it governs least"—and to concluding his piece with an indirect reference to the same minimalist principle of government: "In drugs, as in other areas, persuasion and example are likely to be far more effective than the use of force." In 1989 he developed that argument even more obliquely, alluding only to libertarian "friends of freedom" and to the specter of "an army of enforcers empowered to invade the liberty of citizens" in his conclusion. Friedman depends instead on a resolute account of the practical consequences of his position, on a patient tabulation of the negative consequences of the drug war. Many of his 1972 appeals survive fairly intact in his 1989 argument, therefore—the

---

[5]It could be argued, however, that both the TV series and the 1987 movie are pro-drug-war arguments. Eliot Ness in both is depicted as a saintly government foe of satanic corruption.

harmful impacts on citizens and society, the lack of effective impact on
drug usage, the inappropriate intrusions into the affairs of other nations.
And Friedman's faith in the law of supply and demand is a staple grounds in
both pieces as well: "Of course the problem is demand, ... demand that
must operate through repressed and illegal channels" (paragraph 3). Friedman takes as a basic assumption the argument that drugs are an economic
commodity whose distribution can be understood best in economic terms.

True, economic theory would suggest that a reduction in price might increase use, just as a decrease in the price of any other commodity makes it
more affordable and accessible. But Friedman for some reason claims the
opposite in his "Open Letter": "There would today be far fewer addicts" if
drug use had been legalized years ago, he offers in paragraph six; "the lives
of thousands, perhaps hundreds of thousands of innocent victims would
have been saved." For some reason, Friedman seems to believe that economic "law" will have inevitable consequences sometimes but not always:
legalization will increase supply of drugs, reduce prices, and drive out the
incentive for crime; but somehow "there would today be far fewer addicts"
if drugs were legal—a remark that echoes Friedman's 1972 text. As a result,
Friedman leaves himself vulnerable to counterattack since opponents of legalization and backers of the war on drugs act as they do because they are
committed to an interdiction on a hazardous economic product, as surely
as if it were plutonium. If a substantial reduction in the price of cell phones,
say, coupled with an increase in their supply, will increase exponentially
the number of cell phone users, why will a reduction in the price of drugs
not also result in an increase in the number of drug addicts—with disastrous results?

Precisely on these grounds was Friedman answered. On September 19,
1989, in the *Wall Street Journal*, several letter writers argued that legalization and lower prices for drugs could generate mass addiction. One of
those responses was offered by William Bennett. "We know," he wrote,
that whenever drugs have been cheaper and more easily obtained, drug
use—and addiction—has skyrocketed. ... Professor James Q. Wilson tells
us that during the years in which heroin could be legally prescribed by
doctors in Britain, the number of addicts increased forty-fold. And after
the repeal of Prohibition—an analogy favored but misunderstood by legalization advocates—consumption of alcohol soared by 350%. Could we afford such dramatic increases in drug use? I doubt it." A few days later
Friedman counterresponded to Bennett's response, again in the *Wall
Street Journal*. He reasserted his main points and reaffirmed in a full concluding paragraph the libertarian principles on which he based his position on drugs: The drug war "would have been utterly unacceptable to the
Founders [of our country]. I do not believe, and neither did they, that it is
the right of government to tell free citizens what is right and wrong. That

is something for them to decide themselves." And he refined his economic, supply-and-demand argument to distinguish between innocent and guilty victims of drug use: "Legalization would drastically reduce the number of innocent victims [e.g., crime victims]. That is a virtual certainty. The number of self-chosen victims [of addiction] might increase, but it is pure conjecture that the number would skyrocket. In any event, while both groups of victims are to be pitied, the innocent victims surely have a greater claim on our sympathy than the self-chosen victims." And with that change in the argument between them (a change that might suggest that Bennett "won" the original argument), the direct conversation between Bennett and Friedman ceased.

Not that this analysis need cease. This discussion of the conversation about drugs in 1989 and about Milton Friedman's specific contribution to that conversation could be extended for a long time—indefinitely, in fact. If it were, an understanding of even more details of Friedman's essay would become clear; the traces of his language choices that derive from prior discourses would become even clearer. There is no need to belabor the point, however: My purpose has been simply to illustrate that contextual analysis of a piece of rhetoric can enrich its understanding.

I cannot resist offering one final point: All of this analysis and background suggests that there was nothing particularly original in Friedman's argument. Rather than inventing a new argument with new premises, Friedman was actually consolidating and rearticulating an argument already in circulation in various forms and forums. Contextual analysis usually works that way: It tends to reduce a sense of individual genius attached to specific communications. If the earlier textual analysis of E. B. White tended to confirm an appreciation of him as a uniquely gifted rhetor, the contextualist analysis of Milton Friedman has tended to make his impressive essay appear less original. For good reason, William Bennett happened to open his September 19, 1989 rebuttal to Friedman by saying that "There was little, if anything, new in your open letter to me calling for the legalization of drugs"—a charge that Friedman himself acknowledged as just in his counterresponse: "William Bennett is entirely right that 'there was little, if anything, new in' my open letter to him." Contextual analyses need not diminish respect and appreciation for outstanding rhetorical performance, however. If Friedman's arguments were not especially novel, if he is to be understood as just another contributor to a larger conversation about legalization taking place in 1989, he still deserves credit for the eloquence of his contribution—and for inserting it into a novel setting. At a time when Republicans and Democrats were beginning to line up to make the drug war into a partisan issue (or to pass on it as a done deal), at a time when it might have been expected that social conservatives like the ones who read the *Wall Street Journal* would routinely line up on the side of the Republican president, Friedman succeeded in making the issue non-partisan. And to the extent that he drew new attention to the issue, he can be credited with breathing new intellectual life into its discussion and adjudication—discussion that continues to this day. "Originality" in the sense of unitary genius Friedman did not display in his "Open Letter"; but genius in the sense of original thinking and social relevance and verbal eloquence he most certainly did possess.

CONCLUSION

Effective rhetorical analysis can be generally textual or contextual in nature, then. But let me conclude by emphasizing again that these two approaches to rhetorical analysis should not be understood as mutually exclusive. Indeed, many if not most analysts operate some place between these two extremes; they consider the details of the text, but they also attend to the particulars of context as well. Or they employ both kinds of analysis simultaneously and recursively to get a fuller appreciation of the interplay between text and context, especially since clues about context are often embedded in text. Textual analysis and contextual analysis inevitably complement each other. Perhaps I could have demonstrated that by adding a contextual analysis of E. B. White's "Education" to my textual analysis, or a close textual analysis of my discussion of Friedman's "Open Letter to Bill Bennett."

Then again, that would have been misleading too, for it would have implied that the two approaches together can somehow exhaust appreciation, can open up an understanding of a communication rather completely. Such an impression would be inaccurate. Rhetorical analysis, like any other kind of analysis, should be understood as necessarily and always partial: any approach to rhetorical analysis will be very good at teaching people some things about a particular communication, but it will also keep them from considering other things. In that sense, rhetorical analysis is as much a way of not seeing as it is seeing. In Kenneth Burke's (1954) terms, any approach to analysis (rhetorical or otherwise) is a "trained incapacity"—a way of seeing some things more profoundly that simultaneously blinds people to other things, just as surely as peering into a microscope opens your eyes to what's under the microscope but blinds you to everything else.

In fact, therefore, it might be appropriate for me to conclude this chapter with two challenges: First, try to use elements of both kinds of analysis whenever you would understand a rhetorical event more completely. Resist the distinction between textual and contextual approaches. Rhetoric is "inside" texts, but it is also "outside": **Specific rhetorical performances are an irreducible mixture of text and context**, and so interpretation and analysis of those performances must account for both as well. Second, remember **the limitations of your analysis**; realize that your analysis will always be somewhat partial and incomplete, ready to be deepened, corrected, modified, and extended by the insights of others. As the contributors to a book called *Understanding Scientific Prose* (Selzer, 1993) demonstrated when they offered a dozen or so separate and yet complimentary analyses of a single piece of scientific writing, **rhetorical analysis can itself be part of the unending conversation** that Kenneth Burke celebrated—a way of learning and teaching within a community.

If you keep those two challenges in mind, you will find rhetorical analysis to be a truly rich intellectual experience. Not only that, you will find yourself growing as a writer and speaker as well; if you read critically, you'll begin to adopt and adapt for your own purposes the best rhetorical maneuvers on display in the world. By becoming better able to understand and appreciate the "conversations" going on around you, you'll learn to make more powerful and sophisticated contributions to the discussions that most engage you personally. Critical reading, the art of rhetorical analysis, can make you a better arguer, a better citizen.

ACTIVITIES

1. Now that you have read a *textual* analysis of E. B. White's "Education," do a *contextual* analysis of it. Place it in its original context, and see what that placement does to complement the textual analysis offered in this chapter.

2. Find an ad in a magazine designed for a particular audience (i.e., an ad not in *Time* or *Newsweek* but *Seventeen* or *Car and Driver* or *Esquire* or *Working Mother*). Then analyze how the ad makes its argument to its audience. Consider ethos, logos, pathos, arrangement, style, and visual presentation.

3. Find a Web site for an organization or public interest group. Analyze how (and how well) the site is suited to its aims and audiences.

4. Take your favorite piece of writing—fiction, poetry, essay, report, personal letter whatever—and analyze it as an argument.

FOR FURTHER READING

Some of the items listed under Works Cited offer plenty of additional information about rhetorical analysis. In particular, I would recommend the essays collected in *Understanding Scientific Prose* (1993)—a book intended as a primer on rhetorical analysis of any kind of writing—and Berger et al.'s (1991) *Ways of Seeing* as an introduction to analyzing visual images. Beyond that, anyone can become more expert at rhetorical analysis by reading the following classics: James Andrews, *The Practice of Rhetorical Criticism* (1990); Thomas Benson, ed., *Landmark Essays on Rhetorical Criticism* (1993)—which includes a fine bibliography and many examples; Edwin Black's influential 1978 book *Rhetorical Criticism*; Bernard Brock et al.'s (1989) *Methods of Rhetorical Criticism*; Donald Bryant's (1973) pioneering effort to formalize approaches to rhetorical analysis, *Rhetorical Dimensions in Criticism*; Edward Corbett's (1969) *Rhetorical Analyses of Literary Works* (an important effort to show how rhetorical analysis can open up belletristic works); Sonja Foss' (1989) *Rhetorical Criticism* (a very student-friendly account of many new ways of doing rhetorical criticism); Roderick Hart's (1990) *Modern Rhetorical Criticism* (another student-oriented discussion of methods of rhetorical analysis, especially ones that are employed in the field of speech communication); and Steven Mailloux's (1998) *Reception Histories*, an explanation and illustration of the branch of rhetorical criticism known as reception theory.

APPENDIX A: "EDUCATION" (BY E. B. WHITE)

I have an increasing admiration for the teacher in the country school where we have a third-grade scholar in attendance. She not only undertakes to instruct her charges in all the subjects of the first three grades, but she manages to function quietly and effectively as a guardian of their health, their clothes, their habits, their mothers, and their snowball engagements. She has been doing this sort of Augean task for twenty years, and is both kind and wise. She cooks for the children on the stove that heats the room, and she can cool their passions or warm their soup with equal competence. She conceives their costumes, cleans up their messes, and shares their confidences. My boy already regards his teacher as his great friend, and I think tells her a great deal more than he tells us.

The shift from city school to country school was something we worried about quietly all last summer. I have always rather favored public school over private school, if only because in public school you meet a greater variety of children. This bias of mine, I suspect, is partly an attempt to justify my own past (I never knew anything but public schools) and partly an involuntary defense against getting kicked in the shins by a young ceramist on his way to the kiln. My wife was unacquainted with public schools, never having been exposed (in her early life) to anything more public than the washroom of Miss Winsor's. Regardless of our backgrounds, we both knew that the change in schools was something that concerned not us but the scholar himself. We hoped it would work out all right. In New York our son went to a medium-priced private institution with semi-progressive ideas of education, and modern plumbing. He learned fast, kept well, and we were satisfied. It was an electric, colorful, regimented existence with moments of pleasurable pause and giddy incident. The day the Christmas angel fainted and had to be carried out by one of the Wise Men was educational in the highest sense of the term. Our scholar gave imitations of it around the house for weeks afterward, and I doubt if it ever goes completely out of his mind.

His days were rich in formal experience. Wearing overalls and an old sweater (the accepted uniform of the private seminary), he sallied forth at morn accompanied by a nurse or a parent and walked (or was pulled) two blocks to a corner where the school bus made a flag stop. This flashy vehicle was as punctual as death: seeing us waiting at the cold curb, it would sweep to a halt, open its mouth, suck the boy in, and spring away with an angry growl. It was a good deal like a train picking up a bag of mail. At school the scholar was worked on for six or seven hours by half a dozen teachers and a nurse, and was revived on orange juice in mid-morning. In a cinder court he played games supervised by an athletic instructor, and in a cafeteria he ate lunch worked out by a dietitian. He soon learned to read with gratifying facility and discernment and to make Indian weapons of a semi-deadly nature. Whenever one of his classmates fell low of a fever the news was put on the wires and there were breathless phone calls to physicians, discussing periods of incubation and allied magic.

In the country all one can say is that the situation is different, and somehow more casual. Dressed in corduroys, sweatshirt, and short rubber boots, and carrying a tin dinner pail, our scholar departs at the crack of dawn for the village school, two and a half miles down the road, next to the cemetery. When the road is open and the car will start, he makes the journey by motor, courtesy of his old man. When the snow is deep or the motor is dead or both, he makes it on the hoof. In the afternoons he walks or hitches all or part of the way home in fair weather, gets transported in foul. The schoolhouse is a two-room frame building, bungalow type, shingles stained a burnt brown with weather-resistant stain. It has a chemical toilet in the basement and two teachers above the stairs. One takes the first three grades, the other the fourth, fifth, and sixth. They have little or no time for individual instruction, and no time at all for the esoteric. They teach what they know themselves, just as fast and as hard as they can manage. The pupils sit still at their desks in class, and do their milling around outdoors during recess.

There is no supervised play. They play cops and robbers (only they call it "Jail") and throw things at one another—snowballs in winter, rose hips in fall. It seems to satisfy them. They also construct darts, pinwheels, and "pick-up-sticks" (jackstraws), and the school itself does a brisk trade in penny candy, which is for sale right in the classroom and which contains "surprises." The most highly prized surprise is a fake cigarette, made of cardboard, fiendishly lifelike.

The memory of how apprehensive we were at the beginning is still strong. The boy was nervous about the change too. The tension, on that first fair morning in September when we drove him to school, almost blew the windows out of the sedan. And when later we picked him up on the road, wandering along with his little blue lunch-pail, and got his laconic report "All right" in answer to our inquiry about how the day had gone, our relief was vast. Now, after almost a year of it, the only difference we can discover in the two school experiences is that in the country he sleeps better at night—and *that* problem is more the air than the education. When grilled on the subject of school-in-country vs. school-in-city, he replied that the chief difference is that the day seems to go so much quicker in the country. "Just like lightning," he reported.

APPENDIX B: "AN OPEN LETTER TO BILL BENNETT" (BY MILTON FRIEDMAN)

Dear Bill:

In Oliver Cromwell's eloquent words, "I beseech you, in the bowels of Christ, think it possible you may be mistaken" about the course you and President Bush urge us to adopt to fight drugs. The path you propose of more police, more jails, use of the military in foreign countries, harsh penalties for drug users, and a whole panoply of repressive measures can only make a bad situation worse. The drug war cannot be won by those tactics without undermining the human liberty and individual freedom that you and I cherish.

You are not mistaken in believing that drugs are a scourge that is devastating our society. You are not mistaken in believing that drugs are tearing asunder our social fabric, ruining the lives of many young people, and imposing heavy costs on some of the most disadvantaged among us. You are not mistaken in believing that the majority of the public share your concerns. In short, you are not mistaken in the end you seek to achieve.

Your mistake is failing to recognize that the very measures you favor are a major source of the evils you deplore. Of course the problem is demand, but it is not only demand, it is demand that must operate through repressed and illegal channels. Illegality creates obscene profits that finance the murderous tactics of the drug lords; illegality leads to the corruption of law enforcement officials; illegality monopolizes the efforts of honest law forces so that they are starved for resources to fight the simpler crimes of robbery, theft and assault.

Drugs are a tragedy for addicts. But criminalizing their use converts the tragedy into a disaster for society, for users and non-users alike. Our experience with the prohibition of drugs is a replay of our experience with the prohibition of alcoholic beverages.

I append excerpts from a column that I wrote in 1972 on "Prohibition and Drugs." The major problem then was heroin from Marseilles; today, it is cocaine from Latin America. Today, also, the problem is far more serious than it was 17 years ago: more addicts, more innocent victims; more drug pushers, more law enforcement officials; more money spent to enforce prohibition, more money spent to circumvent prohibition.

Had drugs been decriminalized 17 years ago, "crack" would never have been invented (it was invented because the high cost of illegal drugs made it profitable to provide a cheaper version) and there would today be far fewer addicts. The lives of thousands, perhaps hundreds of thousands of innocent victims would have been saved, and not only in the U.S. The ghettos of our major cities would not be drug-and-crime-infested no-man's lands. Fewer people would be in jails, and fewer jails would have been built.

Colombia, Bolivia, and Peru would not be suffering from narco-terror, and we would not be distorting our foreign policy because of narco-terror. Hell would not, in the words with which Billy Sunday welcomed Prohibition, "be forever for rent," but it would be a lot emptier.

Decriminalizing drugs is even more urgent now than in 1972, but we must recognize that the harm done in the interim cannot be wiped out, certainly not immediately. Postponing decriminalization will only make matters worse, and make the problem appear even more intractable.

Alcohol and tobacco cause many more deaths in users than do drugs. Decriminalization would not prevent us from treating drugs as we now treat alcohol and tobacco: prohibiting sales of drugs to minors, outlawing the advertising of drugs and similar measures. Such measures could be enforced, while outright prohibition cannot be. Moreover, if even a small fraction of the money we now spend on trying to enforce drug prohibition were devoted to treatment and rehabilitation, in an atmosphere of compassion not punishment, the reduction in drug usage and in the harm done to the users could be dramatic.

This plea comes from the bottom of my heart. Every friend of freedom, and I know you are one, must be as revolted as I am by the prospect of turning the United States into an armed camp, by the vision of jails filled with casual drug users and of an army of enforcers empowered to invade the liberty of citizens on slight evidence. A country in which shooting down unidentified planes "on suspicion" can be seriously considered as a drug-war tactic is not the kind of United States that either you or I want to hand on to future generations.

11

Speech Acts, Genres, and Activity Systems: How Texts Organize Activity and People

Charles Bazerman

University of California, Santa Barbara

Part I of this book provides conceptual and analytic tools to show how texts evoke worlds of meaning by representing content and using the resources of language, including relations with other texts, and other media, such as graphics. Part II to this point provides tools to examine how texts arise within and influence the living world of people and events. This final chapter proposes one more set of conceptual and analytic tools for viewing the work that texts do in society. This chapter provides means to identify the conditions under which they accomplish this work; to notice the regularity of texts in carrying out recognizably similar tasks; and to see how specific professions, situations, and social organizations can be associated with a limited range of text types. Finally, it provides methods to analyze how the orderly production, circulation, and use of these texts in part constitutes the very activity and organization of social groups. The analytical approach of this chapter relies on a series of concepts: social facts, speech acts, genres, genre systems, and activity systems. These concepts suggest **how people using text create new realities of meaning, relation, and knowledge**.

Consider a typical academic situation. One university's faculty senate after much debate passes a regulation requiring students to pass six writing intensive courses in order to be granted a B.A. The regulation defines several criteria that a course must meet before it can be approved by the curriculum committee as writing intensive, such as a minimum number of writing assignments with a minimum number of total required words across the term. This requirement then gets written into various administrative documents including the university catalogue and various student advisement documents. Students read these documents (or are reminded by advisors at critical junctures) and know they have to locate and register for courses that will fulfill those requirements if they hope to graduate. Memos and other administrative documents are sent to the faculties of various departments to encourage them to offer such courses. The faculty of those departments write syllabi indicating that students will be required to write the requisite number of assignments and words. Further, the faculty are likely to shape those assignments in relation to the intellectual challenges of their subject matter and the goals of the course such as improving students' ability to understand and use economic models or to interpret 17th-century Spanish verse. The faculty then submit these syllabi for review by faculty committees, according to procedures set out in other administrative documents. Once the appropriate committee approves, the approval is noted in the minutes of the committee, in future editions of the catalogue, and each term's schedule of courses available for registration. Students then register and take these courses using typical registration forms and procedures; at the end of the term the teacher submits grades on an official grade sheet to be inscribed on the student's permanent record. When students get near graduation, these records will be reviewed by some official who will, among other things, add up whether six of these writing intensive courses have been taken. If all graduation requirements have been met, students gain diplomas useful for graduate school admissions, employment, and hanging on a wall. If not, students will be notified they need to take more courses.

In this sequence of events, many texts have been produced. But even more significantly, many social facts have been produced. These facts wouldn't have existed except that people have made them so by creating texts: graduation requirements, course syllabi defining the work of the various courses, criteria for courses to be labeled writing intensive, lists of approved courses, each student's record of writing intensive courses, and so on. In this cycle of texts and activities, we see well articulated organizational systems within which specific kinds of texts flow in anticipatable paths with easily understood and familiar consequences (at least to those people who are familiar with university life). We have highly typified genres of documents and highly typified social structures within which those documents create social facts that affect the actions, rights, and obligations of others.

When we look inside the courses where the required writing is actually done, we see even more typified structures in which writing takes place. In each course we have identifiable cycles of texts and activities, shaped by the syllabus, plans, assigned textbooks and readings, and assignment sheets which structure expectations and consequences. Typically, much of the first class of each course is taken up by laying out these expectations defined in the syllabus. Students then typically project how the course will unfold, how much work will be required, and whether the experience will be interesting and/or worthwhile in order to decide whether to stay in the course or replace it with another. Later in this chapter we look more closely at courses as structured activity systems built upon an infrastructure of genred texts.

This extended example suggests how each text is embedded within structured social activities and depends on previous texts that influence the social activity and organization. Further, this example suggests how each text establishes conditions that somehow are taken into account in consequent activities. The texts within this example create realities, or facts, for students and teachers live both in what they explicitly state and in the structures of relationship and activity they establish implicitly simply by fitting together in an organized way of life. Each successful text creates for its readers a **social fact**. The social facts consist of meaningful social actions being accomplished through language, or **speech acts**. These acts are carried out in patterned, typical, and therefore intelligible textual forms or **genres**, which are related to other texts and genres that occur in related circumstances. Together the text types fit together as **genre sets** within **genre systems**, which are part of **systems of human activity**. I explain more precisely what I mean by each of these terms in the next section.

Understanding these genres and how they work in the systems and circumstances they were designed for, can help you as a writer fulfill the needs of the situation, in ways that are understood and speak to the expectations of others. Understanding the acts and facts created by texts can also help you understand when seemingly well-written texts go wrong, when those texts don't do what they need to do. Such an understanding can also help you diagnose and redesign communicative activity systems—to determine whether a particular set of document used at certain moments is redundant or misleading, whether new documents need to be added, or whether some details of a genre might be modified. It can also help you decide when you need to write innovatively to accomplish something new or different.

Understanding the form and flow of texts in genre and activity systems can even help you understand how to disrupt or change the systems by the deletion, addition, or modification of a document type. While this may tempt textual mischief, it also provides the tools for thinking about social creativity in making new things happen in new ways. If, for example, you are sitting around with friends after dinner, you may have a choice of pulling out the TV listings, mentioning the newspaper's lead political story, taking out the book of photos of your last trip, or turning on the computer to look at the latest Web site. By introducing these different texts not only are you introducing different topics, you are introducing different activities, interactional patterns, attitudes, and relationships. The choice of a text may influence whether you make bets and wisecracks over a football game, debate politics, admire or envy each others' adventures, or make schemes for your own shared projects. Once one of these patterned activities are taken up they can shape opportunities of interaction until the mood is broken and a new activity is installed. In a classroom, a teacher's lessons often serve to define genres and activities, thereby shaping learning opportunities and expectations.

BASIC CONCEPTS

Social Facts and the Definition of the Situation. **Social facts** are those things people believe to be true, and therefore bear on how they define a situation. People then act as though these facts were true. The sociologist W. I. Thomas (1923) states it so: "If [people] define situations as real, they are real in their consequences." If people believe that their country has been offended or threatened by another country, they may even go to war over what they believe to be fact. Sometimes these social facts bear on our understanding of the physical world. As long as some people believe Elvis is around they will act as though it were true, even though most people accept his burial as definitive. Even statements that are socially held as scientifically verified, may not be recognized by some people as true. So even though it is well established that airplanes do fly and have safety records far better than land vehicles, many people do not securely believe such facts and prefer to go by train.

More often though social facts bear on subjects that are primarily matters of social understanding, such as whether or not a mayor has authority to make certain decisions and act in a certain way. That authority is based on a series of historically developed political, legal, and social understandings, arrangements, and institutions. As long as people continue to believe in the legitimacy of those understandings, arrangements, and institutions, they will accept the mayor's authority in appropriate circumstances. These social facts are a kind of self-fulfilling prophecy, for the more the mayor seems to exercise legitimate authority, the more people are likely to recognize and grant that authority. Under certain conditions, however, such as after a conviction for felony or after the violent overthrow of a government, people may no longer respect the authority of that mayor.

Very often social facts bear on the words people speak or write and on the force the utterance carries. If all the students in the class understand the teacher's syllabus to require a paper to be turned in on a certain day, they will act on this. If, on the other hand, they all understand him to have said during one class that the deadline can be extended, many will likely pursue what they perceive as a new option. The professor may or may not share this social belief about what was said, with consequences for conflict or cooperation. Similarly, if my friend and I believe we have made a bet by saying the right verbal formulas in the right situation, then one of us will pay up the other at the appropriate moment. On the other hand, if I believe a bet was being made, and my friend only believes we were making a joke, then there is no shared social fact and conflict may result.

Similarly, my right to attend a college may depend on whether I had enrolled properly, whether I had sent in a check to pay back tuition, whether I had received a diploma from high school, and a whole list of other social facts determined by texts. In order to be allowed to attend, I need to respect the institution's definition of required social facts and then be able to produce acceptable textual tokens of each. If, for example, I claim that in fact I had taken a course at another school but there is no record of it, or the new school rejects the record of that course, we do not share that course as a social fact. For institutional purposes it might as well have been a figment of my imagination.

As discussed in chapter 4, intertextuality often seeks to create a shared understanding of what people have said before and what the current situation is. That is, intertextual reference can attempt to establish the social facts upon which the writer is attempting to make a new statement. In making a plea to the registrar of my school I will need to bring transcripts from the prior institution, perhaps copies of syllabi, and maybe letters from current professors indicating I have the skills that would come from having taken that course.

Many of the social facts, such as the ones described in the last several examples hinge on speech acts, whether certain verbal formulations were accurately and properly done. If properly accomplished, these words are to be taken as fully completed acts that should be respected as having been done.

Speech Acts.   The philosopher John Austin in his book, *How to Do Things with Words*, argued that words not only mean things, they do things. His argument builds on such examples as two friends making a promise or a preacher declaring a pair of people married. These acts are done just by the words themselves. As a result of a set of words said at the proper time in the proper circumstances by the proper person, someone will be obligated to do something, or the life arrangements of two people will change. In considering written documents, you might equally say that applying for a bank loan is carried out purely in the words and numbers you use to fill out and submit the application. Equally, the bank's approval is simply accomplished by a letter being issued saying you have been approved. From such striking examples Austin goes on to argue that every statement does something, even if only to assert a certain state of affairs is true. Thus, all utterances embody **speech acts**.

Of course for our words to carry out their acts these words must be said by the right people, in the right situation, with the right set of understandings. If two potential bettors were strangers likely not to meet after the football game, if no stakes were set, if the event wagered upon had already passed, if the context and intonation suggested a joke rather than a formal bet, or if a thousand other things were not right, one or another of the parties might not believe a real and proper bet had been made. Similarly, if the person making a marriage declaration were not a member of the clergy or judiciary with power in this jurisdiction, or if the people were not legally eligible for marriage with each other, or if they were taking part in a dramatic performance, there would be no real and binding marriage. A loan application by someone under 18 is not a legal application and a letter of approval signed by the night janitor at the bank or that does not set terms of repayment is not a real approval. All these represent **"felicity" conditions** that must be right in order for the speech act to succeed. Without the felicity conditions being met, the act would not be an act, or at least the same sort of act. Austin and John Searle, who continued the analysis of speech acts, pointed out that speech acts operate at three levels. First is the **locutionary act**, which includes a **propositional act**. The locutionary act is literally what is said. So in saying that "it is a bit chilly in this room," I am reporting on a state of affairs and making a certain proposition about the temperature in the room.

Quite possibly the act I was attempting to accomplish, however, was to request my host to raise the thermostat. Or perhaps I was disagreeing with the rather "cold" remarks being made about someone. By speaking indirectly I intended my words to have a specific illocutionary force, which I assume others would recognize given the immediate circumstances and the manner of delivery of the sentence. The act I intend my hearer to recognize is the **illocutionary act**.

The listeners, however, may take my comments to mean something else entirely, such as a complaint about the stinginess of the host or an attempt to change the subject of an unpleasant discussion. Their own further responses will take into account what *they* thought I was doing, and not necessarily what *I* thought I was doing, or even what I literally said. How people take up the acts and determine the consequences of that act for future interaction is called the **perlocutionary effect**. To make the issue even more complicated, listeners may not be happy or cooperative with what they understand me to be doing, and in their further utterances and acts they may not go along with it. I may intend to request an adjustment of the thermostat, and the host may even understand my request, but still might then say something like, "I have been reading how energy shortages may lead to international economic instability." Where did that come from? Why is the host reporting on his economics reading? Perhaps he is trying to tell me that he does not want to waste fuel and intends to keep the thermostat low.

This **three-leveled analysis of speech acts**—what was literally stated, the intended act, and actual effect—is also applicable to written texts. You may write a letter to a friend telling of the latest events in your life, but your illocutionary intent may be to maintain a low-key friendship or to trigger an answering letter that would reveal whether a certain problem had been resolved. And the reader's perlocutionary uptake may be that she believes that you miss her greatly and are trying to rekindle an intense romance. So as not to encourage you, she may never write back.

This three-leveled analysis of speech acts also allows us to understand the status of claims or representations made within texts about states of affairs in the world—the propositional acts, as Searle calls them. Many texts assert propositions, such as a new scientific finding about the health value of chocolate, or the news "facts" of a public demonstration, or the "true meaning" of a poem. Thus the illocutionary force is to gain acceptance of the propositional act. However, only under some conditions will the readers believe these assertions as fact. In the case of the wondrous effects of chocolate, if there are contrary scientific findings or obvious flaws in the procedures followed, or the authors have no medical credentials, or if it becomes known they received major funding from the chocolate manufacturer's association, the proposition may well not be accepted by enough relevant readers to achieve status as a "fact." Other conditions may effect how people take up the assertions about news events or literary interpretation. The only perlocutionary effect may remain that the proposition is seen only as a dubious assertion. With only that more limited act accomplished, the resulting social fact will only be that the authors are trying to convince certain people of this or that claim. If, however, the authors do gain wide acceptance, new social facts about the value of chocolate, an historical event, or the meaning of a poem will be established until someone undermines those facts or replaces them with new "truths." When viewed through this analysis, the matter of arguing for the truth of propositions becomes a matter of meeting those felicity conditions that will lead the relevant audiences to accept your claims as true, thus matching the perlocutionary effect with your illocutionary intent.

Typification and Genres. The three-leveled distinction among what we say or write, what we intend to accomplish by what we say or write, and what people understand us to be attempting points out how much our intentions may be misunderstood and just how difficult may be coordinating our actions with each other. The lack of coordination is potentially much worse when we are communicating by writing, for we cannot see each other's gestures and mood, nor can we immediately see the other's uptake in a perlocutionary effect that does not match our illocutionary intent. That is, we can't notice our host immediately saying, "Oh, I didn't realize that you were uncomfortable" and step toward the thermostat, when we only wished to be ironic about the nasty turn in the conversation. If we spot misunderstandings in face-to-face situations, then we can always repair the damage with a comment like, "Oh, I was just joking." But in writing the opportunities for repair are usually extremely limited, even if we have enough information to suspect we may have been misunderstood.

One way we can help coordinate our speech acts with each other is to act in typical ways, ways easily recognized as accomplishing certain acts in certain circumstances. If we find a certain kind of utterance or text seems to work well in a situation and be understood in a certain way, when we see another similar situation we are likely to say or write something similar. If we start following communicative patterns that other people are familiar with, they may recognize more easily what we are saying and trying to accomplish. Then we can anticipate better what their reactions will be if we followed these standardized, recognizable forms. These patterns are mutually reinforcing. Recognizable, self-reinforcing forms of communication emerge as **genres**.

In creating typified forms or genres, we also come to typify the situations we find ourselves in. If we recognize that when a guest in someone else's house comments about bodily discomfort, the host typically understands that as an obligation to make the guest feel comfortable, then we can adjust our comments so as not to say things that would mistakenly put our host in a state of obligation. The typification gives a certain shape and meaning to the circumstances and directs the kinds of actions that will ensue.

This process of moving to standardized forms of utterances that are recognized as carrying out certain actions in certain circumstances and to standard understandings of situations is called **typification**. Thus in some professions if we wish to seek a position, we need to prepare a resume or curriculum vitae to list all the relevant facts and professional accomplishments of our life and to highlight our desirable qualities for the potential employer. Standard formats direct us toward what information to present, such as address, education, and prior experience. The standard format also directs us how to present that information. Following the standard format, as well, helps the employer find and interpret the information. Further, there are standard differences in format for different professions. In academic employment, publications and research take a central role, whereas in business listing responsibilities in each prior position and a record of specific training and skills are often important. Of course, even within the standard forms people try to express their particular characteristics and make their resume distinctive and memorable, so as to stand out from the others. Yet as soon as someone invents a new element or format that seems to work, it is likely to be picked up by others and become fairly standard within that field. Such, for example, is the newly established practice on resumes for a number of professions of listing computer programs one is familiar with.

The definition of genre presented here is a little different from the everyday sense we have of genres, but is consistent with it. As we walk through life we recognize very rapidly texts as being one or another familiar kind, usually because we recognize some features of the text that signal us what kind of message to expect. On an envelope, bulk rate postage and slogans signal us about junk mail advertisements and solicitations; a memo format signed by someone high up in the organization signals an announcement or directive. So we tend to identify and define genres by those special signaling features, and then all the other textual features that we expect to follow.

This identification of genres through features is very useful knowledge for us to interpret and make sense of documents, but it gives us an incomplete and misleading view of genres. By seeing genres as only characterized by a fixed set of features we come to view genres as timeless and the same for all viewers. Everybody always knows what we know—right? Wrong. Common knowledge changes over time as genres and situations change; "common knowledge" even varies from person to person, or even the same person in different situations and moods. The definition of genres only as a set of textual features ignores the role of individuals in using and making meaning. It ignores differences of perception and understanding, the creative use of communications to meet perceived novel needs in novel circumstances, and the changing of genre understanding over time.

We can reach a deeper understanding of genres if we understand them as **psycho-social recognition phenomena** that are parts of processes of socially organized activities. Genres are only the types individuals recognize as being used by themselves and others. Genres are what we believe they are. That is, they are social facts about the kinds of speech acts people can make and the ways they can make them. Genres arise in social processes of people trying to understand each other well enough to coordinate activities and share meanings for their practical purposes.

Genres typify many things beyond textual form. They are part of the way that humans give shape to **social activity**. When you are at a football game and recognize that the crowd is taking up a chant for your team, as you join in you are being drawn into the spectacle and emotions of the community athletic event. As you read and are convinced by the political pamphlet of a candidate for Congress you are being drawn into a world of politics and citizenship. As you learn to read and use research articles of your field you are drawn into a professional way of being and work. When a new Web site develops and attracts attention, your local community service organization may evolve into a clearinghouse for corporate donation of excess products. You and your fellow volunteers may then find yourselves drawn into an entirely new set of activities and roles.

To characterize how genres fit into and comprise larger organizations, roles, organizations, and activities, several overlapping concepts have been proposed, each grabbing a different aspect of this configuration: genre set, genre system and activity system.

A **Genre Set** is the collection of types of texts someone in a particular role is likely to produce. In cataloging all the genres someone in a professional role is likely to speak and write, you are identifying a large part of their work. If you find out a civil engineer needs to write proposals, work orders, progress reports, quality test reports, safety evaluations, and a limited number of other similar documents, you have gone a long way toward identifying the work they do. If you then can figure out what skills are needed to be able to write those reports (including the mathematical, measuring, and testing skills that are needed to produce the figures, designs, calculations, etc. in the reports) you will have identified a large part of what a civil engineer has to learn to do that work competently. If you identify all the forms of writing a student must engage in to study, to communicate with the teacher and classmates, and to submit for dialogue and evaluation, you have defined the competences, challenges, and opportunities for learning offered by that course.

A **Genre System** is comprised of the several genre sets of people working together in an organized way, plus the patterned relations in the production, flow, and use of these documents. A genre system captures the regular sequences of how one genre follows on another in the typical communication flows of a group of people. The genre set written by a teacher of a particular course might consist of a syllabus, assignment sheets, personal notes on readings, notes for giving lectures and lesson plans for other kinds of classes, exam questions, email announcements to the class, replies to individual student queries and comments, comments and grades on student papers, and grade sheets at the end of the term. Students in the same course would have a somewhat different genre set: notes of what was said in lectures and class, notes on reading, clarifications on assignment sheets and syllabus, email queries and comments to the professor and/or classmates, notes on library and data research for assignments, rough drafts and final copies of assignments, exam answers, letters requesting a change of grade. However, these two sets of genres are intimately related and flow in predictable sequences and time patterns. The instructor is expected to distribute the syllabi on the first day and assignment sheets throughout the term. Students then ask questions about the expectation in class or over email, and then write clarifications on the assignment sheets. The assignment sheets in turn guide student work in collecting data, visiting the library, and developing their assignments. The pace of their work picks up as the assignment deadline approaches. Once assignments are handed in, the professor comments on and grades them. Similarly the instructor prepares, then delivers lectures and classes. Students are expected to take notes on readings beforehand and then on what the instructor says in class; then they study those notes on class and readings before the various quizzes and exams. Typically the instructor looks at the lectures and assigned readings in order to write questions for quizzes and exams. The students then take the exam and the teacher grades them. At the end of the term the instructor calculates by some formula the sum of all the grades to produce the content of the grade sheet, which is submitted to the registrar to enter into an institutional system of genres.

This **system of genres** is also part of the **system of activity** of the class. In defining the system of genres people engage in you also identify a framework which organizes their work, attention, and accomplishment. In some situations spoken genres dominate, but as you move up the educational ladder and into the professional world, the system of written genres become especially important. In some activities physical aspects take on a highly visible and central role, and the spoken and written genres are peripheral or supportive rather than central. Playing basketball may be mostly about moves and ball handling, but there are rules, strategies, cheers, league organization, and newspaper reporting which engage spoken and written genres. Factory production similarly is closely tied to orders, control and quality reports, production records, machine instructions, and repair manuals. In knowledge-based fields, such as medicine, and especially fields where the primary product is making and distributions of symbols, such as journalism, then the activity system is centrally organized around written documents.

Considering the activity system in addition to the genre system puts a focus on what people are doing and how texts help people do it, rather than on texts as ends in themselves. In educational settings, activity puts the focus on questions such as how students build concepts and knowledge through solving problems, how instructional activities make knowledge and opportunities for learning available, how instructors support and structure learning, and how and for what purposes student abilities are assessed.

METHODOLOGICAL ISSUES

The textual analysis in this chapter aims at genre and the larger aggregations (genre sets, genre systems, and activity systems) that genres are part of. The concepts of social fact and speech act provide a basis for understanding the analytical approach of this chapter. We do not, however, in this chapter provide focused analytic tools for investigating social facts and speech acts. Empirical research and analysis of social facts and speech acts would raise many additional methodological concerns of sociology, anthropology, and linguistics than we have space for here. To keep our task simpler, we will keep our analytical focus at the level of genre, and particularly genres of written texts, setting aside methodological issues that pertain primarily to spoken utterances.

Before getting to methods of studying written genres, however, we need to address one issue that arises from considering extended written genres as speech acts. The concept of speech acts was developed by Austin and Searle using brief utterances, for the most part spoken. Linguists and linguistic anthropologists who have used the concept of speech act in the their investigations typically have stayed with brief spoken utterances—typically of the length of a short sentence. The shortness of the utterance makes the task of identifying distinct propositional and illocutionary acts simple. A single sentence can be seen as making a single request, or a single bet, or a single claim, and little more. And the immediate response possible in spoken interaction gives strong clues about the perlocutionary uptake of the listener. Further the initial speaker's response can give evidence of whether he or she felt the intent or force of the initial statement was understood correctly (i.e., whether the perlocutionary force was close or distant from the illocutionary intent).

Written texts typically do not have these advantages for analysis. Written texts are typically longer than a single sentence. The sentences within the texts themselves are typically longer and more complex. So that each sentence may contain many acts, and the many sentences of a text compound the problem infinitely. Nonetheless, we usually see the overall text as having a single or few dominant actions that define its intent and purpose, that we take up as the perlocutionary effect or the fact of social accomplishment for the text. An application to graduate school can be seen as the aggregate of writing numerous identifying and descriptive facts about ourselves, boasting about our accomplishments, presenting our thoughts about our professional goals, photocopying a paper completed earlier in our schooling, requesting several people to write letters of recommendation, filling out forms to several institutions to forward our scores and record, and writing a check to cover the application fee. How do we as analysts recognize this aggregate genre, with the actions and contexts implied?

Further, written texts usually provide little immediate evidence of the reader's uptake. That uptake may be more complex and considered than in response to spoken utterances because the reader may find varying meanings and develop multiple responses in reading through the long text. The reader then may ponder the text for some longer period. Because the reader's response is usually separated in time and space from the moment of writing, and is often buried within the privacy of silent reading, the writer may gain little evidence of any reader's uptake. Furthermore, even with knowledge of readers' uptake, the writer usually has few opportunities for corrections, repairs, or elaborations to resolve misunderstandings or differences between illocutionary intent and perlocutionary effect. Finally, a written text more easily than a spoken utterance can travel into entirely new situations where it may serve unanticipated uses for new readers, as when a private email gets spread around the Internet, or a politician's medical records get into the press.

This methodological dilemma of identifying speech acts in written texts is similar to the dilemma we face as readers and writers of texts. How do we make sense out of the complexity, indeterminacy, and contextual multiplicity that a text presents us with? We use genre and typifications to help us with just this sort of dilemma. As readers and writers we use whatever we have learned through our lives about texts, text types, and situation types to get a sense of the text at hand and to attribute a dominant action for each text. But there are serious methodological difficulties with relying totally on our "native speaker intuitions" as anything more than a first approximation. Technically, relying on our intuitions already makes us assume many of the things we want to investigate. We are already assuming that everybody understands these texts exactly as we understand them— that they share exactly the same kind and level of textual and social knowledge, and that we all share the same textual culture. This in a sense assumes the problem of genre understanding is always trivial and always solved—and in fact requires no education, socialization, or acculturation. If we all understood each other's texts so easily and well, many teachers would be out of a job. But mutual understanding of texts is not so easily achieved. Genre studies are needed precisely because we do not understand the genres and activities of unfamiliar fields that are important to us or to our students. Even those genres and activity systems that we already are to some degree familiar with could bear more analysis, so that we can act more effectively and precisely with a more articulated sense of what is going on.

So how do we get out of this dilemma of multiple understandings of genres and acts? How do we move beyond our "naturalized" user's view of genres and activity systems to a more carefully researched, observed, analyzed knowledge? How do we incorporate an understanding of the practices and knowledge of others—and then understand how these very practices come about and are learned? This is essentially the methodological problem of genre studies to which there is no simple and quick answer. Rather we have only a bootstrapping operation of increasing our knowledge and perspective through research such as examining more texts in a more regularized way; interviewing and observing more writers and readers, and ethnographically documenting how texts are used in organizations. The richer and more empirical a picture develops, the less we are dependent on the limitations of our own experience and training. The following methodological comments are aimed precisely at expending our perspective on genres and the systems they are part of.

Methodological Issues and Analytic Tools: What Is a Genre and How Do You Know One? Over the last few pages I have developed a complicated answer to something we recognize every day in fairly straightforward ways. When we look at documents we notice certain features that seem to signal them to us as belonging to one genre or another and therefore attempting to accomplish a certain kind of interaction with us.

You get a mail offer for a credit card. You immediately recognize what it is, perhaps without even opening the envelope. How do you do this? It is in a standard envelope, but with the glassine window for the address, so we recognize it as business or institutional. We recognize the bulk rate postage, and know it is some kind of impersonal solicitation. We notice the offer to lower our interest rates. We already know that inside the envelope we will find application for a credit card along with a letter. Even more we know whether we want to have anything to do with what they are offering.

You walk into a cafeteria and glance at a newspaper lying on a table. You immediately know many things about what it will contain and what the articles will look like, the style they will be in, how they will be organized, and even where in the newspaper different kinds of articles will be found. Again, this quickly assessed knowledge helps us structure what we do with that newspaper.

Most genres have easy to notice features that signal you about the kind of text it is. And often these features are closely related to major functions or activities carried out by the genre. The bold newspaper headlines mentioning major events are designed to grab your attention by pointing out the exciting news that you will want to read more about. The date and place of the story lets you know where in the world the news comes from (of course this really only became an important feature after telegraph and other forms of distant communication made the newspaper more than a local report). The lead sentence typically gives you *who, what, where*, and *when* so you can decide whether to read on about the details. The cheap paper is chosen because the paper's content gets old fast, and newspapers are usually thrown out within a couple of days. These features direct how we attend to the newspaper and even how long we keep it.

Because genres are recognizable by their distinctive features and those features seem to tell us so much about the function, it is tempting to see genres just as a collection of these features. We then are tempted to analyze the genres by picking out those regular features we notice and tell a story about the reason for these features, based on our knowledge of the world. Much, in fact, can be learned about familiar genres current in our time and community by proceeding in this way, but only because they are part of our immediate cultural world. There are, however, limitations and problems with identifying and analyzing genres by making up plausible reasons for easily spotted features.

First, it limits us to understanding those aspects of genre we are already aware of.

Second, it ignores how people may see each text in different ways, because of their different knowledge of genres, the different systems they are part of, the different positions and attitudes they have about particular genres, or their different activities at the moment. A wanted poster, for example, is read very differently by and has very different meanings for an FBI agent, a parent nervous about the safety of children, and the fugitive. Researchers in a particular field, for another example, may be able to distinguish many different kinds of articles that appear in the journals of their field, while graduate students may only recognize a few, which they will not understand the full implications of. How is a review of the literature at a research front that appears in a top research journal different from a textbook review or a seminar-assigned review of literature? First-year undergraduates may not even know research literatures exist and may think all scientific writing looks like the textbooks they are familiar with. In the business world, someone familiar with the texts that circulate in an insurance company may not be so familiar with those in a wholesale hardware operation. Even within the same industry sets of typical documents may vary in significant respects from one company to another.

Third, such a collecting of features may make it appear that these features of the text are ends in themselves, that every use of a text is measured against an abstract standard of correctness to the form rather than whether it carries out the work it was designed to do. If a news article is printed on high quality paper is it less a news article? If it does not list the "who, what, where, and when" in the opening paragraph is it seriously faulted? Of course, every example of a genre may vary in particulars of content, situation, and writer intent, which may lead to differences in the form. Yet we still use our genre knowledge to understand it. We may even use multiple genre models to understand and use it. The features and genres invoked have their only justification and motive in the understanding and activity that occurs between people, and finally whatever works, counts.

Fourth, consequently, the view of genre that simply makes it a collection of features obscures how these features are flexible in any instance or even how the general understanding of the genre can change over time, as people orient to evolving patterns. Students writing papers for courses have a wide variety of ways of fulfilling the assignment, and may even bend the assignment as long as they can get their professor or grader to go along with the change. Newspaper stories now have a different "feel" than those of a century ago—which can be attributed to changes in the understanding of articles—such as the expectation of rapid communication, the quick dating of stories, the recognition of the role of celebrity and famous people, the critical culture.

To deal with these issues, then, we can suggest several different approaches to identifying and analyzing genres that go beyond the cataloging of features of genres that we already recognize.

First, **to go beyond those features we are already aware of**, we can use a variety of less obvious linguistic, rhetorical, or organizational analytical concepts to examine a collection of texts in the same genre. In that way we can discover if there are consistencies within a genre that go beyond the most obvious identifying features. By examining typical patterns of subject and verbs, we may, for example, consider whether or not state education standards attribute agency, and of what sort to students, or whether those documents put most of the decision making in the hands of teachers, or administrators, or abstract principles of knowledge. Or we may see how science textbooks use graphic images and tables and compare those uses to those in more professional scientific documents to see whether students are being given the opportunity to become familiar with scientific practices of graphic representation. Most of the methods of textual analysis in this book can be considered with respect to genre, although not all of them will necessarily reveal a pattern in any particular genre.

Second, **to consider variation in different situations and periods**, we can extend the sample to include a larger number and range of texts that still might be considered within the same genre. More examples allow us to see how the form of the text varies. Even more importantly, if you are able to gain information about the rhetorical situation of each of the examples, you can analyze how those variations are related to differences in the situation and the interaction being carried out in the situation.

We may further consider how there may be patterned differences between what is called the same genre in different areas or fields. If we start looking at experimental research articles in biology and psychology we can notice characteristic differences between them. We may then consider the way in which these are the same genres and the extent to which you might consider them different. And we can then consider how differences in the form are related to differences in the social and activity organization of the fields.

Similarly, we can compare front-page news articles in different countries to consider the different roles news takes within the differing political, economic, and social lives found in those countries. Or we can compare front-page stories in a national paper of record like the *New York Times* and a tabloid or a local paper. These kinds of investigations will reveal how expectation of genres can become highly specialized in different areas, how what people recognize is very much a local cultural matter, and how news enters into the complex of organized life activities.

Another way to extend your sample is to look historically. With sufficient examples of the genre over time, we can get a sense of how the genre understandings change as a field and historical context change. These changes may be so great that the names of the genres change or very different things count as a genre. The earliest scientific articles look more like letters than anything we see now in *Physics Review*. The more we hold all other aspects of the situation constant, the more we can see how much of the change is due to changes in genre understanding. To compare news stories from a century ago to today, it helps to look at newspapers from the same size town with the same level of readership in a similar region, so as to identify what differences are likely to result from historical changes in newspaper format rather than differences of the audience served.

Third, to deal with the problem of characterizing **genres that you may not be familiar with or that others may understand differently than you do**, you need to gather information not just about the texts, but about other people's understanding of them. One broad way is to ask people in a certain field to name the kinds of texts they work with (i.e., to identify their genre set). If you find that all people in a field make a similar list of kinds of texts that accountants or insurance claims adjusters use, then you may have some sense that they do have common understandings. The existence of a well-known name for a genre within a world of practice suggests that this is indeed common knowledge to practitioners, but people may in fact understand somewhat different things by a single shared name. To check the degree of agreement as to understand the particulars of the genre, collecting samples of what they would consider each of those named genres gives you a chance to examine how similar they are in form and in function they are. Sometimes professional or legal or administrative documents define and specify what must go into various documents and how they are to be used. Procedures and regulations manuals, for example, may identify 12 kinds of forms to be filled out, the occasions on which they are to be filled out, and the manner of completion. However, be careful, because people do not always do things exactly as the regulations tell them to or they interpret the regulations differently, or they try to accomplish other things beyond the mandate of the regulations.

Fourth, to extend beyond the explicit understanding of what people in a field name, in order **to see the full range of implicit practice**, you can do ethnographic research in the workplace, classroom, or other site of text production, distribution, or use. By collecting every text people use over a day, or a week, or a month, as well as noting on what occasions they use them, for what purposes, and how they produce, work with, and interpret these texts, you will get a more complete picture of their textual worlds. If you do this, make sure you are as complete as possible, including such things as email messages, personal notes jotted on the margins of other forms, or other things people might not consider formal documents worth noting. Interviewing people in the process of using texts can give you further insight into the meanings, intentions, uptakes, and activity of the participants.

In the course of this ethnographic work you may also record the sequence particular documents come in, in relation to which activities, and which documents are referred to in the course of reading and writing each new document. This data will help you document and understand the genre set, genre system, and activity system. Examining the genre set allows you **to see the range and variety of the writing work** required within a role, and to identify the genre knowledge and writing skills needed by someone to accomplish that work. Examining the genre system allows you **to understand the practical, functional, and sequential interactions of documents**. Understanding these interactions also allows you to see how individuals writing any new text are intertextually situated within a system and how their writing is directed by genre expectations and supported by systemic resources. Finally, considering the activity system enables you **to understand the total work accomplished by the system and how each piece of writing contributes to the total work**. Analysis of genre and activity systems also allows you to evaluate the effectiveness of the total systems and the appropriateness of each of the genred documents in carrying forward that work. This analysis could help you determine whether any change in any of the documents, distribution, sequence, or flow might improve the total activity system.

METHODOLOGICAL GUIDELINES: HOW TO FRAME AND PURSUE A GENRE INVESTIGATION

1. Frame your purposes and questions to limit your focus. As with any form of research and analysis the first and most important task is knowing **why you are engaged** in the enterprise and **what questions you hope to answer** by it. Depending on your purposes, what you have access to, the amount of time and energy you can commit to the project, you may carry out an investigation at any of the levels discussed in the previous section. Each level has its problems and benefits. No one is right or wrong. You just need to be aware of the limits and values of each.

2. Define your Corpus. Once you know what you are looking for and why, the next task is to **identify the specific texts or collections you want to ex-**

amine, making them extensive enough to provide substantial evidence in making claims, but not too broad to become unmanageable. There is no magic equation to determine what gives you adequate evidence of a genre or stability, but a good rule of thumb is the point of diminishing returns plus a couple more. That is, the sample size should be large enough that adding additional samples will be unlikely to give you major new news or variations. Once you have found that point, add a couple more just to make sure.

On the other hand, if you are examining the history of a journal, or a comparison across several subspecialties, your sample should be rich enough to include more than a few from each period or domain.

If you are gathering the genres from a genre set or a genre system, again the point of "diminished returns plus a couple" is a good guideline. If the genres and work are organized within a limited and coherent cycle, then you can use that cycle to organize and limit your collecting. For example, in looking at a class, you may look at the entire cycle of the term's work; or you may examine the cycle of texts involved in a single unit or assignment sequence. You need not examine every student's paper for every assignment, but you should have a reasonable sample of all assignments, all sets of notes, etc. If you are working with a small peer editing group in the class, all the texts they work with could define your sample of collected work.

3. Select and apply your analytic tools. Based on the purposes of your investigation, you need to **select appropriate analytic tools** to examine the consistencies and variations of features, functions, or relations over the collection. These are the tools discussed in the previous section on how to recognize a genre. As you carry out the analysis, it should be evident whether you are tapping into some fairly stable patterns of text and activity.

After extensive collecting and analysis, **if no stable patterns emerge** this may be because of one of two difficulties.

- The collection does not reflect the actual practices of users or a coherent flow of documents. For example, if you collect all texts looked at or worked on by students sitting in the student center lounge, you may be tapping into so many different activity systems brought there by students who are just passing through, that you will find no coherence. If you wanted to get a sense of the many genres that pass through a student's life, you might do better to follow a single student around over a day or several days.
- The analytical focus may be misplaced. For example, if you are looking at television advertisements assuming the purpose is to give information about the product, you may find in many ads little product information to consider. You may be stymied, because ads often seek variety and novelty in order to gain the attention of jaded viewers and give little information. Sometimes the ads withhold even identifying the product

until the end to keep you wondering. Perhaps, therefore, your analysis might be better framed around novelty and attention gaining devices. The drive for attention gaining novelty may be so strong that the recognizable features of ads change very rapidly, which your analysis will need to take into account.

APPLIED ANALYSIS

The following case demonstrates the value of considering genre, genre sets, genre systems, and activity systems in evaluating the learning potential and consequences of a set of classroom activities. I would like to thank Chris Carrera and Kambiz Ebraham for their help in collecting the data.

Over a 6-week period during the late fall of 1998 in a sixth-grade class in a suburban California public elementary school, students engaged in a social studies learning unit on the Maya, which was to some degree integrated with simultaneous learning units in mathematics, language arts, and video production. As part of this unit they read and wrote a variety of texts. Texts they wrote included worksheet and outline completions, notes on the readings, quizzes, exams, informational reports (with drafts), collaboratively written scripts (with drafts) for an adventure story about an expedition to the land of the Maya, and final reflections on what they learned from the unit. These documents are the genre set of student writing during this unit. Each student's **genre set** was collected in a file of the student's work. The student work also included art on Mayan sports, a map of an imagined Mayan city, collaboratively built models of the imagined cities, a board game about the Maya which incorporated words and text (produced by pairs of collaborating students), and videos of their adventure stories (collaboratively produced in teams of about four students each). We can call this **an extended graphic genre set**, although all parts were not collected and placed within the student file of work—suggesting a difference in the evaluation of these productions. Among their readings were a number of assignment sheets and blank worksheets, packets of information about the Maya, supplementary reference books and Web sites, each other's reports and drafts of reports, and drafts of their mutually constructed projects and scripts. Many of these were collected in the student work files.

In traditional terms the aim of this unit could be described as learning social studies facts and concepts with some reinforcement activities. The inclusion of the final reports, the worksheets, outlines, exams, and information sheets in the work file reinforces that impression. The final reports of most students were collections of facts gleaned from handouts, textbooks, encyclopedias, and online reference materials, presented with only minimal organization and no transition between different topics and the fact sheets, quizzes, and exams equally show only the accumulation of fragmentary facts and ideas. Only a few students were able to achieve a level of articulated synthesis that gave a sense of totality of vision to their papers. On the other hand, students seemed to have understood the expectations of the genre as to require a collection of information. One student, Maria, in the opening sentences of her paper articulates exactly this understanding of what she has to do.

> Okay, before I pour all this information on you, let me introduce you to the Maya. They had six prosperous cities: Tulum, Chichen Itza, Uxmal, Mayapan, Tikal, and Palenque. Got that? Great.
> Here comes the rest . . .
> They were the first people in the New World to have written records. They also had numbers. One was a dot. · Two was two dots.··

This goes on for about 500 words presenting information on chronicles, calendars, ball games, human sacrifice, geographic and historical extent, trading, and demise. In fact, almost all the papers from the class were similar to Maria's in content, organization, and diction, varying mostly in length and amount of information reported.

That students had such an understanding of the task and the genre is not surprising given that the original assignment packet for this unit described this assignment only as a "three-page typed report describing the Mayan culture." This was embedded within a much more elaborate set of activities, described shortly, but the specific genre of this assignment was very narrow. The narrow information collection focus of this assignment was reinforced and supported by a number of other activities that occurred between the original assignment and the due date of the paper (December 4). First, with the assignment packet and in the days after several handouts were distributed to the class photocopied from reference works covering history, calendar, religion, number system, sports, cities, sacrifice, geography, art, and similar topics. Second, each week in class specific topics of the information were reviewed, with an informational quiz on Friday. Third, on November 9, students had to fill out a preprinted informational outline on the Mayan civilization providing four points of information for each of three categories: The Land and Region; Classic Period; Mayan Knowledge (see Fig. 11.1 for Janine's response). Fourth, due November 30 just before the final reports was a research chart to be filled out by students working in pairs, first by hand on the worksheet, and then transcribed on a spreadsheet. For five cities, each pair of students had to identify the location, record an important discovery, describe the region, and select an interesting cultural fact. Figure 11.2 is the research chart produced by Maria and Sau-lin.

Ancient Maya
Outline
November 9, 1998

You are to complete this outline with information from our Maya packet, classroom discussions, and research materials. Remember to keep the information brief and to the point.

I. Maya Civilization
  A. The Land and Region
    1. Harsh living conditions
    2. Jungle, rain forest
    3. Mountains
    4. Mexican southeastern states, Yucatan Peninsula
    Guatemala, south into Guatemala, northern Honduras
  B. Classic Period
    1. Beginnings of Mayan greatness 300 AD
    2. Flourished until 900 AD
    3. Schools
    4. Markets for trading goods
    Centers for practicing religion.
  C. Maya Knowledge
    1. Master astronomers
    2. " " mathematicians
    3. " " architecture
    4. " " writing
    " time & calendars

FIG. 11.1. Informational outline for students to fill in.

The product here is a mechanically organized set of factual fragments, selected and transcribed from the distributed informational sheets. The further transcription of this material onto a spreadsheet beyond providing new technical skills, reinforces the idea that information (and research) consists of such fragments organized into formal categories. Thus it is not surprising that students understand the final research report as they do and do not feel challenged to rise to a higher level of synthesis, analysis, or discussion.

city name	city location	research information	region description	interesting facts
Uxmal	Northwestern part of the Mexican Yucatan.	The magnificent architecture here is adorned with many elaborate decorations and bright colors.	Rugged terrain, and hot ground	The Magician's Pyramid has been said to be built in one night.
Tikal	The middle of dense jungle, north of Guatemala.	This sprawling city consists of numerous residences, temples, pyramids, and ball courts.	Viny, and very colorful	Played a soccer type game called Pok-a-tok.
Tulum	The coast of the Caribbean Sea	Tulum prospers because it can acquire trade goods from the sea.	Water, coast, and very colorful	Sacrificed humans to Gods.
Chichen Itza	North-central part of the Mexican Yucatan	Chichen Itza has grown to great wealth and power because of its central among the Maya trade routs.	North-central rain forest	Attempted to kill other cities.
Palenque	East part of Mexico	Human sacrifices were located here.	Thick Mexican Jungle	They had special ceremonies.

FIG. 11.2. The research chart produced by Maria and Sau-lin.

The apparently student-produced genres of outlines, worksheets, and quizzes are in fact collaboratively produced with the teacher in the very specific sense that the words on the final page include words produced by the teacher and the students. The teacher produces the topics and categories and structure for the outline and chart and the questions for the quiz. He further produces the instructions on each of the assignment sheet. In this latter sense, and also by structuring the intermediate informational assignments we can also see the teacher's hand in the final reports. Thus these genres are strongly shaped by the teacher's decisions of what should be written and how. The students' recognition of the teacher's speech act of assignment shapes their further actions in fulfillment of the assignment, just as the teacher's further assignments are dependent on his recognition of the students' completion of prior acts. And each new student production is dependent on them having completed earlier acts, turning them into facts which they could then rely on and build upon.

In two collaboratively produced teacher–student genres, however, the teacher's decisions structure a very different kind of work for the students. First is the unit final exam, given on December 11, with three questions.

1. What qualities do you think gave strength to the Mayan Empire?
2. In what ways can trade between cities help to create good relationships?
3. Why do you think the Mayan Empire did not go on forever?

Each of the three questions requires students to think evaluatively, causally, and critically, and most of them did so. Maria provided one of the more elaborated set of answers, but not all that different from that of most of her classmates. In answer to Question 1, "What qualities do you think gave strength to the Mayan Empire?" she wrote:

> I think that the accuracy in their calendars, their knowledge of the movements of the stars, their ability to create their own letters gave strength to the Mayan Empire. I also think that no matter what role you had, or what you did, you were important to the Mayan Empire, and that gave strength to the Mayan Empire.

How did such questions and answers count as an appropriate test of what the students had learned if the earlier activities were primarily transcription of fragmented information? And where did the students get the ideas and stance from which they could answer these questions?

Before we answer that let us examine another end-of-the-sequence document, the "Final Thoughts" worksheet filled out 2 days before the final exam. The following example from Desmond covers typical themes (see

Figs. 11.3 and 11.4). Only the first question really evokes in Desmond (and most of the other students) any reference to the factual information, and even then the information is subordinated to an evaluative conclusion. All his remaining responses (as were the responses of most of his classmates) referred to the other activities of building models, the play production and videotaping. And key themes were working together, doing things better, and having fun—all issues of participation and engagement. Given the pre-

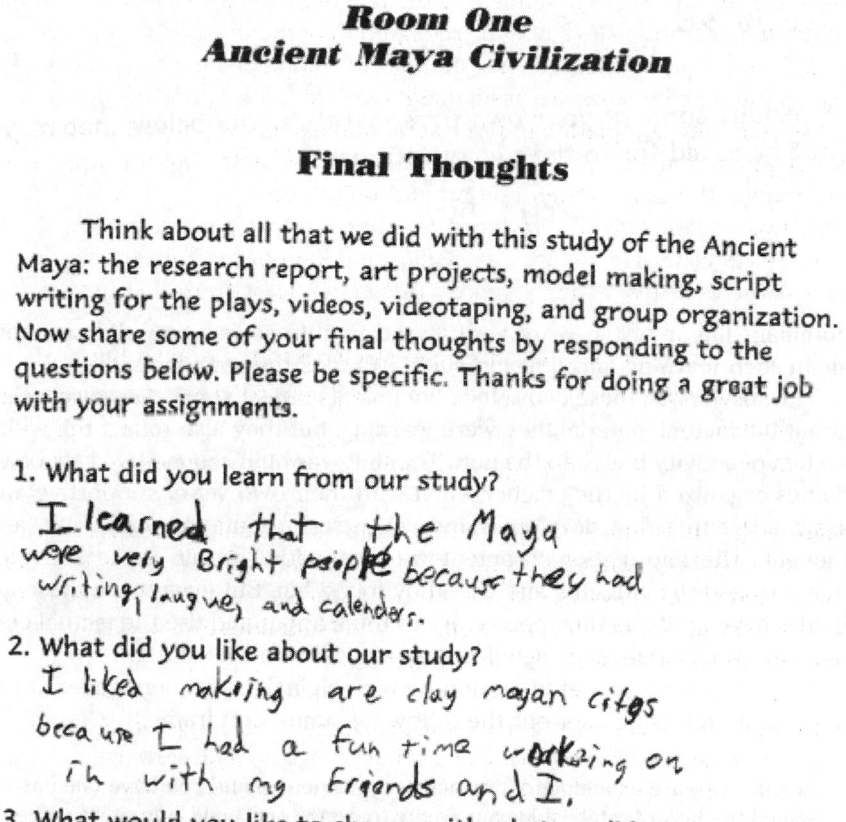

Room One
Ancient Maya Civilization

Final Thoughts

Think about all that we did with this study of the Ancient Maya: the research report, art projects, model making, script writing for the plays, videos, videotaping, and group organization. Now share some of your final thoughts by responding to the questions below. Please be specific. Thanks for doing a great job with your assignments.

1. What did you learn from our study?

I learned that the Maya were very Bright people because they had writing, laugue, and calendars.

2. What did you like about our study?

I liked makeing are clay mayan citos because I had a fun time working on in with my Friends and I.

3. What would you like to change with what we did?

I would like to change the Mayan city time to work on it, I would want more time to loobrk on it. I think it would have been better if we had more time to work on it. But it still turned out good.

FIG. 11.3.

4. What would have made it better and more interesting?
Are play would have been better if we had more cumaperation.

5. How could we have improved our video productions?
It would be better if we were organzed.

* Include some of your own personal thoughts below that may not be asked for in the five questions.
It was very fun.

FIG. 11.4.

dominant flavor of the work we have examined so far, how did students glean such learning and develop such attitudes toward the unit?

The answers on these two sets of documents reflect some class discussion about the factual material they were learning, but they also reflect the wider system of activity built into the unit. The unit was built around two sets of activities organized by the teacher, each with their own set of supportive and assigned genres that developed and rehearsed orientation, creativity, and thought. The informational content was embedded within these activities that engaged the students and that they found fun. But even more these activities gave students the opportunity to think about and use the factual content, and thus to develop significant meanings from the content.

The activities were set in motion by the original assignment sheet at the beginning unit, which set out the following simulation frame:

> Project: You are a member of an ancient Maya people and you have been assigned the task of establishing a new site to design and build a great city. The name of the city will be chosen from one of the following: Tulum, Chichen Itza, Uxmal, Mayapan, Tikal, or Palenque. The task is to be done individually, but you may confer with others to get ideas or give suggestions. Good luck and begin immediately, because the king is not a patient man and needs the city built before invaders arrive.

The sheet goes on to specify three parts of the project: a "three-page typed report on Mayan Culture, an illustration/graphic, and a blueprint of the Mayan City with everything labeled. A fourth final activity is mentioned of group creation of a play with script and costumes and videotaping. Each of these four parts was modified and elaborated in the ensuing 6 weeks.

The original situation frame of designing a new Mayan city gave motive and purpose to the informational and other activities of the first half of the unit. The factual information is what you need in order to be able to know what a Mayan city is and how you should design one to include its typical buildings, institutions, and places for its usual activities. That work became most fully and directly expressed in the map/design each produced, which then became the basis for a scale model. Two additional art projects, however, reflected the same kind of civilization building thinking. One was a board game each had to design to reflect the daily life of residents of the city and the other was to act as the chief Maya artist commissioned to create a design that reflects the style of the culture (students were also learning to use graphic software as part of this assignment). Finally there was a sequence of Mayan math exercises (from a prepared unit) that used standard word and logic problems using objects and situations relevant to the Mayan agriculture, social structure, and culture and that also gave some experience using Mayan number system and calendar. These immersions in Mayan life through simulations did more that rehearse some factual material about the Maya, they drew sixth graders into thinking about the material and how the facts reflected a way of life.

The second half of the unit transformed the situational frame from design into inquiry and the mode of work from individual into collaborative. This shift was initiated by an assignment sheet handed out 4 weeks into the unit on November 20, just after the designs and scale models were finished. The assignment sheet informs the students that they are archeologists who have found an artifact with a map to an undiscovered Mayan City. They are to organize in teams to search for the city and its treasures; they will then script and produce a video documentary of their adventures. The assignment sheet then provides space for the students to sketch out preliminary ideas about setting, characters, events, and story summary for the initial work sessions with the collaborative group (about five students in each group). Also provided is a follow-up framework for the script, in which the characters, setting for each scene, the props and costumes and the production team roles, and other notes are to be listed. These assignment sheets scaffold the work of script writing and production for the students as they make decisions in filling out the blanks and then do the additional work implied in each of their answers.

The research chart discussed earlier finds its meaning within this archeological frame of action. The instructions for the chart describe it as reported from field archeologists back to their colleagues to let them know what has been found. So now the material is not just information to be tested on—it is something the students, in their simulated roles as archeologists, know to be shared with others. The knowledge they have found also becomes subject and material of their videos (which were also produced as live plays).

The scripts for the videos are pretty basic, involving archeologists walking through the city with local informants pointing out aspects of the culture, with lots of dwelling on the ball game with a death penalty for losing and other moments of human sacrifice. Nonetheless, the stories are larded with the facts and names that have cropped up in the various reading and writing genres throughout the unit, so that the students have learned to inhabit the informational space even while engaged in imaginative play. Looking at the limitations of the scripts, one could well understand why a number of students commented that the videos would have been much better if they had learned to work together and everyone learned to do their part. It also becomes evident that the teacher used the lesson of cooperation within successful civilizations to help students reflect on the difficulties of their own collaboration—and thus comments about cooperation being essential to Mayan success turn up as well on the final exam.

When we look at **the total activity system of the classroom** as students participated in each unit, and the kind of work and learning accomplished in the production of each of the teacher-directed genres, we can see that students were doing more than reproducing facts from handouts and books. They were thinking about the material and using the material to engage in other activities, which required understanding and elicited motivated engagement. These various activities were coordinated in a mutually supported sequential system that ended with classroom presentation of reports, airing of the videos produced by each of the several small groups, reflective observations on the activity, and analytical thought on the final exam. The activities each were centrally engaged with well-known, **typified textual and graphic genres**, which afforded students anticipateable access to information, challenges and problem solving, and opportunities for learning. The end result included familiarity with some factual information about the Maya but also a sense of what Mayan life was like, an experience of being an inquirer into another culture, increased skill in synthesizing and presenting information, using knowledge creatively for imaginative productions, and a sense of the practical import of the information. There was also learning and practice of many computing and video media skills. Such complex learning with multiple, varied formal products and such varied forms of cognition and learning could only be evoked and coordinated because of the teacher's practical understanding of the complex interrelated activities set in motion by the assignments and of the roles of specific genres in establishing and focusing activities. Although interviews and conversations with the teacher provided no indication of an awareness of the theoretical framework presented in the chapter, in a practical way the teacher managed precisely the concrete realizations of the concepts presented here.

ACTIVITIES

1. Textbooks
   a. Describe the features, functions, and student activity of a textbook for a single field, such as American History. Write a paper analyzing the genre.
   b. Compare the features, functions, and student activities of the first set of textbooks (e.g., in American History) to the features, functions, and student activities of textbooks in a very different field (such as mathematics). Write a paper comparing the two related genres.
   c. Compare the features, functions, and reader activities of either of the set of textbooks with the features, functions, and reader activities of professional research articles or books in the same field. Write a paper comparing the genre of textbook and research contribution in that field.

2. A Class
   Identify and collect samples of the entire genre set produced by you in a recent class you have taken or are now taking. Then consider the entire genre and activity and system of the class. You may wish to interview the instructor and other students; you may also wish to take observational notes on how texts are produced, distributed, used, and related in the class.

3. A Genre Set of a Professional
   Interview a professor or other professional to determine what kinds of texts receives and writes in the course of a typical day. If possible, collect samples. You may wish to shadow them for a day to notice what kinds of texts they receive and produce. Write a paper analyzing the genre set you have found.

4. Student Assignments
   To examine the range of variation within a genre or the differing understandings of a genre, examine a set of papers of all the students in a class responding to a single assignment. (Be sure to get a copy of the original assignment.) What features are in common? What is the range of variation? How much commonality and variation seems invited by the assignment? By the assignment's place within the course? By the overall nature of schooling? By other cultural factors? How much variation seems to reflect student differences in interests, personality, resources, skills, or resources? You may interview the instructor to determine how much of the variation is ac-

ceptable to the instructor, which variations seem to reduce the instructor's evaluation, and which variations seem to violate the expectations or genre of the assignment. You may also interview the other students to find out what they thought the genre of the assignment asked for, how much they thought they were varying the genre, and what motivated the particular way they varied their paper from what they viewed as the standard response. In a paper report your findings and analysis.

FOR FURTHER READING

In sociology the classic statement on social facts is from Emile Durkheim's (1982) *The Rules of Sociological Method*, and the classic discussion of the social definition of the situation is in a brief passage (pp. 41–44) of W. I. Thomas' (1923) *The Unadjusted Girl*. Robert King Merton's (1968) essay on "The Self Fulfilling Prophecy" brings the two concepts together in a readable and convincing way.

The standard philosophic discussions of speech acts are two thin but dense books, John Austin's (1962) *How to Things with Words* and John Searle's (1969) *Speech Acts*. The former opens up very broadly the ways words perform actions, while the latter attempts to identify a more focused and limited system of acts. Within linguistics and linguistic anthropology this performative approach to language has created the basis for the area of study known as pragmatics. A good introduction to pragmatics is Allessandro Duranti's (1997) *Linguistic Anthropology*. A somewhat more difficult but rewarding presentation is William Hanks' (1996b) *Language and Communicative Practice*.

The sociological and phenomenological concept of typification has its source in the work of Alfred Schutz, particularly *The Structures of the Life World* (Schutz & Luckman, 1973). A very approachable and influential elaboration of his approach is the work of his students Peter Berger and Thomas Luckmann, *The Social Construction of Reality* (1966).

Schutz's phenomenological approach to typification was brought together with rhetorical studies and applied specifically to the concept of genre by Carolyn Miller (1984) in "Genre as a Social Act." There is now an extensive literature on genre as typification in rhetoric and writing studies, including Charles Bazerman, *Shaping Written Knowledge* (1988); Berkenkotter and Huckin, *Genre Knowledge* (1995); Freedman and Medway, eds. *Genre and the New Rhetoric* (1994); and Bazerman and Paradis, eds. *Textual Dynamics of the Professions* (1991).

Bazerman's *Shaping Written Knowledge* also links genre-as-typification to activity theory growing out of the work of Vygotsky, *Thought and Language* (1986) and *Mind in Society* (1978), particularly in relation to Vygotsky's interest in the history of cultural forms. David Russell's two essays (1997a, 1997b) elaborate the ways genre theory is enriched by considering it in an activity theory frame. Bazerman and Russell have edited a special issue of *Mind, Culture and Activity* (1997) as well as *Writing Selves/Writing Society* (2003), an edited electronic collection devoted to activity approaches to writing. Bazerman's (1999) *The Languages of Edison's Light* is an extensive study using the concepts set out in this chapter.

Other related approaches to genre come out of functional linguistics, including Swales (1990), Bhatia (1993), and Cope and Kalantzis (1993). Within literary theory, the history of the way genre has traditional been handled is in Hernadi (1972); Mikhael Bakhtin (1986) and Ralph Cohen (1986) have developed approaches consistent with the approaches here; and Thomas Beebee (1994) has considered how genres are associated with ideology.

References

Achebe, Chinua. (1959). *Things fall apart.* Scanton, PA: Haddon Craftsmen.

Allen, Graham. (2000). *Intertextuality.* London: Routledge.

Altheide, David. (1987). Ethnographic content analysis. *Qualitative Sociology, 10,* 65–77.

Amann, Klaus, & Knorr-Cetina, Karin. (1990). The fixation of (visual) evidence. In Michael Lynch & Steve Woolgar (Eds.), *Representation in scientific practice* (pp. 85–122). Cambridge, MA: MIT Press.

Anderson, James. (1996). *Communication theory: Epistemological foundations.* New York: Guilford Press.

Andrews, James. (1990). *The practice of rhetorical criticism* (2nd ed.). New York: Longman.

Anzaldúa, Gloria. (1987). *Borderlands: La Frontera.* San Francisco: Aunt Lute Books.

Aristotle. (1991). *On rhetoric: A theory of civil discourse* (George A. Kennedy, Trans.). New York: Oxford University Press.

Arnheim, Rudolf. (1982). *The power of the center: A study of composition in the visual arts.* Berkeley: University of California Press.

Atkinson, Dwight. (1999). *Scientific discourse in sociohistorical context: The Philosophical Transactions of the Royal Society of London, 1675–1975.* Mahwah, NJ: Lawrence Erlbaum Associates.

Atkinson, John, & Heritage, John. (Eds.). (1984). *Structures of social action: Studies in conversational analysis.* Cambridge, England: Cambridge University Press.

Atwell, Nancie. (1987). *In the middle: Writing, reading, and learning with adolescents.* Portsmouth: Boynton/Cook Heinemann.

Auer, Peter. (Ed.). (1998). *Code-switching in conversation: Language, interaction and identity.* London: Routledge.

Austin, John. (1962). *How to do things with words.* Oxford, England: Oxford University Press.

Bakhtin, Mikhail. (1981). *The dialogic imagination: Four essays by M. M. Bakhtin* (Caryl Emerson & Michael Holquist, Trans.; Michael Holquist, Ed.). Austin: University of Texas Press.

Bakhtin, Mikhail. (1984). *Problems of Dostoevsky's poetics* (Caryl Emerson, Trans.). Minneapolis: University of Minnesota Press.

Bakhtin, Mikhail. (1986). *Speech genres and other late essays* (Vern McGee, Trans.; Caryl Emerson & Michael Holquist, Eds.). Austin: University of Texas Press.

Bal, Mieke. (1997). *Narratology: Introduction to the theory of narrative* (2nd ed.; Christine van Boheemen, Trans.). Toronto: University of Toronto Press.

Bang, Molly. (1991). *Picture this: Perception and composition.* Boston: Little Brown.

Barthes, Roland. (1972). *Mythologies* (Annette Lavers, Trans. & Ed.). New York: Noonday.

Bartholomae, David. (1985). Inventing the university. In Mike Rose (Ed.), *When a writer can't write: Writer's block and other composing problems* (pp. 104–116). New York: Guilford Press.

Bartlett, Francis. (1932). *Remembering: A study in experimental and social psychology.* Cambridge, England: Cambridge University Press.

Barton, Ellen. (1993). Evidentials, argumentation, and epistemological stance. *College English, 44,* 745–79.

Barton, Ellen. (2002). Inductive discourse analysis: Identifying rich features. In Ellen Barton & Gail Stygall (Eds.), *Discourse studies in composition* (pp. 19–42). Cresskill, NJ: Hampton Press.

Barton, Ellen, Halter, Ellen, McGee, Nancy, & McNeilley, Lisa. (1998). The awkward problem of awkward syntax. *Written Communication, 15,* 69–98.

Barton, Ellen, & Stygall, Gail. (Eds.). (2002). *Discourse studies in composition.* Cresskill, NJ: Hampton Press.

Baynham, Mike. (1993). Code switching and mode switching: Community interpreters and mediators of literacy. In Brian Street (Ed.), *Cross cultural approaches to literacy.* Cambridge, England: Cambridge University Press.

Bazerman, Charles. (1981). What written knowledge does: Three examples of academic discourse. *Philosophy of the Social Sciences, 11,* 361–388.

Bazerman, Charles. (1981, 1985, 1989, 1992, 1995). *The informed writer.* Boston: Houghton Mifflin.

Bazerman, Charles. (1988). *Shaping written knowledge: The genre and activity of the experimental article in science.* Madison: University of Wisconsin Press.

Bazerman, Charles. (1991). How natural philosophers can cooperate. In Charles Bazerman & James Paradis (Eds.), *Textual dynamics of the professions* (pp. 13–44). Madison: University of Wisconsin Press.

Bazerman, Charles. (1993). Intertextual self-fashioning: Gould and Lewontin's representations of the literature. In Jack Selzer (Ed.), *Understanding scientific prose* (pp. 20–41). Madison: University of Wisconsin Press.

Bazerman, Charles. (1994). Systems of genre and the enactment of social intentions. In Aviva Freedman & Peter Medway (Eds.), *Rethinking genre* (pp. 79–101). London: Taylor & Francis.

Bazerman, Charles. (1999). *Languages of Edison's light.* Cambridge MA: MIT Press.

Bazerman, Charles, & Paradis, James. (Eds.). (1991). *Textual dynamics of the professions.* Madison: University of Wisconsin Press.

Bazerman, Charles, & Russell, David. (2003). *Writing selves/writing society: Research from activity perspectives.* Fort Collins, CO: The WAC Clearinghouse and Mind, Culture, and Activity. Available at http://wac.colostate.edu/books/selves_society/

Beaufort, Anne. (1999). *Writing in the real world: Making the transition from school to work.* New York: Teachers College Press.

Beebee, Thomas. (1994). *The ideology of genre: A comparative study of generic instability.* University Park: Pennsylvania State University Press.

Belcher, Diane, & Braine, George. (Eds.). (1995). *Academic writing in a second language.* Norwood, NJ: Ablex.

Bennett, William. (1989, September 19). A response to Milton Friedman. *Wall Street Journal,* p. 15E.

Bennett, William. (1990, March). Should drugs be legalized? *Reader's Digest,* 42–44.

Benson, Thomas. (Ed.). (1993). *Landmark essays on rhetorical criticism*. Davis, CA: Hermagoras Press.

Berelson, Bernard. (1952). *Content analysis in communication research*. Chicago: University of Chicago.

Berger, John. (1972). *Ways of Seeing*. London: BBC-Penguin.

Berger, John, Blomberg, Sven, Fox, Chris, Dibb, Michael, & Hollis, Richard. (1991). *Ways of Seeing*. New York: Penguin.

Berger, Peter, & Luckmann, Thomas. (1966). *The social construction of reality: A treatise in the sociology of knowledge*. Garden City, NJ: Doubleday.

Berkenkotter, Carol, & Huckin, Thomas. (1995). *Genre knowledge in disciplinary communication: Cognition/culture/power*. Hillsdale, NJ: Lawrence Erlbaum Associates.

Berkenkotter, Carol, Huckin, Thomas, & Ackerman, John. (1991). Social context and socially constructed texts: The initiation of a graduate student into a writing research community. In Charles Bazerman & James Paradis (Eds.), *Textual dynamics of the professions* (pp. 191–215). Madison: University of Wisconsin Press.

Bernstein, Janice. (1998). Marked versus unmarked choices on the auto factory floor. In Carol Myers-Scotton (Ed.), *Codes and consequences: Choosing linguistic varieties* (pp. 178–191). Oxford, England: Oxford University Press.

Bhatia, Vijay. (1993). *Analysing genre: Language use in professional settings*. London: Longman.

Biber, Douglas. (1988). *Variation across speech and writing*. New York: Cambridge University Press.

Biber, Douglas. (1994). An analytic framework for register studies. In Douglas Biber & Edward Finnegan (Eds.), *Sociolinguistic perspectives on register* (pp. 31–56). New York: Oxford University Press.

Biber, Douglas, & Finegan, Edward. (Eds.). (1994). *Sociolinguistic perspectives on register*. New York: Oxford University Press.

Birdwhistle, Ray. (1970). *Kinesics and context: Essays on body motion communication*. Philadelphia: University of Pennsylvania Press.

Bissex, Glynda. (1980). *Gnys at wrk: A child learns to write and read*. Cambridge, MA: Harvard University Press.

Black, Edwin. (1978). *Rhetorical criticism: A study in method*. Madison: University of Wisconsin Press.

Black, Max. (1993). More about metaphor. In Andrew Ortony (Ed.), *Metaphor and thought* (2nd ed., pp. 19–41). Cambridge, MA: Cambridge University Press.

Blair, Carole, & Neil, Michel. (2000). Reproducing civil rights tactics: The rhetorical performances of the civil rights memorial. *Rhetoric Society Quarterly, 30*, 31–55.

Bogden, Robert, & Biklen, Sari. (1998). *Qualitative research for education: An introduction to theory and methods*. Boston: Allyn & Bacon.

Bolter, Jay. (1991). *Writing space: The computer, hypertext, and the history of writing*. Hillsdale, NJ: Lawrence Erlbaum Associates.

Bolter, Jay. (1998). Hypertext and the question of visual literacy. In David Reinking, Michael McKenna, Linda Labbo, & Ronald D. Kieffer (Eds.), *Handbook of literacy and technology: Transformations in a post-typographic world* (pp. 3–14). Mahwah, NJ: Lawrence Erlbaum Associates.

Bridwell-Bowles, Lillian, Johnson, Parker, & Brehe, Steven. (1987). Composing and computers: Case studies of experienced writers. In Ann Matsuhashi (Ed.), *Writing in real time: Modeling production processes* (pp. 81–107). Norwood, NJ: Ablex.

Britton, James, Burgess, Tony, Martin, Nancie, McLeod, Alex, & Rosen, Harold. (1975). *The development of writing abilities*, pp. 11–18. London: MacMillan Education, Ltd.

Brock, Bernard, Scott, Robert, & Chesebro, James. (1989). *Methods of rhetorical criticism* (3rd ed.). Detroit: Wayne State University Press.

Bruner, Jerome. (1986). *Actual minds, possible worlds*. Cambridge, MA: Harvard University Press.

Bryant, Donald. (1973). *Rhetorical dimensions in criticism*. Baton Rouge: LSU Press.

Burke, Kenneth. (1954). *Permanence and change* (3rd ed.). Berkeley: University of California Press.

Burke, Kenneth. (1969). *A grammar of motives*. Berkeley: University of California Press. (Original published in 1945)

Burke, Kenneth. (1973). *The philosophy of literary form*. Berkeley: University of California Press. (Original published in 1941)

Calkins, Lucy. (1983). *Lessons from a child: On the teaching and learning of writing*. Portsmouth, NH: Heinemann.

Cameron, Deborah. (2001). *Working with spoken discourse*. Thousand Oaks, CA: Sage.

Carley, Kathleen, & Palmquist, Michael. (1992). Extracting, representing, and analyzing mental models. *Social Forces, 70*, 601–636.

Carruthers, Mary. (1990). *The book of memory: A study of memory in medieval culture*. Cambridge, England: Cambridge University Press.

Carruthers, Mary. (1998). *The craft of thought: Meditation, rhetoric, and the making of images, 400–1200*. Cambridge, England: Cambridge University Press.

Carter, David, & Maligian-Odle, Stanley. (Producers). (1994). *Ecology and the barn owl: A journey of discovery* [Videotape]. Mt. Vernon, Washington: Genesis.

Casanave, Christine Pearson. (1995). Local interactions: Constructing contexts for composing in a graduate sociology program. In Diane Belcher & George Braine (Eds.), *Academic writing in a second language* (pp. 83–110). Norwood, NJ: Ablex.

Casanave, Christine. (2002). *Writing games: Multicultural case studies of academic literacy practices in higher education*. Mahwah, NJ: Lawrence Erlbaum Associates.

Chafe, Wallace. (1982). Integration and involvement in speaking, writing, and oral literature. In Deborah Tannen (Ed.), *Spoken and written language: Exploring orality and literacy* (pp. 35–53). Norwood, NJ: Ablex.

Chafe, Wallace. (1986). Evidentiality in English conversation and academic writing. In Wallace Chafe & Johanna Nichols (Eds.), *Evidentiality: The linguistic coding of epistemology* (pp. 261–272). Norwood, NJ: Ablex.

Chafe, Wallace. (1994). *Discourse, consciousness, and time: The flow and displacement of conscious experience in speaking and writing*. Chicago: University of Chicago Press.

Chafe, Wallace, & Danielewicz, Jane. (1987). Properties of spoken and written language. In Rosalind Horowitz & S. Jay Samuels (Eds.), *Comprehending oral and written language* (pp. 83–113). New York: Academic Press.

Chapman, Marilyn. (1994). The emergence of genres: Some findings from an examination of first-grade writing. *Written Communication, 11*, 348–380.

Chapman, Marilyn. (1995). The sociocognitive construction of written genres in first grade. *Research in the Teaching of English, 29*, 164–192.

Clark, Romy, & Ivanic, Roz. (1997). *The politics of writing*. New York: Routledge.

Clay, Marie. (1975). *What did I write? Beginning writing behaviour*. Portsmouth, NH: Heinemann.

Cohen, Adam. (1998, November 2). Demonizing Gates. *Time*, pp. 58–66.

Cohen, Ralph. (1986). History and genre. *New Literary History, 17*, 203–218.

Cole, Michael. (1992). Context, modularity, and the cultural constitution of development. In Lucient Winegar & Jaan Valsiner (Eds.), *Children's development within social contexts: Vol. 2. Research and methodology* (pp. 5–32). Hillsdale, NJ: Lawrence Erlbaum Associates.

Connor, Ulla. (1996). *Contrastive rhetoric: Cross-cultural aspects of second-language writing*. New York: Cambridge University Press.

Cooper, Marilyn. (1989). Why are we talking about discourse communities? Or foundationalism rears its ugly head once more. In Marilyn Cooper & Michael Holzman (Eds.), *Writing as a social practice* (pp. 202–220). Portsmouth, NH: Boynton/Cook.

Cope, Bill, & Kalantzis, Mary. (1993). *The powers of literacy: A genre approach to teaching writing*. Pittsburgh: University of Pittsburgh Press.

Corbett, Edward. (1969). *Rhetorical analyses of literary works*. New York: Oxford University Press.

Cortazzi, Martin. (1993). *Narrative analysis*. London: Falmer.

Crammond, Joanna. (1998). The uses and complexity of argument structures in expert and student persuasive writing. *Written Communication, 15*, 230–268.

Cross, Geoffrey. (1994). *Collaboration and conflict: A contextual exploration of group writing and positive emphasis*. Cresskill, NJ: Hampton Press.

Damon, William. (1990, April 25). Colleges must help foster a spirit of inquiry in the nation's schools. *Chronicle of Higher Education*, p. A48.

Dautermann, Jennie. (1997). *Writing at Good Hope: A study of negotiated composition in a community of nurses*. Greenwich, CT: Ablex.

Derrida, Jacques. (1974). *Of grammatology* (Gayatri Spivak, Trans.). Baltimore, MD: The Johns Hopkins University Press.

Devitt, Amy. (1991). Intertextuality in tax accounting: Generic, referential, and functional. In Charles Bazerman & James Paradis (Eds.), *Textual dynamics of the professions* (pp. 336–380). Madison: University of Wisconsin Press.

DiPardo, Anne. (1994). Stimulated recall in research on writing: An antidote to "I don't know, it was fine." In Peter Smagorinsky (Ed.), *Speaking about writing: Reflections on research methodology* (pp. 163–184). Thousand Oaks, CA: Sage.

Donovan, Carol. (2001). Children's development and control of written story and information genres: Insights from one elementary school. *Research in the Teaching of English, 35*, 394–447.

Dressler, Richard, & Kruez, Roger. (2000). Transcribing oral discourse: A survey and a model system. *Discourse Processes, 29*, 25–36.

Duranti, Alessandro. (1997). *Linguistic anthropology*. New York: Cambridge University Press.

Duranti, Alessandro, & Goodwin, Charles. (Eds.). (1992). *Rethinking context: Language as an interactive phenomenon*. Cambridge, England: Cambridge University Press.

Durkheim, Emile. (1982). *The rules of sociological method*. New York: Free Press.

Dyson, Anne. (1986). Transitions and tensions: Interrelationships between the drawing, talking and dictating of young children. *Research in the Teaching of English, 20*, 379–409.

Dyson, Anne. (1989). *Multiple worlds of child writers: Friends learning to write*. New York: Teachers College Press.

Dyson, Anne. (1993). *Social worlds of children learning to write in an urban primary school*. New York: Teachers College Press.

Dyson, Anne. (1997). *Writing superheroes: Contemporary childhood, popular culture, and classroom literacy*. New York: Teachers College Press.

Eckert, Penelope. (2001). *Linguistic variation as social practice*. Oxford, England: Blackwell.

Eggins, Suzanne. (1994). *An introduction to systemic functional linguistics*. New York: Pinter.

Ellis, Rod. (1986). *Understanding second language acquisition*. Oxford, England: Oxford University Press.

Emig, Janet. (1971). *The composing processes of twelfth graders*. Urbana, IL: The National Council of Teachers of English.

Engeström, Yrjo, & Middleton, David. (Eds.). (1996). *Cognition and communication at work*. New York: Cambridge University Press.

Erdman, Terry. (1998). *Star Trek action*. New York: Pocket Books.

Erickson, Joan. (1981). Communication assessment of the bilingual bicultural child. In Joan Erickson & Donald Omark (Eds.), *Communication assessment of the bilingual and bicultural child: Issues and guidelines* (pp. 1–24). Baltimore: University Park Press.

Eubanks, Philip. (1999). Conceptual metaphor as rhetorical response: A reconsideration of metaphor. *Written Communication, 16*, 171–199.

Eubanks, Philip. (2000). *A war of words in the discourse of trade: The rhetorical constitution of metaphor*. Carbondale: Southern Illinois University Press.

Exclusive interview with Bill Gates. (1998, May 25). *Time*, pp. 58–59.

Faber, Brenton. (1996). Rhetoric in competition. *Written Communication, 13*, 255–284.

Fahnestock, Jeanne. (1999). *Rhetorical figures in science*. New York: Oxford University Press.

Fairclough, Norman. (1989). *Language and power*. London: Longman.

Fairclough, Norman. (1992). *Discourse and social change*. Cambridge, England: Polity Press.

Fairclough, Norman. (1995). *Critical discourse analysis: The critical study of language*. London: Longman.

Ferreiro, Emilia, & Teberosky, Ana. (1982). *Literacy before schooling* (Karen Castro, Trans.). Exeter, NH: Heinemann.

Finders, Margaret. (1997). *Just girls: Hidden literacies and life in junior high*. Urbana, IL & New York: National Council of Teachers of English & Teachers College Press.

Floriani, Ana. (1993). Negotiating what counts: Roles and relationships, texts and contexts, content and meaning. *Linguistics & Education, 5*, 241–274.

Flower, Linda, & Hayes, John. (1981). Plans that guide the composing process. In Carl Frederiksen & Joseph Dominic (Eds.), *Writing: The nature, development, and teaching of written communication* (pp. 39–58). Hillsdale, NJ: Lawrence Erlbaum Associates.

Flower, Linda, & Hayes, John. (1984). Images, plans, and prose: The representation of meaning in writing. *Written Communication, 1*, 120–160.

Flower, Linda, Stein, Victoria, Ackerman, John, Kantz, Margaret, McCormick, Kathleen, & Peck, Wayne. (1990). *Reading-to-write: Exploring a cognitive and social process*. New York: Oxford University Press.

Foucault, Michel. (1977). *Discipline and punish: The birth of the prison* (Alan Sheridan, Trans.). Harmondsworth, England: Penguin.

Foucault, Michel. (1984). *The Foucault reader* (Paul Rabinow, Ed.). New York: Pantheon.

Foss, Sonja. (Ed.). (1989). *Rhetorical criticism*. Prospect Heights, IL: Waveland.

Foss, Sonja. (1993). The construction of appeal in visual images: A hypothesis. In David Zarefsky (Ed.), *Rhetorical movement* (pp. 210–224). Evanston, IL: Northwestern University Press.

Freedman, Aviva, & Medway, Peter. (Eds.). (1994). *Genre in the new rhetoric*. London: Taylor & Francis.

Friedman, Milton. (1972). Prohibition and drugs. *Newsweek*, p. 87.

Friedman, Milton. (1989, September 7). Open letter to Bill Bennett. *Wall Street Journal*, p. 1E.

Friedman, Milton. (1989, September 29). Bennett fears 'public policy disaster'—It's already here. *Wall Street Journal*, p. 14E.

Fromkin, Victoria. (Ed.). (2000). *Linguistics: An introduction to linguistic theory*. Oxford: Blackwell.

Gallas, Karen. (1994). *The languages of learning: How children talk, write, dance, draw, and sing their understanding of the world*. New York: Teachers College Press.

Garfinkel, Harold. (1967). *Studies in ethnomethodology*. Englewood Cliffs, NJ: Prentice-Hall.

Gates, Bill, Myhrvold, Nathan, & Rinearson, Peter. (1995). *The road ahead*. New York: Viking.

Gee, James. (1996). *Social linguistics and literacies: Ideology in discourse*. London: Falmer.

Gee, James (1999). *An introduction to discourse analysis: Theory and method*. London: Routledge.

Geisler, Cheryl. (1994). *Academic literacy and the nature of expertise: Reading, writing, and knowing in academic philosophy*. Hillsdale, NJ: Lawrence Erlbaum Associates.

Geisler, Cheryl. (2001). Textual objects: Accounting for the role of texts in the everyday life of complex organizations. *Written Communication, 18*, 296–325.

Geisler, Cheryl. (2003). When management becomes personal: An activity-theoretic analysis of Palm technologies. In Charles Bazerman & David Russell (Eds.), *Writing selves/writing societies: Research from activity perspectives* (pp. 125–158). Fort Collins, CO: The WAC Clearinghouse and Mind, Culture and Activity. (Available at http://wac.colostate.edu/books/selves_society/)

Genette, Gerard. (1992). *The architext* (Jane Lewin, Trans.). Berkeley: University of California Press.

Genette, Gerard. (1997a). *Palimpsests* (Channa Newman & Claude Doubinsky, Trans.). Lincoln: University of Nebraska Press.

Genette, Gerard. (1997b). *Paratexts* (Jane Lewin, Trans.). Cambridge, England: Cambridge University Press.

Gere, Anne. (1981). A cultural perspective on talking and writing. In Barry Kroll & Roberta Vann (Eds.), *Exploring speaking-writing relationships: Connections and contrasts* (pp. 111–123). Urbana, IL: National Council of Teachers of English.

Glaser, Barney, & Strauss, Anselm. (1967). *The discovery of grounded theory: Strategies for qualitative research.* Chicago: Aldine.

Golomb, Claire. (1974). *Young children's sculpture and drawing.* Cambridge, MA: Harvard University Press.

Goffman, Erving. (1974). *Frame analysis: An essay on the organization of experience.* Cambridge, MA: Harvard University Press.

Goffman, Erving. (1981). *Forms of talk.* Philadelphia: University of Pennsylvania Press.

Gooding, David. (1990). *Experiment and the making of meaning.* Boston: Kluwer.

Goodwin, Charles. (1994). Recording interaction in natural settings. *Pragmatics, 3,* 181–209.

Goodwin Charles, & Duranti, Alessandro. (1992). Rethinking context: An introduction. In Duranti Alessandro & Goodwin Charles (Eds.), *Rethinking context: Language as an interactive phenomenon* (pp. 1–42). Cambridge: Cambridge University Press.

Goodwin, Charles, & Goodwin, Marjorie. (1996). Seeing as situated activity: Formulating planes. In Yrjo Engstrom & David Middleton (Eds.), *Cognition and communication at work* (pp. 61–95). Cambridge, England: Cambridge University Press.

Grant-Davie, Keith. (1992). Coding data: Issues of validity, reliability, and interpretation. In Gesa Kirsch & Patricia Sullivan (Eds.), *Methods and methodology in composition research* (pp. 270–286). Carbondale: Southern Illinois University Press.

Graves, Donald. (1983). *Writing: Teachers and children at work.* Exeter, NH: Heinemann.

Gray, Paul. (1990, May 9). Society benefits when academics serve on corporate boards. *Chronicle of Higher Education,* p. A48.

Gumperz, John. (1982a). *Discourse strategies.* Cambridge, England. Cambridge University Press.

Gumperz, John. (Ed.), (1982b). *Language and social identity.* Cambridge, England: Cambridge University Press.

Gumperz, John, Aulakh, Gurinder, & Kaltman, Hannah. (1982). Thematic structure and progression in discourse. In John Gumperz (Ed.), *Language and social identity* (pp. 22–56). Cambridge, England: Cambridge University Press.

Gumperz, John, & Gumperz, Jenny-Cook. (1982). Introduction: Language and communication of social identity. In John J. Gumperz (Ed.), *Language and social identity* (pp. 3–21). Cambridge, England: Cambridge University Press.

Gutierrez, Kris, Rymes, Betsy, & Larson, Joanne. (1995). Script, counterscript, and underlife in the classroom: James Brown vs *Brown v. Board of Education. Harvard Educational Review, 65,* 445–471.

Hall, Edward T. (1959). *The silent language.* Garden City, NY: Doubleday.

Halliday, Michael. (1978). *Language as social semiotic.* London: Edward Arnold.

Halliday, Michael. (1998). *An introduction to functional grammar.* London: Edward Arnold.

Halliday, Michael, & Martin, James. (1993). *Writing science: Literacy and discursive power.* Pittsburgh: University of Pittsburgh Press.

Hancock, Mark. (1997). Behind classroom code switching: Layering and language choice in L2 learner interaction. *TESOL Quarterly, 31,* 217–235.

Hanks, William. (1996a). Exorcism and the description of participant roles. In Michael Silverstein & Greg Urban (Eds.), *Natural histories of discourse* (pp. 160–200). Chicago: University of Chicago Press.

Hanks, William. (1996b). *Language and communicative practice.* Boulder, CO: Westview Press.

Harris, Joseph. (1989). The idea of community in the study of writing. *College Composition and Communication, 40,* 11–22.

Harste, Jerome, Woodward, Virginia, & Burke, Carolyn. (1984). *Language stories and literacy lessons.* Portsmouth, NH: Heinemann.

Hart, Roderick. (1990). *Modern rhetorical criticism.* Glenview, IL: Scott Foresman.

Hayes, John, & Hatch, Jill. (1999). Issues in measuring reliability: Correlation versus percentage of agreement. *Written Communication, 16,* 354–367.

Haynes, Cynthia, & Holmevik, Jan Rune. (Eds.). (1998). *High wired: On the design, use, and theory of educational MOOs.* Ann Arbor: University of Michigan Press.

Heath, Christian. (1997). The analysis of activities in face to face interaction using video. In D. Silverman (Ed.), *Qualitative research: Theory, method, and practice* (pp. 183–200). Thousand Oaks, CA: Sage.

Heath, Christian, & Luff, Paul. (2000). *Technology in action.* Cambridge, England: Cambridge University Press.

Heath, Shirley Brice. (1983). *Ways with words: Language, life, and work in communities and classrooms.* Cambridge, England: Cambridge University Pres.

Heller, Monica. (1982). Negotiations of language choice in Montreal. In John J. Gumperz (Ed.), *Language and social identity* (pp. 108–118). Cambridge, England: Cambridge University Press.

Hendrickson, Althea. (1989). How to appear reliable without being liable: C.P.A. writing in its rhetorical context. In Carolyn Matalene (Ed.), *Worlds of writing: Teaching and learning in discourse communities of work* (pp. 302–331). New York: Random House.

Hengst, Julie. (1998). *Big shirts and invisible cheetahs: Tracing alignments in everyday family activities.* Unpublished manuscript. University of Illinois at Urbana.

Hengst, Julie. (2001). *Collaborating on reference: A study of discourse and aphasia.* (Doctoral Dissertation, University of Illinois, 2001*). Dissertation Abstracts International, 62,* 2684.

Hengst, Julie, & Miller, Peggy. (1999). The heterogeneity of discourse genres: Implications for development. *World Englishes, 18,* 325–341.

Hengst, Julie, & Prior, Paul. (1998, December). *Playing with voices: Heterogeneous socialization into language in the wild.* A paper presented at the Modern Language Association Convention, San Francisco, California.

Hernadi, Paul (1972). *Beyond genre.* Ithaca, NY: Cornell University Press.

Hicks, Deborah. (1990). Narrative skills and genre knowledge: Ways of telling in the primary school grades. *Applied Psycholinguistics, 11*(1), 83–104.

Hodge, Robert, & Kress, Gunther. (1988). *Social semiotics.* Ithaca, NY: Cornell University Press.

Hodge, Robert, & Kress, Gunther. (1993). *Language as ideology* (2nd ed.). New York: Routledge.

Hoey, Michael. (2001). *Textual interaction: An introduction to written discourse.* London: Routledge.

Huckin, Thomas. (1992). Context-sensitive text analysis. In Gesa Kirsch & Patricia Sullivan (Eds.), *Methods and methodology in composition research* (pp. 84–104). Carbondale: Southern Illinois University Press.

Huckin, Thomas. (2002). Textual silences and the discourse of homelessness. *Discourse & Society, 13,* 347–372.

Hymes, Dell. (1972). Models of the interaction of language and social life. In John Gumperz & D. Hymes (Eds.), *Directions in sociolinguistics: The ethnography of communication* (pp. 35–71). New York: Holt, Rinehart and Winston.

Hymes, Dell. (1974). *Foundations of sociolinguistics: An ethnographic approach.* Philadelphia: University of Pennsylvania Press.

Irvine, Judith. (1996). Shadow conversations: The indeterminacy of participant roles. In Michael Silverstein & Greg Urban (Eds.), *Natural history of discourse* (pp. 160–202). Cambridge, England: Cambridge University Press.

Jaworski, Adam, & Coupland, Nikolas. (Eds.). (1999). *The discourse reader.* New York: Routledge.

Jefferson, Gail. (1989). Preliminary notes on a possible metric which provides for a "standard maxium" silence of approximately one second in conversation. In D. Roger & P. Bull (Eds.), *Conversation: An interdisciplinary perspective* (pp. 166–196). Clevedon, UK: Multilingual Matters.

Johns, Ann. (1997). *Text, role, and context: Developing academic literacies.* New York: Cambridge University Press.

Johnstone, Barbara. (2002). *Discourse analysis: An introduction.* Oxford: Blackwell.

Kalman, Judy. (1999). *Writing on the plaza: Mediated literacy practices among scribes and clients in Mexico City*. Cresskill, NJ: Hampton Press.

Kamberelis, George. (1993). Tropes are for kids: Young children's developing understanding of narrative, poetic, and expository written discourse genres (Doctoral dissertation, University of Michigan, 1993). *Dissertation Abstracts International, 54*, 4379A.

Kamberelis, George. (1995). Genre as institutionally informed social practice. *Journal of Contemporary Legal Issues, 6*, 115–171.

Kamberelis, George. (1999). Genre development: Children writing stories, science reports and poems. *Research in the Teaching of English, 33*, 403–460.

Kamberelis, George. (2001). Producing heteroglossic classroom (micro)cultures through hybrid discourse practice. *Linguistics and Education, 12*, 85–125.

Kamberelis, George, & Scott, Karla. (1992). Other people's voices: The coarticulation of texts and subjectivities. *Linguistics and Education, 4*, 359–403.

Kaplan, Robert B. (1966). Cultural thought patterns in intercultural education. *Language Learning, 16*, 1–20.

Kaye, Harvey. (1991, June 12). Colleges must prepare the next generation of public intellectuals. *Chronicle of Higher Education*, p. A40.

Kendon, Adam. (1990). *Conducting interaction: Patterns of behavior in focused encounters*. Cambridge, England: Cambridge University Press.

Kepplinger, Hans. (1989). Content analysis and reception analysis. *American Behavioral Scientist, 33*, 175–182.

Kirsch, Gesa, & Sullivan, Patricia. (Eds.). (1992). *Methods and methodology in composition research*. Carbondale: Southern Illinois University Press.

Kostelnick, Charles, & Roberts, David. (1998). *Designing visual language: Strategies for professional communicators*. Boston: Allyn & Bacon.

Krantz, Michael. (1998, June 1). The main event. *Time*, pp. 32–37.

Kreml, Nancy. (1998). Implicatures of styleswitching in the narrative voice of Cormac McCarthy's *All the Pretty Horses*. In Carol Myers-Scotton (Ed.), *Codes and consequences: Choosing linguistic varieties* (pp. 41–61). Oxford, England: Oxford University Press.

Kress, Gunther. (1993). *Learning to write*. London: Routledge.

Kress, Gunther. (1997). *Before writing: Rethinking the paths to literacy*. London: Routledge.

Kress, Gunther. (2000). *Early spelling: Between convention and creativity*. London: Routledge.

Kress, Gunther, & van Leeuwen, Theo. (1996). *Reading images: The grammar of visual design*. New York: Routledge.

Kristeva, Julia. (1980). *Desire in language: A semiotic approach to literature and art* (Leon Roudiez, Ed.; Thomas Gora, Alice Jardine, & Leon Roudiez, Trans.). New York: Columbia University Press.

Kroll, Barry, & Vann, Roberta. (Eds.). (1981). *Exploring speaking-writing relationships: Connections and contrasts*. Urbana, IL: NCTE.

Labov, William. (1972a). *Language in the inner city*. Philadelphia, PA: University of Pennsylvania Press.

Labov, William. (1972b). The social stratification of (r) in New York City department stores. *Sociolinguistic Patterns*. Philadelphia: University of Pennsylvania Press.

Lakoff, George, & Johnson, Mark. (1980). *Metaphors we live by*. Chicago: University of Chicago Press.

Lakoff, George, & Johnson, Mark. (1999). *Philosophy in the flesh*. New York: Basic Books.

Langer, Judith. (1986). *Children reading and writing: Structures and strategies*. Norwood, NJ: Ablex.

Lanham, Richard. (1993). *The electronic word: Democracy, technology, and the arts*. Chicago: University of Chicago Press.

Latour, Bruno, & Woolgar, Steve. (1986). *Laboratory life: The social construction of scientific facts*. Princeton, NJ: Princeton University Press.

Leander, Kevin. (2000). Silencing in classroom interaction: Producing and relating social spaces. *Discourse Processes, 34*(2), 193–235.

Leander, Kevin. (2002). Polycontextual construction zones: Mapping the expansion of schooled space and identity. *Mind, Culture, and Activity, 9*(3), 211–237.

Lee, S. Jean, & Hoon, Tan. (1993). Rhetorical vision of men and women managers in Singapore. *Human Relations, 46*(4), 527–542.

Lensmire, Timothy. (1994). *When children write: Critical re-visions of the writing workshop.* New York: Teachers College Press.

Linell, Per. (1998). Discourse across boundaries: On recontextualization and the blending of voices in professional discourse. *Text, 18*, 143–157.

Lofty, John. (1992). *Time to write: The influence of time and culture on learning to write.* Albany, NY: State University of New York Press.

Luff, Paul, Hindmarsh, Jon, & Heath, Christian. (2000). *Workplace studies: Recovering work practice and informing system design.* Cambridge, England: Cambridge University Press.

Luria, Alexander. (1983). The development of writing in the child. In Margaret Martlew (Ed.), *The psychology of written language: Developmental and educational perspectives* (pp. 237–278). New York: Wiley.

Lyotard, Jean-Francois. (1979). *The postmodern condition: A report on knowledge.* Minneapolis: University of Minnesota Press.

MacDonald, Susan Peck. (1994). *Professional academic writing in the humanities and social sciences.* Carbondale: Southern Illinois University Press.

MacGillivray, Laurie. (1994). Tacit shared understandings of a first-grade writing community. *Journal of Reading Behavior, 26*(3), 245–66.

MacNealy, Mary. (1999). *Strategies for empirical research in writing.* Boston: Allyn & Bacon.

Mailloux, Steven. (1998). *Reception histories: Rhetoric, pragmatism, and American cultural thought.* Ithaca, NY. Cornell University Press.

Martin, James. (1984). Types of writing in infants in primary school. In Len Unsworth (Ed.), *Reading, writing, spelling: Proceedings of the fifth Macarthur reading/language symposium* (pp. 34–55). Sydney, Australia: Macarthur Institute of Higher Education.

Martin, James. (1989). *Factual writing: Exploring and challenging social reality.* Oxford, England: Oxford University Press.

Martin, James, & Rothery, Joan. (1980). *Writing project report 1980* (Working Papers in Linguistics No. 1). Sidney: University of Sidney, Department of Linguistics.

Martin, James, & Rothery, Joan. (1981). *Writing Project Report.* (Working Papers in Linguistics No. 2). Sydney: University of Sydney, Department of Linguistics.

Mathison, Maureen. (1996). Writing the critique, a text about a text. *Written Communication, 13*, 314–354.

Matsuhashi, Ann. (1987a). Revising the plan and altering the text. In Ann Matsuhashi (Ed.), *Writing in real time: Modeling production processes* (pp. 197–223). Norwood, NJ: Ablex.

Matsuhashi, Ann. (Ed.). (1987b). *Writing in real time: Modeling production processes.* Norwood, NJ: Ablex.

Maxwell, Joseph. (1996). *Qualitative research design: An interactive approach.* Thousand Oaks, CA: Sage.

McCarthey, Sarah. (1994). Authors, text, and talk: The internalization of dialogue from social interaction during writing. *Reading Research Quarterly, 29*, 200–231.

McGinley, William, & Kamberelis, George. (1996). *Maniac Magee* and *Ragtime Tumpie*: Children negotiating self and world through reading and writing. *Research in the Teaching of English, 30*, 75–113.

McIntyre, Alasdair. (1981). *After virtue: A study in moral theory.* Notre Dame, IN: University of Notre Dame Press.

Merriam, Sharan. (2001). *Qualitative research and case study applications in education.* San Francisco, CA: Jossey-Bass.

Merton, Robert King. (1968). *Social theory and social structure* (Rev. ed.). New York: Free Press.

Miller, Carolyn. (1984). Genre as social action. *Quarterly Journal of Speech, 70*, 151–167.

Miller, Susan. (1992). Writing theory : : Theory writing. In Gesa Kirsch & Patricia Sullivan (Eds.), *Methods and methodology in composition research* (pp. 62–83). Carbondale: Southern Illinois University Press.

Mishoe, Margaret. (1998). Styleswitching in Southern English. In Carol Myers-Scotton (Ed.), *Codes and consequences: Choosing linguistic varieties* (pp. 162–177). Oxford, England: Oxford University Press.

Mitchell, William. (1986). *Iconology: Images, texts, ideology.* Chicago: University of Chicago Press.

Mitchell, William. (1994). *Picture theory.* Chicago: University of Chicago Press.

Mithun, Marianne. (2001). Who shapes the record: The speaker and the linguist. In Paul Newman & Martha Ratliff (Eds.), *Linguistic fieldwork* (pp. 34–54). New York: Cambridge University Press.

Mulhern, Margaret. (forthcoming). *The literate lives of three Mexican American kindergartners.* Albany, NY: State University of New York Press.

Mullet, Kevin, & Sano, Darrell. (1995). *Designing visual interfaces: Communication-oriented techniques.* Mountain View, CA: Sun Microsystems.

Myers, Greg. (1990). *Writing biology: Texts in the social construction of scientific knowledge.* Madison: University of Wisconsin Press.

Myers-Scotton, Carol. (Ed.). (1998). *Codes and consequences: Choosing linguistic varieties* (pp. 18–38). Oxford, England: Oxford University Press.

Nelson, Jennie. (1993). The library revisited: Exploring students research processes. In Ann Penrose & Barbara Sitko (Eds.), *Hearing ourselves think: Cognitive research in the college writing classroom* (pp. 102–122). New York: Oxford University Press

Nerlich, Birgitte, Clarke, David, & Dingwall, Robert. Clones and crops: The use of stock characters and word play in two debates about bioengineering. *Metaphor and Symbol, 15*, 223–239.

Newkirk, Thomas. (1989). *More than stories. The range of children's writing.* Portsmouth, NH: Heinemann.

Newmeyer, Frederick. (1986a). *Linguistic theory in America* (2nd ed.). New York: Academic Press.

Newmeyer, Frederick. (1986b). *The politics of linguistics.* Chicago: University of Chicago Press.

Newmeyer, Frederick. (1998). *Language form and language function.* Cambridge, MA: MIT Press.

Novak, Viveca. (1999, November 22). The company courts the A.G.s. *Time,* p. 66.

Nunberg, Geoffrey. (Ed.). (1996). *The future of the book.* Berkeley: University of California Press.

Ochs, Elinor. (1979). Transcription as theory. In Elinor Ochs & Bambi Schiefflin (Eds.), *Developmental pragmatics* (pp. 43–72). New York: Academic Press.

Ochs, Elinor, Jacoby, Sally, & Gonzales, Patrick. (1994). Interpretive journeys: How scientists talk and travel through graphic space. *Configurations, 2,* 151–171.

Ochs, Elinor, Schegloff, Emanual, & Thompson, Sandra. (Eds.). (1996). *Interaction and grammar.* Cambridge, England: Cambridge University Press.

Odell, Lee, Goswami, Dixie, & Herrington, Anne. (1983). The discourse-based interview: A procedure for exploring the tacit knowledge of writers in non-academic settings. In Peter Mosenthal, Lynne Tamor, & Sean Walmsley (Eds.), *Research on writing* (pp. 221–236). New York: Longman.

Ong, Walter. (1982). *Orality and literacy: The technologizing of the word.* London: Methuen.

Ortony, Andrew. (Ed.). (1993). *Metaphor and thought* (2nd ed.). Cambridge, England: Cambridge University Press.

Palmquist, Michael, Carley, Kathleen, & Dale, Thomas. (1997). Two applications of automated text analysis: Analyzing literary and nonliterary texts. In Carl Roberts (Ed.), *Text analysis for the social sciences: Methods for drawing statistical inferences from texts and transcripts* (pp. 171–189). Hillsdale, NJ: Lawrence Erlbaum Associates.

Patton, Michael Quinn. (1990). *Qualitative evaluation and research methods* (2nd ed.). London: Sage.

Paul, Danette. (2000). In citing chaos: A study of the rhetorical use of citations. *Journal of Business and Technical Communication, 14,* 185–222.

Penrose, Ann, & Sitko, Barbara. (Eds.). (1993). *Hearing ourselves think: Cognitive research in the college writing classroom.* New York: Oxford University Press.

Perkins, Jane, & Blyler, Nancy. (1999). Introduction. In Jane Perkins & Nancy Blyler (Eds.), *Narrative and professional communication* (pp. 1–34). Stamford, CT: Ablex.

Phelps, Louise. (1990). Audience and authorship: The disappearing boundary. In Gesa Kirsch & Duane Roen (Eds.), *A sense of audience in written communication* (pp. 153–174). Newbury Park, CA: Sage.

Pickering, Andrew. (1995). *The mangle of practice: Time, agency, and science.* Chicago: University of Chicago Press.

Pinker, Stephen. (1994). *The language instinct: How the mind creates language.* New York: William Morrow.

Playboy interview: Bill Gates. (1994, July). *Playboy,* pp. 55–68, 153–154.

Plimpton, George. (Ed.). (1963). *Writers at work: The Paris Review interviews.* (Second Series). New York: The Viking Press.

Porter, James (1986). Intertextuality and the discourse community. *Rhetoric Review, 5,* 34–47.

Pratt, Charlotte, & Pratt, Cornelius. (1995). Comparative content analysis of food and nutrition advertisements in *Ebony, Essence,* and *Ladies' Home Journal. Journal of Nutrition Education, 27,* 11–18.

Prince, Gerald. (1987). *A dictionary of narratology.* Lincoln: University of Nebraska Press.

Prior, Paul. (1994). Response, revision, disciplinarity: A microhistory of a dissertation prospectus in sociology. *Written Communication, 11,* 483–533.

Prior, Paul. (1998). *Writing/disciplinarity: A sociohistoric account of literate activity in the academy.* Mahwah, NJ: Lawrence Erlbaum Associates.

Prior, Paul, Hawisher, Gail, Gruber, Sibylle, & MacLaughlin, Nicole. (1997). Research and WAC evaluation: An in-progress reflection. In Kathleen Blake Yancey & Brian Huot (Eds.), *WAC and program assessment: Diverse methods of evaluating writing across the curriculum programs* (pp. 185–216). Norwood, NJ: Ablex.

Prior, Paul, & Shipka, Jody. (2003). Chronotopic lamination: Tracing the contours of literate activity. In Charles Bazerman & David Russell (Eds.), *Writing selves/writing societies: Research from activity perspectives* (pp. 180–238). Fort Collins, CO: The WAC Clearinghouse and Mind, Culture and Activity. (Available at http://wac.colostate.edu/books/selves_society/)

Propp, Vladimir. (1968). *Morphology of the folktale* (2nd ed.; Laurence Scott, Trans.). Austin: University of Texas Press.

Quirk, Randolph, Greenbaum, Sidney, Leech, Geoffrey, & Svartvik, Jan. (1985). *A comprehensive grammar of the English language.* London: Longman.

Ramo, Joshua. (1996, September 16). Winner take all. *Time,* pp. 58–64.

Riffe, Daniel, Lacy, Stephen, & Fico, Frederick. (1998). *Analyzing media messages: Using quantitative content analysis in research.* Mahwah, NJ: Lawrence Erlbaum Associates.

Roberts, Carl. (1989). Other than counting words: A linguistic approach to content analysis. *Social Forces, 68,* 147–177.

Roberts, Carl. (Ed.). (1997). *Text analysis for the social sciences: Methods for drawing statistical inferences from texts and transcripts.* Mahwah, NJ: Lawrence Erlbaum Associates.

Rorty, Richard. (1979). *Philosophy and the mirror of nature.* New Jersey: Princeton University Press.

Rose, Mike. (1984). *Writer's block: The cognitive dimension.* Carbondale, IL: Southern Illinois University Press.

Rowe, Deborah. (1994). *Preschoolers as authors: Literacy learning in the social world of the classroom.* Creskill, NJ: Hampton Press.

Russell, David. (1997a). Rethinking genre in school and society: An activity theory analysis. *Written Communication, 14,* 504–554.

Russell, David. (1997b). Writing and genre in higher education and workplaces. *Mind, Culture and Activity, 4*, 224–237.

Russell, David, & Bazerman, Charles. (1997). *The activity of writing: The writing of activity.* Special issue of *Mind, Culture and Activity, 4*(4).

Rymer, Jone. (1989). Scientific composing processes: How eminent scientists write journal articles. In David Jolliffe (Ed.), *Advances in writing research volume 2: Writing in academic disciplines* (pp. 211–250). Norwood, NJ: Ablex.

Sacks, Harvey, Schegloff, Emanuel, & Jefferson, Gail. (1974). A simplest systematics for the organization of turn taking for conversation. *Language, 50*, 696–735.

Sandig, Barbara. (1986). *Stylistik der deutschen Sprache* [ ]. Berlin, New York: de Gruyter.

Saville-Troike, Muriel. (2003). *Ethnography of communication: An introduction* (3rd ed.). New York: Blackwell.

Sawkins, Margaret W. (1971). *The oral responses of selected fifth grade children to questions concerning their written expression.* Unpublished doctoral dissertation, State University of New York, Buffalo.

Schaafsma, David. (1994). *Eating on the street: Teaching literacy in a multicultural society.* Pittsburgh: University of Pittsburgh Press.

Schank, Roger, & Abelson, Robert. (1995). Knowledge and memory: The real story. In Robert Wyer, Jr. (Ed.), *Advances in Social Cognition* (Vol. 8, pp. 1–86). Hillsdale, NJ: Lawrence Erlbaum Associates.

Schecter, Sandra, & Bayley, Robert. (1997). Language socialization practices and cultural identity: Case studies of Mexican-descent families in California and Texas. *TESOL Quarterly, 31*, 513–541.

Schegloff, Emanuel. (1996). Turn organization: One intersection of grammar and interaction. In Elinor Ochs, Emanuel Schegloff, & Sandra Thompson (Eds.), *Interaction and grammar* (pp. 52–133). Cambridge, England: Cambridge University Press.

Schickedanz, Judith. (1990). *Adam's righting revolutions.* Portsmouth, NH: Heinemann.

Schieffelin, Bambi. (1990). *The give and take of everyday life: Language socialization of Kaluli children.* New York: Cambridge University Press.

Schieffelin, Bambi, & Ochs, Elinor. (Eds.). (1990). *Language socialization across cultures.* New York: Cambridge University Press.

Schiffrin, Deborah. (1984a). How a story says what it means and does. *Text, 4*, 313–46.

Schiffrin, Deborah. (1984b). Jewish argument as sociability. *Language in Society, 13*, 311–35.

Schiffrin, Deborah. (1994). *Approaches to discourse.* Oxford, England: Blackwell.

Schutz, Alfred, & Luckmann, Thomas. (1973). *The structures of the life-world.* Evanston, IL: Northwestern University Press.

Scollon, Ron. (1997). Contrastive rhetoric, contrastive poetics, or perhaps something else? *TESOL Quarterly, 31*, 352–358.

Scollon, Ron, & Scollon, Suzanne. (1981). *Narrative, literacy, and face in interethnic communication.* Norwood, NJ: Ablex.

Scollon, Ron, & Scollon, Suzanne. (2001). *Intercultural communication: A discourse approach* (2nd ed.). Oxford: Blackwell.

Schriver, Karen. (1997). *Dynamics in document design: Creating texts for readers.* New York: Wiley.

Searle, John. (1969). *Speech acts.* Cambridge, England: Cambridge University Press.

Selinker, Larry. (1974). Interlanguage. In Jack Richards (Ed.), *Error analysis: Perspectives on second language acquisition* (pp. 31–54). London: Longman.

Selzer, Jack. (1993a). Intertextuality and the writing process. In Rachel Spilka (Ed.), *Writing in the workplace* (pp. 171–180). Carbondale, IL: Southern Illinois University Press.

Selzer, Jack. (Ed.). (1993b). *Understanding scientific prose.* Madison: University of Wisconsin Press.

Selzer, Jack, & Crowley, Sharon. (Eds.). (1999). *Rhetorical bodies.* Madison: University of Wisconsin Press.

Shaughnessy, Mina. (1977). *Errors and expectations.* New York: Oxford University Press.

Sheridan-Rabideau, Mary. (2001). The stuff that myths are made of: Myth building as social action. *Written Communication, 18,* 440–469.

Siegel, Marjorie. (1984). Reading as signification. (Doctoral dissertation, Indiana University, 1984). *Dissertation Abstracts International, 45,* 09A.

Silva, Tony, & Matsuda, Paul Kei. (Eds.). (2001). *On second-language writing.* Mahwah, NJ: Lawrence Erlbaum Associates.

Smagorinsky, Peter. (Ed.). (1994). *Speaking about writing: Reflections on research methodology.* Thousand Oaks, CA: Sage.

Smart, Graham. (1999). Storytelling in a central bank: The role of narrative in the creation and use of specialized economic knowledge. *Journal of Business and Technical Communication, 13,* 249–273.

Smith, Keith. (1989). *Text in the book format.* Rochester, NY: Keith A. Smith Books.

Smith, Louis. (1978). An evolving logic of participant observation, educational ethnography, and other case studies. In Lee Shulman (Ed.), *Review of research in education* (pp. 316–377). Itasca, IL: F. E. Peacock.

Smith, Thomas, Sells, Scott, & Clevenger, Theodore. (1994). Ethnographic content analysis of couple and therapist perceptions in a reflecting team setting. *Journal of Marital and Family Therapy, 20*(3), 267–286.

Sroda, Mary. (1998). 'Not quite right': Second-language acquisition and markedness. In Carol Myers-Scotton (Ed.), *Codes and consequences: Choosing linguistic varieties* (pp. 195–214). Oxford, England: Oxford University Press.

Stafford, Barbara. (1996). *Good looking: Essays on the virtue of images.* Cambridge, MA: MIT Press.

Stake, Robert. (1995). *The art of case study research.* Thousand Oaks, CA: Sage.

Steen, Gerard. (2000). Metaphor and language and literature: A cognitive perspective. *Language and Literature, 9,* 261–277.

Strauss, Anselm. (1987). *Qualitative analysis for social scientists.* Cambridge, England: Cambridge University Press.

Suchman, Lucy, & Trigg, Randall. (1993). Artificial intelligence as craftwork. In Seth Chaiklin & Jean Lave (Eds.), *Understanding practice: Perspectives on activity and context* (pp. 144–178). Cambridge, England: Cambridge University Press.

Sulzby, Elizabeth, Barnhart, June, & Hieshima, Joyce. (1989). Forms of writing and rereading: A preliminary report. In Jana Mason (Ed.), *Reading and writing connections* (pp. 31–63). Needham Heights, MA: Allyn & Bacon.

Swales, John. (1984). Research into the structure of introduction to journal articles. In John Swales (Ed.), *Common ground* (pp. 77–86). Oxford: Pergamon Press.

Swales, John. (1990). *Genre analysis: English in academic and research settings.* New York: Cambridge University Press.

Swales, John. (1998). *Other floors, other voices: A textography of a small university building.* Mahwah, NJ: Lawrence Erlbaum Associates.

Syverson, Margaret. (1999). *The wealth of reality: An ecology of composition.* Carbondale, IL: Southern Illinois University Press.

Tannen, Deborah. (1984). *Conversational style: Analyzing talk among friends.* Norwood, NJ: Ablex.

Tannen, Deborah. (1989). *Talking voices: Repetition, dialogue, and imagery in conversational discourse.* Cambridge, England: Cambridge University Press.

Tannen, Deborah. (Ed.). (1993). *Gender and conversational interaction.* New York: Oxford University Press.

Taylor, Denny, & Dorsey-Gaines, Catherine. (1988). *Growing up literate: Learning from inner city families.* Portsmouth, NH: Heinemann.

Taylor, Mark. (1977). *Hiding.* Chicago: University of Chicago Press.

Temple, Charles, Nathan, Ruth, & Burris, Nancy. (1983). *The beginnings of writing: A practical guide to young children's discovery of writing through scribbling, spelling, and composing stages*. Boston, MA: Allyn & Bacon.

ten Have, Paul. (1999). *Doing conversation analysis: A practical guide*. Thousand Oaks, CA: Sage.

They're trying to change the rules. (1999, November 22). *Time*, p. 65.

Thomas, Sari. (1994). Artifactual study in the analysis of culture: A defense of content analysis in a postmodern age. *Communication Research, 21*, 683–697.

Thomas, William. (1923). *The unadjusted girl*. Boston: Little, Brown.

Thompson, Isabelle. (1999). Women and feminism in technical communication: A qualitative content analysis of journal articles published in 1989 through 1997. *Journal of Business and Technical Communication, 13*, 154–178.

Titscher, Stefan, Meyer, Michael, Wodak, Ruth, & Vetter, Eva. (2000). *Methods of text and discourse analysis*. Newbury Park, CA: Sage.

Toulmin, Stephen. (1964). *The uses of argument*. Cambridge, England: Cambridge University Press.

Trachtenberg, Alan. (1989). *Reading American photographs*. New York: Hill and Wang.

Trudgill, Peter. (2001). *Sociolinguistics: An introduction to language and society* (4th ed.). London: Penguin.

Turner, Mark. (1996). *The literary mind*. New York: Oxford University Press.

van Dijk, Teun. (1991). *Racism and the press*. New York: Routledge.

van Dijk, Teun. (1993). *Elite discourse and racism*. Newbury Park, CA: Sage.

van Dijk, Teun. (Ed.). (1997a). *Discourse as social interaction*. Thousand Oaks, CA: Sage.

van Dijk, Teun. (Ed.). (1997b). *Discourse as structure and process*. Thousand Oaks, CA: Sage.

Van Dijk, Teun. (1997c). The study of discourse. In Teun Van Dijk (Ed.), *Discourse as Structure and Process* (pp. 1–34). London: Sage.

van Dijk, Tuen. (Ed.). (1997d). *Discourse studies: A multidisciplinary introduction*. Vol. 1–2. Thousand Oaks, CA: Sage.

van Dijk, Tuen. (1998). *Ideology: A multidisciplinary approach*. Newbury Park, CA: Sage.

Villanueva, Victor. (1993). *Bootstraps: From an American academic of color*. Urbana, IL: National Council of Teachers of English.

Volosinov, Valentin. (1986). *Marxism and the philosophy of language* (Ladislav Matejka & Irwin Titunik, Trans.). Cambridge MA: Harvard University Press.

Vygotsky, Lev (1978). *Mind in Society*. Cambridge MA: Harvard University Press.

Vygotsky, Lev. (1986). *Thought and language*. (Alex Kozulin, Trans.). Cambridge, MA: MIT Press.

Vygotsky, Lev. (1987). *Thinking and speech* (Norris Minick, Ed. & Trans.). New York: Plenum.

Wertsch, James. (1991). *Voices of the mind: A sociocultural approach to mediated action*. Cambridge, MA: Harvard University Press.

White, Elwyn Brooks. (1944). *One man's meat*. New York: Harper & Row.

Wilke, John, & Buckman, Rebecca. (2000, May 25). U.S. judge calls abrupt end to Microsoft trial. *Wall Street Journal*, pp. A3–A4.

Williams, Robin. (1994). *The non-designer's design book: Design and typographic principles for the visual novice*. Berkeley, CA: Peachpit.

Wilt, Timothy. (1998). Markedness and references to characters in Biblical Hebrew narratives. In Carol Myers-Scotton (Ed.), *Codes and consequences: Choosing linguistic varieties* (pp. 89–99). Oxford, England: Oxford University Press.

Wittgenstein, Ludwig. (1958). *Philosophical investigations*. (Gertrude Anscombe, Trans.). Oxford, England: Basil Blackwell.

Wodak, Ruth, & van Dijk, Teun. (Eds.). (2000). *Racism at the top: Parliamentary discourses on ethnic issues in six European states*. Klagenfurt, Austria: Drava Verlag.

Wolcott, Harry. (1994). *Transforming qualitative data: Description, analysis, and interpretation*. Thousand Oaks, CA: Sage.

Wolfram, Walt, Adger, Carolyn, & Christian, Donna. (1999). *Dialects in schools and communities.* Mahwah, NJ: Lawrence Erlbaum Associates.

Wortham, Stanton. (2001). *Narratives in action: A strategy for research and analysis.* New York: Teachers College Press.

Yule, George. (1996). *The study of language* (2nd ed.). New York: Cambridge University Press.

Zamel, Vivian. (1997). Toward a model of transculturation. *TESOL Quarterly, 31*(2), 341–351.

Zecker, Liliana. (1991). Young children's early literacy across genres (emergent literacy). (Doctoral dissertation, University of Michigan, 1991). *Dissertation Abstracts International, 52,* 03A.

Zecker, Liliana. (1996). Early development in written language: Children's emergent knowledge of genre-specific characteristics. *Reading and Writing: An Interdisciplinary Journal, 8,* 5–25.

Author Index

A

Abelson, Robert, 36, 353
Achebe, Chinua, 111, 112, 441
Ackerman, John, 95, 181, 183, 199, 343, 346
Adger, Carolyn, 60, 81, 355
Allen, Graham, 95, 341
Altheide, David, 20, 26, 341
Amann, Klaus, 200, 341
Anderson, James, 26, 341
Andrews, James, 304, 341
Anzaldúa, Gloria, 98, 99, 119, 120, 341
Aristotle, 42, 43, 280, 283, 284, 341
Arnheim, Rudolf, 162, 341
Atkinson, Dwight, 58, 63, 65, 82, 341
Atkinson, John, 236, 252, 341
Atwell, Nancie, 190, 341
Auer, Peter, 121, 341
Aulakh, Gurinder, 101, 120, 347
Austin, John, 313, 314, 320, 338, 341

B

Bakhtin, Mikhail, 95, 116, 118, 183, 241, 254, 267, 339, 341, 342
Bal, Mieke, 34, 54, 342
Bang, Molly, 162, 342
Barnhart, June, 242, 250, 277, 354
Barthes, Roland, 95, 285, 342
Bartholomae, David, 100, 117, 272, 342
Bartlett, Francis, 185, 342
Barton, Ellen, 9, 16, 30, 69, 70, 71, 82, 203, 239, 342
Bayley, Robert, 98, 353

Baynham, Mike, 101, 342
Bazerman, Charles, 9, 10, 48, 61, 65, 67, 82, 95, 96, 105, 170, 198, 200, 224, 242, 245, 292, 338, 339, 342, 353
Beaufort, Anne, 200, 342
Beebee, Thomas, 339, 342
Belcher, Diane, 121, 342
Bennett, William, 296, 300, 302, 306, 307, 342
Benson, Thomas, 304, 343
Berelson, Bernard, 13, 343
Berger, John, 281, 303, 343
Berger, Peter, 338, 343
Berkenkotter, Carol, 22, 23, 95, 338, 343
Bernstein, Janice, 121, 343
Bhatia, Vijay, 61, 339, 343
Biber, Douglas, 14, 63, 64, 65, 202, 203, 343
Biklen, Sari, 251, 343
Birdwhistle, Ray, 212, 236, 343
Bissex, Glynda, 277, 343
Black, Edwin, 304, 343
Black, Max, 43, 44, 343
Blair, Carole, 162, 343
Blomberg, Sven, 303, 343
Blyler, Nancy, 35, 56, 352
Bogden, Robert, 251, 343
Bolter, Jay, 162, 343
Braine, George, 121, 342
Brehe, Steven, 172, 343
Bridwell-Bowles, Lillian, 172, 343
Britton, James, 277, 343
Brock, Bernard, 304, 343
Bruner, Jerome, 34, 35, 343
Bryant, Donald, 304, 343
Buckman, Rebecca, 49, 50, 355

Buell, Marcia, 9
Burgess, Tony, 277, 343
Burke, Carolyn, 277, 348
Burke, Kenneth, 285, 292, 293, 302, 303, 344
Burris, Nancy, 277, 355

C

Calkins, Lucy, 277, 344
Carley, Kathleen, 14, 344
Cameron, Deborah, 81, 344
Carley, Kathleen, 20, 26, 27, 351
Carruthers, Mary, 162, 344
Carter, David, 262, 344
Casanave, Christine, 102, 121, 344
Chafe, Wallace, 62, 63, 64, 70, 72, 81, 344
Chapman, Marilyn, 277, 344
Chesebro, James, 304, 343
Chomsky, Noam, 59
Christian, Donna, 60, 81, 355
Cicero, 284
Clarke, David, 56, 351
Clark, Romy, 239, 344
Clay, Marie, 242, 277, 344
Clevenger, Theodore, 26, 354
Cockburn, Alexander, 296
Cohen, Adam, 47, 48, 344
Cohen, Ralph, 339, 344
Cole, Michael, 240, 344
Connor, Ulla, 102, 121, 122, 344
Cooper, Marilyn, 67, 344
Cope, Bill, 339, 344
Corbett, Edward, 304, 344
Cortazzi, Martin, 252, 344
Coupland, Nikolas, 235, 348
Crammond, Joanna, 23, 24, 344
Cromwell, Oliver, 297, 298
Cross, Geoffrey, 175, 199, 200, 344
Crowley, Sharon, 281, 354

D

Dale, Thomas, 20, 26, 27, 351
Damon, William, 73, 345

Danielewicz, Jane, 62, 344
Dautermann, Jennie, 65, 345
de la Luna, Lenora, 10, 105, 195, 198, 224
Derrida, Jacques, 240, 241, 345
Devitt, Amy, 95, 345
Dibb, Michael, 303, 343
Dingwall, Robert, 56, 351
DiPardo, Anne, 193, 345
Donovan, Carol, 248, 277, 345
Dorsey-Gaines, Catherine, 261, 277, 354
Dressler, Richard, 210, 345
Duranti, Alessandro, 81, 206, 236, 338, 345, 347
Durkheim, Emile, 338, 345
Dyson, Anne, 195, 196, 200, 277, 345

E

Eckert, Penelope, 237, 345
Eggins, Suzanne, 81, 345
Ellis, Rod, 121, 345
Emig, Janet, 180, 199, 345
Engeström, Yrjo, 235, 236, 345
Erdman, Terry, 185, 345
Erickson, Joan, 174, 175, 345
Eubanks, Philip, 9, 21, 27, 29, 37, 46, 110, 216, 291, 345

F

Faber, Brenton, 23, 345
Fahnestock, Jeanne, 55, 345
Fairclough, Norman, 5, 252, 345, 346
Ferreiro, Emilia, 277, 346
Fico, Frederick, 16, 30, 352
Finders, Margaret, 200, 346
Finegan, Edward, 14, 343
Floriani, Ana, 245, 346
Flower, Linda, 180, 181, 183, 199, 346
Foss, Sonja, 163, 304, 346
Foucault, Michel, 274, 346
Fox, Chris, 303, 343
Freedman, Aviva, 338, 346

Friedman, Milton, 293, 296, 346
Fromkin, Victoria, 81, 346

G

Gallas, Karen, 277, 346
Garfinkel, Harold, 204, 346
Gates, Bill, 48, 346
Gee, James, 110, 236, 246, 272, 346
Geisler, Cheryl, 172, 183, 199, 346
Genette, Gerard, 95, 346, 347
Gere, Anne, 64, 347
Glaser, Barney, 251, 347
Goffman, Erving, 100, 109, 116, 170,
    204, 212, 236, 347
Golomb, Claire, 277, 347
Gonzales, Patrick, 233, 351
Gooding, David, 200, 347
Goodwin, Charles, 199, 206, 236,
    345, 347
Goodwin, Marjorie, 199, 236, 347
Goswami, Dixie, 189, 351
Grant-Davie, Keith, 82, 347
Graves, Donald, 199, 347
Gray, Paul, 73, 347
Greenbaum, Sidney, 69, 352
Gruber, Sibylle, 189, 352
Gumperz, John, 81, 101, 120, 237,
    347
Gumperz, Jenny-Cook, 347
Gutierrez, Kris, 209, 347

H

Hall, Edward, 212, 347
Halliday, Michael, 61, 81, 347
Halter, Ellen 69, 70, 71, 342
Hancock, Mark, 98, 347
Hanks, William, 338, 347
Harris, Joseph, 67, 347
Harste, Jerome, 277, 348
Hart, Roderick, 304, 348
Hatch, Jill, 18, 27, 348
Hawisher, Gail, 189, 352
Hayes, John, 18, 27, 180, 199, 346,
    348

Haynes, Cynthia, 125, 348
Heath, Christian, 199, 206, 236, 348,
    350
Heath, Shirley Brice, 81, 261, 348
Heller, Monica, 120, 348
Hendrickson, Althea, 174, 348
Hengst, Julie, 212, 213, 348
Heritage, John, 236, 252, 341
Hernadi, Paul, 339, 348
Herrington, Anne, 189, 351
Hicks, Deborah, 257, 348
Hieshima, Joyce, 242, 250, 277, 354
Hindmarsh, Jon, 199, 350
Hodge, Robert, 241, 348
Hoey, Michael, 5, 348
Hollis, Richard, 303, 343
Holmevik, Jan Rune, 125, 348
Hoon, Tan, 22, 350
Huckin, Thomas, 8, 9, 18, 22, 23, 24,
    46, 57, 65, 66, 82, 95, 239, 249,
    338, 343, 348
Hymes, Dell, 59, 60, 99, 236, 237,
    348

I-J

Irvine, Judith, 100, 348
Ivanic, Roz, 239, 344
Jacoby, Sally, 233, 351
Jakobsen, Roman, 52
Jaworski, Adam, 235, 348
Jefferson, Gail, 210, 348, 353
Johns, Ann, 61, 67, 68, 348
Johnson, Mark, 30, 42, 44, 55, 349
Johnson, Parker, 172, 343
Johnstone, Barbara, 81, 348

K

Kalantzis, Mary, 339, 344
Kalman, Judy, 200, 349
Kaltman, Hannah, 101, 120, 347
Kamberelis, George, 10, 105, 195,
    196, 198, 200, 224, 239, 240, 242,
    248, 249, 277, 349, 350
Kantz, Margaret, 181, 183, 199, 346

Kaplan, Robert, 102, 122, 349
Kaye, Harvey, 73, 349
Kendon, Adam, 212, 236, 349
Kepplinger, Hans, 26, 349
Kirsch, Gesa, 82, 349
Knorr-Cetina, Karin, 200, 341
Kostelnick, Charles, 163, 281, 349
Krantz, Michael, 42, 349
Kreml, Nancy, 121, 349
Kress, Gunther, 76, 163, 200, 241, 281, 348, 349
Kristeva, Julia, 95, 349
Kruez, Roger, 210, 345
Kroll, Barry, 64, 349

L

Labov, William, 60, 100, 269, 349
Lacy, Stephen, 16, 30, 352
Lakoff, George, 30, 42, 44, 55, 349
Langer, Judith, 249, 277, 349
Lanham, Richard, 163, 349
Larson, Joanne, 209, 347
Latour, Bruno, 195, 199, 200, 349
Leander, Kevin, 10, 65, 100, 105, 207, 212, 227, 239, 350
Lee, S. Jean, 22, 350
Leech, Geoffrey, 69, 352
Lensmire, Timothy, 277, 350
Linell, Per, 96, 350
Lofty, John, 277, 350
Luckmann, Thomas, 338, 343, 353
Luff, Paul, 199, 348, 350
Luria, Alexander, 242, 350
Lyotard, Jean-Francois, 35, 36, 54, 350

M

MacDonald, Susan Peck, 65, 82, 350
MacGillivray, Laurie, 277, 350
MacLaughlin, Nicole, 189, 352
MacNealy, Mary, 16, 18, 27, 28, 350
Mailloux, Stephen, 304, 350
Maligian-Odle, Stanley, 262, 344
Martin, James, 61, 277, 347, 350
Martin, Nancie, 277, 343

Mathison, Maureen, 20, 21, 350
Matsuda, Paul Kei, 121, 354
Matsuhashi, Ann, 195, 199, 350
Maxwell, Joseph, 251, 350
McCarthey, Sarah, 277, 350
McCormick, Kathleen, 181, 183, 199, 346
McGee, Nancy, 69, 70, 71, 342
McGinley, William, 239, 277, 350
McIntyre, Alasdair, 242, 350
McLeod, Alex, 277, 343
McNeilley, Lisa, 69, 70, 71, 342
Medway, Peter, 338, 346
Merriam, Sharan, 251, 350
Merton, Robert King, 338, 351
Meyer, Michael, 31, 355
Middleton, David, 235, 236, 345
Miller, Carolyn, 338, 351
Miller, Peggy, 212, 348
Miller, Susan, 67, 351
Mishoe, Margaret, 121, 351
Mitchell, William, 163, 351
Mithun, Marianne, 72, 351
Mulhern, Margaret, 277, 351
Mullet, Kevin, 163, 351
Myers, Greg, 82, 99, 100, 103, 104, 105, 200, 254, 351
Myers-Scotton, Carol, 100, 104, 120, 121, 351
Myhrvold, Nathan, 48, 346

N

Nathan, Ruth, 277, 355
Neil, Michel, 162, 343
Nelson, Jennie, 185, 351
Nerlich, Birgitte, 56, 351
Newkirk, Thomas, 277, 351
Newmeyer, Frederick, 59, 81, 351
Novak, Viveca, 42, 351
Nunberg, Geoffrey, 163, 351

O

Ochs, Elinor, 61, 212, 233, 236, 351, 353

Odell, Lee, 189, 351
Ong, Walter, 203, 223, 351
Ortony, Andrew, 55, 351

P

Palmquist, Michael, 14, 20, 26, 27,
    344, 351
Paradis, James, 338, 342
Patton, Michael Quinn, 105, 351
Paul, Danette, 24, 352
Peck, Wayne, 181, 183, 199, 346
Penrose, Ann, 180, 352
Perkins, Jane, 35, 56, 352
Phelps, Louise, 179, 352
Pickering, Andrew, 270, 352
Pinker, Stephen, 81, 352
Plimpton, George, 185, 199, 352
Porter, James, 95, 352
Pratt, Charlotte, 19, 20, 26, 27, 352
Pratt, Cornelius, 19, 20, 26, 27, 352
Prince, Gerald, 34, 352
Prior, Paul, 9, 10, 65, 67, 100, 102,
    105, 109, 177, 185, 186, 187, 189,
    192, 198, 199, 212, 213, 214, 224,
    239, 247, 260, 348, 352
Propp, Vladimir, 34, 54, 352

Q-R

Quintillian, 284
Quirk, Randolph, 69, 352
Ramo, Joshua, 47, 352
Reynolds, W. Ann, 76, 77, 78
Riffe, Daniel, 16, 30, 352
Rinearson, Peter, 48, 346
Roberts, Carl, 15, 26, 27, 352
Roberts, David, 163, 281, 349
Rorty, Richard, 98, 99, 352
Rose, Mike, 193, 352
Rosen, Harold, 277, 343
Rothery, Joan, 277, 350
Rowe, Deborah, 277, 353
Russell, David, 240, 339, 342, 353
Rymer, Jone, 199, 353
Rymes, Betsy, 209, 347

S

Sacks, Harvey, 204, 353
Sandig, Barbara, 14, 353
Sano, Darrell, 163, 351
Saville-Troike, Muriel, 59, 61, 100,
    236, 353
Sawkins, Margaret, 249, 353
Schaafsma, David, 277, 353
Schank, Roger, 36, 353
Schecter, Sandra, 98, 353
Schegloff, Emanual, 204, 210, 236,
    351, 353
Schickedanz, Judith, 277, 353
Schieffelin, Bambi, 61, 353
Schiffrin, Deborah, 58, 59, 61, 81,
    353
Schriver, Karen, 163, 353
Schutz, Alfred, 338, 353
Scollon, Ron, 60, 61, 122, 353
Scollon, Suzanne, 60, 61, 353
Scott, Karla, 196, 239, 277, 349
Scott, Robert, 304, 343
Searle, John, 314, 315, 320, 338, 353
Selinker, Larry, 101, 353
Sells, Scott, 26, 354
Selzer, Jack, 10, 38, 82, 123, 281, 303,
    353, 354
Shaughnessy, Mina, 64, 354
Sheridan-Rabideau, Mary, 56, 354
Shipka, Jody, 192, 352
Siegel, Marjorie, 277, 354
Silva, Tony, 121, 354
Sitko, Barbara, 180, 352
Smagorinsky, Peter, 180, 354
Smart, Graham, 38, 354
Smith, Keith, 163, 354
Smith, Louis, 247, 354
Smith, Thomas, 26, 354
Sroda, Mary, 121, 354
Stafford, Barbara, 163, 354
Stake, Robert, 247, 354
Steen, Gerard, 44, 354
Stein, Victoria, 181, 183, 199, 346
Strauss, Anselm, 251, 347, 354
Stygall, Gail, 82, 342

Suchman, Lucy, 233, 354
Sullivan, Patricia, 82, 349
Sulzby, Elizabeth, 242, 250, 277, 354
Svartvik, Jan, 69, 352
Swales, John, 16, 61, 67, 82, 90, 91, 113, 339, 354
Syverson, Margaret, 195, 199, 354

T

Tannen, Deborah, 61, 204, 236, 354
Taylor, Denny, 261, 277, 354
Taylor, Mark, 148, 149, 150, 151, 152, 153, 354
Teberosky, Ana, 277, 346
Temple, Charles, 277, 355
ten Have, Paul, 206, 236, 355
Thomas, Sari, 28, 29, 355
Thomas, William, 312, 338, 355
Thompson, Isabelle, 21, 355
Thompson, Sandra, 236, 351
Titscher, Stefan, 31, 355
Toulmin, Stephen, 285, 355
Trachtenberg, Alan, 281, 355
Trigg, Randall, 233, 354
Trudgill, Peter, 51, 81, 355
Turner, Mark, 36, 44, 54, 55, 355

V

Vann, Roberta, 64, 349
van Dijk, Tuen, 26, 61, 81, 235, 355

van Leeuwen, Theo, 163, 276, 281, 349
Vetter, Eva, 31, 355
Villanueva, Victor, 122, 355
Volosinov, Valentin, 95, 355
Vygotsky, Lev, 185, 242, 274, 277, 338, 339, 355

W

Walker, Jeffrey, 280
Wertsch, James, 183, 184, 240, 355
White, Elwyn Brooks, 286, 291, 302, 304, 305, 306, 355
Wilke, John, 49, 50, 355
Williams, Robin, 163, 355
Wilt, Timothy, 121, 355
Wittgenstein, Ludwig, 68, 178, 355
Wodak, Ruth, 31, 61, 355
Wolcott, Harry, 251, 355
Wolfram, Walt, 60, 81, 355
Woodward, Virginia, 277, 348
Woolgar, Steve, 195, 199, 200, 349
Wortham, Stanton, 252, 356
Wysocki, Anne, 9, 54, 197, 198, 203, 281

Y-Z

Yule, George, 81, 356
Zamel, Vivian, 122, 356
Zecker, Liliana, 249, 356

Subject Index

A

activity systems, 311, 319, 336, 245-246
animation, 136
argument, 35, 38
arrangement, 284
audience, 293
authorship, 169-171
awkward sentences, 68-71

C

charts and graphs, 134-136
code-switching, 97-101
coding, 182-183
cognition, 36, 38
color, 132
composing, 168-169
conceptual analysis, 14
conceptual metaphor, 44 - 46
construct, 16-17
content, 13-14
context, 15, 240, 243, 250, 258-260, 266-271
contextual analysis, 291-293
contrastive rhetoric, 101-102
conversation analysis, 203-204
corpus, 17, 63, 326-327,
critical discourse analysis, 5, 61

D

deliberative rhetoric, 283
delivery, 284
discourse analysis, 1-6, 57-64, 252-253
discourses, 246
drawings, 133-134

E

embodied activity, 212
epideictic rhetoric, 284
ethnography, 26, 105-106 113-117, 247-248
ethos, 284
evaluation, 88
evidentials, 72-75

F

felicity conditions, 314
fieldnotes, 194-195, 206, 248
footing, 170, 204-205, 260
forensic rhetoric, 283
function (linguistic function), 60-61

G

genre, 4, 61, 89, 245, 311, 315-328
genre sets, 311, 318, 328
genre systems, 311, 318-319

H-I

hypothesis, 16
illocutionary act, 314
image schema, 44, 48
indexicality, 241, 243
inductive analysis, 251-253
inscription, 168-169
intercontextuality, 245
interdiscursivity, 244-245
interlanguage, 101-102
interpretive analysis, 103-4, 107-111
intertextual reach, 89-90
intertextuality, 84-91, 103-105 , 111-113, 170, 173-179, 244-245, 249, 313

interview, discourse-based, 189-191
interview, semi-structured, 187-188
interview, stimulated elicitation,
    188-193
invention, 284

L

layout, 130-131
linguistics, 58-61
literacy, types of, 202-203
locutionary act, 314
logos, 284

M

meaning, 13-14
metaphor, 3, 42-46
methodological issues, 5, 16-19. 36-
    38, 65-67, 91-93, 103-106, 137,
    140, 172-196, 205-214, 247-253,
    282-283, 319-328
metonymy, 50-52
myth, 39-40

N-O

narrative, 3, 34- 36
natural attitude, 7-8
observation, 193-195
orality, types of, 202-203
oral vs. written language, 62-65

P

participant accounts, 179-193
participation structure, 170, 204-
    205
pathos, 284
perlocutionary act, 314
persuasion, 280, 285
photographs, 132-133
politics, 240, 260-261, 271-274
postmodernism, 35-36
propositional act, 314
process logs, 185-187

Q

qualitative research, 14-15, 20-25, 63
quantitative research, 14-15, 19-20,
    22-25, 63-64
quotation, 85, 88

R

recontextualization, 90-91
relational analysis, 14
research question, 16
retrospective accounts, 184-185
rhetoric, 2-3
rhetorical figures, 52
rhetorical situation, 282
rich feature analysis, 65-67

S

semiotics, 202-203
simile, 43
social fact, 311, 312-313
social identity, 100-101
speech act, 311, 313-315, 320-321
spoken language, 1
story (see narrative)
structure (linguistic structure), 58-60
student writing, 67-68, 71-72
style, 284
subjectivity, 247

T

talk and text, 179, 201-202, 214, 231
tape (video or audio) recording, 193,
    206-208
text, 240-242, 254-258, 265-266
text, definition of, 6-7, 168-169
textual analysis, 283-285
think-aloud protocols, 180-184
transcription, 208-214
turn-taking, 204
typefaces, 127-130
typification, 316-317

U-V-W

units of analysis, 17
video, 135
visual presentation, 123-126
writing practices, 171, 239-240, 242
writing processes, 4, 7, 171